India's Eastward Engagement

From Antiquity to Act East Policy

S.D. Muni
Rahul Mishra

ATLANTIC
PUBLISHERS & DISTRIBUTORS (P) LTD

ATLANTIC
PUBLISHERS & DISTRIBUTORS (P) LTD

7/22, Ansari Road, Darya Ganj, New Delhi
Tel.: +91-11-4077 5252, 2327 3880
E-mail: orders@atlanticbooks.com
Web: www.atlanticbooks.com

Published by Atlantic Publishers & Distributors (P) Ltd 2024

Previously Published by SAGE Publications in 2019

Printed & bound in India by Atlantic Print Services

Advance Praise

I am an admirer of Professor S. D. Muni. He with Rahul Mishra has written an excellent book on India's deep connections with Southeast Asia.

—Tommy Koh, Ambassador-at-large, Ministry of Foreign Affairs, Republic of Singapore

With rising Chinese power and the emergence of the Indo-Pacific concept reshaping Southeast Asia's destiny, what is India's response and role? This well-researched and timely book is indispensable for anyone looking for an answer and for understanding India's 'Act East' Policy.

—Amitav Acharya, Professor, American University; President of International Studies Association; Author of East of India, South of China: Sino-Indian Encounters in Southeast Asia

India's Eastward Engagement reflects the authors' intimate familiarity with India's extended neighbourhood to the east, in both its historical and contemporary contexts. The authors bring to the subject the rigour of an academic and the perspective of a practising diplomat—a rare combination. This book will command a wide audience, given its broad historical sweep and its penetrating political insights.

—Shyam Saran, Former Foreign Secretary; Chairman of Research and Information Systems for Developing Countries

Contents

List of Abbreviations vii
Preface xi

1. Introduction: India's Idea of the East 1
2. Waves of History: Ancient to Pre-Independence Era 29
3. The Nehru Wave (1927–1964): Hopes Belied 65
4. After Nehru: Did India Get Distanced? 114
5. Look East Policy (1992–2014): Streamlining and Restructuring Engagement 152
6. Act East Policy (2014–): How Different, How Successful? 196
7. Prospects: Challenges of Deeper and Wider Engagement 244

Annexure A. Exchange of Visits 264
Annexure B. India's Trade with ASEAN and Its Dialogue Partners 296
Annexure C. India's Exports to ASEAN 300
Annexure D. India's Imports from ASEAN 304
Annexure E. FDI Inflows and Outflows between ASEAN and India 308
Annexure F. Military Exercises 316
Index 320
About the Authors 328

List of Abbreviations

ADMM+	ASEAN Defence Ministers Meeting+
AEM	ASEAN Economic Ministers
AEP	Act East Policy
AIADMK	All India Anna Dravida Munnetra Kazhagam
AIIB	Asian Infrastructure Investment Bank
APEC	Asia-Pacific Economic Cooperation
ARC	Asian Relations Conference
ARF	ASEAN Regional Forum
ARO	Asian Relations Organisation
ASEAN	Association of Southeast Asian Nations
BCIM	Bangladesh, China, India and Myanmar
BIMSTEC	Bay of Bengal Multi-Sectoral Initiative for Technical and Economic Cooperation
BIST–EC	Bangladesh, India, Sri Lanka and Thailand–Economic Cooperation
BJP	Bharatiya Janata Party
BRI	Belt and Road Initiative
BRICS	Brazil, Russia, India, China and South Africa
CENTO	Central Treaty Organization
CLMV	Cambodia, Laos, Myanmar and Vietnam
DoNER	Development of the North Eastern Region
DPA	Development Partnership Administration
EAEC	East Asia Economic Caucus
EAEG	East Asia Economic Group
EAS	East Asia Summit
FIPIC	Forum for India–Pacific Islands Cooperation
FTA	Free Trade Agreement
FTAAP	Free Trade Area for Asia Pacific
GAGAN	GPS-aided GEO Augmented Navigation
GDP	Gross Domestic Product

HAL	Hindustan Aeronautics Limited
ICAI	Institute of Cost Accountants of India
ICC	International Control Commission
ICP	Integrated Check Post
ICWA	Indian Council of World Affairs
IIL	Indian Independence League
IISS	International Institute of Strategic Studies
IMF	International Monetary Fund
INA	Indian National Army
ISAS	Institute of South Asian Studies
ITEC	Indian Technical and Economic Cooperation
KMT	Kuomintang
LAC	Line of Actual Control
LEP	Look East Policy
MAPHILINDO	Malaysia, the Philippines and Indonesia
MEA	Ministry of External Affairs
MGC	Mekong–Ganga Cooperation
MOS	Minister of State
NAM	Non-Aligned Movement
NDA	National Democratic Alliance
NER	North Eastern Region
NSG	Nuclear Suppliers Group
NSS	National Security Strategy
ODA	Official Development Assistance
ONGC	Oil and Natural Gas Commission
OPEC	Organization of the Petroleum Exporting Countries
PBD	Pravasi Bharatiya Divas
PDR	People's Democratic Republic
PIC	Pacific Island Countries
PIOs	persons of Indian origin
PLAN	Peoples' Liberation Army Navy
PQI	Partnership for Quality Infrastructure
Quad	Quadrilateral
RCEP	Regional Comprehensive Economic Partnership
SAARC	South Asian Association for Regional Cooperation
SAGAR	Security and Growth for All in the Region

SEATO	Southeast Asia Treaty Organization
SOM	Senior Officers Meeting
TAC	Treaty of Amity and Cooperation
TPP	Trans-Pacific Partnership
UN	United Nations
UNSC	United Nations Security Council
UPA	United Progressive Alliance
USSR	Union of Soviet Socialist Republics
ZOPFAN	Zone of Peace, Freedom and Neutrality

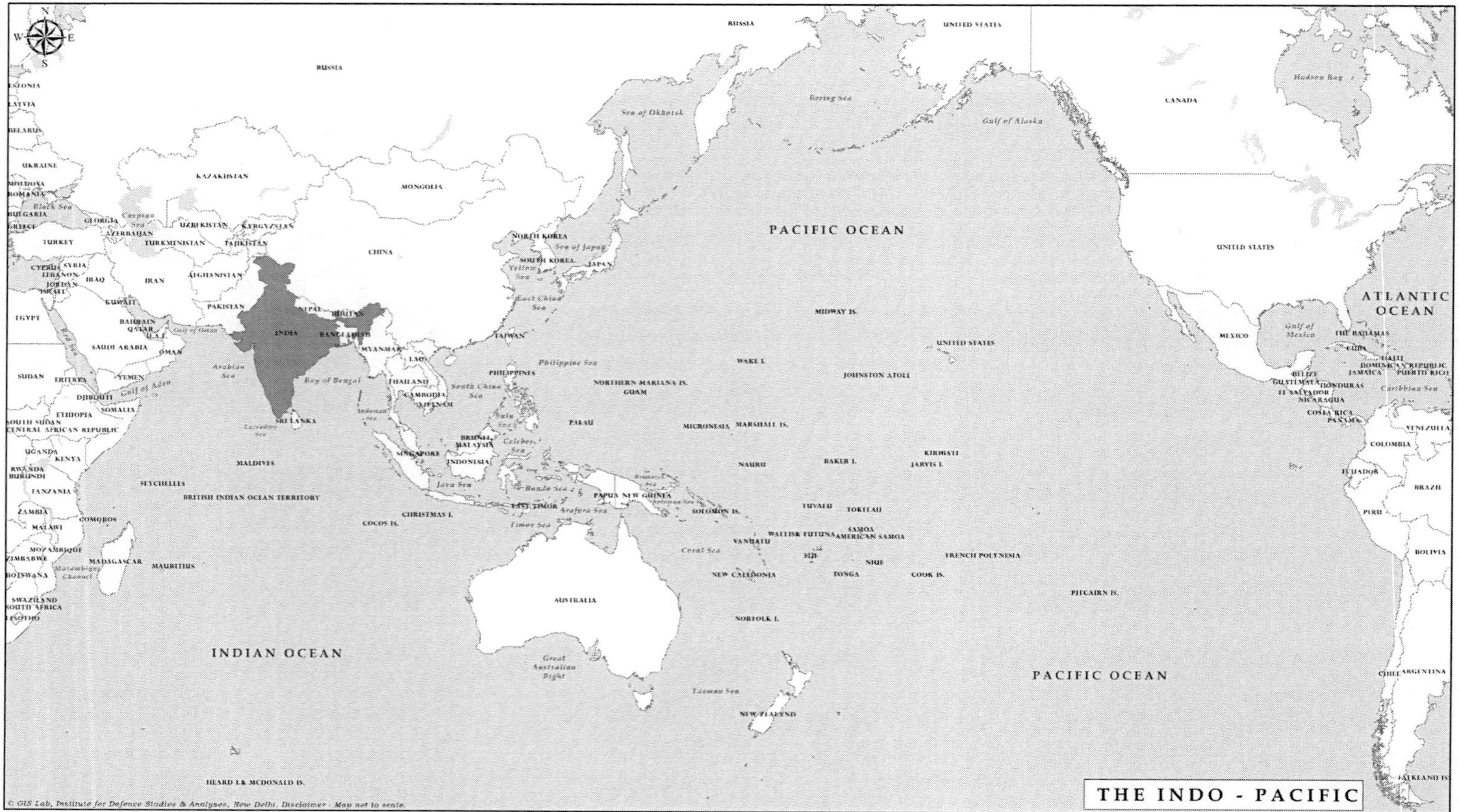

Disclaimer: This map is for representation purpose only.

Preface

The idea of writing this book came out of my sense of unease and discomfort from the repeated criticism heard during my decade-long stay in the Southeast Asia region, between 1995 and 2013, both as a diplomat and as a researcher/academic, that India was responsible for not keeping adequately engaged with the countries of the region. Many of the foreign service officers and the documents of the Ministry of External Affairs, including speeches and statements by important leaders, seemed to be endorsing this criticism. There was no logic in assuming that India would be indifferent to this dynamic region without any rhyme or reason. Even when there were disruptions in India's engagement with the East, was it a unilateral Indian decision that was exercised even at the cost of its vital interests? Or were there factors and forces on both sides—of India and the eastern region—that periodically distanced India and its extended eastern neighbours from each other?

When one starts looking deeply into these questions, it becomes clear that, contrary to the widespread perception, India's Look East Policy did not just begin in the early 1990s. India's engagement with the East is more than two millennia old, maybe even older than that. I drew attention to this as my first response in my contribution to Ambassador A. N. Ram's *Two Decades of India's Look East Policy*. In that contribution, I also underlined that India never stopped looking East, and it alone has not been responsible for the periodic slumps in the eastward engagements. Then suddenly came a near rebuke from President Obama to the Indian parliamentarians and policymakers in November 2010 with regard to their Look East approach to the region. According to Obama, the approach of the parliamentarians was not adequate and they needed to engage with the region more actively. This was an avoidable intellectual provocation because it flew in the face of India's very long cultural and civilizational history, almost since antiquity. India has always remained extensively engaged with the region, even prior to the birth of the present-day USA. Although the UPA government ignored Obama's reprimand, the Modi government implicitly endorsed it by changing the name of India's Look East Policy into the Act East Policy. Most of the books that have come after India's Look East Policy have ignored its broader historical evolution and initial civilizational context.

The idea of writing this book was accordingly set against three tasks: First, to highlight the historical and civilizational context of India's eastward engagement, almost from antiquity, because the engagement is as old as that. In that sense, India has had a persistent engagement with its eastern neighbours, and what we call as India's Look East and/or Act East Policies constitute only different phases of the same continuum. Second, we do not hold India alone responsible for the phases of eastward engagement that were low-key and not very dynamic. An objective attempt has been made to explore, scrutinize and understand the causes of erosion in India's eastward engagement during the British colonial period as also from the mid-1960s until the end of the Cold War. This was clearly not India's choice or option, but the then operating circumstances made it so. India had its own security and economic constraints and concerns against sustaining the 1950s, vigour and vitality to its eastward relationships. The global forces were not so supportive of a deeper engagement by India in the region. And above all, the countries of Southeast Asia had their own domestic compulsions and foreign policy priorities not to look towards India, as India too was constrained by its own, to add. The end of the Cold War made India more confident to broaden and deepen its external outreach, and it brought about a basic change in regional and global contexts, resulting in a sudden spurt in India's eastward enthusiasm.

Finally, we also try to explore if changing the name from 'Look' to 'Act' East has done anything radically different and positive to the content and conduct of the policy, except perhaps in frontloading the civilizational dimension on it and injecting a great deal of energy and speed in its manifestation. Researching for all these tasks appeared daunting to me. While I was still collecting my confidence to launch the book project, one of my dear students, and a dedicated scholar of the Look East Policy, Dr Rahul Mishra, came to visit me. When I sounded out the idea of the book to him and sought his help in this regard, he enthusiastically endorsed the proposal, and we decided to collaborate in writing the book.

It has been exciting for both me and Rahul, working in tandem within these three parameters for writing this book. However, our efforts were made unexpectedly difficult and time consuming due to unexpected developments. Rahul moved to Malaysia and I shifted my place of work from the Institute for Defence Studies and Analyses (IDSA) to Jawaharlal Nehru University, New Delhi. As a result of this dislocation, the reading and re-reading of the chapters and coordinating the process of writing cost us more time and effort. In the long period covered in the study, many of the concerned countries changed not only their policies but also their territorial contours and names. Burma became Myanmar, and Ceylon became Sri Lanka. Cambodia has been oscillating between Khamboj, Cambodia, Khmer and Kampuchea. Civilizational India was partitioned into India and Pakistan, and Bangladesh emerged out of the partitioned Pakistan. The civilizational entities of Java and Sumatra became integral parts of Indonesia, and the Malay Union became Malaysia and Singapore. Even the Asia-Pacific region has emerged in a new *avatar* (incarnation) of the Indo-Pacific region, enlivening and reinforcing the memories of India's civilizational links. We have not gone into the anatomy and dynamics of these changes and have taken them as they occurred. We have also used the new and old names of the countries concerned freely.

We have tried our best to present the historical and civilizational context of the 'Look East' and 'Act East' policies as objectively as possible, and explain as to why the periodic distancing between India and its Eastern neighbours was almost inevitable, dictated by forces and powers beyond India and its neighbours. But such phases were transient, short lived, and at no time India wanted, relished or completely gave up its eastward engagement. We leave it to the readers to judge the extent to which our efforts have been of any use.

I wish to thank Rahul for joining me in this project because without his moral encouragement and solid contribution, I would not have been able to muster the courage and confidence to undertake it all by myself. Both Rahul and I are also thankful to Chandraveer Singh Bhati, a young and enthusiastic scholar and teacher from Rajasthan, who helped us in preparing the annexures for the book, listing the exchange of visits and military exercises between India and the Indo-Pacific region. Prabir Dey of the Research and Information System for Developing Countries, ASEAN-India Centre helped us generously in getting the data on trade and investments by allowing us access to many of the centre's studies. I hope that the readers find all this data computation useful. Rahul and I deeply appreciate the efforts of Shri Mukesh Jha (Senior Library Assistant, IDSA) in helping us with the library resources. Shri Rajesh Dey of SAGE deserves our sincere thanks for agreeing to accept and facilitate the publication of this book through SAGE. We hope that the book will attract the attention of students, scholars/analysts and policymakers who are interested in India's role in the emerging Indo-Pacific region.

S. D. Muni

CHAPTER 1

Introduction

India's Idea of the East

India's idea of the East has evolved through the centuries. It has been shaped by geographical location, civilizational and cultural moorings, economic aspirations and strategic concerns. Broadly, the East to India is a geographically contiguous source of energy, life and light: civilizationally and culturally, it is compatible and responsive; economically, it is dynamic; and strategically, this region has not only never posed any security challenge to India and vice versa but also even looks towards India for active involvement in balancing other powers like the USA and China. Let us look at these aspects in some details.

Sun Worshippers

India is a civilizational country of Sun worshippers. It has, therefore, been looking towards the East since antiquity with reverence and devotion. The Sun is a source of light and energy not only to India but to the whole world. India, like some other countries such as Egypt, Iran and Japan, has integrated this relationship into its culture and civilization, with many aspects of India's philosophy and spiritualism rooted in the Sun. India's geographical location is such that the Sun is neither too harsh as on the equator nor too mild and dim as on the poles. It is seen as an essential component of nature that sustains human life. The ethos of the Vedic civilization, believed to be initiated by the Aryans around the year 1500 BC, are woven around the Sun. Hundreds of references to the different energies and virtues of the Sun are scattered in the four Vedas.[1]

The reverence for the Sun in India is institutionalized. There is a Sun Temple in Konark on the east coast of Odisha (earlier Orissa) state of India. People from Bihar, parts of Jharkhand and eastern Uttar Pradesh, and also the Terai people (Madhes) from Nepal, celebrate a social festival called *Chhath Puja*, generally in the month of October (the sixth day of the Hindu calendar month of *Kartika*) to worship the Sun god. This festival has references to the Indian epics of Ramayana and Mahabharata. In Mahabharata, one of the important characters, Karna, was born of the association between his mother Kunti—the mother of the Pandavas—and the Sun god. India's health system of yoga which has now been propagated all over the world begins with a series of postures of bowing to the Sun called *Surya Namaskar*. In real estate also, the east is considered auspicious, and it is preferred that any home or new building face the east so as to get the blessings of the rising Sun.

Civilizational Exchanges and Cultural Diffusion

Culturally and civilizationally, the East, especially Southeast Asian countries, has been seen in India as being sympathetic and responsive. India's civilizational and cultural spread has been absorbed and amalgamated resiliently and harmoniously in the East. This is largely due to the fact that there is an inherent compatibility between the Indian and the Southeast Asian cultures.[2] This is evident in numerous living icons of culture and civilization in Southeast Asian countries. The temples of Bali and Borobudur in Indonesia, Angkor Wat in Cambodia and Luang Prabang in Laos, and the imprints of Champa civilization in

[1] Justin Norris, 'Lost Civilizations of the Sun', in *The Path of Spiritual Sun: Celebrating the Solstices and Equinoxes*, eds. Belsebubb and Angela Pritchard (Perth: Mystical Life Publications, 2016).

[2] Milton Osborn, *Southeast Asia: An Introductory History* (Australia: Allen and Unwin, 1979), 24–25; D. R. Sardesai, *Southeast Asia: Past and Present* (Boulder, CO: Westview Press, 1994), 16.

Vietnam, are internationally acknowledged in this respect. The cultural diffusion between India and the East took place in the waves of religious spread, beginning with Hinduism and followed by Buddhism and Islam. With religion also came language and literature, art and architecture, social and cultural festivals, and norms and values of governance and administration.

Southeast Asian countries evolved a synthesis of influences coming from India to make it their own. They accepted Hinduism for its strong spiritual thrust and rich philosophical approach. Besides being the vehicles of cultural diffusion, Hinduism and Buddhism also helped the Southeast Asian kingdoms to legitimize themselves in the given local context. The Hindu kingdoms identified themselves with 'Shiva (as in Champa, and in Fourteenth century Majapahit) or Vishnu (as in the case of Airlangga in the Eleventh century Java and Suryavarman II in Eleventh century Cambodia)'.[3] When Hinduism was followed by Buddhism, they converted their temples by replacing the idols of Hindu gods with the statues of Buddha in the *sanctum sanctorum*, leaving the rest of the temple architecture intact. It is indeed unique that mostly Islamic and Buddhist countries of the region continue to celebrate different forms of the Hindu epic Ramayana as a cultural and art form.[4] Most of their linguistic scripts trace their roots in Sanskrit and Pali.[5] Most of the names of individuals continue to remain Sanskritized in the whole region, except in Vietnam.

The process of civilizational and cultural diffusion between India and the East, based primarily on Hinduism and Buddhism, was most active during the first millennium of the Christian era. It is believed that India directly led this diffusion until the seventh century, after which China also joined as the Indian influence went partly through China by

[3] Heine-Geldern, as quoted in Amitav Acharya, *Civilizations in Embrace: The Spread of Ideas and the Transformation of Power, India and Southeast Asia in the Classical Age* (Singapore: Institute of Southeast Asian Studies, 2013), 33.

[4] V. Raghavan, *The Ramayana Tradition in Asia* (New Delhi: Sahitya Akademi, 1980); Devdutt Pattanaik, 'Ramayana Is a Bridge That Connects India with ASEAN', *The Hindustan Times*, 27 January 2018.

[5] J. Gonda, *Sanskrit in Indonesia* (New Delhi: International Academy of Indian Cultures, 1952).

the land route (via Myanmar, Thailand and Laos), and partly directly by the sea route. The rise of the Mughal Empire in India did not quite stop the process of cultural diffusion but slowed the momentum as the Mughals had greater interaction with their western and north-western neighbours. Trade and voyages continued between India and Southeast Asia during the Mughal Empire also, securing a prominent place for cultural diffusion. The theory that the Arabs were directly responsible for the spread of Islam in Southeast Asia does not seem convincing. Considering the distance, lack of connectivity and dependence of trade on wind directions, it could not have been possible for the Arab traders to reach Southeast Asia directly. They transited through India and took the help of Indian merchants. It was the descendants of Arab Muslims settled in India—the mixed population of Arabs and Tamil/Malayalam-speaking Muslims—who acted as intermediaries in the spread of Islam to the East. According to Ronit Ricci,

> [T]he coasts of Southeast India and Indonesia were part of the Indian Ocean's commercial network that was permeated—beginning in the fifteenth century—by an Islamic ethos, where goods and shared texts and values crossed the seas carried by Muslim merchants, pilgrims, soldiers and scholars, and where coastal towns, which functioned as important trade centres and ports, developed into major centres of Islamic learning and culture.[6]

Opinions differ on the issue of who introduced the region to Islam. A range of perspectives can be seen highlighting the role of Arabia, China, Bengal in eastern India, Gujarat in western India and, last but not least, South India as the possible sources of Islamization of Southeast Asia. However, it is widely understood that the South Indian Muslims, especially from Ma'bar[7]/Malabar, played an important role in the introduction of Islam, especially in the Malay world. It may be noted here that the earliest pieces of evidence of Arab trade

[6] Ronit Ricci, 'From Jewish Disciple to Muslim Guru: On Literary and Religious Transformation in Late Nineteenth Century Java', in *Islamic Connections: Muslim Societies in South and Southeast Asia*, eds. R. Michael Feener and Tarenjit Sevea (Singapore: ISEAS Books, 2009), 68–85.

[7] A name given by the Muslims to the Coromandel Coast and the region of Madura. The area roughly represents today's Kerala and Tamil Nadu.

with Southeast Asia are of the seventh century AD. Arab topographies and geographical dictionaries are replete with repeated mentions of Southeast Asian places:

> There had been an increase in the volume of trade due largely to changes in the political geography of the region.... This period synchronised with the rise of the Fatimids in Egypt, the Cholas in South India and the Sung dynasty in China as well as the expansion of the agricultural base and political growth of the Khmer and Burmese states.[8]

The difference between the flavours of the Arabic Islam on the one hand and the other Islam that grew and prospered in India and the East on the other hand is quite visible and distinct. The Sufi moderation was the distinct flavour of the Indian subcontinent, and that is evident in Southeast Asia also. The fact that Islam in Indonesia and Malaysia continues to happily coexist with other powerful icons and traits of Hinduism and Buddhism underlines a remarkable similarity with the composite culture of India.

Three Schools

There are three schools of thought on the extent and process of Indian civilizational spread and cultural diffusion in Southeast Asia. The first one is led by the French and Dutch historians. They were closely followed by the Indian historians (some of whom studied under their European professors), especially those who organized themselves as the Greater India Society.[9] U. N. Ghoshal, one of the leading members of this society, quotes the well-known French historian Sylvain Levi who recognized India's significant contribution in cultural diffusion all over the world:

[8] B. A. Hussainmiya, 'India and the ASEAN: The Islamic Linkage of the Past', in *Civilizational Dialogue Asian Inter-connections and Cross-Cultural Exchanges*, ed. Anjana Sharma (New Delhi: Manohar, 2013), 244.

[9] The following discussion draws from Kwa Chong-Guan, ed., *Early Southeast Asia Viewed from India: An Anthology of Articles from the Journal of the Greater India Society* (New Delhi: Manohar, 2013); and Amitav Acharya, *Civilizations in Embrace*.

> From Persia to the Chinese Sea, from the Icy regions of Siberia to the Islands of Java and Borneo, from Oceana to Socotra, India has propagated her beliefs, her tales and her civilization. She has left indelible imprints on one fourth of the human race in the course of a succession of centuries. She has the right to reclaim in universal history the rank that ignorance has refused her for a long time and to her place among the great nations, summarising and symbolising the spirit of human history.[10]

The scholars of the Greater India Society described the Southeast Asian kingdoms as 'Indianized kingdoms' and 'Indian colonies'. They ran a journal of the society to encourage many other historians and researchers to share their findings on India's civilizational and cultural engagement with Southeast Asia. Historians such as R. C. Majumdar, Kalidas Nag, K. A. Nilakanta Shastri, and U. N. Ghoshal were among the leading figures of the Greater India Society to explore the civilizational and historical engagement between India and the East. Most of them, like their European predecessors, were of the opinion that the process of diffusion has predominantly been one-way, from India to the East. In his essay on Indian internationalism, well-known historian Kalidas Nag said:

> Thus from the beginning of the Christian era, India started playing her role of internationalism not only through her lofty academic philosophy or through the vigorous propagation of a royal personality, but as a whole people following mysteriously a divine impulse, an ecstatic inspiration to sacrifice the *Ego* for the *All.* This grand movement of spiritual conquest, this noble dynamic of cultural imperialism—a legacy of Asoka—soon won for India, the inalienable empire over the vast continent, right across Tibet and China to Corea and Japan on the one hand and across Burma and Indo-China to Java and Indonesia on the other.[11]

The Greater India Society worked under the blessings of Rabindranath Tagore. He cautioned the Indian historians not to be carried away

[10] U. N. Ghoshal, 'Progress of Greater India Research, 1917–1942', *Progress of Indie Studies* 36, no. 98 (1945): 65–145.

[11] Kalidas Nag, 'Greater India: A Study in Indian Internationalism', *Greater India Society Bulletin,* no. 1 (1926), as quoted in Kwa Volume, 18.

by unduly nationalist interpretations of India's international engagements. Tagore had extensively travelled in China and Southeast Asia. During his travels to Malaysia and Indonesia, he wrote a poem entitled 'Sribijiyalakshmi', in which he said:

In the distant unrecorded age
We had met, thou and I
When my speech became entangled in thine and my life in thy life…
The East Wind had carried thy beckoning call
Through an unseen path of the air…[12]

India's first prime minister, Jawaharlal Nehru, was also exploring India's historical engagement with the world. He appears to have been influenced by the researches carried out by the Greater India Society. He wrote in his *Discovery of India* referring to R. C. Majumdar's work:

> During the past quarter of a century, a great deal of light has been thrown on the history of this widespread area of South-East Asia, which is sometimes referred to as Greater India. There are many gaps still, many contradictions and scholars continue to put forward their rival theories….
>
> From the first century of the Christian era onwards wave after wave of Indian colonists spread east and south-east reaching Ceylon, Burma, Malaya, Java, Sumatra, Borneo, Siam, Cambodia, and Indo-China. Some of them managed to reach Formosa, the Philippine Islands and Celebes. Even as far as Madagascar the current language is Indonesian with a mixture of Sanskrit words. It must have taken them several hundred years to spread out in this way, and possibly all of these places were not reached directly from India but from intermediate settlement. There appear to have been four principal waves of colonisation from the first century AC to 900 AC, and in between there must have been a stream of people going eastward. But the most remarkable feature of these ventures was that they were evidently organised by the state. Widely, scattered colonies were started almost simultaneously and almost always the settlements were situated on strategic points and on important trade routes. The names that were given to these settlements were old Indian names. Thus Cambodia, as it is known now, was

[12] As quoted in Kwa Chong-Guan, *Early Southeast Asia Viewed from India*, xxi.

> called Kamboja, which was a well-known town in ancient India, in Gandhara or the Kabul valley. This itself indicates roughly the period of this colonisation, for at that time Gandhara (Afghanistan) must have been an important part of Aryan India.[13]

The second school is represented by those who challenge the one-way process of diffusion through colonization by India. They do not find this logically compatible with the process of cultural evolution and diffusion all over the world. Some of the Dutch scholars like Jacob Cornelis van Leur later challenged the theories of the Greater India Society, saying that India was not the initiator of this cultural diffusion. In his doctoral dissertation on *Indonesian Trade and Society*, van Leur held that

> [W]hether carried on as Indonesian shipping or through the intermediary of Indian shipping, the Indonesian rulers and aristocratic groups came in contact with India, perhaps seeing it with their own eyes. In the same sort of attempt at legitimizing their interests involved in 'international trade' (in the first place vis-a-vis Indian traders themselves) and (though this was probably of secondary importance) organising and documenting their states and subjects, they called Indian civilization to the east—that is to say, they summoned the Brahmin priesthood to their courts.... There was then no 'Hindu colonisation'...no 'Hindu colonies' from which the primitive indigenous population and first of all its headmen took over the superior civilization from the west; and no learned Hindus in the midst of Indian colonists as 'advisers' to their countrymen.[14]

Underlining the give and take aspect of cultural diffusion against the Indian cultural primacy, Amitav Acharya contends that the Southeast Asians adopted and assimilated only those aspects of Indian culture that suited their local genius and conditions. In the process of this civilizational engagement, the Southeast Asians also gave ideas to India. His conclusion is that:

[13] Jawaharlal Nehru, *Discovery of India* (New Delhi: Penguin India, 2004), 213–214.

[14] As quoted in Kwa Chong-Guan, *Early Southeast Asia Viewed from India*, xxviii.

> The insights from the flow of ideas between India and Southeast Asia show that interaction among civilizations should be understood not just in material terms, but also in ideational ones. Analyzing such interactions through the lens of local initiative, localization and convergence demonstrates that the process of such inter-civilizational encounters can be pacific, and their outcome productive.[15]

It appears that the questioning of the 'Greater India Society's' Indian initiatives and Indian primacy in cultural diffusion with Southeast Asia sometimes may be emotional and exaggerated because of the terms used like 'colonization'. Some of the historians from the region have themselves endorsed the Greater India Society's line of argument. Indian historians have however been clear that this was not the colonization on those lines that followed in the region from the Western powers. R. C. Majumdar said: 'The Hindus did not regard their colonies as mainly an outlet of their excessive population and an excessive market for their growing trade.... They were not the dominant notes of the colonial policy of ancient India'. He even accepts the role of the local cultures and the give and take aspect of the cultural diffusion when he says: 'The Hindu social institutions were adapted to the needs and habits of the people, and both religion and literature were transformed to a certain extent by the influence of the indigenous elements'.[16]

The third school has emerged out of this debate that accepts the give and take aspect and even goes to the extent of underlining the parallel. This view has lately been accepted by Indian historians as well. G. C. Pande in his introduction to *India's Interactions with Southeast Asia* (2006) asserts the 'common and parallel civilizational trails in India and Southeast Asia through a long process of interchange. For a time classical Indian languages, religions, and art were creatively adapted and developed in Southeast Asia'.[17]

The process of cultural diffusion between India and Southeast Asia remained smooth in the first millennium of the Christian era.

[15] Acharya, *Civilizations in Embrace*, 71.

[16] Ibid.

[17] As quoted in Kwa Chong-Guan, *Early Southeast Asia Viewed from India*, xi.

Subsequently, India got fragmented into internecine political rivalries, which was followed by the rise of Mughal Empire first and of the British later. Interaction between India and the East remained restricted and was transformed due to various factors that will be discussed in the next chapter. However, the inherent mutual cultural compatibility and resilience remained between the two, gaining momentum whenever a suitable environment was created. The respect for Ramayana, and for Buddhist pilgrimages, remain as strong as ever in the East even at present, and Bollywood is considerably popular even in Muslim countries such as Indonesia and Malaysia, as also in predominantly Chinese society of Singapore, not to mention Myanmar. A vigorous cultural revival and projection by India in the region, to be pursued hopefully under the Act East Policy (AEP), may further strengthen its civilizational and cultural bonds with the East.

The question arises here: Why was this India-led cultural diffusion, of which even Nehru seemed convinced, not integrated with India's post-Independence policy towards this region? Nehru's approach towards Southeast Asia will be discussed in the subsequent chapters, but two possible factors may be identified here in answer to this question. First, soon after Independence, India got absorbed not only with the decolonization struggle in Asia but also with the consequences of partition and the Cold War. There were also intra-Asia conflicts that kept India preoccupied, such as with Pakistan and China. There were conflicts and divisions, prompted and encouraged by the Cold War, also within the Southeast Asian region. All this did not allow the cultural synergies between the two sides to express themselves. Second, India might also have been inhibited by the secular thrust of its post-Independence polity which did not encourage projecting India's religious linkages in its foreign policy. This hesitation was especially understandable with reference to Muslim countries of the East such as Malaysia and Indonesia.

Economic and Strategic Dimensions

Cultural diffusion between India and the East had been carried out through the exchanges of priests and preachers, scholars and voyagers, artists and artisans, and above all by the traders. There were generally two routes of such exchanges: one, the land-based route from India to Indo-China (Laos, Cambodia and Vietnam) through Myanmar, and the other, the sea-based route through sailors and commercial cargoes led by traders (Bay of Bengal through South China Sea). The East has been a great economic attraction for India and vice versa. The region comprising Thailand and Indo-China was known as *Swarnbhumi* (Land of Gold) and Sumatra as *Swarndeep* (Golden Island). India was also known as the Golden Bird (*Sone ki Chidiya*) of the East. India's East was rich in minerals, and India traded in textiles and spices with the East, as far as China. There were the rich Indian merchants who carried trade with Southeast Asia to build mutual prosperity. Evidence is also available of strong trading missions from Indonesia to India's South.[18] India was a source of trade with the region not only directly but also as a transit to the eastward trade from Africa and the Arab world.

It is difficult to put any precise date on when the two-way trade between India and the East started, but there are evidences of this trade going as far back as the year 300 BC.[19] Indian exports included textiles, opium, metal wares and artefacts, crafted gold and silver jewellery and the imports varied from spices (such as cloves, nutmeg and mace from Indonesia), camphor minerals (tin from Malaysia), rubber and precious stones from Burma, to Chinese silk and agricultural products. Textiles going from India were of different varieties, ranging from the fine Dhaka muslins and Gujarat silk embroideries to the coarse cotton of Coromandel. It was the coarse cotton textile, manufactured in bulk and being inexpensive, which was in greater demand as it was used by common people. It may be interesting to note that Thai elephants were also imported by India.[20] Along with the traders Hindu and Buddhist priests also went to carry forward the cultural exchanges. The trade and economic exchanges between India and Southeast Asia continued

[18] Van Leur and Jacob Cornelis, *Indonesian Trade and Society: Essays in Asian Social and Economic History* (Published by Dutch Scholars, Vol. 1) as cited in Kwa Chong-Guan, *Early Southeast Asia Viewed from India*, xlvii.

[19] K. P. Rao, 'Early Trade and Contacts between South India and Southeast Asia (300 BC–200 AD)', *East and West* 51, no. 3–4 (December 2001): 385–394.

[20] Om Prakash, 'Trading World of India and Southeast Asia in the Early Modern Period', *Archipel* 56 (1998): 31–42.

until the British destroyed India's manufacturing capacities through 'deindustrialization' and diverted Southeast Asian trade and economic relations directly to Great Britain. They also introduced plantation economy as a strong factor in harnessing the economic potential of Southeast Asia and Sri Lanka. It is, however, the continuation of this inherent economic dynamism between the two regions that is now manifesting in India's renewed drive towards the East in the form of Look East and Act East policies.

Cultural and economic exchanges between India and Southeast Asia flourished peacefully due to mutual compatibility and advantage. This was a peaceful engagement of civilizations, unlike the later theories of scholars like Huntington who propounded the notion of the clash of civilizations (mainly between Islamic and Christian, in the aftermath of 9/11). Both Hinduism and Buddhism from India, as also the Southeast Asian local cultures, displayed a phenomenal spirit of mutual accommodation and adaptation. Even the flow of Islam did not precipitate in any conflict in the East of India. The only exception of a clash is a reference to the Chola kings from South India having a conflict with the empire of Srivijaya in the eleventh century. The Cholas did have some military encounters with Palembang, Srivijaya empire's capital, in 1025 AD. But some of the Western scholars like George Coedes maintain that the encounter was a reaction against the obstructions caused by the Srivijaya rulers in the trade flows of the Cholas towards China. Dr Nilakanta Shastri, an Indian historian on the Chola period, asserts that 'there was no attempt by the Cholas to rule over these lands…at best they might have received periodical tributes'.[21] After the Cholas, who are credited with having a vision of becoming a naval power, during the seventeenth and eighteenth centuries, Maratha ruler Shivaji's commander, Kanhoji Angre, and the king of Mysore, Tipu Sultan, also paid a lot of attention to strengthening their naval capabilities for ensuring coastal security, but they never succeeded in doing so and were soon subdued by the British.

[21] As quoted in Navrekha Sharma and Baladas Ghoshal, *India's Relations with Indonesia* (Singapore: Market Asia Books, 2014), 18; Sanjeev Sanyal, *The Ocean of Churn: How the Indian Ocean Shaped Human History* (New Delhi: Penguin, Random House, 2016), 130–134.

The strategic factor between India and Southeast Asia was seemingly introduced by the British Empire in India. Pre-colonial India's spirit of engagement was replaced by that of territorial expansion, consolidation and control by the British, when they came in conflict, first with the competing European empires of the French and Portuguese in the region and then with the regional empires in China and Japan. They used Indian and other subcontinental soldiers like the Gurkhas of Nepal in the service of the Empire, which distorted the idea of India in the perception of the East by adding a military and aggressive dimension to it. The perception of the East about India was also dented because Indian leaders like Subhas Chandra Bose sought liberation from the British militarily by joining hands with the Japanese forces during the Second World War.

However, post Independence, India has seldom been seen as a security threat to Southeast Asia, with some exceptions. One was in 1965, when Indonesia threatened to blockade India's Andaman and Nicobar Islands during the India–Pakistan conflict in support of Pakistan.[22] The Indonesian move was largely driven by the Islamic identity with Pakistan. There was no attempt to understand the causes of the war and who started it. It was entirely imposed by Pakistan, on India. Then again, during the mid-1980s, a statement of the Indian Naval Officer to plan for a blue-water navy was interpreted by media in Australia and some Southeast Asian countries as an aggressive move by India. There has been Western unhappiness over India's demand, along with some of its neighbours like Sri Lanka during the early 1970s, that the Indian Ocean be left free of the great power military presence. India was in no position to raise a blue-water navy due to its financial constraints, nor did it ever have any aggressive design on any of its eastern neighbours. As we shall see in the subsequent chapters, the unfounded scare that was raised died out soon.

Contrary to such scares, many of the Southeast Asian countries have sought India's support and cooperation in security matters. Singapore's Lee Kuan Yew wrote to former Indian Prime Minister Lal Bahadur Shastri to help him raise a strong army for the new State. He

[22] Sharma and Ghoshal, *India's Relations with Indonesia*.

was also one of the few world leaders who suggested India to go nuclear after the Chinese nuclear explosion.[23] India did not respond to the request for help in building up the Singapore army partly because of its own resource constraints but primarily because India did not want to get entangled in the region's internal rivalries and conflicts. India also thought that helping Singapore in defence matters may not go well with another friendly country, Malaysia. Despite this disappointment and notwithstanding his reservations on India's pace of development, Lee continued to believe that 'India alone could look China in the eye'.[24] India's reservations on building defence and security ties with Southeast Asian countries have started melting away under its Look East and Act East policies, as will be seen in the subsequent chapters.

Making Sense of Transitions in India's Eastward Engagement

The idea of the East for the European powers was very different from that of India's idea of the East. Perhaps, the 'Indianized states or Greater India' of the Southeast Asian region were seen as being engulfed within India. During the entire European medieval ages, most of the Eastern civilization was manifested by China, Japan and India. India was known by a number of expressions such as 'upper India', 'greater India', 'little India' and 'farthest India', terms which have also been used to define the entire landmass comprising the Indian subcontinent, Southeast Asia and beyond. As George Coedes states,

> Culturally speaking, Farther India today is characterised by more or less deep traces of the Indianisation that occurred long ago: the importance of the Sanskrit element in the vocabulary of the languages spoken there; the Indian origin of the alphabets with which those languages have been or still are written; the influence of Indian law and administrative organisation; the persistence of certain Brahmanic and Buddhist traditions in the countries

[23] Lee Kwan Yew, *From Third World to the First: The Singapore Story 1965–2000* (Singapore: Harper Collins, 2000).

[24] Sunanda K. Datta-Ray, *Looking East to Look West: Lee Kuan Yew's Mission India* (Singapore: Institute of Southeast Asian Studies, 2009).

> converted to Islam; and the presence of ancient monuments which, in architecture and sculpture, are associated with the arts of India and bear inscriptions in Sanskrit.[25]

Throughout the sixteenth and seventeenth centuries, almost all the territories east of the Indus river were called *India*, and the geographic maps of *India Orientalis* showed the entire region stretching from India to the entire Southeast Asian landscape.[26]

India intra Gangem (India within the Ganges) was the Latin name that Europeans used for several centuries while referring to the Indian subcontinent. It was Herman Moll, a British cartographer, who in 1710 drew a map of India showing it for the first time as a part of the Indian subcontinent. He redrew the map in 1726 and entitled it India Proper or the Empire of the Great Mogul. 'This led to increasing understanding in Britain that [the] Indian subcontinent should be seen as a different geographic and cultural entity.... It also manifested the desire to leave behind the confusion that reigned until then with regard to the use of the term India for all of Asia'.[27] Subsequently, mapmaking became an integral part of colonization, thus leading to the re-drawing of regions based on convenience of the colonial powers. Eventually, in 1799, James Rennell drew the first modern map of India, depicting India as a part of the Indian subcontinent. The cumulative effect of cartographic divisions, colonial compartmentalization of countries of the region, and eventually cultural differentiations due to the impact of Islam and the Western colonial rule led to the emergence of the argument that India and countries of the East were different from one another and, therefore, should have their own distinct identities. This, however, was a faulty notion, and it remained predominant only till the colonial powers ruled India and the countries of Southeast and East Asia. For India and its people, the East always remained an important aspect of its philosophical, religious and cultural space.

[25] G. Coedes, *The Indianised States of Southeast Asia* (Honolulu: East-West Center, 1968), xvi.

[26] Pekka Korhonen, 'Monopolizing Asia: The Politics of a Metaphor', *Pacific Review* 10, no. 3 (1997): 347–365.

[27] Susan Gole, *India within the Ganges* (New Delhi: Jayaprints, 1983): 64.

Clearly, ideas such as South Asia, Southeast Asia and even Asia were formulated and imposed by the European colonial powers.[28] It was the idea of colonial powers which aimed at restraining the popular discourse in the East that they all are part of a cultural continuum, full of vices and devoid of significant virtues, placed alongside each other in this part of the world.

In his book *Glimpses of World History*, Jawaharlal Nehru wrote that Asia and Europe were no more than geographical terms. This terminology acquired momentum as the European countries began colonization of the countries of the 'East'. However, this could not make an impact on its own. The real change began when the countries which were colonized started appropriating such nomenclatures on their own.[29] Eventually, from the mid-twentieth century onwards, geographical subsets came into existence, thus deconstructing the idea of the East. For instance, the term 'Southeast Asia' was first used in 1839 by an American pastor Howard Malcolm in his book entitled *Travels in South-Eastern Asia*.[30] The Allies used the term in official documents for the first time during the Second World War, through the formation of the South East Asia Command in 1943.[31] The concept of South Asia did not exist at the time of the Asian Relations Conference (ARC) in 1947; because of this, the nations of the Indian subcontinent belonged to the Southeast Asian unit.

In India's millennia-old Eastward engagement, several highs and lows have come and gone. For instance, after the glorious Hindu and Buddhist period came the medieval times, which also gave birth to the rise of the Chinese quest for influence in its neighbourhood. Thus, as the golden era of Indian interface with its East was fading by the seventh/eighth century AD, the Chinese influence fastened the receding Indian

[28] Isabelle Saint Mezard, *Eastward Bound India's New Positioning in Asia* (New Delhi: Manohar, 2006), 17.

[29] Ibid.

[30] Joshua Eliot, Jane Bickersteth and Sebastian Ballard, *Indonesia, Malaysia & Singapore Handbook* (New York, NY: Trade & Trade & Travel Publications, 1996).

[31] Park Seung Woo and Victor T King, eds., *The Historical Construction of Southeast Asian Studies: Korea and Beyond* (Singapore: Institute of Southeast Asian Studies, 2013).

influence. Several Southeast Asian countries that were administratively, politically and societally influenced by India also moved in the political orbit of China because of their geographic position. In the fourth century, Samudragupta's victory in the Ganges valley and southern India and the expeditions of the Chola emperors of Thanjore in the eleventh century had ramifications on the other side of the Bay of Bengal.[32] Coedes argues,

> The Chinese never looked with favour on the formation of strong states in the southern seas, as it is a fact worth noting that the periods of greatest strength of Funan (Cambodia), which was essentially a Hindu Kingdom, and the Javanese and Sumatran kingdoms, correspond in general to the period of weakness of the great Chinese dynasties. In addition, the countries of 'farther' India are bound together by geographic and economic ties, and any revolution in the interior of one, by stirring up the populace, has had repercussions on the others. The disintegration of the Funan empire, the birth of the Sumatran kingdom of Srivijaya, the accession of Anoratha in Pagan or Suryavarman II in Angkor, the founding of the Thai kingdom of Sukhothai, all had distinct effects beyond the borders of the countries in which these events took place. There are, then, critical dates which constitute real 'turning points' in the history of Southeast Asia which make it possible to delimit a certain number of epochs, each having its own characteristics, each marked by the imprint of a strong personality or by the political supremacy of a powerful state.[33]

From this, it is clear that India's idea of the East has metamorphosed over time, denoting different philosophical and material values at different times. Traditionally, it is believed that as Sun worshippers, India has always been looking towards the East, as has been already noted. Considered auspicious in the Hindu mythology, Indians have traditionally been attaching great philosophical, religious and symbolic value to the East. For instance, at one point in history, for India, Japan was considered a country situated in the East. This was also in conformity with the Japanese traditional belief that Japanese people are the sons of the Sun god.

[32] Coedes, *The Indianised States of Southeast Asia*, xviii–xix.
[33] Ibid.

Bali Jatra is a landmark example of spiritual-religious aspect of India's eastward engagement, which exists even today. The term literally means 'a voyage to Bali'. In the Indian state of Odisha, this festival is held on Gadagadia Ghata of the Mahanadi River in Cuttack to mark the day when ancient *sadhabas* (Oriya mariners) would set sail to the distant lands of Bali as well as to Java, Sumatra, Borneo and Sri Lanka for trade and cultural expansion.[34] Also known as *Boita Bandana*, the festival of *Bali Jatra* 'witnesses people gathering near river banks or sea shores to float miniature boats (*boita*) as a symbolic gesture that they will leave for faraway islands of Bali, Java, Sumatra, Borneo and Ceylon (Sri Lanka) to which their ancestors once sailed'.[35] It is celebrated in October–November every year for five consecutive days before the full moon. The idea is to memorize the maritime legacy of Odisha and to remember the strong commercial ties that used to exist between India and countries to its East.[36]

After the advent of the Renaissance and the Industrial Revolution, and the subsequent rise of the 'West', particularly during the colonial period, most of the newly colonized countries, particularly those falling in Asia, were considered as the 'East', and India too was a part of this wider 'East'. Suddenly, the East was identified with poverty and illiteracy, and with lack of scientific temper and knowledge, and modernity. The East became a synonym of the colonies with a rich ancient heritage, which were later defined as Asia. According to Maura Cunningham,

> [D]erived from the Greco-Roman conception of the world, the concept of Asia has a perverse genealogy as Europe's other. Asians have experienced 'Asia' in ephemeral, uneven, and fleeting modes. At its heart lie the limits of inherited geographical categories. Nevertheless, the concept of Asia retains great power in the political imagination. It serves as a critique of geography as a historical category and of the Asian nation-states that are today asserting

[34] For details, see the official website of the Orissa tourism, http://odishatourism.gov.in/?q=node/155, accessed 16 August 2018.

[35] Ibid.

[36] Ibid.

> themselves politically, economically, and geographically by invoking older and mythic forms of Asian culture and genealogies.[37]

Apparently, there were several specific identifiable points, sometimes stereotypes, which were attached to the East during the colonial era. Some of these included lack of enough modern education and industrialization, poverty and diseases, and, more importantly, the inability to compete with the newly industrialized Western countries.[38]

However, that begun to change in the second half of the twentieth century. As India's economic growth started to take shape, with the success of the economic reforms, its strategic vision expanded and thus its need to look at East in a more comprehensive fashion increased. That, arguably, is the reason why in the post-2000 phase, Japan has begun to figure more prominently in India's Look East Policy (LEP) discourse.

The Indo-Pacific

The strategic dimensions of India's East have been changing. Recent developments are redefining the geopolitics of India's idea of the East as it is being extended to the Pacific. The process was triggered in August 2007 when Japan's Prime Minister Shinzo Abe first raised it during his visit to India. Explaining the new need for bringing the Indian and the Pacific Oceans into one geostrategic space of Indo-Pacific, he said in his address to the Indian Parliamentarians that

> Pacific and the Indian Oceans are now bringing about a dynamic coupling as seas of freedom and of prosperity. A 'Broader Asia' that broke away geographical boundaries is now beginning to take on a distinct form. Our two countries have the ability—and the responsibility—to ensure that it broadens yet further and to

[37] Maura Elizabeth Cunningham, Association of Asian Studies, http://www.asian-studies.org/Conferences/AAS-in-Asia-Conferences/India-2018-Home-Page/Call-for-Proposals, accessed 16 August 2018.

[38] Edward W. Said in his excellent book *Orientalism* argues that the Western view of the East is based on their imagination and on stereotypes popularized through a colonial view of these countries. For details, see Edward W. Said, *Orientalism* (New York, NY: Pantheon Books, 1978).

> nurture and enrich these seas to become seas of clearest transparence.... This is the message I wish to deliver directly today to the one billion people of India. That is why I stand before you now in the Central Hall of the highest chamber, to speak with you, the people's representatives of India.[39]

There is an attempt to see the Pacific (especially Western Pacific) with the Indian Ocean linked as one region by the inclusion of South Asia, particularly India, as one single strategic theatre. In the US official articulation of the 'pivot policy', the concept of 'Indo-Pacific' was first used by Secretary Clinton in 2010 as an imperative of the emerging geostrategic reality of the region. Explaining 'America's Engagement in the Asia-Pacific' at Honolulu, Hawaii, on 28 October 2010, she said:

> [O]ur military presence must evolve to reflect an evolving world. The Pentagon is now engaged in a comprehensive Global Posture Review, which will lay out a plan for the continued forward presence of U.S. forces in the region. That plan will reflect three principles: Our defense posture will become more politically sustainable, operationally resilient, and geographically dispersed.... *And we are expanding our work with the Indian navy in the Pacific, because we understand how important the Indo-Pacific basin is to the global trade and commerce.*[40] (Emphasis added)

Explaining the salience of an integrated view of the Indian and Pacific Oceans, and redefining the Asia-Pacific in the Indo-Pacific terms, she again wrote in her *Foreign Policy* article:

> Asia-Pacific has become a key driver of global politics. Stretching from the Indian subcontinent to the western shores of the Americas, the region spans two oceans—the Pacific and the India(n)—that

[39] The complete text of Japanese Prime Minister Shinzo Abe's address 'Confluence of Two Seas' on 22 August 2007 is available via the Ministry of Foreign Affairs Japan, https://www.mofa.go.jp/region/asia-paci/pmv0708/speech-2.html, accessed 16 August 2018.

[40] The complete text of then Secretary of State Hillary Rodham Clinton's speech on 'America's Engagement in the Asia-Pacific' on 28 October 2010 is available via the website of US Department of State, https://2009–2017.state.gov/secretary/20092013clinton/rm/2010/10/150141.htm, accessed 16 August 2018.

> are increasingly linked by shipping and strategy. It boasts almost half of the world's population. It includes many of the key engines of the global economy, as well as the largest emitters of greenhouse gases. It is home to several of our key allies and important emerging powers like China, India and Indonesia.[41]

Following Secretary Clinton, the use of Indo-Pacific as a concept in the US official statements became frequent. Secretary of Defence Leon E. Panetta reaffirmed it while addressing defence experts in New Delhi on 6 June 2012, saying that under the rebalancing strategy, 'We will expand our military partnership and our presence in the arc extending from the western Pacific and east Asia into Indian Ocean region and South Asia'.[42] For instance, Kurt Campbell, Assistant Secretary of State for East Asia and the Pacific, in one of his interactions said:

> We have to create an operational concept that links more the Indian Ocean with the Pacific. These are going to be the two dynamic oceans of our future. We are going to have to be more geographically dispersed. We are going to have to work with more nations that will sustain a strong American presence in the Asia Pacific.[43]

The Indo-Pacific concept has gradually been integrated into US strategic thinking. It has found a place in the America First National Security Strategy (NSS) announced by the Trump administration in December 2017. Under the regional pillar of the strategy document, it is said:

> A geopolitical competition between free and repressive visions of world order is taking place in the Indo-Pacific region. The region,

[41] Hillary Rodham Clinton, 'America's Pacific Century', *Foreign Policy*, 11 October 2011.

[42] The complete text of the speech by former Defence Secretary of State Leon Panetta on 'Partners in the 21st Century' on 6 June 2012 is available via the IDSA website, https://idsa.in/keyspeeches/LeonEPanettaonPartnersinthe21stcentury, accessed 16 August 2018.

[43] Mr Campbell was interacting with the strategic community at the Foreign Policy Initiative forum in December 2011. For details, see http://www.foreignpolicyi.org/content/obama-administration-pivot-asia#pictures, accessed 16 August 2018.

> which stretches from the west coast of India to the western shores of the United States, represents the most populous and economically dynamic part of the world. The U.S. interest in a free and open Indo-Pacific extends back to the earliest days of our republic.[44]

Accordingly, territorial and maritime limits of the Indo-Pacific region are defined here, and India is given an important place as a strategic partner in the implementation of the strategy. Following on this direction, the USA has renamed its Pacific Command as the Indo-Pacific Command. The US Defence Secretary John Mattis, announcing this change of name in Hawaii in May 2018, said:

> It is our primary combatant command, it's standing watch and intimately engaged with over half of the earth's surface and its diverse populations, from Hollywood to Bollywood, from polar bears to penguins....
>
> In recognition of the increasing connectivity between the Indian and Pacific oceans, today we rename the U.S. Pacific Command to U.S. Indo-Pacific Command.... Over many decades this command has repeatedly adapted to changing circumstances and today carries that legacy forward as America focuses west.[45]

Following on the USA's lead, the concept has also been deeply integrated into the official strategic discourse and policy articulation of Australia.[46]

Indonesia has also emerged as a strong supporter of the concept of Indo-Pacific. Its first indication came in 2013 when the then Indonesian Foreign Minister Dr Natalegawa in an international conference in Washington, DC, proposed a treaty for Indo-Pacific

[44] As quoted in Ayres Alyssa, *Our Time Has Come; How India is Making Its Place in the World* (New York, NY: Oxford University Press, 2018).

[45] The complete text of the press release is available via the website of the US Department of Defence, 30 May 2018, https://translations.state.gov/2018/05/30/remarks-at-u-s-indo-pacific-command-change-of-command-ceremony/ accessed 16 August 2018.

[46] For a detailed discussion of the use of the term, see David Scott, 'The Indo-Pacific–New Regional Formulations and New Maritime Frameworks for US–India Strategic Convergence', *Asia-Pacific Review* 19, no. 2 (2012): 85–109.

Friendship and Cooperation. The objective behind this proposal was to underline a 'commitment by states in the region to build confidence, to solve disputes by peaceful means and to promote a concept of security that is all encompassing'.[47] This concept is being vigorously pursued under the powerful and dynamic leadership of Indonesian President Joko Widodo, where ASEAN (Association of Southeast Asian Nations) centrality is underlined and the concept is being projected as different and independent of what is being propagated by the USA and Japan. Indonesian leadership proposes to present this concept as the key foreign policy strategy of Indonesia at the forthcoming ASEAN Summit in November 2018, because Indonesia envisages itself as being the 'global maritime axis' or 'fulcrum'.[48]

The Indo-Pacific concept has not found any favour with China. There has not been any strong official reaction but the academic and strategic debate in China has not endorsed the concept. They see it as a vague, still undeveloped and at best a negative concept that aims at containing China's rise.[49] Russia supports China in this respect. Russian Deputy Foreign Minister Igor Morgulov, addressing a conference in Beijing on 29 May 2018, said that

> The attempts to reshape the architecture of international relations are eroding the foundations of the current system in Asia-Pacific. I am referring in part, to the idea of the Indo-Pacific region, which the United States and Japan are actively advocating. Essentially it is designed to divide the regional countries into friends and foes, the good and the bad, or democratic and not-very-democratic countries. It goes without saying that the authors of this idea reserve

[47] The complete text of the speech is available via the Center for Strategic and International Studies, http://csis.org/files/attachments/130516_Marty_Natalegawa, accessed 16 August 2018.

[48] Jansen Tham, 'What's in Indonesia's Indo-Pacific Cooperation Concept', *The Diplomat*, 16 May 2018, https://thediplomat.com/2018/05/whats-in-indonesias-indo-pacific-cooperation-concept/, accessed 16 August 2018.

[49] Han Guo, 'Why China Takes Issues with Trump's Indo-Pacific Concept', *Institute For China-America Studies,* 21 December 2017, http://chinaus-icas.org/bulletin/why-china-takes-issue-with-trumps-indo-pacific-concept/, accessed 16 August 2018. Also see Dingding Chen, 'What China Thinks of the Indo-Pacific Strategy', *The Diplomat*, 27 April 2018, https://thediplomat.com/2018/05/what-china-thinks-of-the-indo-pacific-strategy/, accessed 16 August 2018.

> the right to decide which is which. Both Russia and China hold a diametrically opposite view. They are against creating blocks and believe that an effective and system-wide response to security challenges in Asia-Pacific must include a comprehensive military and political détente and uniform rules of the game.[50]

The credit for conceiving of and introducing the concept should however go to the Indian official strategic discourse. And this goes back to earlier than Abe's use of the term. The *Indian Maritime Doctrine* articulated by the Ministry of Defence in 2004 underlined 'the shift in global maritime focus from the Atlantic-Pacific combine to the Pacific–Indian Ocean region'.[51] Senior officials in the Ministry of External Affairs (MEA) have been using the term quite frequently by now. India's then Ambassador in the USA, Mrs Nirupama Rao, had been using the term soon after the announcement of the pivot strategy by the USA. Speaking at Brown University on 4 February 2013, she said:

> It has also been observed how the geographical subtext of India's engagement in the Asia-pacific is also manifest in the term 'Indo-Pacific' which is increasingly defining the cultural, economic, political and security continuum that straddles the Indian and the Pacific Ocean regions, and is fast becoming a geo-strategic construct to comprehend common opportunities, the intersecting maritime and security interests, and challenges confronting the region.[52]

[50] The complete text of the speech of Deputy Foreign Minister Igor Morgulov is available via the website of Russian Ministry of Foreign Affairs, http://www.mid.ru/en/diverse/-/asset_publisher/zwI2FuDbhJx9/content/vystuplenie-zamestitela-ministra-inostrannyh-del-rossii-i-v-morgulova-na-cetvertoj-mezdunarodnoj-konferencii-rossia-i-kitaj-sotrudnicestvo-v-novu-u-epo?_101_INSTANCE_zwI2FuDbhJx9_redirect=http%3A%2F%2Fwww.mid.ru%2Fen%2Fdiverse%3Fp_p_id%3D101_INSTANCE_zwI2FuDbhJx9%26p_p_lifecycle%3D0%26p_p_state%3Dnormal%26p_p_mode%3Dview%26p_p_col_id%3Dcolumn-1%26p_p_col_pos%3D2%26p_p_col_count%3D6, accessed 16 August 2018.

[51] For details, see *Indian Maritime Doctrine, First Edition, Integrated Headquarters* (New Delhi: Ministry of Defence (Navy), Government of India, New Delhi, 2004), 91.

[52] The complete text of the speech of former Indian Ambassador in the USA, Mrs Nirupama Rao, is available via the website of the Indian embassy, Washington, DC, http://www.indianembassy.org/includes/page.php?id=2097, accessed 16 August 2018.

Former Indian Foreign Secretary Ranjan Mathai also used the term 'Indo-Pacific' as a synonym of the Asia-Pacific region while underlining India's convergence of interests with the USA in this region, in February 2012.[53] The greatest legitimacy to the term in the Indian official lexicon was given by the then Prime Minister Dr Manmohan Singh when addressing the commemorative India–ASEAN Summit in New Delhi on 20 December 2012 when he said: 'I, feel, our future is interlinked and a stable, secure and prosperous Indo-Pacific region is crucial for our own progress and prosperity'.[54] Earlier, former Defence Minister A. K. Antony, while addressing the Maritime Power Conference in New Delhi on 26 February 2012, had acknowledged the 'relevance of the Indian-Ocean-Pacific or the Indo-Pacific' in the emerging great power relations.[55]

The endorsement of the usage of 'Indo-Pacific' is also widely reflected in the strategic discourse at unofficial levels in India. In contemporary strategic writings, it was used as early as in January 2007, well before the use of the term by the Japanese prime minister.[56] India's senior former officials such as former Navy Chief Arun Prakash and former Special Envoy to the Prime Minister and former Foreign Secretary Shyam Saran have also been using the term, besides several other scholars.[57] To the Indian analysts and policymakers, the concept of Indo-Pacific comes naturally, rooted as it is in historical and civilizational experiences and geostrategic reality. An Indian

[53] The complete text of the speech of former Foreign Secretary Ranjan Mathai on the subject is available via the website of the Indian MEA, http://meaindia.nic.in/mystart.php?id=530118985, accessed 16 August 2018.

[54] The complete text of the speech of former Indian Prime Minister Dr Manmohan Singh at the Plenary Session of India-ASEAN Commemorative Summit on 20 December 2012 is available via the website of Press Information Bureau, http://www.pib.nic.in/newsite/erelcontent.aspx?relid=91052, accessed 16 August 2018.

[55] The complete text of the speech by former Minister of Defence A. K. Antony is available via the website of the Press Information Bureau, http://pib.nic.in/newsite/erelcontent.aspx?relid=80543, accessed 16 August 2018.

[56] Gurpreet Khurana, 'Security of Sea-Lines: Prospects of India-Japan Cooperation', *Strategic Analysis*, January 2007.

[57] Shyam Saran, 'Mapping the Indo-Pacific', *The Indian Express*, 30 October 2011; C. Raja Mohan, *Samudra Manthan: Sino-Indian Rivalry in the Indo-Pacific* (Washington, DC: Carnegie Endowment for International Peace, 2012).

historian, Kalidas Nag, wrote a book, *India and the Pacific World*, in 1941 concluding that:

> The expansion of Indian culture into the Pacific world is a grand chapter of human history.... What parts of this cultural complex could reach the Eastern pacific basin and New World are problems for future anthropologists and antiquarians.... This colossal cultural drama is reappearing to us like an ancient mutilated play with many acts and interludes still missing which future research alone would probably restore and reconstruct. But whatever portions have already been recovered inspire us with awe and admiration.... There was no sordid chapter of economic exploitation or political domination in the development of Greater India which coming as a legacy from Emperor Asoka of third century BC continued for over 1000 years to foster the fundamental principles of *maître* (fellowship) and *kalayana* (universal well-being) which form the bed-rocks of Hindu-Buddhist idealism.[58]

Historically, India was a principal player in the 'spice' trade that flowed from the Indian Ocean to the Western Pacific Region. Even before this trade flourished, India's cultural and civilizational footprints in the countries of the Western Pacific such as Cambodia, Laos, Vietnam and Indonesia had been firmly established. The process started in the first century or even earlier, and it was carried out by cultural and commercial means. The British Indian Empire added new features like the presence of Indian diaspora (the Indian indentured labour taken to work on plantations) in Southeast Asian countries, and a security and strategic perspective covering the Indian Ocean as also the South China Sea (Hong Kong). These footprints have played a foundational role in India's LEP to which we shall return later. Geographically, India's out-stretched island territories comprising Andaman and Nicobar, sitting on the mouth of the Malacca Strait, provide a strategic link between the Indian Ocean and the Western Pacific. Strategically also, in recent years, the interventionist moves by the US Pacific Command during the war of liberation in Bangladesh in December 1971, when the USS

[58] U. N. Ghoshal, review of *India and the Pacific World*, by Kalidas Nag, *Journal of the Greater India Society* IX, no. 1 (1942): 39–41, as cited in Kwa Chong-Guan, *Early Southeast Asia Viewed from India*, 51–52.

Enterprise sailed from the Pacific Ocean to the Bay of Bengal to force India to stop the operation of liberating Bangladesh, left no doubt in the minds of the Indian strategic planners that the Pacific was linked with the Indian Ocean when it comes to India's security.

India's initial response has been one of caution and hesitation in accepting this concept. The reservations arise from the perception that accepting this concept would amount to India being seen as getting strategically close to the USA at the cost of its strategic autonomy. Over the past few years, India has shed off these reservations and accepted the Indo-Pacific concept. It would have been better if India did not have these reservations at all because this concept is rooted in India's cultural engagement with the region and has been nursed by a long history. Unfortunately, India's official responses to critical policy options are not very apt in grounding themselves in history. Prime Minister Abe also did not present the concept as his original idea. He referred to a book authored by India's Mughal Emperor Aurangzeb's brother Dara Shikoh entitled *Confluence of Two Seas* (1615). Dara Shikoh was, however, writing about the two different seas of culture and civilizations, perhaps Hinduism and Islam, wherein he perceived the need for 'confluence'.

India's idea of the East covered the Western Pacific Region and extended up to the west coast of the Americas. From India's perspective, the geopolitics of the Indo-Pacific was part of its historical, cultural and civilizational space. Kalidas Nag also underlines this in his essay 'Indian Internationalism', included in Kwa Chong-Guan's book. More than nearly seven decades before the USA's call on India to play a greater role in the 'Indo-Pacific' region, India's first prime minister, Nehru, even before India's Independence, envisaged this. In his *Discovery of India*, he almost predicted the rise of the Indo-Pacific:

> The Pacific is likely to take the place of the Atlantic in the future as a nerve centre of the world. Though not directly a Pacific state, India will inevitably exercise an important influence there. India will also develop as the centre of economic and political activity in the Indian Ocean, in Southeast Asia and right up to the Middle

> East. Her position gives an economic and strategic importance in a part of the world which is going to develop rapidly in future.[59]

Indian policymakers, with a sense of history and India's civilizational evolution, should have not only readily endorsed but also been an active proponent of the Indo-Pacific concept from the beginning, as it gives India a unique chance to make culture as a powerful instrument in its strategic diplomacy. As we have noted earlier, the initial hesitation has been shed off, and the Indo-Pacific concept has become an acknowledged part of India's foreign policy discourse, even before announcing the change in policy from Look East to Act East. This has become clear, looking at Prime Minister Modi's visits to the region during May–June 2018. In Indonesia, he signed a 'shared vision' statement on 'Maritime Cooperation in the Indo-Pacific' with the host President Joko Widodo on 30 May 2018. Again, on 1 June 2018, he projected India's view on ensuring a 'free, open and inclusive' Indo-Pacific region at the Shangri La Dialogue in Singapore. Defining the geographical limits of the region, Modi said, 'from the shores of Africa to that of the Americas'. There is, however, some confusion here. India has also been insisting on the ASEAN centrality in the Indo-Pacific dynamics. If that is so, then how can ASEAN relate to 'from the shores of Africa…' that covers the western front of the Indian Ocean. The latest Indian definition of the Indo-Pacific stretch is also at variance with that of the US definition. The former covers a larger area than defined by the US NSS (December 2017) covering the 'west coast of India to the western shores of the United States'.

It is hoped that with renewed emphasis on culture-based soft power in India's policy under Modi, the AEP will soon integrate India's traditional civilizational and cultural links with the Eastern region into its strategic and foreign policy perspectives. It is being realized that in the evolution of the idea of East for India, the Indo-Pacific concept has come to represent the multidimensional strategic reality of the region, encompassing within itself the aspects of culture and civilization, economy and development, and strategic imperatives and security.

[59] Nehru, *Discovery of India*, 597.

CHAPTER 2

Waves of History

Ancient to Pre-Independence Era

Introduction

As elaborated in the previous chapter, India's interaction with the East dates back to the prehistoric times.[1] The imprint of Indian influence on the East has been indelible, cutting across various aspects of human life. No matter how uninformed, an Indian tourist's casual visit to the countries of the East and of Southeast Asia mesmerizes him (or her) with the remarkable similarities between India and the region. For one, a mirror image of sorts of the Ajanta and Ellora caves (near Mumbai) can be seen in Prambanan, Central Java, in the form of the Plaosan temple. The Indian epics Ramayana, Mahabharata and Pali Nidesa repeatedly mention the eastern cities and countries.

While it is true that India never (with one or two exceptions) colonized the countries of the region—something which has been acknowledged and appreciated by the giants of the ancient Greco-Roman empire such as Claudius Ptolemy (100 AD–170 AD)—it is equally unimaginable that such heavy influence on the region

[1] For instance, the archeological evidences found in some parts of Thailand, dating back to first millennium BC, have remarkable similarity with artefacts found in archeological sites of northern and north-central parts of India.

happened without any direct or indirect intervention of the Indian kings and their peoples, as will be seen later.

India's engagement with the East can be divided into seven distinct phases or waves. Beginning with the first wave of ancient Hindu–Buddhist influence and then the Islamic wave, the British era could be considered a wavelet of the third wave, which was effectively countered by the counter-wavelet in the form of the Indian freedom struggle. The fourth wave was led by Nehru as the chief architect of Indian foreign policy and of India's eastward engagement in the twentieth century. The post-Nehru phase, which we have considered as the fifth wave, was followed by the Look East phase which lasted till 2014. The Act East phase may be considered as the seventh ongoing phase.

The three initial waves of India's eastward engagement—(a) Hindu–Buddhist, (b) Islamic and (c) the British colonial period and the freedom movement—offer a fascinating mix of wavelets of engagement. During the Hindu–Buddhist phase, the spread of Hinduism and Buddhism complemented each other, and in several ways they brought together a holistic picture of Indian influence on the East. The Islamic phase, beginning from the twelfth to the thirteenth century onwards, remained rather solitary and deprived of royal patronage. The third, that is, the Colonial rule and the freedom struggle phase, had two contrasting wavelets working with different objectives and led by opposing actors, but both of them contributed to India's engagement with the East in varying degrees.

This chapter does not intend to approach the history of India, and countries of the East and of Southeast Asia, from a historian's point of view. It is meant for scholars and students of international relations and India's foreign policy who wish to have a basic understanding of India's past engagement with the region. Thus, the scholarly debates are not focused upon in this chapter nor are the history research tools such as numismatics, archaeology, inscriptions, and ancient and medieval archival sources analysed and debated.

Ancient Indian influence on Southeast Asia has been given several terms. 'Indianization' has so far been the most accepted term to understand and explain the Indian influence on the East. This came into vogue with the work produced by George Coedes entitled *Indianised States of Southeast Asia.* Another term used to analyse Indian influence has been 'Hinduization' but it does not quite encompass the essence of the waves of Indian influence on the region as it tends to overlook the influence of Buddhism and Islam emanating from India to these regions. The term Hinduization is often attached to the Hindu nationalist historians who were of the view that Indian kingdoms had established religious colonies in Southeast Asia. While the concepts of Hinduization and Greater India have their own limitations, keeping in view the history of religions, and of mass religious conversions and the role of missionaries, mercenaries, and monarchs in it, it is hard to argue (and believe) that the Southeast Asian countries accepted and embraced Hindu and Buddhist rituals on their own, and that it was the Southeast Asian kings who happened to embrace Indian concepts of monarchy. This theory does not sufficiently explain the process. The history of religion across centuries clearly demonstrates that without the kingdoms or missionaries playing the role of active propagators, it is impossible for people to just accept another culture or religion. This view is often advanced by the Western colonial era scholars who tend to brush off the Indian influence on the region. Terming the linguistic, artistic, architectural, culinary, literary, social and societal, religious and philosophical influences of India on the region as a voluntary adaptation that was led just by priests and traders is inexplicable at best. Hinting at the biases of such scholars, Majumdar aptly says,

> Some historians were so much obsessed by the present-day conditions of India that even the detailed account of that book (*The Periplus of the Erythraean Sea*) would not convince them that the Indians could ever cross the sea and apply themselves to trade and maritime activity. One of them says, 'The trade thus carried on was very extensive but appears to have been conducted by Greeks and Arabs'. It is perfectly true that many evidences of the trade activity of the Indians which we know today were unknown when they wrote.[2]

[2] R. C. Majumdar, *India and South East Asia* (Delhi: B.R. Publishing Corporation, 1975), 5.

Arguably, the truth lies somewhere between what scholars such as R. C. Majumdar and George Coedes proposed and what the likes of J. C. Van Leur argued against.[3]

'Sanskritization' is another term which owes its origin due to the fact that Sanskrit was adopted as a script for some of the Southeast Asian languages. (Sanskritization here does not mean the term used in sociology by M. N. Srinivas and others to explain the process of a particular form of social change in the Indian society.) Evidences also suggest that in the ancient times Sanskrit was used as the official language, especially during the coronation of kings in Southeast Asia. Interestingly, in Malaysia, even today, the sultans follow the traditional Indian rituals at the time of their coronation.

> Sanskrit, as the sacred language of both Hinduism and Mahayana Buddhism, had a major impact on the 'original' lowland languages of Southeast Asia: Javanese, Malay, Mon, Khmer, and Cham. Thai and Lao, by contrast, were more heavily influenced by Pali, used in Theravada Buddhism (as was the case with Burmese), and much of their linguistic Indianization occurred through the mediation of Khmer. These cultures were pre-literate when they acquired the use of Sanskrit, and it was thus in that language that their earliest inscriptions were written. Later they wrote in their own languages, using scripts derived from various writing systems in India.[4]

Even today, across the region, Sanskrit has an impact on the Southeast Asian languages.

The Era of Hindu and Buddhist Wave

The First Wave: Hindu Engagement with the East

The first signs of India's interaction with the East begin almost in the prehistoric times. Over the centuries, as the political consolidation

[3] Dutch scholar J. C. Van Leur had a rather dismissive view of Indian influence on Southeast Asia. He calls it no more than a superficial flake on the Southeast Asian culture. For further details, see J. C. Van Leur, *Indonesian Trade and Society: Essays in Asian Social and Economic History* (The Hague: W. Van Hoeve, 1975).

[4] M. C. Ricklefs, Bruce Lockhart, Albert Lau, Portia Reyes and Maitrii Aung-Thwin, *A New History of Southeast Asia* (New York: Palgrave Macmillan, 2010), 23.

in India led to the birth of a stronger polity, the Indian engagement with the East also began to grow. 'The religious artefacts of Southeast Asia from the first millennium CE are almost completely Hindu or Buddhist, as is much of its most famous architecture'.[5] According to renowned historian Kalidas Nag,

> From the 3rd Century A.D. we find inscriptions in Indian language and script, in different parts of Indo-China, specially in Champa and Cambodge. In the early centuries of the Christian era, the Chinese already entered Tong-King, and Indian religion and art influenced profoundly the life of the people for about 1,000 years. Champa was divided into four provinces: Panduranga, Kauthara, Vijaya, and Amaravati.[6]

One also finds a mention of Indian migrants to Southeast Asia in Kautilya's *Arthashastra*. H. G. Q. Wales states that

> [The spread of Indian culture in Southeast Asia] proceeded in a number of successive waves of which he counts five: the Amaravati (second and third centuries AD), the Gupta (fourth to sixth century AD), the Pallava (550–750 AD), the Pala (first in-between 750–900 AD and then in the 12th and 13th centuries).[7]

The Periplus of Erythraean Sea, which was written in 70 AD, notes that the Indian ships and merchants were frequently spotted along the Southeast and East Asian ports. The Buddhist *Jatakas* also highlight the role of Indian traders in building trade linkages with Suvarnabhumi.

In describing the geographic expanse of ancient India's engagement with the 'East', scholars such as R. C. Majumdar use terms like

[5] Ibid., 22.

[6] Kalidas Nag, *Discovery of Asia* (Calcutta: The Institute of Asian African Relations, 1957), 32.

[7] H. G. Q. Wales, *The Making of Greater India: A Study in Southeast Asian Cultural Change* (London: B Quaritch, 1951), cited in Prakash Nanda, *Rediscovering Asia Evolution of India's Look-East Policy* (New Delhi: Lancer Publishers & Distributors, 2003), 54–55.

'Greater India' and 'India beyond the Ganges', which clearly depicts the variation from the British scholarship which essentially overlooked and underestimated Indian contribution to the making of the 'East'. Majumdar, Raychaudhuri and Datta argue:

> Some stories represent young Kshatriya princes, dispossessed of their hereditary kingdoms, sailing to Suvarnabhumi to restore their fortunes, to some such Kshatriya enterprise we perhaps owe the foundation of Indian political power in these far-off regions. From the second century AD onwards we find reference to kingdoms ruled by persons with Indian names. Their religion, social manners and customs, language and alphabet are all Indian and we may therefore regard these States as Indian colonial kingdoms. Between the second and fifth centuries AD, such kingdoms were established in the Malay Peninsula, Cambodia, Annam, and the islands of Sumatra, Java, Bali and Borneo. The history of these kingdoms is known, partly from the Sanskrit inscriptions found in those countries, and partly from the accounts preserved by the Chinese.[8]

Coedes represents the stream of unbiased scholars who present India's contribution in a positive way. He states:

> The geographic area here called 'Farther India' consists of Indonesia, or island Southeast Asia except for the Philippines; and the Indochinese Peninsula, or India beyond the Ganges, including the Malay Peninsula. Excluded are Assam, which is simply an extension of India and Bengal, and northern Vietnam, whose history developed outside Indian influence.[9]

Coedes, however, differs from R. C. Majumdar in the sense that he highlighted the role of trade linkages in boosting India's eastward engagement. The first Sanskrit inscription found in Vo Canh in Southern Vietnam is believed to be from the third century AD 'One of

[8] R. C. Majumdar, H. C. Raychaudhuri and Kalikinkar Datta, *An Advanced History of India* (Delhi: Macmillan, 1974), 206.

[9] George Coedes, *The Indianized States of Southeast Asia* (Hawaii: East West Center, 1968), xv.

the earliest known South Indian merchants, the Mannigraman (from Sanskrit *Vanik-graman*, "guilds of merchants") is mentioned in the copper plate inscriptions from the ninth century. They record grant of certain trade privileges on the Malabar coasts to its merchants'.[10] Thus it is clear that without some amount of royal/institutional support, traders and priests could not have managed to travel to so many islands across the region over centuries, and also to set a firm footing in the Southeast Asian region.

From this it is clear that India had a strong influence on several countries of the East, to the extent that at least some countries of the East were considered as an extension of sorts of India. Explaining the precise meaning of what 'Farther India' meant to him, Coedes explains:

> Culturally speaking, Farther India today is characterized by more or less deep traces of the Indianization that occurred long ago: the importance of the Sanskrit element in the vocabulary of the languages spoken there; the Indian origin of the alphabets with which those languages have been or still are written; the influence of Indian law and administrative organization; the persistence of certain Brahmanic traditions in the countries converted to Islam as well as those converted to Singhalese Buddhism; and the presence of ancient monuments which, in architecture and sculpture, are associated with the arts of India and bear inscriptions in Sanskrit.[11]

However, Coedes does not mince his words in highlighting that an inward-looking India, especially from the medieval ages, had forgotten its immense contribution and substantial linkages with the 'East'. Coedes argues:

> Curiously, India quickly forgot that her culture had spread over such vast domains to the east and southeast. Indian scholars have not been aware of this fact until very recently; it was not until a small group of them, having learned French and Dutch, studied

[10] R. Michael Feener and Tarenjit Sevea, *Islamic Connections Muslim Societies in South and Southeast Asia* (Singapore: ISEAS, 2009).

[11] Coedes, *The Indianized States of Southeast Asia.*

> with the professors of the Universities of Paris and Leyden that they discovered, in our works and those of our colleagues in Holland and Java, the history of what they now call, with justifiable pride, 'Greater India'.[12]

With the goal to assess the role of India in shaping up the countries of the East, Kalidas Nag argues that 'the oriental nations in general, and India and China in particular, have made great contributions to the exploration and settlement of the Pacific World'.[13] The earliest migrations traced so far, from the Indian Ocean to the Pacific, may be divided into the following principal ethnic-cum-cultural currents:

I. The Negritos who proceeded from some part of Africa along the coastal belts leaving traces of their stock in South India, in the Malayan Peninsula and beyond, as far as the Philippines.

II. The Proto-Australoids or the Pre-Dravidians, whose descendents are the Todas of Nilgiri and the Veddahs of Ceylon, likewise reached the far-off Australasian Continent where their cousins came to be isolated as the aboriginal races of Australia and Tasmania.

III. In the closing centuries BC and in the early centuries of the Christian era, we find mass migration of Indians to Malaysia and Indonesia where we find place-names in Sanskritic languages in Sumatra, Java, Champa, Kambuja, Suvarna-Bhumi and Suvarna Dvipa, being unmistakable evidences of the early cultural and commercial, if not also political, colonization of the Western Pacific by the Indians. The earliest inscriptions so far traced in Champa (Vietnam), Java and Borneo were written in Sanskrit and in purely Indian scripts. Isolated centres of trade and commerce, founded by the Indian merchants and mariners, developed gradually into big cultural zones and finally into the Hindu colonies and empires like that of the 'Shree Vijaya' in Indonesia and of the Hinduised Kingdoms of Champa and Cambodia in Indochina. Small local sanctuaries gradually developed into colossal architectural marvels like

[12] Ibid.

[13] Nag, *Discovery of Asia*, 57–58.

> the 'Borobudur' and 'Prambanan' of Java and the 'Bayon' and 'Angkor Wat' of Indo-China.[14]

The extent of Sanskrit's influence is evident from the fact that

> [A]ll the known examples of scripts found in the inscriptions in Southeast Asia demonstrate different types of Brahmi script, dating to the period from the 2nd century to the 5th century. The earliest inscriptions are written in a script that is strongly reminiscent of that of the Kushan inscriptions of probably the 2nd Century, while apparently later inscriptions are in a kind of Gupta script.[15]

So far as the influence of the Hindu wave on the East is concerned, it is clear that from the earliest times till the thirteenth century, several Indian kingdoms and places contributed to building India's links with the East. From the Mauryan Empire to the Gupta and Harsha periods, and from the Pallavas to the Pala kingdom, all contributed a lot, of course with the active involvement of the merchants and traders. The contribution of the Chola kingdom, however, should be specifically mentioned as the Cholas took a proactive interest in widening and deepening India's multidimensional role in shaping the East. The Tamil merchant guilds actively expanded their activities to some parts of the region, which is substantially proved by the discovery of several inscriptions. The 'Tamil inscriptions have been found in Sumatra, peninsular Thailand (Nakhon Si Thammarat) and in Pagan. There are also references to traders from various parts of India in Javanese epigraphy during the same period'.[16]

During the rule of the Chola kingdom, both traders and priests were given royal patronage. K. M. Panikkar states:

> The naval activity of the Hindus was controlled by organized corporations of which the most important were the Manigramam Chetties and the Nanadesis. Of the Manigramam Chetties who

[14] Ibid.

[15] Shashibala, ed., *Sanskrit on the Maritime Route* (New Delhi: Bharatiya Vidya Bhavan, 2017), 2.

[16] Ricklefs et al., *A History of Southeast Asia*, 123. Also see Prakash Nanda, *Rediscovering Asia Evolution of India's Look-East Policy.*

> traded all over the world we have authentic records in grants and inscriptions. The Bhaskara Ravi Varman plate of the Kerala King grants certain special privileges to the Manigramam guild. This body was given a charter practically similar to that given to the European East India Companies including 'the sword of sovereign merchant ship' and monopoly rights of trading. In an inscription discovered at Takopa near the Isthmus of Kra, the temple and tank of Sri Narayana are placed under the protection of this body of merchants.[17]

However, it must be noted that except for the Chola kings, who had a few military expeditions run against the Sri Vijaya Empire, primarily due to conflicting trade and political interests, there is no authentic evidence of India invading the countries of the East.

> [The ancient Chinese texts] allude to the adventures of an Indian in Funan (consisting of parts of Vietnam and Cambodia). A Chinese source of the fourth century AD alludes to an Indian who became the ruler of Funan and his name is given as Chuchai-t'an—'Chu' refers to a person of Indian origin.[18]

The Batak people of Sumatra followed Hinduism including Hindu deities as also the Indian astronomy. In Laos, there is not just a hill-top called *Linga Parvat* (mountain with a Shiv *linga*) in the southern Savannakhet town, but hundreds of Shiv lingas were discovered in the Mekong basin in that area. Even today, the Black Thai of north-western Vietnam and eastern Laos use a writing system derived from an Indian script. It seems that Bali has had most profound impact of Hinduism, or perhaps it has remained largely insulated after the Hindu influence on it. That is the reason why Bali has remained predominantly Hindu even today, and attracts a lot of Indian tourists.

In terms of influence, the focus of Hinduism remained somewhat confined to the Southeast Asian region, something which widened with the transmission of Buddhism in the region. It must be noted,

[17] K. M. Panikkar, *India and the Indian Ocean: An Essay on the Influence of Sea Power on Indian History* (London: George Allen & Unwin Ltd, 1945), 29.

[18] Nanda, *Rediscovering Asia Evolution of India's Look-East Policy*, 46.

however, that Northern Vietnam is the only area where one may not find many traces of Indian influence, but Lord Ganesha's statue in a temple in central Hanoi reminds one of Champa civilizational bonds. The Philippines remained marginal to the Indian linguistic and Hindu religion's influence.

Buddhism in East and Southeast Asia

Buddhism was and remains, even today, one of the most fundamental contributions of India in shaping the philosophical, spiritual and religious contours of the Eastern world. In India, the predominant form of Buddhism was the Mahayana cult, which believed in seeking complete enlightenment by following the teachings of the Bodhisattva. In Mahayana Buddhism, Sanskrit is used as the prime language for both religious texts and rituals. Today Mahayana Buddhism is the majority sect of Buddhism, with its variants practiced in Japan, Korea, Taiwan and China. Historically though, when Buddhism begun to recede in India, Sri Lanka emerged as a major hub of Buddhist teaching. Since majority of Buddhists in Sri Lanka were Theravada, gradually, the conversions to Theravada school also happened.

Unlike the Southeast Asian region, where all seven waves of India's eastward engagement registered their significant presence, in East Asia—especially in China, Japan and Korea—the engagement begun with the Buddhist wave (or wavelet, since it is clubbed with the Hindu era), having no significant presence of the Hindu, Islamic and colonial waves. Thus, in terms of expanse and reaching out to countries across the East, the Buddhist wave has contributed the most.

> Buddhism, originating in the 6th century BC, became the dominant religion in India during the Mauryan emperor Ashoka (273–232 BC) and spread throughout his empire from Bengal to Afghanistan. As a result, Buddhism eventually reached the Hellenised neighbour, the Kushan and Bactria Kingdom which under the Kushanas dominated the areas of Hindukush into Kabul, Gandhara, northern Pakistan and northwestern India after the decline of the Mauryan empire. Under the great Kushana king Kanishka (144–172 AD), Buddhism further flourished and spread, and Gandhara, now in Pakistan became not only a great Buddhist settlement but also

> served as a cradle to a distinctive Graceo-Buddhist art form. During next few centuries, Buddhism along the Silk Road spread to Hadda, Bamiyan and Kondukistan. Bamiyan now in Afghanistan became one of the most important Buddhist centres by the 4th century AD because of its strategic location at the intersection of roads to Persia, India, Tarim Basin and China.[19]

Buddhism transmitted from India to China around the second century BC. India's interactions with China were strong not only due to the maritime linkages, which were the mainstay of global trade until the Arabs begun to dominate trade on India's western sectors, but also because of the Silk Road that connected India with China through the rugged terrains of Afghanistan, Central Asia and Persia. Both India and China were great hubs of land and maritime trade until the beginning of the dark ages of colonial rule in the seventeenth century.

> [During this] period of the Silk Road history roughly in the early Christian era, northwestern Indians who lived near the Ganges river started playing prominent role as middlemen in the China-Mediterranean silk trade as soon as they understood that silk was a lucrative product of the Chinese Empire. The trading relationship between China and India mostly in barter form, developed with increased Han expansion into the central Asia. The Chinese traded their silk with Indians for precious stones and metals such as gold, silver and jade, and then Indians would trade silk with the Roman empire. Thus, in a sense India came to be the middle point for trade and commerce between China and Rome, the east and the west. The antiquity of India's participation in the silk trade can be attested by the use of word 'Sinapatta' for the Chinese equivalent of silk in the great Indian text of political economy *Arthashastra*, written by Kautilya in the 4th century BC.[20]

As stated earlier, the predominant form of Buddhism in India was Mahayana Buddhism. The same flourished in China as well through

[19] Subhakanta Behera, 'India's Encounter with the Silk Road', *Economic and Political Weekly* 37, no. 51 (21–27 December 2002): 5077–5080.

[20] Ibid.

India with the help of Indian and Chinese monks and some royal patronage. Buddhism from India rapidly grew during the Tang dynasty in China (AD 618–907). It is believed that the Empress Wu (AD 705–712) proactively pursued the cause of the propagation of Buddhism in China. Her biggest contribution, however, was in trying to make Buddhism a 'State religion' of the kingdom. However, by the ninth century, Buddhism begun to decline in China.

During the first wave, India's engagement with China was also at its peak—so much so that the stories of Chinese monks and travellers, particularly Fa Hsien (fifth century AD), Huan Tsang and Yi-Tsing (seventh century AD), who visited India during the ancient and early medieval times, are part of Indian school textbooks even today, which is remarkable if compared with European and West Asian travellers who came visiting India in early medieval, medieval and colonial periods. Kashyapa Matanga was a prominent Indian academic and monk who travelled to China and also taught Buddhism in China. Indian academics and translators translated Buddhist works in Chinese, thus facilitating the spread of Buddhism in China. One such scholar was Kumarajiva who stayed for 12 years in China to translate the Buddhist texts. Kumarajiva's associates Buddhayasa, Dharmayasa and Punyatrata carried on his work after his death (AD 413). Since the fifth century AD, India–China interactions substantially grew due to the travels of scholars from both countries.

While the spread of Buddhism to China happened largely through direct links and via Tibet, its transmission to Japan and Korea happened via China. It is believed that after the sixth and seventh centuries AD, strong Buddhist establishments had developed in China who took the religion further south and east. India's ties with Korea are also more than two millennia old. According to the historical texts, in the middle of the first century AD, Queen Huh, who was an Indian princess hailing from Ayodhya,[21] was married to the legendary King Suro, the founder

[21] To highlight the millennia-old linkages between India and South Korea, the mayors of Ayodhya and Kim-Hae (Gimhae) city signed a sister city bond in March 2001. Thanks to the appallingly slow Indian bureaucratic system, the project has not witnessed anything worth its name except the monument of the Korean queen Heo Hwang-ok which too was brought in by the Korean side.

of the Karak Kingdom.[22] Amongst the Buddhist monks, Kyomik is believed to be the first Korean monk to travel to India for learning the nuances of Buddhism. However, it was Hyech'o whose memoir entitled *Wango Chon Chuk Kuk Chon* (*Memoirs of Five Kingdoms of India*) provides a detailed account of his travels to India, and of India's political, social, economic and religious features. The decline of Buddhism in India and the simultaneous rise of Confucianism in Korea led to the receding of ties, which reduced further with Mughal and British rule in India.

Japan has also been a recipient of Buddhism transmitting from India directly as also via China. According to the Ministry of Foreign Affairs of Japan,

> Exchange between Japan and India is said to have begun in the 6th century when Buddhism was introduced to Japan. Indian culture, filtered through Buddhism, has had a great impact on Japanese culture, and this is the source of the Japanese people's sense of closeness to India.[23]

According to a brief published by the MEA, 'India's earliest documented direct contact with Japan was with the Todaiji Temple in Nara, where the consecration or eye-opening of the towering statue of Lord Buddha was performed by an Indian monk, Bodhisena, in 752 AD'.[24] It is also widely accepted that Baramon Sozo and Dharmabodhi significantly contributed to the propagation of Buddhist learning in Japan.

[22] V. N. Arora, 'South Korea's Ayodhya Connection', *The Times of India*, 12 September 2004, https://timesofindia.indiatimes.com/india/South-Koreas-Ayodhya-connection/articleshow/847880.cms, accessed 16 August 2018.

[23] For details on India–Japan relations, see the website of Ministry of Foreign Affairs of Japan, available at https://www.mofa.go.jp/region/asia-paci/india/data.html, accessed 16 August 2018.

[24] For details on India–Japan relations, see the website of MEA, Government of India, http://mea.gov.in/Portal/ForeignRelation/Japan_Relations_13_12_2016.pdf, accessed 16 August 2018.

The Emergence of 'World-class' Centres of Learning

Another significant contribution of the Hindu Buddhist wave was opening and establishing the world-class centres of learning, a dimension that no other wave of India's eastward engagement has been able to achieve so far.

The foremost among the prominent centres of learning was the Nalanda University. It was founded in the fifth century AD, which led to the emergence of a major learning centre of Mahayana Buddhism, attracting students and scholars from across East and Southeast Asia. For centuries, it remained a key hub for Buddhist studies as well as Indian philosophy and Pali and Prakrit languages. The Gupta Empire during the fifth century AD, and later Harsha in the sixth century AD, provided patronage to the Nalanda University, and thus helped it remain the centre of learning in the region, with students and scholars coming from Japan, Korea, China and the entire Southeast Asian region. The archaeological evidences have proved that a king from the Shailendra dynasty of Indonesia had also built a monastery in the Nalanda compound.

After the gradual decline of the Nalanda University, Vikramshila University was established (near today's Bhagalpur, Bihar) under the rulership of King Dharmapala (AD 783–820). Vikramshila remained a key regional hub for learning until it was destroyed by Muhammad bin Bakhtiyar Khilji around AD 1193.

It is a pity that more than 1,500 years later, despite its Look East and Act East policies, India has not been able to come up with a single university on sciences and social sciences which belongs to the global 'ivy league' or ranks even in the list of top 50 universities in the world. The attempts to revive the Nalanda University have also fallen victims to red-tapism, nepotism and bureaucratic hurdles. Till date, the revived Nalanda University remains a half-hearted, politicized and reluctant attempt to bring back India's glory as a regional and global hub of higher learning.[25]

[25] S. D. Muni, 'Nalanda: A Soft Power Project', *The Hindu*, 30 August 2010.

From this, it is clear that the first wave of India's interaction with East and Southeast Asia was led by trade and by Hindu and Buddhist linkages. This wave remained strong till the twelfth century AD, and it did not disappear even with the arrival of Islam in Southeast Asia from the thirteenth century onwards. As the historical records to substantiate whether India had a direct control over Southeast Asia are scant, the matter remains debated among the scholars. However, it is widely believed that in the seventh century, the Chalukya King Vinayaditya, and in the ninth century, the Pallava King Nandivarman III had also exercised some influence over parts of the region.

The real use of force was exercised by the great Chola King Rajendra Chola of Tanjore (AD 1012–1044), who took extreme care and interest in expanding his empire far and wide. Historical evidences suggest that during the reign of Rajendra Chola, his army raided Sri Vijaya's empire on several occasions. The Shailendras had a strong control over the Southeast Asian region. Their kingdom lasted for around seven centuries, albeit in varying levels of expanse and strength. The Cholas fought with the Shailendra empire primary over the access to trade points and piracy issues, and not over territorial annexation.

It has also been recorded that Rajendra Chola had sent diplomatic missions to China also and had established good contacts with the Chinese emperors. However, over a period of time, the Chola empire weakened. Other kingdoms too gradually weakened, and eventually due to infighting and rivalries among the kings in the southern parts of India, they found it too difficult to take an active interest in the Southeast Asian region, let alone maintain control over the region.

The Second Wave: Spread of Islam in Southeast Asia

Islam in Southeast Asia owes much of its origin to India, making that the second wave of India's eastward engagement which begun to take shape from late twelfth/early thirteenth century onwards.

During the Islamic phase in India, the first few centuries were full of turmoil. Finally when the Mughals established their control over Delhi, some stability was restored in the country that had been looted and plundered by invaders from across the north-western parts of India. Indian rulers' obsession with the north-western frontiers as the primary source of threat loomed large, leaving strategic priorities, resources and the vision for the East and Southeast Asian countries at the periphery. For instance, during the reign of Akbar, despite the fact that the Mughals had an impressive navy, they only strived to set up a naval base in Dekka (Dhaka) with the primary motive to confront the Arakanese (inhabitants of today's Arakan province of Myanmar) and the Portuguese. Even at the peak of their empire, the Mughals never looked beyond the land boundary of India, and thus contributed to India's lopsided approach of excessive focus on land boundary at the cost of its short- to long-term interests on the maritime matters. It must be added, however, that the Mughal rulers never tried to control or stop the trade or religious activities of Indians to the East, as mentioned in the previous chapter. Though the Muslims rulers in India had their origins from outside of the country, and Islam was not a native religion of India, Muslim rulers are still considered a part of the Indian civilization, because unlike the British and the Portuguese, they came to India and settled down in the country, thus, trying to make themselves a part of India or the other way round (with Jizya tax, forceful contributions from majority community for the Haj visits, destruction of temples and forceful conversions—all of which hound the Indian polity today in their convoluted forms). By the time the Mughal Empire declined, the Dutch, the Portuguese and the British East India Company had entered India and the countries of the East. It is interesting to note here that the Malabar Coast (and southern India), which had an important role in spreading Islam in the Southeast Asian region, was not under the control of the Mughals but was controlled by regional Muslim kingdoms.

With the East India Company gaining strength in India, and the Dutch and other European powers taking control of the East and the Southeast Asian countries, India's influence begun to wean away. Until the arrival of leaders of the Indian freedom struggle—Rash Behari Bose, Mahatma Gandhi, Jawaharlal Nehru and Subhas Chandra Bose—the relationship at best remained a tool at the hands of the British empire, with frequent people-to-people linkages. However, as mentioned in the introductory chapter, except for making the strategic dimension an integral part of India's eastward engagement, the contribution of the British largely remained negative. Indians employed with the British government garnered a bad reputation for themselves as they were perceived as the 'local tools of oppression' at the hands of the British empire, and the labourers who migrated to Southeast Asia were seen as alien communities which posed a threat to the lower economic strata of the host society. Both these factors mar the image of both India and Indians in Southeast Asia even today. Despite living in Southeast Asia and the Pacific Island Countries (PIC) for more than three centuries, the people of Indian origin are mostly considered outsiders and not one of the their own. A cursory comparison with the Bumiputra in Malaysia, Burmese in Myanmar, and Han in China depicts the multicultural nature of Indian society despite its pitfalls and follies.

Unlike the first wave, where the origin points in India were primarily Pataliputra (Patna), Sarnath, Bodh Gaya, Prayag (Allahabad), Sanchi, Vidisha, Ujjain, Kaveri delta, Tamralipti, Amravati, Madurai (and other cities of today's Tamil Nadu),[26] and the eastern coasts of Odisha and Bengal, the nodal points for the spread of Islam in Southeast Asia were confined primarily to south and east Indian states (with Gujrat playing its traditional role as a trade hub). This included the coastal cities of Malabar and Coromandel, as also cities in Bengal.

During both the first and the second waves of engagement, there was an uninterrupted flow of visitors from India, some of whom also settled down in the region. Some Indian historians are of the view that Asoka's war on the Kalinga empire, in which hundreds of thousands Kalingan people were killed, had led to the mass migration of the people of Kalinga to the Southeast Asian region. These immigrants were later known as Klings. The Tailang people of Burma, who were migrants from the eastern and northern parts of India and Tibet, also owed their origin to Kalinga.[27] It is also widely accepted that by the

[26] Early Hindu architecture and artefacts found in Western Java and Thai were inspired by the 7th and 8th century Pallava style, whereas in Cambodia the influence has been both of Cholas and Pallavas.

[27] R. D. Banerjee, *History of Orissa Vol. I* (Delhi: Bharatiya Publishing House, 1980).

turn of the first millennium, Indian traders had begun to establish huge settlements in places such as Aceh and Melaka.

Thus, contrary to popular belief, the roots of the Indian diaspora are not of colonial origin but date back to more than a millennium. Of course, with each 'wave' of India's eastward engagement, a new set of Indians visited the region, and some stayed there forever. That said, it must be highlighted that while the Hindu–Buddhist wave was overtaken by the Islamic wave, the first wave never came to a dead stop, and the flow, howsoever little, kept going uninterrupted until the British colonized India.

The details of India's linkages with the East during the Islamic age are scant and bleak, and therefore it is rather difficult to analyse the medieval phase in great detail. One thing however is clear: India's eastward engagement during the medieval period had economic, trade and cultural linkages as the fulcrum of India's eastward engagement. Islam too had played a key role in such an engagement.[28] Links between the Malabar Coast and Southeast Asia, which was uninterrupted during the Chola and Vijayanagara empires, continued unabated during the Islamic wave as well. The theory that merchants from Malabar not only had robust trade linkages with Southeast Asia but also influenced the religious contours of the region is 'supported by a thirteenth century inscription from Pagan, noting a donation made to a local *nanadesi* temple by a native of the Malabar coast who was connected to a South Indian merchant group'.[29] Marco Polo also mentions the strong trade ties between Malabar and China.

So far as the spread of Islam is concerned, it begun with traders and religious missionaries landing in the Southeast Asian waters. The liberal-Sufi inclusive variant of Islam coming from India attracted the Southeast Asian chieftains. Like the Hindu–Buddhist wave, during

[28] Due to paucity of both time and resources, we do not intend to dwell upon this section in much detail, and thus leave it for the next edition.

[29] Sebastian R. Prange, 'Like Banners on the Sea: Muslim Trade Networks and Islamization in Malabar and Maritime Southeast Asia', in *Islamic Connections Muslim Societies in South and Southeast Asia*, eds. R. Michael Feener and Tarenjit Sevea (Singapore: ISEAS, 2009), 25–47.

the second wave also, traders and spiritual leaders contributed to the propagation of a new religion—Islam—in Southeast Asia.

> From the thirteenth century onwards, many Muslim traders and religious leaders active in Southeast Asia hailed from India rather than the traditional Arab heartland, and the new (local) Muslim courts patronised religious scholars. 'Islamising courts of Southeast Asia still imported teachers from India and beyond, much as their Indianised predecessors had welcomed multi-ethnic expertise to establish their entrepots in earlier periods'.[30]

Snouck Hurgronje, a Dutch scholar and administrator, was one of the earliest to establish that Southeast Asian Islam traces its origin to South India. In his second volume of *De Atjehers* published in 1894, he proves the linkages between the two.[31] G. E. Morrison also states that the Tamil-speaking territory in South India played a direct and crucial role in the Islamization of Southeast Asia.[32] This was also the phase when the focus of India's trade with the region shifted from Tamralipti, that is, the Orissa–Bengal coast, to southern India, with Malabar and Ma'bar playing key roles.

The spread and expansion of Islam across India's eastern seaboard, especially in Southeast Asia and the Indian Ocean littoral countries, had a massive impact on societies, polities and cultural domains of the region. India itself came under the heavy influence of Islam not only because of the Muslim rulers who had captured the political space of the country, especially from the fifteenth century onwards until the dawn of the British rule in India, but also due to the fact that Muslim rulers—whether the Khalji (1290–1320), Tughlaq (1321–1414), Sayyid (1414–1451) or Lodi dynasty (1451–1526) or the Mughals—all had a vociferous missionary wing which vehemently

[30] Quoted in Prange, 'Like Banners on the Sea: Muslim Trade Networks and Islamization in Malabar and Maritime Southeast Asia', 38.

[31] Ibid., 247.

[32] G. E. Morrison, 'The Coming of Islam to the East Indies', *JMBRAS (Part 1)*, (1951): 28–37.

practiced conversions to Islam in India. That aspect, however, was not witnessed beyond the Indian waters. The spread of syncretic Islam in Southeast Asia was advanced by the Sufi saints. A significant part of that aspect is the fact that the Bahmani Sultanate, the first independent Muslim kingdom of South India, which ruled parts of southern India (primarily Deccan) between AD 1347 and AD 1527, had Shia Islam as the state religion.

The rise of Islamic rulers in India led to two simultaneous things: First, whatever little State/institution support to propagation of Hinduism and Buddhism was being given came to a complete stop, and the propagation of Islam benefitted in the process. Second, Muslim rulers in India never tried to either stop or take undue extractive advantage of India's eastward engagement. Stripped of the royal/institutional patronage, India's engagement with the East remained largely confined to trade and commerce, and religious and cultural propagation through traders and common people. Islam also rose because by the end of the twelfth century, Buddhism declined in India, thus, leading to a remarkable slowdown in engagement with the East in terms of Buddhist linkages. Over the centuries, while Buddhism became a mainstay of several countries of the East, India turned out to be largely a non-Buddhist country with Buddhism as a minority religion.

It is widely accepted that the process of Islamization in Southeast Asia and beyond was largely an offshoot from India, coupled with the influence of Muslim merchants and Sufis who travelled to and settled in parts of the region over several centuries. Places such as Penang, Malacca, Johor and Martaban are classic examples in that regard. In Islam, its central religious text (the Quran) mentions and its preachers and believers believe that Islam originated from a particular place, which is centred around Mecca and Medina; the Arab-centric approach has led to the substantiation of the point that religious conversions, voluntary or otherwise, led to spread of Islam across the East in the majority of instances. Of course, the traders also contributed their bit in that regard, but that too was due to intermingling with the local women.

It may be noted here that the very reason why Buddhism got so much popularity during pre-Mauryan, Mauryan and post-Mauryan periods (till the end of the Kushans) is that it was not rigid in terms of practice, and was more accommodative and inclusive. The *shrenis* (trade guilds) during the era of the Sixteen Mahajanpads actively promoted Buddhism. Likewise, the strand of Islam that became popular in the East, especially in the maritime Southeast Asia and Indian Ocean littorals, was liberal and was an amalgamation of strands of other religions too. The Perankan community in Singapore, Malaysia and elsewhere is a classic example in that regard.

The Third Wave: Colonial Rule—A Wavelet Imposed; and Freedom Struggle—A Wavelet Created from Within

From the early seventeenth to the mid-twentieth centuries, the Indian engagement with the East was shaped by two predominant coalescing and contrasting wavelets. First, the colonial rule in India and elsewhere in the East, and second, the freedom struggle in India which was linked with and influenced the freedom struggles across Asia.

From the time the British established their control over India in the sixteenth century, until the rise of the Indian National Congress and its leaders such as Jawaharlal Nehru and Subhas Chandra Bose in Indian politics in the 1920s and the 1930s respectively, the period may be called the 'dark ages of India's eastward engagement', where India's engagement with the East was reduced to the level of a mere tool at the hands of the East India Company and later the British empire, and the petty traders and moneylenders who did more harm to India (and to themselves too in the long run) than positively contribute to India's engagement with the East. But the British did revive and widen the strategic dimension to India's eastward engagement vis-à-vis its geopolitical location in the region.

Indian Diaspora

Beginning with the acquisition of Penang in 1786 until almost mid-twentieth century, Britain drove millions of Indians to its colonies in the region as plantation and mining workers. In terms of numbers, it was roughly the following:[33]

Malaya	1,911,000
Burma (Myanmar)	1,164,000
Mauritius	455,000
Fiji	61,000

It is also estimated that around 1.5 million individuals left India during the nineteenth century to engage in commerce.[34] It is commonly believed that Indian plantation workers, merchants and other migrants eventually settled down in the then British colonies. However, historical evidences underline that Indian people visited and some settled in east, south-east, and south-west Pacific from the prehistoric times. As mentioned in earlier paragraphs, during Emperor Asoka's time (272–232 BC), the people of Kalinga migrated and settled in Southeast Asia. There are layers and layers of Indian migration to the East, which has gone on regardless of time.

The systematic migration of Indian people to Southeast Asia and elsewhere in British colonies with an aim to create and establish a consolidated group of lower and lower-middle class in those societies was designed and executed by the British. It must be pointed out here that at later stages, especially in the nineteenth and twentieth centuries, some Indians also migrated on their own in search for better prospects. Upon acquiring the colonies, the British began to identify the places from where raw materials could be extracted to fuel their industrial demands and scale up their productions. Mining and plantations turned out to be the key activities in the British-ruled Southeast Asia, for which they made use of Indian and Chinese labour that came almost free of cost.

[33] Quoted in Marina Carter, 'Indians and the Colonial Diaspora', in *Rising India and Indian Communities in East Asia*, eds. K. Kesavapany, A. Mani and P. Ramasamy (Singapore: ISEAS, 2008), 12.

[34] Ibid.

With the British acquisition of Malaya, it was turned into a major exporter of primary commodities to serve the trade and commerce interests of the British Empire, including the production of rice, sugarcane, pepper, tea and coffee, and most importantly rubber.

> Malaya emerged as the world's largest exporter of Tin and rubber. Migrant Chinese and Indian labour played a major role in the production of these commodities. While Chinese dominated the mining labour force, the large-scale entry of the Indian labour was associated with the development of the rubber industry. The recruitment of Indian labour involved two separate political entities necessitated a certain degree of control and regulation by the Indian colonial government.[35]

The 'rubber rush' which reached its zenith in the early twentieth century demanded more and more workers and quicker production.

Strategic Dimensions of India's Eastward Engagement

While it is true that the British Empire added a more comprehensive strategic element to India's eastward engagement, it must be added that it was the Chola King Rajendra Chola I, who ruled from AD 1014 to AD 1042, provided, for the first time, a strategic dimension to India's eastward engagement. He used the Andaman and Nicobar Islands as a naval base to launch military expeditions against the Srivijaya empire, which is a substantive proof in that regard. The details of Rajendra Chola's expedition against the kingdom are found in the Thanjavur inscription, which is dated AD 1050. According to K. M. Panikkar,

> Till the end of the tenth century, that is, for a period of nearly 500 years, the Sri Vijaya kings were Lords of the Ocean. But in 1007 the Chola emperor fitted out a powerful navy and challenged the

[35] Amarjit Kaur, 'The Movement of Indians in East Asia', in *Rising India and Indian Communities in East Asia*, eds. K. Kesavapany, A. Mani and P. Ramasamy (Singapore: ISEAS, 2008), 31.

> might of Sri Vijaya. He not only defeated the opposing navy but captured Kedah and established the Chola power on the Malaya peninsula. Numerous inscriptions bear witness to this fact. Having created a base on the eastern side of the sea and extended their rule over the peninsula, the Cholas carried on war against the Sri Vijaya Kings in their own home waters.[36]

Panikkar does not leave any doubts while emphasizing:

> From the ports on the East coast of India argosies have sailed this sea from the dawn of history and the colonisation of the Pacific islands by the Hindus shows the extent to which this sea had been explored and navigated at least 2,000 years ago. The Gulf of Malacca is like the mouth of a crocodile, the Peninsula of Malaya being the upper and the jutting end of Sumatra being the lower jaw. The entry to the Gulf can be controlled by the Nicobars and the narrow end is dominated by the island of Singapore.[37]

Thus, while the British did not discover the strategic dimension to India's eastward engagement, they certainly revived it, and widened its scope to make it a key feature of Indian strategic thinking. As a matter of fact, when Japan invaded Southeast Asia during the Second World War, it inadvertently provided the entire landmass lying east of India and south of China a new geopolitical meaning. For the first time, this region in totality acquired the entity of a single unit, though for unfortunate reasons.

The Japanese occupation awakened the Western colonial powers as well as India and China to the hidden but immense strategic importance of mainland (Indo-China) and maritime Southeast Asia as a compact unit. Arguably, before the Japanese occupation, the Southeast Asian region was not only divided amongst the colonial powers but each had its own perspective of looking at its colonies also. The post-war history is a simple manifestation of how major regional and global powers have jostled for influence in the region that now encompasses 11 countries.

[36] Panikkar, *India and the Indian Ocean*, 33.
[37] Ibid., 33–34.

Great Britain acquired Burma in 1824 and subsequently made it a part of British India. The phenomenon added a completely new dimension to the country's positioning vis-à-vis the Southeast Asian region. With Burma under its control, the British India opened its frontiers deep in today's Southeast Asia, with Thailand as the next-door neighbour. Turning the Bay of Bengal again into India's Bay, the British also felt more secure about their position in those waters. During the British rule, Calcutta (now Kolkata) was the capital of India until 1911. Calcutta's proximity with Bay of Bengal and Southeast Asia added a greater focus on maritime waters extending up to the Malacca straits.

The British also had Malaya under their control, which was considered the strategic gateway to the Pacific. British control over India and Malaya provided the British strategists with a perspective that together these two colonies formed a solid conclave and could control two of the most important choke points and trade routes of the world, that is, the Malacca Straits and the Indian Ocean. The British also made good use of the Andaman and Nicobar Islands for their strategic purposes. For instance, in 1789, they set up a naval base on the Chatham Island next to Great Andaman, which is today's Port Blair.

During the Second World War, the strategic importance of India came sharply into focus. 'The fall of Singapore in 1942 made it clear that India's security was intricately linked up with the security of the countries along the rim of Indian Ocean'.[38] Saroj Pathak argues,

> Southeast Asia occupies an important place in the strategic thinking on Indian defence since 1942. This area is of paramount significance for India both land-wise and sea-wise. Actually, this area is regarded as 'core area' of India's security extending from Durand Line to the borders of Burma. South-East Asia and the Persian Gulf constitute the first circle of Indian security while the Indian Ocean region the second one.[39]

[38] Saroj Pathak, *India and South-East Asia: A Study of Indian Perspective and Policy Since 1962* (New Delhi: Atma Ram and Sons, 1990), 25.

[39] Ibid.

Thus, the strategic interests and compulsions of the British Empire before and during the Second World War led to the widening and deepening of the strategic dimensions of India's eastward engagement. The induction of Indian soldiers as part of the British imperial forces in the region also started distorting the image of India as a source of commerce and culture in the region.

Freedom Struggles in Asia and the Birth of Linkages between the Leaders of India and the East

A major unintended consequence of the British colonial rule on India's eastward engagement was the establishment of linkages between the political elite of India and the countries of the East. Being victims at the hands of the colonial European oppressors, leaders of the Asian countries felt that they had a common oppressor, and a common goal: to push the colonial rulers away from their nation. This led to the gradual emergence of camaraderie amongst the leaders of Asia, with Sun Yat-sen, Jawaharlal Nehru, Chiang Kai Shek, Aung San, Mohd Hatta, Soekarno, Mahatma Gandhi and Subhas Chandra Bose playing key roles. Since its formation in 1885, the Indian National Congress took an active interest in world affairs, especially in the colonized countries of Asia and Africa. Countries of the Southeast Asian region, especially Indonesia, Malaya, and Burma, China, and Japan, figured regularly in the deliberations and resolutions of the Indian National Congress. For instance, in the first session held in December 1885, P. M. Mehta moved a resolution criticizing the British annexation of Burma. This was echoed again in the 1891 session by Dinshaw Wacha. In 1899, when the Indian soldiers of the British Indian army were sent to China (also in May 1927) and South Africa, the Indian National Congress again opposed the British policy.

> The general advance in the outlook of the Indian National Congress between 1918 and 1929, was clearly reflected in its attitude towards the world affairs. As it begun to think in terms of free India...it begun to think about India's relationship with other countries and to formulate her policy towards the various

> developments in the world, untrammeled by any consideration for British imperialist interests.[40]

This trend only grew stronger over the years, with Nehru playing an active role.

Tagore's Contribution

Rabindranath Tagore is considered one of the pioneers in providing the intellectual impetus to India's eastward engagement. Tagore is credited with popularizing Professor Lowes Dickinson's *Letters of John Chinaman* in Bangla through his essay *Chinamaner Chithi (1905–06)*.[41] In 1923, Tagore was invited by Liang Chi-chao and other leaders of the Chinese Republic. The Vishwa Bharti delegation comprising Kshitimohan Sen, Nandalal Bose, Kalidas Nag and Tagore himself visited China. The visit of the delegation not only led to scholarly debates and works on India–China interactions but also facilitated greater engagement between India and the 'East'. In one of his lectures during his visit, Tagore said, 'I shall consider myself fortunate if through this visit China comes nearer to India and India to China—for no political or commercial purpose but for disinterested love and nothing else'.[42]

A year later, in 1924 Tagore visited China again. Professor Liang Chi-chao, the then president of Universities' Association, underscored the significance of the re-emergence of the two civilized races. Appreciating India's religious, philosophical and cultural contribution to the world, Chi-chao said,

> Both in character and geography, India and China are like twin brothers. Before most of the civilised races became active, we two brothers had already begun to study great problems which concern

[40] Bimla Prasad, *The Origins of Indian Foreign Policy* (Calcutta: Bookland Private Limited, 1960), 61–62.

[41] Nag, *Discovery of Asia*.

[42] Kalidas Nag, 'Tagore in Asia', in *Rabindranath Tagore: A Centenary Volume, 1861–1961* (New Delhi: Sahitaya Akademy, 1961).

> the whole of mankind. We had already accomplished much in the interest of humanity. India was ahead of us, and we the little brother, followed behind.[43]

In his speech, he emphasized on the more-than-millennia-old linkages between India and China and India's influence on China, cutting across political, economic, social, spiritual and material domains. He stated,

> India taught us to embrace the idea of absolute freedom—that fundamental freedom of mind, which enables it to shake off all the fetters of past tradition and habit as well as present customs of particular age—that spiritual freedom which castes off the enslaving forces of material existing. In short, it was not merely that negative aspect of freedom which consists in ridding ourselves of outward oppression and slavery, but that emancipation of the individual from his own self, through which men attain great liberation, great ease and great fearlessness.[44]

During the freedom struggle, Mahatma Gandhi and Nehru kept a close watch on developments in Korea, especially after Japan's annexation of Korea in 1910–1911. Tagore's sympathies with Korea were aptly depicted through his poems 'Song of the Defeated' and 'Lamp of the East'. His poem, 'Lamp of the East', which was published in a Korean newspaper the *Dong-A Ilbo* on 2 April 1929, depicted Korea as given here.

In the golden age of Asia,
Korea was one of its lamp-bearers,
and that lamp is waiting to be
lighted once again for the
illumination of the East[45]

[43] Liang Chi-chao, 'China's Debt to India, from a Speech of Welcome to Rabindranath Tagore', *The Vishva-Bharati Quarterly*, 2 (1924): 251–252.

[44] Ibid., 253.

[45] Quoted in Theresa Hyun, 'Translating Indian Poetry in the Colonial Period in Korea', in *Decentering Translation Studies: India and Beyond*, eds. Judy Wakabayashi and Rita Kothari (Amsterdam: John Benjamins, 2009), 147.

Even today, Tagore remains one of the most admired Indian icons in South Korea. In 1927, Tagore sailed for Indonesia to establish scholarly linkages with Indonesian leaders based in Bali and Java. While returning back from Indonesia, he also visited Burma, Malaya and Siam.

Sun Yat-sen and the Revolutionary Freedom Struggle in India

Being the victims of colonial oppression, India and China found each other on the same side of the war against the colonial powers. The 1911 nationalist revolution in China led by Dr Sun Yat-sen was received with awe and appreciation in India. Sun Yat-sen, the father of modern China, was reinstalled as the President of China in 1916 after five years of struggle against the Manchu dynasty and its remnants. Dr Sun Yat-sen's Three Principles of the Peoples were also influenced by the Non-cooperation Movement led by Mahatma Gandhi. More importantly, Dr Sun Yat-sen played an active role, since 1905, in putting the Indian revolutionaries in touch with the Japanese so that they could be more equipped in fighting the British.[46]

M. N. Roy was amongst the foremost revolutionaries who visited countries across the East including China, Japan and the Soviet Union to launch a sustained armed struggle against the British rule in India. In pursuance of that goal, he also met with Dr Sun Yat-sen. Roy and Dr Sun Yat-sen had also agreed to work together in putting their collective strengths by passing on some arms from Yunnan and Sichuan with the help of the Germans.[47] However, despite honest efforts by the Indian, Chinese and German sides, the plan could not materialize, due to an unfortunate turn of events.[48] M. N. Roy devised several other plans with the support of Dr Sun Yat-sen and his associates, but he could not lead them to reality due to shortage of enough support on the ground. Rash Behari Bose, another prominent Indian revolutionary, sought and received active support of Dr Sun Yat-sen after he left India for Japan in 1912.

[46] B. R. Deepak gives a fascinating account of India–China relations in the first half of the 20th century. See B. R. Deepak, *India-China Relations in the First Half of the 20th Century* (New Delhi: A.P.H. Publishing Corporation, 2001).

[47] Ibid.

[48] Ibid.

In 1914, the two Indian revolutionaries Satyendra Nath Sen and Vishnu Ganesh Pingle went to China to meet Dr San Yat-sen and Tehl Singh who was the leader of the Indian patriots in Shanghai.[49] The other prominent revolutionaries who worked closely with Dr Sun Yat-sen include Barakatallah and Satindranath Sen. 'The early nationalists like Borohan and Bose who formed the Association for Asian Harmony with Zhang Taiyan, Sun's aide also might have kept their association with Sun Yat-sen'.[50] Dr San Yet-sen had great empathy for the Indian freedom movement (particularly the revolutionary struggle). Assessing the role of the British imperialist curse on India, he stated: '[T]he Indian must overthrow the British rule in India first, until then there would be no hope for weaker nations. It was a sacred and historic duty of the Indian to help humanity by liberating India'.[51]

It was primarily because of the strong linkages between the leaderships of India and China that the Indian National Congress registered a strong protest against the deployment of Indian soldiers to China. As a matter of fact, in its Patna meeting, the All India Congress Committee expressed its sympathy with the Chinese people in their tireless effort to keep the country united.[52] Later on, during the 43rd session of the All India National Congress in 1928 in Calcutta, the Congress leaders supported the peoples of China in their struggle. As a gesture of moral support, Madame Sun Yat-sen (wife of Dr Sun Yat-sen) was also invited by the leaders, but she could not attend the 1928 Calcutta session as the British denied her the visa.[53]

Jawaharlal Nehru, the Indian National Congress and Freedom Struggles across Asia

Leaders of the Indian National Congress provided the key moral support to the freedom fighters in the Southeast Asian countries. This was especially the case with Burma and Indonesia. A more direct ideational

[49] Ibid.

[50] Ibid.

[51] Ibid.

[52] *The Indian National Congress* (Allahabad: All India Congress Committee, 1926), 24.

[53] She was denied visa by the British government in 1927 also.

and moral contact begun with the February 1927 conference entitled 'Congress of the Oppressed Nationalities' that was held in Brussels, Belgium, in which more than 170 representatives from 31 countries participated. Jawaharlal Nehru represented India in the Brussels conference. Upon his return from Brussels, Nehru submitted a report to the Indian National Congress, and one of his recommendations was that India should build greater ties with China, something which was present in the set of resolutions of the Brussels congress also. In his 1927 report, Nehru suggested that national organizations of Asian countries should have direct linkages through visits and exchange of publications.[54] In the 1927 annual session of the Congress, M. A. Ansari also brought up the idea of an Asian federation. The idea hovered around the minds of Indian leaders, including Gandhi and Nehru, for the next two decades, but nothing substantial could be done.

Later, in 1931, when Japan invaded Manchuria, a province of China, India supported the Chinese. Over the years, India's support for the Chinese freedom grew in quantum and vigour to the extent that on 26 September 1937, with the Indian National Congress playing an active role, the China Day was observed across India in solidarity with the Chinese peoples' struggle against Japan. On 9 January 1938, another China Day was observed across the country. Later, on 1 September 1938, a medical mission comprising five doctors was sent to China to help the war-ravaged country. Nehru's ties with Chiang Kai-shek also gained strength over the years, and Chiang Kai-shek accompanied by his wife visited India in February 1942. In 1940, Nehru also spoke of 'a federation of China, Burma, Ceylon, Afghanistan, and other countries like Siam, Malaya and Iran'.[55] Expressing his solidarity and sympathy with China, Mahatma Gandhi wrote a letter to Chiang Kai-shek on 14 June 1942 to state

[54] For further details, see 'Report submitted by Jawaharlal Nehru to the All India Congress Committee on the International Congress against Imperialism' held in Brussels in February 1927. Reproduced as Appendix I in Prasad, *The Origins of India's Foreign Policy*, 262–280.

[55] Asis Kumar Majumdar, *South-East Asia in Indian Foreign Policy: A Study of India's Relations with South-East Asian Countries from 1962–82* (Calcutta: Naya Prokash, 1982), 25.

that 'he could not purchase India's freedom at the cost of China's and wanted India to play the rightful part in preventing Japanese domination, but this could not happen so long as the British clung to their rule in India'.[56] He also wrote a letter to the Japanese, warning them of Indian protests against Japanese invasion of India and the region.

In May 1935, the Indian National Congress established a foreign affairs department under the leadership of Nehru and with support of Acharya J. B. Kripalani and Ram Manohar Lohiya. The establishment of the foreign affairs department provided an institutional anchor to the Indian National Congress in understanding and engaging the leaders of freedom movements across Asia. In 1946, Nehru visited Malaya and Singapore. In a speech in Singapore on 18 March 1946, Nehru said,

> The independence that India wants is not merely for herself. You cannot have the world half-free and half-slave. If India aspires for freedom, it is for a free world, and when India is free, every ounce of its energy shall be used for the freedom of all subject countries. This is true of Indonesia, Malaya or any other country in the world.[57]

Nehru played an active role in bringing India closer to Indonesia which was ruled by the Dutch at that time. His active campaigns in organizing the Southeast Asia Day, and the Indonesia Day in solidarity with the freedom struggle in Indonesia has been remarkable. In 1944, Nehru wrote that though India is not a Pacific power, it would have a remarkable influence, assuming the role of the centre of political and economic activities in Southeast Asia, Indian Ocean and even the Middle East.[58] Nehru also convened the '18-nation conference on Indonesia' on 20 January 1949. Between 1946 and 1949, when the Indonesian struggle against the Dutch was at its peak, India did

[56] Prasad, *The Origins of Indian Foreign Policy*, 204.

[57] Quoted in V. Suryanarayan, *Together in Struggle India and Indonesia 1945–1949* (New Delhi: Prabhat Prakashan, 2018), 61.

[58] Jawaharlal Nehru, *Discovery of India* (New York, NY: John Day, 1946), 547–548.

its level best to support Sukarno and his colleagues, which will be discussed in the next chapter.

Likewise, on the question of North Vietnam's fight led by Ho Chi Minh against the French colonial rule, in December 1946, the Indian leadership supported Ho Chi Minh. Mahatma Gandhi, Nehru, and J. B. Kripalani (then the president of the Congress) expressed their support to North Vietnam. However, Nehru was firm in not endorsing Sarat Chandra Bose's idea of sending a brigade of Indian volunteers to support Ho Chi Minh in his armed struggle against the French.

Nehru also supported General Aung San's attempt to free Burma from the British rule and the Japanese imperialist forces. Nehru's contribution will be discussed in detail in the subsequent chapters.

Subhas Chandra Bose and the Azad Hind Fauj

Japan's victory over Russia had boosted the morale of freedom fighters across Asia. In the first decade of the twentieth century, Japan was looked at as a role model for other Asian countries. Naturally, therefore, the Indian leadership sought to build closer ties with Japan. For instance, in 1903, the Japan–India Association was set up, which is today the oldest international friendship body in Japan.[59]

The victory of Japan, an Asian country, ignited hope among both the revolutionary leaders and the supporters of peaceful means for freedom movement. Jawaharlal Nehru writes in his *Glimpses of World History:*

> Japan's victory lessened the feeling of inferiority from which most of us suffered. A great European power had been defeated, thus Asia could still defeat Europe as it had done in the past.[60]

[59] For details on India–Japan relations, see the website of Ministry of Foreign Affairs of Japan, available at https://www.mofa.go.jp/region/asia-paci/india/data.html.

[60] For details, see David Wells and Sandra Wilson, eds., *The Russo-Japanese War in Cultural Perspective, 1904–05* (London: Palgrave Macmillan, 1999).

In the years that followed, Japan provided support and supplies to the Indian revolutionary leaders in their fight against the British rule. M. N. Roy, Rash Behari Bose and Lala Lajpat Rai sought the support of Japan in the armed struggle against the British rule. In 1910, Barakatallah, another prominent leader, formed the 'Islamic fraternity in Tokyo'. Swami Vivekananda and Rabindranath Tagore were also heavily influenced by Japan, though Tagore openly criticized Japan's annexation of Korea.

However, the Japanese aggression in East and Southeast Asia was not appreciated by the Indian leadership. As mentioned earlier, the Indian National Congress organized the China Day in support of China against the Japanese aggression. The leaders of the Indian National Congress were also not favourably disposed towards the Japanese military support for India's liberation against the British. Nehru and Rajendra Prasad openly opposed the Japanese idea that Japan had invaded the Asian countries to support them in their struggles against the colonial rulers.

However, Subhas Chandra Bose had a contrarian perspective. In his opinion, it was more important to fight the British rulers than to raise objections to the Japanese activities in China and Southeast Asia. The Indian National Army (INA), formed on 1 September 1942 under the leadership of Mohan Singh, was later led by Subhas Chandra Bose. On 21 October 1943, Subhas announced the formation of the provisional government of the *Azad Hind.* Within a fortnight, on 6 November 1943, Japan declared its support for Subhas's independent provisional government and offered to hand over the Andaman and Nicobar Island for Subhas's provisional government to rule. Subsequently, with the support of the Japanese forces, the *Azad Hind Fauj* invaded British India from the north-eastern side, and occupied Mowdok and Kohima. However, later, the Japanese forces succumbed to the British forces in Manipur and had to flee. The Azad Hind Fauj found it difficult to sustain the British military capabilities. Subsequently, on his way from Formosa (Taiwan) to Tokyo, Subhas Chandra Bose allegedly died in a plane crash, and with him ended Japan and the *Fauj*'s cooperation in fighting the British forces.

Concluding Remarks

India's engagement with the East, which acquired its most wholesome multidimensional form with the Hindu wavelet of engagement, reached far and wide beyond the Southeast Asian region, to Japan, Korea, China and elsewhere with the Buddhist wavelet. That somewhat receded with the Islamic wave of eastward engagement as it no longer remained the only fountain of inspiration for the East. Lack of institutional support and active engagement weakened it further. With the British setting foot in India, the priests, gurus and teachers, big merchants and Sufis from India were outnumbered and were gradually replaced by the moneylenders (mostly Tamil-origin Chettiyars), lower and middle-rung bureaucrats, and indentured labour of the British, thus setting the bar of Indian peoples' presence to an all-time-low level. After gaining independence, the governments of some of the countries also made laws that adversely affected the Indian diaspora. In Burma, Fiji and Indonesia, Indian community had to suffer at the hands of majoritarian elements (Burma: 1938 and 1962 onwards; Indonesia: the 1965 Asian Games), but the Government in India never got itself involved in those matters.

Another reason for that the appalling state of Indians was that some of them had supported the Azad Hind Fauj (and the Indian Independence League [IIL]) in their armed struggle against the British. The fact that INA and IIL worked closely with the Japanese forces did not go well with the emergent nationalist forces in Southeast Asia.

That said, the British revived a comprehensive strategic element to India's eastward engagement, particularly the maritime dimension, which still awaits its full realization. Running parallel to the twentieth century British rule, the Indian leadership added a new dimension of closer ties among the political elite[61] of India and of the East and the Southeast Asian region in their respective freedom struggles.

[61] Use of 'political elite', a term from political science, here should not be confused with its generic meaning.

CHAPTER 3

The Nehru Wave (1927–1964)

Hopes Belied

> *Just as a bright star cannot help influencing all heavenly bodies around it, Panditji's great influence has not been confined to India. Under his leadership India's peace preserving efforts, have today come not only to be generally recognized, but even to be widely sought. We Asians are happy, indeed, to acknowledge these great achievements of India under her great Prime Minister.*
>
> —U. Nu[1]

> *Politically, Nehru is my father.*
>
> —Soekarno[2]

Introduction

The fourth wave of India's eastward engagement began with the arrival of Jawaharlal Nehru, a freedom fighter, Mahatma Gandhi's protégé

[1] Former Burmese Premier U. Nu's message to a special newsreel broadcast by the All India Radio, Delhi, on 14 November 1960.

[2] O. Sutomo Roesnadi, 'Indian-Indonesian Relations—Past, Present and Future', in *Self-Reliance and National Resilience*, ed. K. Subrahmanyam (New Delhi: Abhinav Publications, 1975), 180.

and India's first Prime Minister-cum-Minister of External Affairs, at the centre stage of Indian politics. Over the decades, Nehru not only influenced but also decisively shaped the broad contours of India's worldview. Arguably, the Nehru wave, as this phase of India's eastward engagement may be called, began in 1927 with his participation in the Brussels International Congress against Colonial Oppression and Imperialism. He attended the congress as the representative of the Indian National Congress. His influence and clout in Asia receded to its lowest point during the India–China war in 1962. The next phase of India's eastward engagement began with his demise in 1964.

The years when Nehru played a decisive role in Indian politics, before and after Independence, deserve to be considered as a phase in itself, as no other Indian leader single-handedly contributed as much to India's external relations in general and relations with Asia in particular, and projected India's international profile and eastward engagement as he did. At the same time, what Nehru said and did in the area of foreign policy was the predominant voice of India's Independence movement before 1947, where so many actors and influences were involved. After 1947, his bureaucracy and the system of India's governance, as also his close associates and other party leaders, did help him shape and execute his ideas and policies, although he was the final arbiter. And yet, Nehru's India was not exactly what India's Nehru would have preferred it to be. In translating his vision and perspective into specific policy decisions and actions, he had to work within the constraints of the Indian system, and the influences of those who mattered in the given context. This must be kept in mind when looking at the developments during the Nehru's phase of India's eastward engagement.

The two most powerful drivers of Nehru's eastward engagement were his deep impressions of India's civilizational and cultural connectivity with the countries of the East, and his passionate commitment to the struggle against colonialism and imperialism. He was driven by the vision of a decolonized, free, independent and resurgent Asia that was culturally homogenous and politically harmonious. Much before the ARC (1947) and the Bandung Conference (1955), Nehru took over the moral leadership of Southeast Asians' struggle against the colonial powers. Nehru's attitude to the anti-imperialist struggles in Southeast Asia and elsewhere in Asia and Africa was of empathy and camaraderie since the early 1930s.

Among his contemporaries, in fact, in the entire league of Indian leaders from 1857 onwards, no other leader stands out to match Nehru's deep and comprehensive understanding and articulation on how India should draft and craft its foreign relations. Although it would be unfair to argue that thinkers such as Rabindranath Tagore and Bal Gangadhar Tilak did not have a vision for Asia or India's place in the world, the fact that only Nehru could effectively contribute to the making of Indian foreign policy should be factored in while evaluating his role. As discussed in the previous chapter, collectively, the Indian National Congress leaders substantially contributed to India's eastward engagement. However, none of the key leaders, starting from Mahatma Gandhi to C. Rajagopalachari, C. F. Andrews, Sardar Patel, etc., was particularly inclined to give a concrete shape to India's foreign policy. In that long list of leaders, only Subhas Chandra Bose stands out close to Nehru regarding commitment to Asia. However, the major point of difference between Nehru and Bose is that the latter's ideas and operational aspects were in complete contrast to both Nehru and the majority of the Indian freedom fighters led by Gandhi. Nehru's thoughts on foreign policy, including India's relations with the East, were more comprehensive and systematic, reflecting a vision. The ideas Nehru had and the vision that he propagated remained the guiding principles of India's foreign policy for decades after him. Of course, the fact that he served as independent India's first foreign minister made his impact even more powerful. Highlighting the prime role Nehru played in shaping India's engagement with the East, Amitav Acharya argues:

> The first important ideas about constructing Asia's regional architecture after the Second World War came from India—more precisely, Jawaharlal Nehru. It was India's first prime minister who articulated the earliest version of a regional order that emphasized Asian unity, advancement of decolonization and anti-racialism, and rejection of great-power intervention. He hosted two of the initial intra-regional gatherings of Asian leaders, called the ARCs, in 1947

> and 1949. He was perhaps the most influential ideational force behind the holding of the Asian–African Conference in Bandung, Indonesia, in 1955. Nehru's India was not only the dominant voice in Asian interactions but also played the chaperon to communist China (People's Republic of China), as it sought acceptance from its sceptical and fearful Asian neighbours.[3]

It is worth underlining here that the 'Nehru wave' was not fundamentally different from the anti-imperialist force that was led by both the peaceful (*naram-dal*) and revolutionary (*garam-dal*) groups of freedom fighters within the Indian National Congress. It was more of a coalescing wave, which by all accounts was stronger than other wavelets of the Indian freedom struggle. Perhaps, the most rigorous assessment of Nehru would suggest that he started as one of the contributors to the wavelet during the Indian freedom struggle, but gathered momentum and strength to turn into a wave himself, shaping the course of India's eastward engagement.

Evolution of India's Eastward Engagement under Nehru

Led by Nehru, India's eastward engagement unfolded in three layers. These could be identified as:

- Before India's Independence;
- From 1947 until the mid-1950s;
- From the mid-1950s until 1964.

These three layers reflected the evolution of Nehru's approach and actions in engaging the East, keeping in mind the context of the national, regional and international political realities of the time. The pre-Independence period clearly had two streaks—one led by India's independence movement and Nehru, and the other represented by Subhas Chandra Bose who joined the Second World War to defeat

[3] Amitav Acharya, *East of India, South of China: Sino-Indian Encounters in Southeast Asia* (New Delhi: Oxford University Press, 2017), xiv.

the British imperialism militarily in the eastern theatre of the war. For Nehru, the period from 1927 to 1947 was a period of struggle when India was not an independent country and he was not in a position to take firm decisions and implement them as prime minister. The second layer brought out the best in Nehru when he actively supported Asian struggles for independence and mobilized Asians through international conferences such as the ARC (1947) and the Bandung Conference (1955) to display the collective Asian will for freedom and mutual support. This period marked the rise of Nehru's charisma and clout in international politics, with Bandung as its zenith. But then from Bandung onwards, Nehru's influence declined due to factors beyond his control, in Asia and the world at large, with each passing day till his death on 27 May 1964. However, even during this third layer, India continued to play an active role, for example on issues concerning Tibet, Korea and Indo-China. We may, therefore, deal with the second and the third layers as a continuum since the policies and initiatives taken before the mid-1950s spilled over into the period until Nehru's death and even beyond.

Before Indian Independence

During the freedom struggle, Nehru's conceptions were to a great extent shaped by the Indian freedom struggle, his student life spent in Harrow and Cambridge, and the years spent in jails during freedom struggle where he could find time to read, write and think.

The years preceding India's Independence were marked at the international level by two major elements: the two world wars and the anti-imperialist struggles across Asia and Africa. These two developments hugely influenced Nehru's worldview. His views on imperialism and India's role in the fight against imperialism took a concrete shape with the conference in Brussels in 1927. During his days in jail, Nehru realized the greatness of 'oriental' civilizations: China, Turkey, Iran and India among others. His fascination for India's historical and civilizational evolution, beginning especially with Buddha and Asoka, also influenced his perspective on Southeast Asia. This is very much evident in his writings: *The Discovery of India*, *Glimpses of World History* and *My Autobiography*. Nehru writes in *The Discovery of India*:

> From the first century of the Christian era onwards, wave after wave of Indian colonists spread east and south-east, reaching Ceylon, Burma, Malaya, Java, Sumatra, Borneo, Siam, Cambodia and Indo-China. Some of them managed to reach Formosa, the Philippine Islands and Celebes. Even as far as Madagascar the current language is Indonesian with a mixture of Sanskrit words....[4] (A longer version of this quotation has been given in Chapter 1.)

From this, it is quite evident how deep an understanding Nehru had of India's place in the world, and in Southeast Asia.

Nehru's commitment to fight colonialism in Asia was reinforced with his participation in the International Congress against Colonial Oppression and Imperialism, held in Brussels in February 1927. The basic objective of the conference was

> [T]o bring together the colonial people of Africa, Asia and Latin America struggling against imperialism and the working people of the capitalist countries fighting against capitalism. Nehru was elected one of the honorary presidents of the Conference along with Albert Einstein, Romaine Rolland, Madame Sun Yat-Sen and George Lansbury.[5]

In Brussels, Nehru also got the opportunity to meet, among others, Southeast Asian leaders like Mohd Hatta of Indonesia and Ho Chi Minh of Vietnam.

The conference gave Nehru a first-hand opportunity to understand the scale and quantum of anti-imperialist struggle across the world. He strongly criticized the British colonial rule for its destructive impact on India.

[4] Jawaharlal Nehru, *The Discovery of India* (New Delhi: Oxford University Press, 1985), 202.

[5] Bipan Chandra, *India's Struggle for Independence* (New Delhi: Penguin, 2000), 417–418.

> In his speeches and statements at the Conference, Nehru emphasised the close connection between colonialism and capitalism and the deep commitment of Indian nationalism to internationalism and to anti-colonial struggles the world over. A major point of departure from previous Indian approaches was his understanding of the significance of US imperialism as a result of his discussions with Latin American delegates.[6]

Upon his return to India, Nehru prepared a confidential report for the working committee of the Indian National Congress. In the report Nehru noted:

> Most of us, especially from Asia, were wholly ignorant of the problems of South America, and of how the rising imperialism of the United States, with its tremendous resources and its immunity from outside attack, is gradually taking a stranglehold of Central and South America. But we are not likely to remain ignorant much longer, for the great problem of the near future will be American imperialism, even more than British imperialism.[7]

After the deliberations, the participants to the Brussels conference agreed

> [T]o found the League Against Imperialism and for National Independence. Nehru was elected to the Executive Council of the League. The Indian National Congress was also affiliated to the League as an associated member. At its Calcutta session, the Congress declared that the Indian struggle was a part of the worldwide struggle against imperialism.[8]

Since then, Nehru played an active role in formulating the Congress party's approach on world affairs. The 1936 annual session of the Indian National Congress adopted the resolution saying:

[6] Ibid. A detailed analysis of Nehru's participation and role in Brussels Conference can be found in Sarvepalli Gopal, *Jawaharlal Nehru: A Biography, Volume One: 1889–1947* (New Delhi: Oxford University Press, 1975), 100–104.

[7] Cited in Hari Jaisingh, *India and the Non-aligned World Search for a New Order* (New Delhi: Vikas Publishing House, 1983), 49.

[8] Chandra, *India's Struggle for Independence*, 418.

> The Congress sends greetings to our fellow-countrymen overseas and its assurances of sympathy and help in their distressful condition and the continuing deterioration in their status in the territories in which they have settled. The Congress is ready and willing to take all action within its power to ameliorate their condition, but desires to point out that a radical amelioration in their status must ultimately depend on the attainment by India of independence and the power to protect her nationals abroad.[9]

In order to address the challenges faced by Indians abroad, the Indian National Congress established the foreign department in 1936, the objective of which was to liaison with the international community and international organizations. The department tried to reach out to a range of countries to have a better grasp of the situation. Nehru personally visited Malaya (Malaysia) and Burma (Myanmar) in 1937, which also helped in building the bridge between India and other Asian countries. 'In 1940, Nehru spoke of a federation of China, Burma, Ceylon, Afghanistan and other countries like Siam, Malaya and Iran'.[10] In 1946, he spoke again of 'a Federation of Asian countries which would include India and lands to the West of (the) Southeast Asia'.[11] From the early 1940s, India under the leadership of Indian National Congress took an active interest in the political developments in Southeast Asia. In the initial stage, that is,

> [F]rom early 1940s to 1955, Indian policy in South-East Asia met with spectacular success. During this period, India was held in high esteem by the Southeast Asian countries. Judged by any standard, India's performance demonstrated existence of deep interest and dynamism in her approach to the region.[12]

The firm evidence of India's commitment for the freedom struggles in Southeast Asia was provided by its pivotal role in Indonesia's fight for

[9] N. V. Rajkumar, *Indians Outside India: A General Survey, with Resolutions of the Indian National Congress on the Subject from 1885 to the Present Day* (New Delhi: All-India Congress Committee, 1951).

[10] Deva Narayan Mallik, *Development of Non-alignment in India's Foreign Policy* (Allahabad: Chaitanya Publishing House, 1967), 26.

[11] Charles H. Heimsath and Surjit Mansingh, *A Diplomatic History of Modern India* (Calcutta: Allied Publishers, 1971), 402.

[12] Acharya, *East of India, South of China*.

liberation against the Dutch rule. On 17 August 1945, leaders of the Indonesian freedom struggle, M. Hatta and Soekarno, proclaimed the independence of Indonesia and established the Indonesian Republic. However, Indonesia's independence was recognized neither by Britain nor by the Dutch. The India National Congress extended its full moral support to Indonesia in the latter's struggle against Dutch colonialism. In India, there was naturally widespread sympathy for the Indonesian Republic.[13] On 9 October 1945, in an interview with the Associated Press of India, Nehru said:

> I should like to tell Dr. Soekarno that if I can be of any service to the cause of Indonesian freedom, I shall gladly visit Java in spite of urgent and important work in India. I believe that our freedom in India or Java or elsewhere hangs together and if I can serve the cause of freedom in Java now better than in India, I shall certainly go there.[14]

Nehru called for withdrawal of the British troops (deployed to help the Dutch forces) and immediate recognition of Soekarno's provisional government. Nehru stated in Moradabad on 28 October 1945: 'The people of India will stand by the Indonesian demand for independence and will give all the help they can'. The All India Congress Committee in its 1946 resolution stated: 'Inevitably whatever the future of the world organization is, India and the countries of South-East Asia must hang together and work'.

On 7 September 1946, six days after the formation of India's interim government, Nehru formulated the contours of his Southeast Asia policy in his speech:

> We are of Asia, and the peoples of Asia are nearer and closer to us than others. India is so situated that she is the pivot of Western, Southern and South-East Asia. In the past, her culture flowed to all these countries and they came to her in many ways. Those contacts are being renewed, and the future is bound to see a closer union between India and South-East Asia on the one side and

[13] Thien, *India and South-East Asia*, 88.

[14] Important speeches of Jawaharlal Nehru being a collection of most significant speeches delivered by Jawaharlal Nehru from 1922 to 1946. Available at: https://archive.org/stream/in.ernet.dli.2015.459342/2015.459342.Being-A_djvu.txt

> Afghanistan, Iran and the Arab world on the other. To the furtherance of that close association of free countries we must devote ourselves.[15]
>
> On 9 March 1947, Kundan, the Indian interim envoy at Batavia (in Indonesia), told a press conference that KLM passenger planes would be forbidden to land at Indian airports, and that the Indian government had undertaken to reject all offers to conclude commercial treaties with the government of the Dutch East Indies, but was prepared to establish trade relations with the government of the Indonesian Republic.[16]

At the domestic front also, India did all that it could. For instance, at its meeting in August 1946, the Congress passed a resolution conveying to the Republic of Indonesia its congratulations and assuring the people of Indonesia of the 'goodwill of the Indian people and their desire to cooperate in the fullest measure in the promotion of the freedom and in the advancement of the nations and peoples of Asia'.[17] Furthermore, in Delhi, the new Central Legislative Assembly, which met for the first time in January 1946, carried a motion of censure against the Government of India (British) for permitting the use of Indian troops in Indonesia.

The Indian National Congress' support for the Indonesian struggle had been registered even before the Dutch police action. In terms of peoples' action, there were several steps. For instance, on 14 November 1945, Indian seamen recruited to man a Dutch ship in Bombay harbour by replacing the Indonesian seamen refused to work.[18] On 22 July 1947, a member of the Legislative Assembly of Orissa, Biju Patnaik, who had flown Dr Hatta back to Indonesia, helped Dr Sjahrir to escape out of Indonesia by piloting him in a Dakota plane.[19] Patnaik was praised by Nehru at a press conference on 28 July for being a 'very

[15] Jawaharlal Nehru, *India's Foreign Policy, 1946–1961* (New Delhi: Publications Division, 1961), 3.

[16] *North China Daily News*, 11 March 1947, as quoted in Thien, *India and South-East Asia*, 90.

[17] N. V. Rajkumar, *The Background of India's Foreign Policy* (New Delhi: All India Congress Committee, 1952), 85.

[18] Thein, *India and South-East Asia*, 91.

[19] Thein, *India and South-East Asia*, 91–92.

gallant airman', for his great efficiency in flying and for his 'adventurous and daring spirit'.[20]

The Indian National Congress also wanted to assess the post-war political situation and the conditions of the Indians living in some of the neighbouring countries. In pursuance of that task, Nehru visited Singapore, Malaysia, Burma and Indonesia. The British administration in Malaysia and other countries did not permit him to visit initially, but later, with the intervention of Lord Mountbatten, then posted as the Supreme Allied Commander in Singapore, he succeeded in visiting these countries under some conditions.[21] In Singapore, Nehru visited the INA (set up by Subhas Chandra Bose) Memorial to pay tribute to the brave soldiers, but he avoided a public function or a ceremonial parade by the INA personnel in deference to the wishes of Lord Mountbatten. Nehru's visit to Malaysia enthused the Indian community and brought them closer to other ethnic communities like that of the Chinese.[22]

On his way back, Nehru had a night's halt in Rangoon where he met Gen. Aung San of Burma. The Indian National Congress, since 1931 (27–28 March Resolution), had been asking for separation of Burma from the British Indian Administration.[23] Many of the Indian leaders such as Gandhi and Nehru visited Burma during the freedom struggles in the two countries. During these visits, Indians settled in Burma were advised to learn the Burmese language and live like the Burmese.[24] The British had periodically lodged Indian freedom fighters in Burmese jails in Mandalay. Nehru had established close contacts with the Burmese freedom fighter Gen. Aung San who sought Nehru's guidance on the Burmese struggle for independence. Nehru deeply

[20] Ibid. Also see V. Suryanarayan, *Together in Struggle: India and Indonesia, 1945–49* (New Delhi: Prabhat Prakashan, 2018).

[21] These conditions related to his interaction with Subhas Bose's INA soldiers and supporters. See Gopal, *Jawaharlal Nehru: A Biography, Volume One*, 309.

[22] Ibid., 310–311.

[23] Thin Thin Aung and Soe Myint, 'India-Burma Relations', in *Challenges to Democratization in Burma: Perspectives on Multilateral and Bilateral Responses* (Stockholm, Sweden: Institute for Democracy and Electoral Assistance, 2001), 87–116.

[24] Rajiv Bhatia, *India-Myanmar Relations: Changing Contours* (New York: Routledge, 2016), 74–76.

mourned the assassination of Gen. Aung San and his interim cabinet ministers in July 1947, much before the grant of independence to Burma. Nehru expressed his unhappiness with the British use of Indian troops in Indonesia and Indo-China to suppress the freedom struggles against the Dutch and French imperialists in these countries.[25]

The engagement with the countries of Southeast Asia by Subhas Chandra Bose was in contrast to the approach by the Indian National Congress and Nehru. He had fallen out with the Indian National Congress because of differences regarding their methods of fighting British imperialism: the Indian National Congress believed in fighting peacefully and constitutionally, while Subhas Chandra Bose believed in military methods. He first went to Germany in 1941 to join hands against the British and Allied forces where he raised the Free India Legion with about 3,000 fighters. However, he soon moved to Southeast Asia and impressed by the Japanese victories against the Western imperialists, joined hands with the Japanese forces by raising Azad Hind Fauj (INA) from the persons of Indian origin (PIOs) in these countries to fight in Singapore, Malaysia and Burma.

> Bose also used Burma as the headquarters for his INA and marched towards Indian borders with the help of the Japanese to liberate India from the British rule. When Burma again came under the British control, the headquarters of the INA were shifted to Thailand—again a Southeast Asian country; the Thais gave full support and sympathy to the INA in its struggle against the British.[26]

The INA–Japan joint attack from the Burmese side awakened British India to the strategic challenges and opportunities that the Northeast and Southeast Asia pose to India. 'The developments during the Second World War also point out to the fact that the security of India and the security of South-East Asia are interdependent'.[27] The year 1942 is considered a watershed year in that regard. The fall of Singapore in 1942 exposed India to the fact that its safety and security

[25] Ibid.

[26] Saroj Pathak, *India and South-East Asia: A Study of Indian Perspective Since 1962* (Delhi and Lucknow: Atma Ram & Sons, 1990), 26.

[27] Ibid., 23.

was directly linked to the security of Southeast Asia and the Indian Ocean Region at large.

> The loss of Singapore had exposed the coastline of India to combined air and naval attacks from the seas. Malaya, Singapore, Indo-China and Burma were, therefore, in the east a sphere of vital interest to India, analogous to Afghanistan and Iran in the west. A hostile power in Cam Ranh Bay would be no less dangerous than it would be in the Persian Gulf. What happened in Bangkok was of as much interest to India as what happened in Basra.[28]

With the support of the Japanese, Subhas Chandra Bose also established the Provisional Government of Free India in Andaman and Nicobar. His endeavours, however, came to an end with the defeat of the Japanese at the hands of the USA and the Allied forces.[29]

From 1947 until the Mid-1950s and Beyond (Second and Third Layers)

The first decade of India's Independence may be considered as one of the best phases of India's and Nehru's foreign policy, especially in relation to Asia. This was the period of Asia's resurgence, led and promoted by India under Nehru's leadership. Former British Prime Minister Winston Churchill acknowledged Nehru's leadership in Asia and described him as the 'light of Asia'. In a letter to Nehru on 21 January 1955, Churchill wrote:

> I hope you will think of the phrase 'The Light of Asia'. It seems to me that you might be able to do what no other human being could in giving India the lead, at least in the realm of thought, throughout Asia. With the freedom and dignity of the individual as the ideal rather than the Communist Party drill book.[30]

[28] Sir Ahmad, quoted in Ton That Thien, *India and South-East Asia 1945–1960* (Geneva: Libraine Droz, 1963), 68–69.

[29] For details on Subhas Bose's struggle, see Sugata Bose, *His Majesty's Opponent: Subhas Chandra Bose and India's Struggle Against Empire* (New Delhi: Penguin India, 2013).

[30] As quoted in Sarvepalli Gopal, *Jawaharlal Nehru: A Biography, Volume Two: 1947–1956* (Cambridge, MA: Harvard University Press, 1980), 236–237.

> [He] felt that if newly independent nations like India joined either of the camp in order to safeguard their national security and to get financial assistance, it would mean surrender of their freedom of action in international field. Moreover, they would be involved in the international power game and could easily become victims of Cold War politics.[32]

Thus, Nehru contemplated a 'positive, dynamic, active and independent role for India in international affairs, and he decided to keep her out of power politics by 'not joining any camp and by following the path of non-alignment'.[33] In that endeavour, India was joined by Indonesia, Malaysia and Burma among others. In order to promote cultural ties, the Indian Council of Cultural Relations was established in 1949.

The Asian Relations Conference, 1947

Organizing the first ARC in March–April 1947 turned out to be a great moment, not only for the newly independent Asian countries but also for India's foreign policy and for Nehru. The conference was called with the purpose of getting the aspiring Asian countries together. The intent was not to forge a block or a group and, therefore, specific issues of cooperation in the areas of economy and defence were not put on the agenda. In his inaugural address, Nehru stated; 'the time has come for us, peoples of Asia, to meet together, to hold together and to advance together'.[34] Echoing Nehru's thought, the Burmese leader Aung San said that the conference would be guided by 'a new consciousness of the oneness of Asia and also by the supreme necessity on the part of all the countries of Asia to stand together in weal and woe'.[35] Likewise, Cheng Yin-fun (Nauking), the head of the Chinese delegation, described the conference as 'a bridge between Asia and

[32] Pathak, *India and South-East Asia*, 34.

[33] Ibid.

[34] Bimal Prasad, 'Trends in Asian Relations, 1947–1987', in *Asian Relations*, ed. Eric Gonsalves (New Delhi: Lancer International, 1991), 66.

[35] Ibid.

At the international stage also, India strived to support Indonesia. India raised the issue of Indonesian independence at the UN. 'On 30 July 1947, the Government of India cabled instructions to the permanent delegation of India in New York to draw the attention of the United Nations Security Council (UNSC) on the Indonesian question'.[40] At the Security Council, India gave Indonesia its full support.

> At the 193rd meeting of the Council, on 22 August 1947, the Indonesian delegate requested the Council to set up two commissions: one for supervising the implementation of the ceasefire and the other to settle all points of dispute between the parties by mediation or arbitration. India supported the Indonesian request on both counts. The Indian action contributed to the Council setting up a consular commission on 25 August and a Committee of Good Offices on 1 November.[41]

The Dutch, however, found the UN resolutions too weak to deter them in their atrocities in Indonesia. Nehru strongly reacted to the second Dutch police action in Indonesia saying, 'The action has been started by the Dutch, but I may warn them that they will not be able to achieve their objective. The days of imperialism are over. The reaction to the Dutch action will be heard all over the Asiatic countries'.[42]

This was the context for calling an international conference on Indonesia by India from 20 to 23 January 1949. Explaining the rationale of the conference further, Nehru said in his inaugural speech:

> It was not without deep thought and earnest consideration that we decided to hold this conference. Believing as we do that the United Nations must be strengthened as a symbol of the New World Order, we were reluctant to take any steps which might appear to weaken its authority … but when the will of the Security Council was itself flouted then it became clear that we must confer together

[40] Thein, *India and South-East Asia*, 92.

[41] Ibid., 94.

[42] As quoted in Navrekha Sharma and Baladas Ghoshal, *India's Relations with Indonesia* (Singapore: Market Asia Books, 2014), 78.

> to strengthen the United Nations and to prevent further deterioration of a dangerous situation.... Ours is therefore a regional conference to which we invited both Australia and New Zealand whose interest in the tranquillity and contentment of Indonesia is as great as that of any of us.[43]

Linking Indonesian independence with India's own national security, Nehru argued: '[I]f some kind of colonial domination continues in Indonesia, if it is permitted to continue, it will be a danger to the whole of Asia, to us in India as well as to other countries'.[44]

Nehru's opening address at the conference was also a statement of India's attitude towards Indonesia as well as the problem of Asian freedom in general. He stressed that feelings had been roused all over Asia and in other parts of world at the recent happenings in Indonesia, and said:

> We meet today because the freedom of a sister country of ours has been imperilled, and dying colonialism of the past has raised its head again and challenged all the forces that are struggling to build up a new structure of the world. That challenge has a deeper significance than might appear on the surface for it is a challenge to a newly awakened Asia which has so long suffered under various forms of colonialism.[45]

The Conference was attended by 15 countries: Afghanistan, Australia, Burma, Ceylon, China, Egypt, Ethiopia, Iraq, Lebanon, Nepal, Pakistan, the Philippines, Saudi Arabia, Syria and Yemen. Thailand and New Zealand sent observers. The invitations to Australia and New Zealand had been calculatedly extended to avoid any impression that the conference was an attempt to forge any anti-West group. It was explained that disturbances in Indonesia would affect these two neighbouring countries as well. It was called a regional conference. In

[43] Ministry of Information and Broadcasting, *Jawaharlal Nehru's Speeches September 1946–May 1949*, Vol. I (New Delhi: Publications Division, Ministry of Information and Broadcasting, 1967), 324–329.

[44] Ibid.

[45] Ibid.

the meantime, Burma, Ceylon, Pakistan, Saudi Arabia and Iraq had followed Nehru's lead in the banning Dutch flights over their territories in reaction to the Dutch police action in Indonesia.[46]

Nehru's successful convening of the Conference on Indonesia yielded positive results and influenced the international opinion. Subsequently, a resolution was adopted at the UNSC on 28 January 1949. On 23 January the conference passed three resolutions. The first, which was the main one, made the following recommendations to the Security Council:[47]

1. The Republic's leaders and all political prisoners should be restored to freedom.
2. An interim government should be formed comprising representatives of the Republic and representatives of the territories of Indonesia before 15 March 1949.
3. The Republican government should be enabled to function freely.
4. The interim government should enjoy full powers of government, and the Dutch forces should withdraw from all of Indonesia.
5. The freedom of the interim government in external affairs should be determined in consultation of the Indonesian government, the Netherlands government, the Committee of Good Offices and anybody appointed by the Security Council.
6. Elections for a Constituent Assembly of Indonesia should be held before 1 October 1949.
7. Power should be completely transferred to the United States of Indonesia by 1 January 1950; the relations of Indonesia with the Netherlands should to be determined by negotiation with the latter.

The conference called by India on Indonesia played a critical and decisive role in advancing Indonesia's struggle for independence. Soon after the achievement of independence, the Indonesian leader Soekarno, within weeks of his assuming office, paid a visit to India to say his thanks. He was invited as the chief guest on India's first Republic Day on 26 January 1950. Nehru's unconditional and active

[46] Thein, *India and South-East Asia*, 90–91.
[47] Ibid., 101.

support to Indonesia brought limitless goodwill. President Soekarno, on the eve of proclamation of the United States of Indonesia said: 'On the eve of the rebirth of our nation, I am trying vainly to measure the gratitude the Indonesian people owe to India and to her Prime Minister personally for the unflinching and brotherly support in our struggle in the past'.[48] Within six months, Nehru paid a return visit to Indonesia in June 1950. He travelled extensively, accompanied by Soekarno, and received overwhelming popular acclaim. It was during this visit that Soekarno described Nehru as his 'political father' and Nehru invited Soekarno to join him in his mission for Asian resurgence and solidarity. Nehru said: 'We should work together for peace, advancement and equilibrium in Asia'.[49]

Since their independence, India and Indonesia followed the same line in international affairs. Both steered clear of power blocs and military pacts, following the policy of non-alignment. At the international stage, the similarity of views between India and Indonesia was so close that Premier Sastroamidjojo of Indonesia could say that foreign policy of Indonesia 'ran parallel' with Indian foreign policy and that for an Indonesian to speak of Indonesian problems to an Indian audience was like 'speaking into a sounding board'.[50] In their mutual perceptions, it was called 'India–Indonesia *Sama*' (India, Indonesia are the same and equal).

Both Nehru and Soekarno were dynamic personalities. Their visions of the world and of their respective new States had strong synergies. Nehru had a great personal rapport with Indonesian leaders, especially Soekarno. Both of them had a similar approach to Asian issues, and were strongly committed to fighting imperialism and colonialism at the global level. In one of his letters, Nehru wrote to Soekarno: 'Fortunately, you and I as individuals have so much in common that we take to each other spontaneously'.[51] They refused to mix religion with politics in building their societies and States. While Nehru strived

[48] United Nations 1949, Security Council Official Records. No. 1. (New York: UN).

[49] As quoted in Sharma Ghoshal, *India's Relations with Indonesia*, 98.

[50] Ibid., 97.

[51] Ibid.

to lay strong foundations for a secular state in India, Soekarno turned down the idea of making Indonesia an Islamic state, which was in conformity with Pundit Nehru's ideas on the nature of the State.

Following Nehru's visit to Indonesia, an Indian trade delegation visited Indonesia in November 1950, and the first trade agreement was concluded between the two countries in January 1951. The objective of this trade agreement was to revive textile trade between them that had been disrupted severely during the colonial period. Trade picked up fast between them in the following years and peaked by 1956. Thereafter, however, this trade started dwindling as China entered into the Indonesian market in a big way as a competitor of India.[52]

Soon after concluding the trade agreement in January 1951, India and Indonesia also entered into a bilateral Treaty of Perpetual Peace and Unalterable Friendship on 3 March 1951. This was the first treaty of its kind that India and Indonesia had entered into with any other country so soon after their respective independence. Article 1 of this treaty stated that 'there shall be perpetual and unalterable friendship' between the two countries; Article 3 stipulated that 'the two governments agree that their representatives shall meet from time to time and as often as occasion requires to exchange views on matters of common interest and to consider ways and means for mutual cooperation in such matters'.[53] India and Indonesia also decided to cooperate in cultural and educational fields. An agreement to that effect was signed between the two countries in 1955 to have educational exchanges and collaboration in science, literature and arts.

The Bandung Conference

The common approach and common thinking between the Indian and Indonesian leaders led to a very important initiative in the form of the Afro-Asian Conference in Bandung (Indonesia). The idea first emanated from the Indonesian leaders in the Conference of

[52] Ibid., 100–102.

[53] Soe Myint, *Burma File: A Question of Democracy* (New Delhi: India Research Press, 2003), 482.

the Colombo Powers in Kandy (Sri Lanka) in 1954 in the midst of Western moves of carving out military blocks in Asia. The idea was to keep the African and Asian countries out of such military alliances and to create an area of peace in Asia and Africa. Nehru enthusiastically endorsed the Indonesian proposal and suggested that such a conference be sponsored by all the Colombo powers, namely, Indonesia, India, Burma, Sri Lanka and Pakistan, with all the five countries also sharing its expenses. The sponsors were pressurized by the West, the USA and the UK not to invite China, but in vain.[54]

The conference concluded with the Bandung Declaration of 10 points as principles to be adopted by all the participants in their mutual relations. They included respect for sovereign equality and human rights, non-interference, abstention from big-powers-led military alliances and 'threats of aggression and the use of force against the territorial integrity or political independence of any country'. The countries participating in the conference raised the problems of dependent peoples and countries, and committed themselves to building mutual economic and cultural cooperation.[55] There were sharp divisions in the conference on defining 'colonialism' as some of the participants like Sri Lanka also wanted to name the Eastern European countries as being under the Soviet 'colonial control', while most others, especially India, Indonesia and Burma, were focussed on colonialism of the Western powers. Finally, the consensus formulation adopted said that 'colonialism in all its manifestations' must be condemned.[56]

In retrospect, the Bandung Conference may also be viewed as the first attempt at building an Asian strategic architecture, for which

[54] Inder Malhotra, 'Memories of Bandung', in *Masala Bumbu: Advancing the India-Indonesia* Partnership, ed. Gurjit Singh (Jakarta: Bertia Satu Media Holdings, 2015), 56–59. For detailed study of the Bandung Conference, see George McTurnan Kahin, *The Asian African Conference, Bandung Indonesia April 1955* (Ithaca, NY: Cornell University Press, 1956); G. H. Jansen, *Afro Asia and Non-alignment* (London: Prager, 1966).

[55] S. D. Muni, 'The Bandung Spirit: India and Indonesia in Resurgent Asia', in *Masala Bumbu: Advancing the India-Indonesia Partnership*, ed. Gurjit Singh (Jakarta: Bertia Satu Media Holdings, 2015), 51–52.

[56] Malhotra, 'Memories of Bandung', 59.

serious efforts are evident these days. The principles contained in them may be termed as the fundamental tenants of such an architecture which underlined that wars be avoided, conflicts and disputes be peacefully resolved, dominance and hegemony be resisted, and peace and development cooperation be promoted. This looked like a step towards building collective and cooperative security in Asia and the developing world.[57]

The Bandung Conference, may be termed as the zenith of India's multilateral diplomacy, especially in the context of its eastward engagement. But this conference also turned out to be a watershed in India's efforts to build Asia as a strong force of peace and solidarity in a region that was fast getting polarized into the Cold War and regional rivalries. This conference was one of its kind as it neither had a precedence nor could create a successor as a second Afro-Asian Conference could not be held. Nehru saw this conference as launching pad not only for Asia in world affairs but also for India and himself to lead Asia in defining the new nature of world politics. He was accordingly very meticulous and went to the extent of micro managing the organization of the conference that was otherwise being handled by the Indonesians. Concerned even with trivial organizational matters, he said:

> Above all, one fact should be remembered, and this is usually forgotten in Indonesia. This fact is an adequate provision of bathrooms and lavatories, etc. People can do without drawing rooms, but they cannot do without bathrooms and lavatories.[58]

The Indonesians took Nehru's instructions seriously but not quite comfortably. They saw them as a reflection on their ability and commitment to organize international gatherings.

Post-Bandung Setback for India

India and Nehru emerged from the Bandung Conference as losers, both in their eastward engagements and in their aspired role in Asia.

[57] Muni, 'The Bandung Spirit: India and Indonesia in Resurgent Asia', 52.
[58] Gopal, *Jawaharlal Nehru: A Biography, Volume Two*, 235.

There were several factors that account for this. The West was obviously not happy with the idea of Asian mobilization and solidarity, and they saw this conference as a challenge to their vision of world politics and their strategy of carving out military blocks and areas of influence in the Afro-Asian world. The Western media leaders like *Time Magazine*, *Washington Post* and *the New York Times* did not take the conference lightly, and they sought to belittle its significance by highlighting even small lapses and by distorting the statements and observations made by important leaders. The Western media also projected the differences voiced among Asian leaders at the Conference. The Western attempts to sabotage the conference were suspected as being behind the incident of where an Air India plane named 'Kashmir Princess' in Hong Kong carrying the Chinese delegation was blown up.[59] The West appeared to be determined not to let the Asian solidarity and Afro-Asian movements succeed.

Then there were rivalries within Asia as well. Bandung provided the first regional platform for China to engage with other Asian countries and to cultivate Pakistan in what came to constitute in future—the attempts to thwart India's leadership in Asia. India's subsequent conflict with China that precipitated the border war of 1962 between the two Asian giants did huge damage to India's influence and clout in Asia, as we shall see further. And lastly, Indian leaders like Nehru and his close associate Krishna Menon, alienated many in Asia by their otherwise well-meaning but what was perceived to be their overbearing and arrogant behaviour vis-à-vis the other conference participants.[60]

Keen observers of political dynamics at the Bandung Conference also discerned that India was not alone in aspiring for Asian leadership. Indonesia was a potentially strong candidate for this. It has been noted earlier that China was introduced to this Afro-Asian forum by India, Indonesia and others, despite Western pressures. India was even keen

[59] Malhotra, 'Memories of Bandung', 56; Sharma and Ghoshal, *India's Relations with Indonesia*, 124. Also see Ampiah Kweku, *The Political and Moral Imperatives of the Bandung Conference: The Reactions of the US, UK and Japan* (Folkestone: Global Oriental, 2007).

[60] This point has been discussed by Sharma and Ghoshal, *India's Relations with Indonesia*, 112–126.

to get China rehabilitated among the Southeast Asian countries who were battling China-supported communist insurgencies. Nehru had instructed his Ambassador in Jakarta to 'sell China to Indonesia'.[61] He had also persuaded U. Nu of Myanmar (then Burma) to soften his stand towards China. Conscious of its position, China maintained a suave, low profile in Bandung deliberations but prepared the ground for its assertion later by connecting with various leaders at the conference. The results of the Chinese diplomacy at the Bandung became evident as India's differences deepened with China, leading to the Chinese war against India in 1962, as we shall see below.

At the Bandung Conference, Nehru's primary goal was to frustrate the American strategic designs manifested through the Southeast Asia Treaty Organization (SEATO) and Central Treaty Organization (CENTO). The Sino-India competition perceived by many conference participants might have dented this goal. Acharya comments in this respect that

> The perceived rivalry between India and China might have put off the smaller and weaker Asian nations to join either of both in forming any regional association. With the two largest Asian countries unacceptable as a regional leader, the space opened for the region's smaller and weaker countries to take the initiative in forming ASEAN–Asia's first viable regional association.[62]

Beginning with the Bandung Conference, the India–China War and Chinese efforts to export communism in Southeast Asia proved both India and China as losers in the long run in Asian regionalism. Pathak argues that between 1947 and 1964, that is, the Nehru era, India carefully maintained a non-interventionist posture towards countries of the Southeast Asian region.

> She has watched the developments in the area with deep concern and sincere interest, but her stand has always been characterised by certain degree of caution and reservation.... The sole exception to

[61] Badr-ud-din Tyabji, *Memoirs of an Egoist* (New Delhi: Roli Books, 1988), 326.

[62] Acharya, *East of India, South of China*, 121.

> this has been India's actions with regard to Indonesia from 1947 to 1949.[63]

In his overall assessment of the Bandung legacy for world politics as a whole, Amitav Acharya says:

> The role the Bandung Conference played in India's strategic and normative approach to Asian security and world order was a key element in the evolution of Nehru's non-alignment policy, especially its rejection of the Cold War military alliances. In this respect, it marked a turning point in Nehru's break with the West led by the US. Whether this was a gain or loss for India is debatable, but *Indian foreign policy would never be the same after Bandung....* Nehru was not able to use the Bandung Conference to bring about a long-term engagement of communist China.... Bandung thus proved to be a crucial stage for the encounters between India, China, and Southeast Asia and also for the evolution of the overall post-war regional and international order.[64]

The minor organizational differences on the conduct of the Bandung that cropped up between India and Indonesia were perhaps the reflections of the strong personalities of their leaders Nehru and Soekarno and the ideological differences in the visions that these two great Asian leaders cherished for the Asian and the world order. Such differences had manifested even earlier, like on the Japanese peace treaty and war reparations from Japan.

> When the United States government convened a conference in San Francisco in September 1951 for the purpose of signing a peace treaty with Japan, India declined to attend. She also waived all war reparations. Indonesia, on the contrary, attended this conference, signed the peace treaty and later demanded reparations from Japan.[65]

But these differences were lost in the Indian–Indonesian enthusiasm and commitment for anti-colonial struggle in Asia. However, the situation had changed after the mid-1950s.

[63] Pathak, *India and South-East Asia*, 39.
[64] Acharya, *East of India, South of China*, 60.
[65] Thein, *India and South-East Asia*, 114.

The events that unfolded during the Bandung Conference adversely affected India's ties with Indonesia. The two countries also had differing perceptions about each other's territorial disputes. For Indonesia, the West Irian (popularly known as Western New Guinea or West Papua) issue was of immense importance as it was more than a third of total Indonesian territory chipped away by the Dutch while conceding the independence to Indonesia. Taking a principled stand on the matter, India supported Indonesia's claim over West Papua but with caveat that the Indonesian efforts should be peaceful and in sync with the wishes of the people. Both Nehru and Mrs Vijaya Lakshmi Pandit, India's High Commissioner in London, reiterated India's position that it supported a peaceful settlement of dispute. When Soekarno, in July 1958, during his visit to India reaffirmed his wishes to use force to recapture West Papua, Nehru steered away from Soekarno's point of view. Sadly, on both Kashmir and West Papua, India and Indonesia could not make each other understand their respective positions.

According to Thein,

> [I]n matters involving Indonesia's major interests, India was not able to bring Indonesia to side with her if those interests did not coincide with those of India. But on matters in which no major Indonesian interests were involved, Indonesia fully supported India. For example, Indonesia gave unqualified support to India's claims to Goa, to India's dispute with South Africa on the question of Apartheid, to India's opposition to United States aid to Pakistan.[66]

He further states that,

> where western imperialism was absent and where no Indonesian major interest was involved, Indonesia's attitude was non-committal. This is evident in the Indo-Pakistan dispute. This is also evident in the case of Tibet. In 1959, together with India, all the other Southeast Asian countries—except North Vietnam—joined

[66] Thein, *India and South-East Asia*, 115.

in condemning Chinese action. Indonesia alone remained persistently silent.[67]

Nehru's approach to the issues of colonialism and imperialism was comparatively conservative in contrast to Indonesia's radical approach. The stridency in Indonesia's views in this respect became clearer gradually. Indonesia was also keen on organizing a second Afro-Asian Conference, for which Nehru was not very enthusiastic as he had moved towards supporting a bigger Non-Aligned Movement (NAM) going beyond Asia and Africa and taking in its fold the countries of Latin America and even Europe, like Yugoslavia. Nehru, who was also anxious to avoid any public display of Asian internal disunity, and conscious of the certainty that a new Afro-Asian conference would lead to that result, consistently avoided committing himself to another Bandung. Since such a conference would not be worthy of the name without Indian participation, Indonesia had to shelve the idea. India's lack of interest in supporting a Second Afro-Asian conference was read in Jakarta as India's softening towards colonialism and imperialism. These differences erupted in the open in the process of convening the 1961 Conference of Non-aligned States in Belgrade. At the Belgrade Conference, Nehru said:

> The task of non-aligned nations is to create proper atmosphere for negotiations between the Soviet Union and America. This could only be done by articulating their demand for peace and exerting their collective pressure for negotiations. For nations of meagre military and economic strength to attempt more than this was futile. More important, any specific suggestion made by the Belgrade participants would be likely to irritate one side or the other and thus exacerbate tensions.[68]

During the Belgrade Conference, Nehru tried to mellow down his earlier critique of colonialism, stating that the 'age of classical colonialism was over'. For him, the greater challenge was the rising tensions between the two superpowers who were the leaders of the

[67] Thein, *India and South-East Asia*, 117.

[68] Jawaharlal Nehru, 'Proceedings of Conference of Heads of States or Government of Non-aligned Countries' (Belgrade, Yugoslavia: 1961).

Communist and the Western block respectively. Calling colonialism as 'not an urgent threat' and putting great power rivalry as the biggest concern, Nehru invited criticism from several leaders. That had visibly upset Nehru, and he felt isolated. When Soekarno's turn came, he not only highlighted the difference between Indian and Indonesian approaches but also turned a bitter critique of Nehru. Later, when India supported the Malaysia plan that was also not to the good taste of Indonesia, which criticized India of being supportive of the British colonial agenda with regard to Malaya. Indonesia, of course, was a leading member in that regard and had been voicing support of militant anti-colonialism in Africa, Asia and elsewhere. Accusing Nehru as a supporter of imperialism in disguise was uncalled for, but India's growing dispute with China, and Indonesia's desire to replace India as the leader of the NAM, made it an unfortunate reality. The state of affairs between India and Southeast Asia became worse and got totally exposed when China attacked India in 1962.

Nehru was also not very happy with the radicalization of internal politics in Indonesia by Soekarno during 1957–1958 wherein he centralized administration and set aside the idea of federalism by introducing guided democracy and by proclaiming himself as 'president for life'. These differences dampened the warm relations between India and Indonesia that was evident before the Bandung Conference.[69]

Despite its growing differences with India, Indonesia looked towards the former for support and sought defence cooperation to meet the challenge of domestic insurgencies. Indonesia signed separate agreements with India related to cooperation with its air force, navy and army in 1956, 1958 and 1960, respectively, for training and joint exercises as well as for supply of weapons. India had always been hesitant in supplying weapons to other countries, partly because of its stated position to keep away from all military matters and conflicts, and partly also due to insufficient surpluses in India. India was also careful in avoiding getting involved in the developing rivalries within Southeast Asia, and therefore moved cautiously when it came to

[69] Some details of these issues have been discussed in Sharma and Ghoshal, *India's Relations with Indonesia*, 92–143. On Indonesia's internal political changes under Soekarno, see Daniel S. Lev, *The Transition to Guided Democracy: Indonesian Politics, 1957–59* (Singapore: Equinox Publishing, 2009).

military support and defence cooperation. Gradually, Indonesia found better support forthcoming from its other friends such as Pakistan and China in defence matters.[70] India's differences with China further added to the distancing in India–Indonesia relations. In 1964, Nehru died, and in 1965, the Soekarno regime was also thrown away by its military. Ever since the Bandung Conference (1955) and the Belgrade Non-aligned Conference (1961), India–Indonesia relations lost its warmth, reaching to their lowest in 1965 when Indonesia not only supported Pakistan during the Indo-Pak war but also threatened to attack India. Indonesia also threatened to invade and take over the Andaman and Nicobar Islands, though that would have been a sheer miscalculation, potentially turning into a disaster for Indonesia.

Impact of the Sino-Indian Conflict

The India–China war of 1962 turned out to be a massive military failure and diplomatic disaster for India. During the war,

> [I]nstead of expressing sympathy and support with India in her hour of crisis, almost all the countries of South-East Asia, with sole exception of Malaya (Malaysia), had mixed reactions between reservations and disbelief. The situation suggested that something [very wrong had gone] somewhere in respect of Indian foreign policy in the region so that the things had deteriorated to such a low ebb. Reactions of some of her neighbours like Indonesia and Burma were particularly a rude shock to Indian government and public as these two nations were considered as the closest friends of India.[71]

Indonesia was non-committal to the India–China war of 1962; Indonesia neither supported nor sympathized with India. If in 1959 China had become an aggressor and imperialist power in the eyes of India, to Indonesia, it was still an anti-imperialist friend and supporter. The 'Bandung spirit' was dying in Delhi but was still alive in Jakarta.[72]

[70] B. D. Arora, *India-Indonesia Relation 1961–1980* (New Delhi: Asian Educational Services, 1981).

[71] Pathak, *India and South-East Asia*, 2.

[72] Thien, *India and South East Asia*, 115.

The Malaysian exception could perhaps be explained with reference to old strong links with India. It may be recalled here, 'after Mahatma Gandhi was assassinated, his ashes were taken to Malaya on March 15, 1948. For nearly a fortnight, his ashes were kept for people of Malaya to pay homage to Gandhi Ji'.[73] India remained closer to both Malaysia and Singapore because it not only supported the *Malaysia Plan* but also supported them in their anti-communist struggle. In 1962, for instance, Malaysia supported India in the India–China war, with Tunku Abdul Rehman setting up the 'Save Democracy Fund', and contributing 1 million rupees to India. There were also regional factors behind the Malaysian position as its relations with Indonesia were gradually becoming tense. Indonesia had declared a policy of *konfrontasi* (Indonesian/Malay term for Borneo confrontation).

Analysing the India–China war of 1962, Acharya states that India's defeat in the war not only led to the loss of territory (and face) to China, but also the loss of respect of the Southeast Asian countries. That, along with India's own compulsions and limitations, made India almost a non-entity in Southeast Asian politics, and their regionalism drive manifested in the form of ASEAN. Focusing on post-1962 developments, Acharya addresses the question of whether India's loss meant China's gain:

> To some extent it did, but with a qualification.... China's triumph at Bandung was short-lived. The goodwill achieved at Bandung by the 'charm offensive' strategy of Chou En-Lai ... dissipated quickly due to China's aid to communist insurgencies in Southeast Asia. While India suffered a loss of prestige ... in the 1962 Sino-Indian war, China did not necessarily win the diplomatic-political relations contest in Southeast Asia either. Its support for the communist movements challenging Southeast Asian governments invited mistrust and isolation.[74]

[73] Asis Kumar Majumdar, *South-East Asia in India's Foreign Policy: A Study of India's Relations with South-East Asian Countries* (Calcutta: Naya Prokash, 1982), 31.

[74] Acharya, *East of India, South of China: Sino-Indian Encounters in Southeast Asia*, xv–xvi.

The effect of the India–China war was twofold on India's eastward engagement. First, it resulted in a loss of reputation for India, and second, it increased the fear among Southeast Asian countries about China's hegemonic designs. 'Things changed rapidly after Bandung, and especially after the Sino-Indian War in 1962. India's leading role in Asian diplomacy quickly faded. From being the major champion of Asian regionalism, India almost became a non-entity—if not a pariah—particularly in Southeast Asia by the 1980s'.[75]

Support for Burma (Myanmar) Stability, Order and State Building

Burma's struggle for independence was not as difficult and challenging as that of Indonesia. As noted earlier, Burma's leaders received guidance and support from India in their negotiations with the British for their independence. Burma became free from colonial rule on 4 January 1948. India offered the services of its Constitutional expert Sir B. N. Rau in helping Burma draft its constitution. Dr Rajendra Prasad, the president of Constituent Assembly of India, represented India in Rangoon for the celebration of its independence in January 1948. Speaking to the citizens of Burma, Dr Prasad said that 'free Burma could always count on India's assistance and services whenever she needed them'.[76]

Burma's principal challenge soon after attaining independence was the restoration of internal peace, stability and order. There were two major threats to Burma's internal stability: the conflict between the new Burma government and the ethnic minorities, and the presence of nearly 12,000 Kuomintang (KMT) troops, fully armed and fighting with the Chinese communist revolutionaries. Burma looked towards India for support in facing these challenges, and India responded positively and decisively.

The ethnic challenge to Burma's new government was led by the Karens, an ethnic group. The Karens, who were joined by the Communist Party of Burma, had the full support of the new Chinese

[75] Acharya, *East of India, South of China*, xiv.
[76] Aung and Myint, 'India-Burma Relations', 88.

for jute goods, textiles, and oil and steel products from India'.[83] This helped Burma immensely, as in 1954, it faced a peculiar situation of huge surplus of rice, much beyond its own needs. The neighbouring countries such as Thailand and Vietnam themselves being rice surplus countries would not buy rice from Burma. Considering the dire state of Burma, India agreed to purchase 900,000 tons of its surplus rice on extremely generous terms, almost four times the prevailing market price, suggested by the then Premier U. Nu.[84] The unsubsidized rice was sold in the Indian market, and the Indian consumers paid for it. In 1955 again, India granted a US$42 million loan to Burma. India never pressed for the repayment of the loan.

India also dealt softly on the question of the Indians living in Myanmar being pushed out as a result of new internal laws in favour of economic nationalism. The then government in Burma enacted a new Land Nationalisation Act of 1948 which most adversely affected the rich Indian landlords. This move had been triggered because some of the Indians were seen as helping the outside powers in Myanmar during the war years. There were nearly 4,000 Indians who were dispossessed of their land and had nowhere to go. The Indian Embassy successfully evacuated these Indians with the support of the Government of Burma (Myanmar) and other non-governmental agencies. The number of repatriated Indians increased to 13,000 by 1949–1950. The Indian Embassy in Myanmar also provided financial relief and worked for their repatriation. As stated in the MEA report of 1948–1949, 'the repatriation of those Indians who are not likely to be reabsorbed in the economy of Burma in the near future. Shipping accommodation for Indians wishing to return to India because of disturbed conditions in Burma has also been arranged'.[85] India also managed to work out an understanding with the Myanmar

[83] For the complete text of India's engagement with the East in 1951–1952, see MEA's *Annual Report 1951–52*.

[84] For the complete text of India's engagement with the East in 1955–1956, see MEA's *Annual Report 1955–56*.

[85] For the complete text of India's engagement with the East in 1948–1949, see MEA's *Annual Report 1948–49*.

government for a proper compensation for the Indians affected by the Land Nationalisation Act of 1948.[86]

The government also made efforts to let Indians permanently settle in Siam (Thailand) and to abolish a discriminatory tax known as '*impot gradue*' imposed by the French government on the Indians in Indo-China. Through the efforts of the Indian Consulate in Saigon, the government helped Indians send remittances to India.[87] Similar efforts were made to support Indian merchants based in Sinkiang (Xinjiang) and Shanghai in China, as also the Indian workers based in Malaysia. This speaks volumes about India's efforts to look after its people even when India had just emerged as an independent nation overstressed with the partition and repatriation of millions of Indians from West and East Pakistan.

The driving factor behind Nehru's involvement in Myanmar's affairs and his softer approach manifested in not making an issue out of evacuating Indians from Myanmar while raising loans for Myanmar and importing its rice on generous terms, was his close understanding and friendship with the Myanmar leader U. Nu. Both the leaders shared perspectives on the anti-colonial struggle and Asian solidarity. Nehru relied on U. Nu for support and help in various Asian conferences organized by him. The personal touch in their relationship was underlined by the fact that occasionally U. Nu would even send exotic fruits like mangostein to Nehru.[88] Nehru had also deferred India's recognition of the Peoples' Republic of China in 1949 to let Burma take lead in this respect. He knew that Burma's need was greater in accommodating China in view of the presence of KMT troops in Burma and the rebellion faced by the Karan ethnic groups and the Communist Party of Burma.

Northeast India and U. Nu

U. Nu had not only accepted Nehru's leadership in Asia but was also willing to help India in dealing with one of its most serious internal

[86] Ibid.

[87] Ibid.

[88] Jawaharlal Nehru Memorial Fund, *Selected Works of Jawaharlal Nehru, Second Series* (New Delhi: Jawaharlal Nehru Memorial Fund, 2014), 59: 424.

security challenge of the Naga insurgency in its Northeast region bordering Burma. Launched by Angami Zapu Phizo in 1946 under the banner of the National Council, the Naga separatists vowed for a Naga state separate from India. Nehru tried to persuade Phizo to give up his separatist demand as India was willing to accommodate him otherwise. Having failed to get Phizo to come round to his point of view, Nehru tried to appeal to the Naga people directly. In this initiative, he requested U. Nu of Burma to join him as the Nagas spilled over both the countries and sought sanctuaries across the Indian border in Burma. Nehru, joined by U. Nu, toured the Naga areas in April 1953 and met many groups of the Nagas. At some places, however, some Nagas walked out of the meeting being addressed by U. Nu and Nehru. In reaction to this act of discourtesy, not only to him but also to U. Nu, Nehru dropped his initiative.[89] Later, Nehru created a state of Nagaland within the Indian Union. But some sections of the Nagas continued to remain on the fringe, seeking external support, from the countries such as Pakistan, China and even the United Kingdom, in their struggle for independence. It is no wonder that the problem still awaits a peaceful and credible resolution.

Containing the Cold War in Korean Peninsula and Indo-China

The foregoing discussion underlines Nehru's quest for Asian solidarity and resurgence in the post-war world. His deep engagement with Indonesia and Myanmar was driven, besides the quest for Asian solidarity, by the imperatives of centuries-old civilizational and cultural bonds as also of neighbourly interests in the areas of security, economic development and political stability. The developing Cold War compelled and constrained this engagement with close neighbours. However, the Cold War also created opportunities for India under Nehru's leadership to play the role of a peacemaker in the Indo-Pacific region: in Korea and Indo-China.

[89] Gopal, *Jawaharlal Nehru: A Biography, Volume Two*, 208. Also see Preet Malik, *My Myanmar Years* (New Delhi: SAGE Publications, 2016), 47.

The Korean Crisis

Korea was the first major Cold War conflict that dragged Nehru and India deeply into it. War broke out in the Korean peninsula in June 1950. India endorsed the UNSC Resolutions holding North Korea responsible for the aggression and inviting all other countries to join hands with the UN in ensuring cessation of hostilities and in forcing North Korea to withdraw its forces to the 38th parallel. While Nehru got the UNSC resolution approved by his Cabinet as that represented the situation on the ground, he was personally not comfortable with just that and wanted to work for stopping the war from escalation. He did not want the Western powers to link the situation with the Republic of Formosa and Indo-China to engulf the whole of Asia into conflict.[90] While he tried to plead with the USA not to seek military solution by destroying North Korea, he also tried to persuade China and the Soviet Union to keep patience and refrain from getting militarily involved in the Korean peninsula. Nehru's prescription was to grant UN membership to the Peoples' Republic of China in the place of Nationalist China to work out a negotiated solution of conflict.[91] He, however, did not succeed in stopping escalation of the war. The US-led forces crossed the 38th parallel, which brought the Chinese into the Korean War.

After crossing the 38th parallel however, it dawned on the USA that it may not be easy to sustain the war as it may become a long drawn one. But for signing the ceasefire, both the USA and China wanted to ensure that their prisoners taken by the opposing camp were repatriated to them. While the USA did not have more than a couple of thousand of its troops held as prisoners, the Chinese and North Koreans held by the US-led forces in South Korea were estimated to be in the range of 200,000. Out of this huge number, the Chinese prisoners were estimated to be 170,000 and China was insisting on

[90] Gopal, *Jawaharlal Nehru: A Biography, Volume Two*, 105.

[91] Sandeep Bhardwaj, 'India and the Korean War: Damned are the Peacemakers', *Revisiting India: Indian History Recounted*, 3 February 2014, https://revisitingindia.com/2014/02/03/india-and-the-korean-war-damned-are-the-peacemakers/, accessed 17 August 2018.

at least 100,000 Chinese prisoners to be repatriated to them. The US side was insisting that the repatriation should be on voluntary basis and only those prisoners should be repatriated who wanted to be repatriated. The underlying assumption was that many of the Chinese and Koreans would not want to go back. The resolution of ceasefire and armistice got stuck on an *all* versus *voluntary* repatriation. To resolve this issue, India's Krishna Menon moved a proposal to appoint a UN repatriation commission.[92] After initial resistance, the idea was eventually accepted, and Korean armistice was signed on 27 July 1953. The Neutral Nations Repatriation Commission appointed by the UN had Sweden, Switzerland, Poland and Czechoslovakia as its members with India as the chairman. Its mandate was to explain the correct position to the prisoners and help them decide what their preferences were in terms of repatriation.

Nehru confronted many challenges in steering Indian diplomacy in the Korean crisis. He was moved by a missionary zeal to work for the ceasefire and de-escalation of the conflict. He was also keen that India played a 'useful role' without being either overwhelmed by the US and Western powers or pressured by China. There were reservations among his Cabinet colleagues, and his Ambassadors dealing with the issue in different contexts lacked coordination on India's specific goals. On the top of this, China's stand on Tibet had complicated Indian assessment of the Chinese role in the Korean crisis.[93] As the Indian work in the Repatriation Commission began, the ground reality of dealing with the prisoners with limited resources and stiff opposition from the diverse stakeholders made the task far more challenging then envisaged. This being the first major global peacekeeping assignment, India also lacked adequate experience and exposure in handling such a complicated matter. The Repatriation Mission was eventually dissolved in February 1954 without any formal declaration of the end of the Korean War.[94] Notwithstanding this failure, Nehru's involvement

[92] For detailed discussion, see Gopal, *Jawaharlal Nehru: A Biography, Volume Two*, 139–140, 144.

[93] Ibid., 101–105.

[94] Eric Gonsalves, 'Resolving the Korean Crisis', *Indian Foreign Affairs Journal* 2, no. 2 (April–June 2007): 116–128.

in the Korean issue brought out his commitment for world peace with growing demands on his statesmanship in a world that was dangerously divided. Hopefully, the outcome of North Korean leader Kim and the US President Trump Summit in June 2018 may lead to the official closure of the Korean War, nearly 64 years after Nehru's efforts.

Peacemaking in Indo-China

The struggle for independence in the Indo-China region, comprising Vietnam, Laos and Cambodia, presented a different challenge to India. The region was under French colonial rule. But during the Second World War, the Japanese pushed the French out and established their own control in 1941. A new nationalist force, Viet Minh, had emerged there under the leadership of Ho Chi Minh. The defeat of the Japanese in the world war in 1945 encouraged the countries of the Indo-China region to declare independence. Ho Chi Minh declared independence of the Democratic Republic of Vietnam in 1945. The Potsdam Conference in July 1945 assigned responsibility to China and Britain to clear the Japanese troops from the northern and the southern parts of Indo-China. While the Chinese let the Viet Minh to manage their areas of control in North Vietnam, the British collaborated with the French to let them re-establish their hold on the remaining region. Subsequently, the Americans joined the French, which eventually led to a long and bloody war in Vietnam and Indo-China that continued until 1975.

Ho Chi Minh resisted the French in Vietnam. North Vietnam controlled by Ho Chi Minh, approached independent India for help in its struggle because the British had been supporting the French and were even allowing them to get reinforcements by using the Indian territory. It was a great disappointment to Vietnam when Nehru did not respond. He invited two delegations from Vietnam at the ARC in New Delhi in March 1947, ignoring Ho Chi Minh's request to recognize only his delegation as the true and sole representative of Vietnam. Invitation to both North and South Vietnam at the conference amounted to accepting the division of the country and the legitimacy of the French control of South Vietnam. India's caution in not getting involved in the Indo-China struggle for independence was clearly reiterated by Nehru in Indian Parliament on 17 March 1950. He said:

> The policy we have pursued in regard to Indo-China has been one of absolute non-interference. Our interference could at best be a theoretical one. I don't think that either a theoretical or any other kind of interference in the affairs of a country struggling for freedom can do any good, because the countries which have been under colonial domination invariably resent foreign interference. Their nationalism cannot tolerate it; and even if interference comes with the best possible motives, it is often regarded as a kind of weapon in the hands of those who are opposed to nationalism. Besides, interference exposes them to the possible slur that their nationalism is not a free independent nationalism but one that is controlled by others. That is why we have sought deliberately not to interfere with Indo-China and we intend to continue this policy.[95]

In the same speech, Nehru had spoken about India's support to Indonesia and Myanmar (Burma), and lauded India's role in resurgent Asia. So the question arises: Why was he hesitant in extending support to Indo-China?

It seems that Nehru was constrained by the British who were supporting the French in Indo-China. He was also negotiating with the French regarding the liberation of French possessions in India and therefore wanted to play safe, giving priority to India's own immediate core interests against the cause of Asian decolonization. Then there was Chinese support to Indo-China, and with the Chinese use of force in Tibet, Nehru was wondering if he should be facilitating their strategy in Indo-China. Though Cambodia was civilizationally very close to India, it was Vietnam that was the biggest and strategically most important player.

[95] Ministry of Information and Broadcasting, *Jawaharlal Nehru's Speeches August 1949–February 1953*, Vol. II (New Delhi: Publications Division, Ministry of Information and Broadcasting, 1963), 226.

India had not been able to take a firm and clear position initially, with respect to the movement led by Ho Chi Minh in North Vietnam and the latter's relations with South Vietnam. South Vietnam was still dominated by France. While Nehru had conveyed to the French that controlling South Vietnam by force would not serve the French interests in the long run, the support was not of the same intensity when it came to Ho Chi Minh and North Vietnam.[96]

Bao Dai, the French puppet emperor of Annam (South Vietnam), made repeated requests to India for raising the issue at the UN, but Nehru did not accept his request. Later, in 1950, when the Ho Chi Minh government was recognized by several Asian countries including China and the USSR (Union of Soviet Socialist Republics), the US-led Western block recognized the French-dominated South Vietnam led by the Bao Dai government. India took an absolutely ambivalent position and did not recognize either of the two sides. In India's perception, Indo-China had been divided along the Cold War rivalries and, therefore, it was prudent to keep away from it. According to D. R. SarDesai, India became 'progressively cautious' in supporting Ho Chi Minh. When the conflict broke out between North and South Vietnam, India decided to send a medical mission to the North but fell short of sending the Indian Air Force. Some scholars are of the opinion that Nehru refused to send the forces because of apprehensions of involvement of Subhas Chandra Bose's brother in Vietnam.[97] Later, in January 1950, the Commonwealth Conference was held in Colombo. During the conference, Nehru successfully convinced the members not to support Bao Dai. Explaining India's continuing caution regarding Indo-China, Nehru said that the situation in the region was 'extraordinarily complicated' and there were 'larger considerations' as well.[98] These larger considerations included deference to French and British involvement in Vietnam.

[96] D. R. SarDesai, *Indian Foreign Policy in Cambodia, Laos, and Vietnam 1947–1964* (Los Angeles, CA: University of California Press, 1968).

[97] Ibid.

[98] Ramesh Thakur, *Peace Keeping in Vietnam: Canada, India, Poland and International Commission* (Canada, University of Alberta Press, 1984), 37.

Nehru, it seems, had clearly given weightage to Vietnam's communist ideology initially. However, as it gradually emerged that under this ideology there was the robustly nationalist character of its struggle against colonial forces, Nehru's position started changing. The Western domination in the Cold War had also started affecting India's own vital security concerns in relation to Pakistan and in Kashmir. The USA was seeking unilateral action in Vietnam and was helping France militarily to keep its hold there. This was not acceptable to India. India feared that this could lead to a direct confrontation between China and the USA in Vietnam. Revisiting his Indo-China policy, Nehru appealed for ceasefire and said on April 1954 in the Parliament:

> Indo-China is an Asian country and a proximate area. Despite her heavy sacrifices, the conflict finds her enmeshed in intervention, and the prospect of her freedom is jeopardized. The crisis in respect of Indo-China, therefore, moves us deeply and calls from us our best efforts to avert an extension and intensification of the conflict and to promote the trends that might lead to a settlement.[99]

He proposed a six-point plan that called for ceasefire, independence of all the Indo-China states, direct negotiations between them and non-interference from outside under the UN monitoring.[100] He also called for the Colombo Powers' Conference and got this plan approved there despite reservations from Pakistan and Myanmar.[101] All this was to prepare India for a role in the Geneva Conference on Indo-China called by four major powers—the USA, the Soviet Union, Britain and France—in April 1954. India was not an invitee

[99] As quoted in Chapter 1, 'India and Cambodia 1947–69: A Historical Background', in *Shodhganga*, shodganga.infibnet.ac.in/bitstream/10603/461/7/07_Chapter1.pdf, accessed 27 April 2018 (hereafter referred as 'shodhganga'). See also Jawaharlal Nehru, *India's Foreign Policy Speeches: September 1946–April 1961* (New Delhi: Publications Division, Ministry of Information and Broadcasting, 1983), 398–399. Also see *Parliamentary Debates* V, no. 52 (24 April 1954): Col. 5581.

[100] *Shodhganga*, 'India and Cambodia 1947–69: A Historical Background', 20–22.

[101] Gopal, *Jawaharlal Nehru: A Biography, Volume Two*, 191.

but participated in it as an observer and played a critical role. Krishna Menon, who represented India at the Geneva Conference, became a much sought-after go-between among all the contending players. He softened the conflicting interests and informed Nehru that the 'opinions in Geneva have converged on India'.[102] The first phase of the Geneva Conference succeeded in calling for the withdrawal of external forces from Laos and Cambodia. The Geneva Conference also constituted a UN International Control Commission (ICC) to monitor peace process in the Indo-China region. India accepted the responsibility to Chair this commission which had Canada and Poland as its other members.

Nehru travelled to China and North Vietnam in October 1954. Nehru wrote about Ho Chi Minh's warm meeting with him during this visit; 'He came forward—almost leapt forward—and embraced and kissed me'.[103] That brought an end to any ambivalence, if it existed, in Nehru's thinking on Vietnam and marked the beginning of a long, warm and cooperative relationship between India and Vietnam. Later, in 1958, Ho Chi Minh visited India. During his visit, he also extended his country's support to India on critical and sensitive issues like Kashmir. India–Vietnam relations evolved smoothly thereafter.

While analysing India's engagement with the East during the Cold War years, scholars have often (mistakenly) attributed most of India's diplomatic failures to its policy of non-alignment. However, such a perception emanates from poor understanding of India's freedom struggle in general and Nehru's worldview in particular. A grossly overlooked fact by many of scholars is that for Nehru, the biggest issue and threat was colonial oppression. Arguably, it was not because India was non-aligned but because of the fact that some Southeast Asian countries had started playing into the hands of the USA. As the Cold War intensified, small states of Southeast Asia succumbed to that pressure.

[102] Ibid., 192.
[103] Ibid., 227.

Relations with Japan

India's relations with Japan have seen many phases of warmth and indifference. As early as in 1948, the Indian government had realized the special importance of Japan. As the MEA *Annual Report 1948–49* states,

> Japan's future is of special interest to India and India maintains a Liaison Mission there, partly to keep in touch with the political development of Japan as a democratic pawn and partly for the furtherance of India's economic interest. The Mission is particularly useful in securing facilities for Indian businessmen visiting Japan and in securing Japanese equipment and technicians for the development of Indian industries.[104]

In 1948, India entered into a trade agreement with Japan. In order to pursue greater trade with Japan, an Indian delegation was sent to Japan in 1948 to study and analyse Japan's cottage industries. Upon their return,

> [The Indian delegation] brought with them numerous exhibits of cottage industry products from Japan, machinery to set up similar cottage industries in India and also a team of Japanese technicians to train our refugees to work the machinery imported from Japan.[105]

Relations with Thailand

With Thailand, India had a sort of formal relation than anything else. Thailand, being a close ally of the USA, found it difficult to understand India's position. When Nehru convened the 18-nation conference on Indonesia, Thailand refused to participate. Though cultural, religious and spiritual ties bind India and Thailand together, but a critical element missing in their ties in the first half of the twentieth century was that unlike India, Indonesia, Burma, Malaya and the rest of Southeast Asia, Thailand never had to face colonial oppression. Of

[104] MEA's *Annual Report 1948–49.*
[105] MEA's *Annual Report 1949–50.*

course, in 1949, joining the Conference on Indonesia was politically incorrect for Thailand as it was a close partner of the USA. That said, Thailand succumbed to the peer pressure of the countries of the region and subsequently sent an observer to the conference.

Clearly, the Indian and Thai priorities were somewhat different in the early 1950s. Not surprisingly, in 1954, India and Thailand found each other on opposite sides of the spectrum. Thailand requested the UN in 1954 to send observers to study the potential dangers to the Thai sovereignty arising out of the war in Indo-China. It was natural for Nehru and the Indian MEA to believe that the Thai move had the American promptings behind it as the latter was not in favour of the Geneva Conference and the developments therein.

Appraisal

India achieved a distinct and important stature in the Asian politics after Nehru's ascendance to Indian politics in general, and the Prime Minister's Office in particular. Unfortunately though, India's diplomatic footwork was not backed either by enhancing military prowess or economic capabilities. As D. R. SarDesai argues, 'India's role in international affairs was certainly disproportionately large when compared with India's economic and military strength'.[106]

The period and contribution of Nehru underlined the depth and sweep of India's eastward engagement that could be traced to the years even before India's Independence. India was both acting and counteracting in the East under Nehru: acting to lead the Asian struggles for decolonization to build and reinforce the Asian resurgence, and counteracting to the persisting presence of colonial and imperial stakeholders under the garb of the Cold War. India was also resisting the spread of the Cold War in Asia at the cost of Asian solidarity, peace and stability. Indian efforts and initiatives brilliantly succeeded in advancing decolonization and peace as was evident in Indonesia, Myanmar and

[106] SarDesai, *Indian Foreign Policy in Cambodia, Laos, and Vietnam 1947–1964*, 1.

Indo-China, particularly Laos and Cambodia. However, India could not achieve what it aimed for in the Korean peacekeeping efforts, in avoiding war in Vietnam and in building the Asian solidarity. Its success in the organization of Asian conferences, especially the Bandung Afro-Asian Conference, also brought in a message that Asia was not responsive and receptive to India's leadership despite the global recognition that India and Nehru were the 'light of Asia'.

There were many reasons that contributed to the shattering of Nehru's Asian dream by the fading years of his life. The roots of Western colonialism and imperialism were rather stronger than Nehru had envisaged. The Cold War greatly facilitated them to retain as much of their stakes in Asia as possible under different forms and shapes. Then there were intra-Asian conflicts and rivalries that were easily exploited by the outside powers that did not want to leave their control and domination of Asia. India was particularly constrained by its own conflicts, first with Pakistan and then with China. Nehru's diplomatic style characterized by a well-meaning arrogance and affectionately overbearing attitude alienated many smaller Asian countries from India. India's military humiliation in the Himalayas at the Chinese hands not only subverted the dream of peaceful coexistence between the two Asian giants but also dented and deterred India's leadership in the rest of Asia. It exposed India's lack of military and economic capabilities needed to help Asia assert itself. Then there was widespread political turbulence within the Asian countries, fuelled and fired by the interventionist Cold War forces as also by the complexities of building new independent state structures after centuries of subjugation and exploitation by others.

Some scholars and analysts have ignored these constraints and blamed Nehru for India's failures. For instance, D. R. SarDesai is of the opinion that Southeast Asia was not given sustained and consistent attention during the prime ministership of Jawaharlal Nehru, and he finds Nehru's engagement with the 'East' patchy. In his views,

> The intensity of Indian interest in the countries of Southeast Asia has, however, varied from time to time. The periods of closest

> attention were 1947–1949, 1954–1955, and 1959–1961.... It may be suggested at the very outset that part of this neglect is owing to deliberate de-emphasis in Indian foreign policy on local or regional problems and a corresponding stress on global issues affecting Communism and anti-Communism, coexistence and confrontation, peace and war. But even in this wider context, Communist China has loomed large in the mutations of Indian thinking on world affairs.[107]

M. Brecher goes even notches ahead in overlooking Nehru's contribution in India's engagement with the East saying:

> India's lack of interest was reflected in India's policy of inaction and indifference in the region during the fifteen years following her initiative in the Dutch-Indonesian colonial struggle at the Delhi Conference of 1949. No efforts at regional integration worthy of the name was made by India. All states in Southeast Asia were classified at Category C, the least desirable and important in the diplomatic service hierarchy, with the result of inferior diplomatic representation ... India abdicated from any role of leadership or catalyst in the area and exerted her influence only in negative terms, to prevent intrusion from great powers, as with the emphatic rejection of SEATO. In short, Southern Asia was backward for India's foreign policy.[108]

A closer look at Brecher's argument suggests the ideological, value loaded and West-biased assessment made by him. Why should opposition to Southeast Asia Treaty Organization (SEATO) and 'prevention of intrusion from great powers' in the region be considered 'negative'? These Indian stances, in fact, turned out to be good moves in the long run. The first one was endorsed at later stages by almost all the countries of the region, and their regional groupings ASEAN and SEATO fell victim to their own narrow approach and could not sustain the test

[107] SarDesai, *Indian Foreign Policy in Cambodia, Laos, and Vietnam 1947–1964*, 2.

[108] M. Brecher, *India and World Politics: Krishna Menon's View of the World* (London: Oxford University Press, 1968), 315 as cited in Kripa Sridharan, *The ASEAN Region in India's Foreign Policy* (Brookfield: Dartmouth, 1996), 27.

of time. While one accepts Brecher's argument regarding the inferior representation of the Indian diplomats in Southeast Asia, a fair evolution must include a comparative study of the deployment of foreign policy personnel by other major powers such as USSR, USA, China and Japan. What category did they put the Southeast Asian countries in for their diplomatic representation?

That said, Nehru has been unanimously accredited by the world leaders, historians, policymakers, and international relations experts with intellectually anchoring the Bandung Conference and with injecting life and intellectual vigour to the anti-colonial movement in Asia and Africa, as has already been discussed. Under Nehru, India's engagement with Indonesia was one of the most robust partnerships the two countries had with any other country in the 1950s. The factors that subjected Nehru to regional and international pressures from the mid-1950s, and more importantly after the 1962 Chinese aggression on India, that rip the latter off its diplomatic profile so meticulously built and nurtured by a visionary Nehru have been underlined. Nehru, with his firm belief in internationalism, unquestionable anti-imperialist spirit of newly independent Asian countries, and faith in the normative power of international and regional institutions and agencies, could not comprehend the Chinese motives in time, and by the time reality started dawning on him, it was too late. Nonetheless, he left a strong legacy for his successors to be proud of and to pursue under different circumstances.

CHAPTER 4

After Nehru

Did India Get Distanced?

Introduction

As we have seen in the previous chapter, by the time the Nehru era ended, India's hopes for shaping the dynamics of the 'East' were belied. However, that does not in any way belittle Nehru's contribution in positioning India as a formidable stakeholder and an inspirational source in its eastward engagements. The contributions of India led to the rise of independence and decolonization struggles in Asia and the emergence of a confident and independent Indonesia. India's failure on building Asian solidarity was not just because of its own lapses and shortcomings alone, as we have seen in the previous chapter. There were forces and circumstances that impinged heavily on the region and were beyond India or any of the regional players. Under the post-Nehru Indian leadership, while India could not pursue its eastward engagement with the vigour of Nehru's first decade, it did not remain completely detached from its eastern neighbours. It tried to intervene and react to most of the important developments in the Indo-Pacific region, tried to shape the outcome of critical issues such as the conflict in Indo-China and kept itself in touch with all the major players, no matter how ineffective those interventions turned out to be.

Turbulent Post-Nehru Transition

Following the 1961 Belgrade Non-aligned Conference, India's military humiliation in the 1962 war with China, and later Nehru's sad demise in 1964, the Nehru era came to an end. With Nehru's passing away, so many intertwined aspects of India's foreign policy and worldview also came to an end. Immediately after Nehru, India turned into an inward-looking, overly cautious and diplomatically conservative country. This was mainly due to a difficult transition that India had to navigate through. India faced a deteriorated security situation resulting from the two full-scale wars inflicted by two of its immediate neighbours, China in 1962, and quickly followed by Pakistan in 1965. There were, in addition, constraints imposed by the Cold War, wherein the USA and its Western allies kept India trapped within the subcontinent. India also had domestic pressures emanating from political transition after Nehru. This was a two-stage transition: the first phase, when Nehru was succeeded by Lal Bahadur Shastri. India was then facing a severe food crisis and had to cope with a Pakistan-imposed war on Kashmir in 1965. Shastri's leadership proved to be short-lived, and he did not have a flair for foreign relations. The second phase of transition witnessed an internal political struggle for leadership within the ruling Congress party. Though Mrs Indira Gandhi, Nehru's daughter, was chosen to succeed Lal Bahadur Shastri following his mysterious and unexpected demise in Tashkent in January 1966, after signing a peace agreement with Pakistan under the Soviet mediation, the Congress party establishment was not quite prepared to accept her as the new leader of the party. The senior Congress leaders, who came to be known as the 'syndicate', preferred to keep her in the front just to tighten their own hold on the party organization and the government. Mrs Gandhi was not amenable to this. This internal struggle precipitated into a division in the party, leading to a formal and open split in November 1969. Majority of the Congress members sided with Mrs Gandhi, and she emerged victorious.

India started regaining its self-confidence only after its internal politics were settled. The creation of Bangladesh in 1971, and an unprecedentedly impressive military victory against Pakistan that was backed by the USA and China, helped India shed off its past humiliation. This was followed by India's first 'peaceful' nuclear explosion in 1974. In its moves to regain the lost regional clout, India helped Sri Lanka in 1971 to defeat its domestic revolt by the Sinhala radical group Janatha Vimukthi Peramuna, conceded sovereignty of a disputed island Kachchativu to Sri Lanka in 1974, and integrated Sikkim as an Indian state through a masterly manoeuvre of democratic politics and diplomacy in 1975. In 1971, India also joined the non-aligned initiative to keep the Indian Ocean free of militarization and great power rivalry. The Sri Lankan move at the UN to get the Indian Ocean declared as a 'zone of peace' was fully backed by India.

Mrs Gandhi's dominance in Indian politics and its foreign-policymaking was interrupted only briefly for two-and-a half-years between 1977 and 1979. During this period, a coalition government formed by all the non-Congress opposition groups, led, first by Morarji Desai and later, for a few months, by Charan Singh, replaced her government. The Janata Party government tried to add its own flavour to foreign policy, but largely continuity rather than any change characterized India's approach, especially in relation to the Indo-Pacific region. The ideological and political stance of the non-Congress coalition government was that Mrs Gandhi had taken India too close to the Soviet Union and that it would like to restore 'genuine non-alignment' in India's foreign policy.[1] However, as the government got down to the business of dealing with the ground reality of regional and international politics, it realized the value of strong relations with the Soviet Union in the given context of India's vital security interests. Mrs Gandhi returned to power in January 1980 and continued to lead India's destiny until 1984 when she was assassinated. She was followed by her son Rajiv Gandhi, giving a continuity to the Nehru–Gandhi dynasty of India. In several of their statements, Mrs Gandhi and Rajiv Gandhi recalled Nehru's sayings. Rajiv Gandhi also seemed to be guided by his mother's direction in

[1] S. D. Muni, 'Foreign Policy: New face of Non-alignment', *Economic and Political Weekly*, 12, no. 44 (29 October 1977): 1044–1045.

foreign policy. In its eastward engagement, India under Nehru's successors remained consistent in its broad principles and basic tenants, albeit in a pragmatic and reactive mode that may appear to be less dynamic and much less inspiring. Let us look at how India's contacts and interaction were maintained with the East during the different transition phases of the post-Nehru wave.

Lal Bahadur Shastri (1964–1966)

After Nehru passed away, it was very difficult to imagine how India would run its foreign relations, as Lal Bahadur Shastri, Nehru's successor to the office of the Prime Minister of India, was no match to Nehru in diplomacy and foreign relations. During Shastri's term in the Prime Minister's Office, not much could be done on the issue of India's eastward engagement. India's foreign relations in the 1960s were viewed through the lens of external support to India as its focus was mostly on the India–Pakistan War of 1965. Though never officially stated, India seemingly began to identify countries on the basis of who was on its side during the difficulties of the Pakistan-inflicted war. Singapore's then Prime Minister Lee Kuan Yew expressed his sympathies for India—a country which was first to recognize Singapore.[2] While Singapore and Laos actively supported India, Malaysia was initially neutral. A goodwill delegation led by D. P. Karmarkar (Minister of Cabinet rank but not a member of the Cabinet) visited Malaysia and Singapore to explain India's stand on the Indo-Pakistan conflict.[3] Later, in September 1965, in the UN, the permanent representative of Malaysia in the UNSC supported India. This irked Pakistan and it severed diplomatic ties with Malaysia, which were restored only in 1966 through the efforts of the Shah of Iran, Mohammad Reza Pahlavi.

[2] As quoted in Ho Ai Li, 'India, Pakistan at War with Each Other', *The Strait Times*, 6 September 2015, https://www.straitstimes.com/singapore/india-pakistan-at-war-with-each-other, accessed 17 August 2018.

[3] For the complete text of India's engagement with the East in 1965–1966, see MEA's *Annual Report 1965–66*.

While the support on the issue of war was visible, these countries remained mute on the issue of Kashmir.[4] The Philippines and Thailand remained neutral and decided not to take sides. As far as Vietnam was concerned, it somewhat tilted towards Pakistan. Interestingly, the Indo-Pak war had its worst effect on India's relations with Indonesia. The sign of bonhomie between Pakistan and Indonesia was noticed long before the Indo-Pak War of 1965. President Soekarno visited Pakistan several times during 1963–1965 and seemed to have given some psychological comfort to Pakistani leaders in their aspirations to wean Kashmir away from India.[5] In September 1965, thousands of Indonesians demonstrated outside the Indian and the US embassies, accusing India and the USA of working together in waging a war against Pakistan—an Islamic country. On 9 September, the protest rally turned violent. While the protestors ransacked the Indian Embassy in Jakarta and looted several Indian shops, the Indian flag was torn off and was given by the demonstrators to the then Indonesian Foreign Minister Dr Subandrio who was reported to have 'appreciated the actions of the Jakarta youths in their condemnation of India as an aggressor against Kashmir and Pakistan'.[6] The Nahdlatul Ulama (Islamic Party of Indonesia) offered the Indonesian leader Soekarno to send volunteers to Kashmir to fight against Indian forces.[7] In fact, Indonesia attempted to offer military support to Pakistan. President Soekarno sent the Indonesian Chief of Staff, Vice Marshall Omar Dhani, to China for a secret mission to obtain spare parts for military airplanes as Indonesia was arranging to dispatch them for military assistance to Pakistan. Then Indonesia gave eight MiG-19 jet fighters to Pakistan without seeking approval

[4] Dennis Kux, 'India's Fine Balancing', *Foreign Affairs* 81, no. 3 (May–June 2002): 93–106.

[5] L. P. Singh, 'Dynamics of Indian-Indonesian Relations', *Asian Survey* 7, no. 9 (September 1967): 660.

[6] *The Hindu*, 'From the Archives—Dated September 10, 1965', 10 September 2015, http://www.thehindu.com/archives/from-the-archives-dated-september-10–1965/article7633831.ece, accessed 17 August 2018.

[7] Gede Wahyu Wicaksana, 'Islam and Sukarno's Foreign Policy, with Reference to Indonesia-Pakistan Relations 1960–1965', *International Journal of Indonesian Affairs*, 1 (2013): 73.

of the original supplier, the Soviet Union.[8] More importantly, the Chief Commander of the Indonesian navy claimed that India did not deserve to be in the Andaman and Nicobar Islands, as in his views, these islands were an extension of the Indonesian territory of Sumatra, and were located between Indonesia and East Pakistan.[9] Indonesia had offered to blockade the Andaman and Nicobar Islands in order to put military pressure on India in favour of Pakistan.[10] In addition to that, Indonesia's support to Pakistan was also motivated by its desire to be a part of the China–Pakistan (anti-India) partnership and convert it into a strategic triangle, then termed as the Beijing–Jakarta–Rawalpindi axis. Although Jakarta returned back as a friend of India after Soekarno's fall, the Beijing–Rawalpindi strategic tie-up became an 'all-weather friendship', and it continues to pose a security challenges to India even today.

In January 1966, *Indonesian Herald*, which had substantial links with the Indonesian Ministry of Foreign Affairs (MFA), warned India that 'she could not continue to bully Pakistan into accepting her expansionist policies and was praising Pakistan's burning will and invincible strength in standing by what was legally and legitimately her right in Kashmir'.[11] Indonesian President Soekarno's statements added insult to India's injury when he said:

> The sympathy and prayers of the Indonesian people are dedicated to the people of Kashmir and the people and Government of Pakistan, who are courageously and historically defending their independence and sovereignty.[12]

[8] Ibid., 71.

[9] Ibid., 71–72.

[10] This was disclosed by Pakistan's then Air Chief, Air Marshal Mohammad Asghar Khan, in his memoirs: Asghar Khan, *The First Round: Indo-Pakistan War, 1965* (New Delhi: Vikas Publishing House, 1979).

[11] L. P. Singh, 'Dynamics of Indian-Indonesian Relations', *Asian Survey* 7, no. 9 (September 1967): 664–665.

[12] Cited in O. Sutomo Roesnadi, 'India-Indonesia Relations: Past, Present and Future', in *Self Reliance and National Resilience*, ed. K. Subramanyam (New Delhi: Shakti Mill, 1975).

One of the primary reasons for Indonesia to take Pakistan's side was India's position on the issue of Malayan independence. India supported the proposal for Malaysia's independence and the formation of the Malaysian federation. According to the official statement, 'in view of the clear and unequivocal findings of the UN Secretary-General in favour of Malaysia in Sarawak and North Borneo, India has maintained its support to the inauguration of Malaysia'.[13] Initially, Indonesia did not object to India's position on Malaysia, but later, on the occasion of the 10th anniversary of Afro-Asian Conference in April 1965, Indonesia's then Deputy Foreign Minister Ganis Harsono expressed discontent with India's stand. He stated, 'We consider India's attitude towards Indonesia, particularly in regard to Malaysia, as unfriendly and unwise'.[14]

The second reason for Indonesia's unhappiness with India was Nehru's decision to turn down Soekarno's proposal for the second Bandung Conference, as has already been discussed in the previous chapter. Due to varying perceptions between India and Indonesia on the role and outcome of the Bandung Conference, the commemoration of the 10th anniversary of the Bandung Conference was not attended by any high-level leader but by the then Minister of Food and Agriculture C. Subramaniam, who represented India for the event. Indonesia's hostility towards India was primarily driven by Indonesia's domestic politics and regional considerations, such as the opposition to Malaysia and proximity with China, during Soekarno's last turbulent years. This had nothing to do with the causes of the Indo-Pak war or the rationality of India's claims on Kashmir. As soon as the Soekarno regime was thrown out and General Suharto assumed office, there was a sudden and dramatic turnaround in Indonesia's relations with India during Mrs Gandhi's time, as we shall see later.

While some Southeast Asian countries extended support to India, a few were on Pakistan's side for unexplainable reasons. One could blame poor efforts on India's part to explain its case. For instance,

[13] For the complete text of India's engagement with the East in 1964–1965, see MEA's *Annual Report 1964–65*.

[14] Ibid.

North Vietnam accused the USA of inciting the Indo-Pak war. It is important to note that it was supporting Pakistan while hugely putting the blame on the USA. The official newspaper of Vietnam, *Nhan Dan*, not only criticized the USA but also accused India of launching an attack on Pakistan. It noted:

> At the recent meeting of the SEATO military bloc, Pakistan expressed her disagreement with the US aggressive policy in Vietnam and acts of war of the USA and its henchmen in Asia. This attitude has infuriated the US imperialists. The attack on Pakistan by Indian troops, in fact, is closely connected with the US scheme of bringing pressure to bear upon Pakistan, and it is completely incompatible with the Indian people's interest.[15]

Under Nehru–Gandhi Successors (1966–1989)

Mrs Gandhi assumed the office of Prime Minister of India in January 1966, and soon after, she had to face the general elections in India in 1967, where the Congress party returned to office with a smaller majority. Indira Gandhi was prime minister for three consecutive terms as well as a fourth term after a brief hiatus. Her first tenure lasted for 11 years from 1966 to 1977, while the second tenure was from 1980 until her assassination in 1984. While facing challenges to her own leadership and to India's economic and political stability, Mrs Gandhi was quite responsive to the changes taking place in India's immediate neighbourhood and in Southeast Asia.

The post-Nehru period witnessed transitions not only in India but also in Southeast Asia. Indonesia witnessed a change in regime by the military takeover of the Soekarno regime to thwart a suspected Communist coup. Malaysia and Singapore emerged as sovereign independent entities, and Myanmar consolidated its military regime under Gen. Ne Win. Externally, the United Kingdom announced the 'east of the Suez' military presence and handed over the island of Diego Garcia to the USA for its development as a strong naval base.

[15] Asis Kumar Majumdar, *South-East Asia in Indian Foreign Policy: A Study of India's Relations with South-East Asian Countries from 1962–82* (Calcutta: Naya Prokash, 1982), 85.

The USA started to feel the burden of its military intervention in Vietnam. China started asserting itself in regional affairs while supporting communist insurgencies in the region. There were diplomatic moves to form regional groupings, possibly even with military ties amongst its members.

The challenge before Mrs Gandhi was to carry forward the best of her father's legacy in the changing context of regional and domestic developments. Since she had risen to power through a bitter struggle, there was a strong infusion in her thinking and actions of pragmatism and hard-core realism, where success mattered. The blending of Nehruvian vision for Asia with pragmatic realism accordingly came to characterize the approach of Nehru's successors, from Indira Gandhi to Rajiv Gandhi, in India's foreign policy. As their approach evolved for the coming nearly two decades towards the eastern neighbours, five key aspects can be identified. They are:

1. Sustained resistance to great power intervention and military groupings in the Indo-Pacific region;
2. Responding to the formation of ASEAN;
3. India's commitment to peace and stability in the Indo-China region;
4. Normalization of relations with China;
5. Expanding and strengthening bilateral economic and developmental cooperation with the countries of the region.

Let us look at these aspects in some detail as they evolved.

Resistance to Great Power Interventions and Military Groupings

Opposition to the great powers' interventions and resistance to military alliances was a part of Nehru's legacy in India's foreign policy. We have noted earlier that the Indo-Pacific region was undergoing strategic transition when Mrs Gandhi assumed power in India. With the Western powers, the USA and the UK, in a withdrawal mode and the fears of China seeking to fill in the vacuum thus created, the region had been pushed into a state of anxiety and concern. Western strategic analysts looked towards South and Southeast Asia as the most dangerous hotspots in the world, and suggested the coming together of the Asian major players such as India, Japan and Australia in a mutual security arrangement, presumably under the US umbrella, to provide a safe balance. The director of the London-based International Institute of Strategic Studies (IISS), Alastair Buchan, suggested:

> There is now an instinct throughout the world, felt as keenly in Warsaw as in Tokyo, in Chicago as in Canberra, that for the next generation southern Asia is the most dangerous area of the world, that if a major conflict should ever occur again, its *casus belli* will be found somewhere between the Khyber Pass and the China Sea…Vietnam and other developments in Asia might drive the United States into a new era of isolationism. The requirements of Asian security have, for complex reasons, reduced the United Kingdom almost to impotence in influencing either Asian or European events…. What seems worth contemplating is not any form of integrated military alliance of the stronger Asian powers, each with a subordinate sphere of responsibility of its own. The core of the system would be a treaty of mutual cooperation between India, Australia and Japan (such a treaty need not be too specific on the subject of cooperation).[16]

There were strong constituencies in Australia and Japan that gave credence to such views. Former Australian Foreign Minister Paul Hasluck argued:

> If we are to think of a contribution to the rebuilding of Asia, it seems to me that the three powers best fitted to make a massive contribution, in the region itself, to the rebuilding of Asia are Japan, India and Australia. I like to think of them as possibly the three points on which the legs of a tripod might rest in order to support a great contribution to Asia.[17]

[16] Alastair Buchan, 'An Asian Balance of Power?', *Australian Journal of Politics and History* 12, no. 2 (August 1966): 278.

[17] As quoted in Kripa Sridharan, *The ASEAN Region in India's Foreign Policy* (Singapore: Dartmouth, 1996), 39. This point has been discussed in detail.

It may be interesting to note the circular nature of these arguments, as they find a loud and clear echo in what is being pursued in the Indo-Pacific context even today where 'tripod' has been elevated to a 'quad', as we shall discuss in the subsequent chapters.

Indian leaders were not unaware of this debate. They were conscious of the retreat mode of the USA and UK, and the possibility of China asserting itself could not be ruled out in view of India's own experience of 1962 as also China's nuclear explosions in 1964. In its annual report for the year 1969–1970, the MEA underlined the situation of 'continuing fluidity' in the region and observed:

> The new policy of the United States, the increasing interest taken by Japan and the Soviet Union in the region, the impending British withdrawal, the attempts at accommodation between the major powers and the increasing disenchantment with military alliances were some of the more significant developments. A major unsettling factor was the Chinese policy of seeking domination by encouraging subversive groups or elements within most countries of the region. At the same time there was heartening evidence of the forces of nationalism exerting themselves within each country and the attempts for the establishment of suitable regional groupings for economic cooperation.[18]

Mrs Gandhi's short-time successor Morarji Desai also had a critical view of China's role in Southeast Asia. He said:

> China has always been an imperialist country, as can be seen from its past history of many centuries. The present Communist regime of China has not only welcomed their inheritance but is more fanatically determined about it. It has designed on several countries in South-East Asia and also wants huge chunks of territory from the Union of Soviet Socialist Republics.[19]

India was, however, not amenable to the power vacuum theory and to the need for such a vacuum to be filled by specific regional security

[18] For the complete text of India's engagement with the East in 1969–1970, see MEA's *Annual Report 1969–70*.

[19] Majumdar, *South-East Asia in Indian Foreign Policy*, 87.

arrangements. India in any case rejected any form of military alliance or arrangements to ensure regional security. The indications of the moves to dissolve SEATO and CENTO had already discredited such arrangements and exposed their irrelevance. It had faith in the strength of Asian nationalism, and was prepared to work for regional economic cooperation to build capabilities and strength. Answering a question on the security of Malaysia and Singapore in the aftermath of British withdrawal, Mrs Gandhi said:

> We reject the 'power vacuum' theory. We believe that the best defence of a nation is its own nationalism and its economic strength. We have no desire whatever to use our defence forces for any purpose beyond our borders except for international missions of peace of the kind which the United Nations has asked us to undertake.[20]

The Indian leaders continuously emphasized the strength of Asian nationalism and disapproved of the 'power vacuum' theory. This was reiterated by Mrs Gandhi while addressing the One Asia Assembly in New Delhi in February 1973. Blaming the colonial powers for perpetuating their military presence in Asia 'in the name of filling a vacuum or to wage a crusade against communism or other doctrines', she said:

> In India, we have always rejected what we consider the rather naïve theory of political vacuum. Europe shed its colonies not out of altruism or caprice, but because of the rising presence of Asian nationalism. With this assertive nationalism, how can there be any vacuum? The very theory of power vacuum is thus a continuation of colonial outlook in another garb.[21]

[20] Ministry of Information and Broadcasting, Government of India, *The Years of Challenge: Selected Speeches of Indira Gandhi, January 1966–August 1969* (New Delhi: Publications Division, Ministry of Information and Broadcasting, Government of India, 1973), 49.

[21] Indira Gandhi, *Selected Speeches and Writings, 1972–77* (New Delhi: Publications Division, Ministry of Information and Broadcasting, Government of India, 1984), 639.

India recognized the security threat posed to the countries of Southeast Asian region by subversion that was being supported and encouraged by communist China. Answer to this lay in strengthening nationalism and regional economic cooperation. The elements of this approach were emphasized by Mrs Gandhi during her visit to the Southeast Asian countries in 1968. They included regional economic cooperation among the developed and developing countries and 'an international guarantee by the big powers that neutrality and independence of aspiring nations would be preserved to help them develop their nationalism through popular governments'.[22] India's hesitation in keeping away from defence arrangements came out of its own constraints in being of much help in this respect. Its own security problems were serious in view of Pakistani and Chinese hostilities, and there was no way it could move in the direction of stretching its capabilities to undertake additional security obligations in Southeast Asia. Explaining this, India's Minister of State (MOS) for External Affairs stated in Parliament in April 1968:

> If there was a defence arrangement, it would only mean India committing her manpower to the defence of areas which is beyond our capacity at present. We have enough troubles of our own. Our security forces are fully committed to the defence of our own borders and some of our immediate neighbours. If we dispersed our efforts and took on responsibilities that we are not capable of shouldering, it will not only weaken our defence but would create a false sense of security and might even provoke a greater tension in this area.[23]

Linking up with ASEAN

It was within this frame of mind that India approached the question of the formation of ASEAN. Even while battling domestic challenges, Mrs Gandhi was keenly pursuing India's engagement with the East. Southeast Asia had been experimenting with regional groupings such as Association of Southeast Asia (ASA, 1961) and Malaysia, Philippines and Indonesia (MAPHILINDO, 1963) Federation,

[22] As summarized in Sridharan, *The ASEAN Region in India's Foreign Policy*, 38.
[23] Ibid., 43.

which did not really work on a lasting basis. By 1966, ideas were being moved for another organization. Mrs Gandhi sent her foreign minister, Mohd Carim Chagla, to visit Indonesia in January 1967, and Malaysia and Singapore in May 1967. The purpose of the visits was to discuss the problems of the conflict-ridden Indo-China region, particularly Vietnam and Cambodia, and assess the prospects of the new organization—ASEAN—that was being contemplated by the Southeast Asian countries with encouragement from the USA but in pursuance of their interests of fighting internal communist subversion supported by the Chinese. In Singapore, Chagla said:

> We will be very happy to have bilateral arrangements with Singapore, with regard to trade, commerce, and economic cooperation. But if Singapore chooses to join any regional cooperation, we will be happy to join such a grouping, if other members want India to do so. If others want to have a small grouping, India will be very happy to remain outside and help such a grouping.... India does not want to dominate any regional grouping.[24]

India was facing a dilemma in responding to the formation of ASEAN. It welcomed the grouping of the countries to defend themselves against communist subversion and China. It therefore did not voice any objection to the ideological thrust of the ASEAN which included only non-communist countries of Southeast Asia. At the same time, India had deep interests in peace and stability in Vietnam and the whole of Indo-China, which could not be ensured without cooperation and understanding of the ASEAN countries. Neither was India too keen to join ASEAN nor were some of the ASEAN members keen on India becoming one of its founding members. India knew that the organization was being encouraged by the USA, with which it did not want to be identified strategically, more so as the possibility of military cooperation in ASEAN could not be ruled out in view of the US war in Vietnam. However, India was not averse to the US role in the region as such, since it was seeking US support on many fronts, including against China and in meeting its food

[24] As quoted in K. P. Saksena, *Cooperation in Development: Problems and Prospects for India and ASEAN* (New Delhi: SAGE Publications, 1986), 53.

and economic difficulties. Some of the ASEAN countries were not comfortable with India being strategically closer to the Soviet Union. Indonesia, being the biggest ASEAN power, did not want India in ASEAN as that could overshadow its own leadership aspirations within the new organization. Singapore and Malaysia were quite favourably inclined towards India's participation, but did not want to press for it in view of the reservations of other members: Thailand, Philippines and Indonesia. When formed in August 1967, ASEAN did not invite India for membership. From South Asia, Sri Lanka was asked to join, but it could not.

India's preference was for a broad-based Asian grouping, focused mainly on economic and developmental agenda. Such an organization could be inclusive, not excluding anyone, and could be called 'Asian Council' or 'Council of Asia'. This had been indicated by India's the Minister of External Affairs M. C. Chagla during his visits to Singapore and Malaysia in May 1967. The idea was further explored by his foreign secretary, T. N. Kaul, when he told his hosts in Singapore that India would even financially contribute to such a broader organization without claiming any advantages. The junior Minister of External Affairs Bali Ram Bhagat explained in the Parliament in April 1968 the idea of a broad-based organization:

> [A] broad based economic organisation of all countries in Asia (should be formed) so that no single country or group of countries from Asia or outside can dominate any country in Asia. We do not want such an organisation to have any political undertones or military overtones, for that would divide Asia into conflicting groups and make them the camp followers and satellites of bigger powers. All the same we do not want to gatecrash into any regional organisation that may be there.[25]

A few months later, reiterating this, Mrs Gandhi said that

> [R]egional cooperation is no longer a remote idea. It was a vital necessity; the forms of cooperation could be many—sub-regional,

[25] As quoted in Sridharan, *The ASEAN Region in India's Foreign Policy*, 46.

> nationalism or internationalism.... It is in this context that we have welcomed and supported the objectives and the achievements of the Association of South-East Asian Nations (ASEAN).... We have followed its remarkable progress from Bali to Kuala Lumpur, and thereafter with great interest. We regard it as a genuine and legitimate instrument of cooperation.... There are many areas of common interest and concern in which we can work closely with ASEAN, and I hope, it should be possible soon to initiate a dialogue to identify concrete areas of joint endeavour.[30]

Prime Minister Morarji Desai sent Dinesh Singh in May 1979 as his Special Envoy to Southeast Asia in pursuance of the twin objectives of explaining India's stand on Indo-China and seeking association with ASEAN. He visited Singapore, Malaysia, Indonesia, the Philippines, Thailand, Vietnam and Laos, and had extensive discussions with the leaders in these countries. India also 'submitted a memorandum to the ASEAN Secretariat indicating possible areas of cooperation'.[31] The persisting reservations of some ASEAN members on India's role in Indo-China and its strategic proximity with the Soviet Union did not make matters move, though it was now generally accepted that India was a deserving and serious candidate for joining ASEAN.

Mrs Gandhi carried the efforts forward in her second term that started in January 1980. The then Secretary in the MEA Eric Gonsalves was sent in May 1980 to Burma, Thailand, the Philippines, Singapore, Indonesia and Malaysia. Gonsalves' brief was to pursue the ASEAN matter and also assess the possible reactions of the ASEAN members on India's recognition of the Vietnam-backed Heng Samrin regime in Kampuchea. Mrs Gandhi had promised to recognize the new Kampuchean regime in her election manifesto of 1980.[32] Eric Gonsalves returned with an invitation for India to join an ASEAN

[30] Atal Bihari Vajpayee, *New Dimensions of India's Foreign Policy* (New Delhi: Vision Books, 1979) 213.

[31] For the complete text of India's engagement with the East in 1979–1980, see MEA's *Annual Report 1979–80*.

[32] *Shodhganga*, 'India-ASEAN Relations', http://shodhganga.inflibnet.ac.in/bitstream/10603/135169/8/08_chapter%202.pdf, accessed 17 August 2018.

ministerial meeting in Kuala Lumpur in June 1980. It was hoped that this would be the beginning of India's status as a 'dialogue partner' of ASEAN. India's then Foreign Minister P. V. Narasimha Rao, however, skipped that meeting under the pretext of his mother's illness. Another reason extended for this Indian failure was that Mrs Gandhi, under the persuasion of Vietnam and the Soviet Union, had decided to hasten the recognition of the Heng Samrin regime which was bound to infuriate the ASEAN members. Accordingly, she advised Rao to skip the meeting and avoid any possible diplomatic embarrassment. Some analysts also suggest that Rao skipped the ASEAN Summit in view of Sanjay Gandhi's (Mrs Gandhi's son) death in an accident.[33] India recognized the Kampuchean regime on 7 July 1980, much to the displeasure of ASEAN:

> The Minister of External Affairs announced in Lok Sabha on 7 July, the decision of India to establish immediately diplomatic relations with the Government of People's Republic of Kampuchea headed by President Heng Samrin. The ASEAN countries expressed disappointment and unhappiness over this decision of India. India, however, patiently explained the rationale of this decision and the positive results that could flow from it. It was pointed out that it was recognition of the reality of the political situation inside Kampuchea.[34]

This brought to an end India's ASEAN mission until the beginning of LEP during the early 1990s. Mrs Gandhi was assassinated in October 1984 and was succeeded by her son Rajiv Gandhi. Both Mrs Gandhi and Rajiv Gandhi made periodic efforts to join ASEAN, but the Kampuchean conflict kept the issue at bay. The intensity of engagement between ASEAN and India was adversely affected between 1980 and 1985, on account of the Kampuchean issue.

[33] Kripa Sridharan, 'India-ASEAN Relations: Evolution, Growth and Prospects', in *China, India and Japan and Security of Southeast Asia*, ed. Chandra Jeshurun (Singapore: ISEAS, 1993).

[34] For the complete text of India's engagement with the East in 1980–1981, see MEA's *Annual Report 1980–81*.

Peace and Stability in Indo-China

Nehru's successors carried forward India's international commitments as a peacemaker in the Indo-China region which was seriously trapped in both internal and external conflicts. There were clearly two sets of challenges for India: one related to the interventionist war in Vietnam and another to the subversion and internal factional fights both in Cambodia and in Laos. There was not much that India, despite its best efforts, could do to resolve internal conflicts within the Indo-Chinese countries, though it tried to bring the contending factions together to help them resolve their differences and seek peaceful solutions. But the situation was deteriorating in the region, and the ICC headed by India was confronting a serious financial crunch. Eventually, the ICC was adjourned sine die in June 1969 in response to the Cambodian suggestion. The situation in Laos got stabilized after the victory of Vietnam in 1975, but Cambodia got embroiled in a more serious situation by 1978, as we shall see later.

On Vietnam, India gradually accepted the nationalist force behind the communists dominating North Vietnam. Though it shied away from strong criticism of the USA in view of its own constraints identified earlier (containing China, and helping in food and economic difficulties), India took a clear position that aerial bombings on Vietnam must come to an immediate and unconditional end in order to create conditions for a peaceful and negotiated resolution of the conflict. Outlining the broad contours of India's policy, Mrs Gandhi in a national broadcast on 7 July 1966 said:

> It is necessary to secure the withdrawal of all foreign forces from Vietnam and to insulate that unhappy country from every foreign interference so that the people of Vietnam determine their own future free of external pressures. Looking further ahead, it might be desirable for the Geneva Conference to guarantee the integrity and independence of a neutral Vietnam and, indeed of the neighbouring states of Laos and Cambodia—as envisaged by the Geneva Agreement. The Geneva powers could also underwrite a rehabilitation and development plan for all three states to repair the grim ravages of war. Such a settlement would be a victory for all and, more so, for the brave and long-suffering people of Vietnam.

> I offer these proposals as no more than an idea. India is committed to a peaceful solution and not a particular solution. We would be willing to support any alternative proposal that offers hopes of success. But of one thing I am certain, there must be an early and immediate turning away from war in Vietnam.[35]

India lobbied on these lines with ASEAN and other regional powers such as Japan and Australia. India also raised the issue repeatedly in the UN and non-aligned conferences. All this, however, did not make much difference to the USA. But as the financial and human costs of war escalated, and its results frustrated, a change came in the USA. The war fatigue eventually led to its defeat in 1975. India heartily welcomed Vietnam's victory, and within hours of the fall of the South Vietnamese regime, it extended diplomatic recognition to the Provisional Revolutionary Government on 30 April 1975. India also recognized the unification of Vietnam in 1976.

The Cambodian conflict became complicated with the military intervention of Vietnam in December 1978 against the Khmer Rouge regime headed by Pol Pot that had established the worst records in political repression and violation of human rights. China launched a month-long punitive war on Vietnam in support of the Khmer Rouge in February 1979. ASEAN and the USA also were in support of the Khmer Rouge regime. They strongly disapproved of the Vietnamese military intervention in Cambodia and demanded immediate withdrawal of the Vietnamese forces. India took a strong exception to the Chinese punitive action against Vietnam. India's then Minister of External Affairs Atal Bihari Vajpayee, who was on a state visit in China, cut short his visit as a mark of protest. Making a statement on this in the Indian Parliament on 22 February 1979, Vajpayee said:

> The People's Republic of China is guilty of committing aggression against the Socialist Republic of Vietnam.... On the question of Vietnam, there is no difference of opinion. Only this morning, I met the Ambassador of the Republic of Vietnam. He congratulated

[35] Mrs Gandhi's broadcast over All India Radio on 7 July 1966; Ministry of Information and Broadcasting, Government of India, *The Years of Challenge*, 327.

> the Government of India and the people of India for the massive support that we have extended to the people of Vietnam....
>
> [A]s soon as I came to know of the massive (Chinese) attack, I informed the Chinese authorities in Peking through their Ambassador who was accompanying me, that what had been done was a matter of grave concern for us. And I decided to cut short my visit. This is the civilised way to act, to protest.[36]

Initially, however, the Janata Party government wanted to take a somewhat neutral stand, disapproving of both the Vietnamese intervention in Cambodia and the Chinese attack on Vietnam. This was to underline its proclaimed 'genuine non-alignment'. There was, however, no way for India to remain neutral between China and Vietnam. When pressed for any Indian initiative to defuse the situation in Indo-China, Vajpayee said: 'All countries and particularly the great powers have to exercise restraint and put pressure on the People's Republic of China to withdraw from the Vietnamese territory'.[37] Vajpayee also lobbied in Colombo in June 1979 (at the preparatory meeting for the Non-aligned Summit to be held in Havana later) for the recognition of the Heng Samrin regime to represent Kampuchea. He did not succeed, and the Cambodian seat was left vacant. As has been noted, India itself recognized the Heng Samrin regime only in July 1980 after Mrs Gandhi returned to power. This further underlines the basic continuity in India's approach to Indo-China, irrespective of political complexion of the government in New Delhi.

The key elements of India's approach to the Kampuchean issue were that it had no contacts with the Pol Pot regime and its Khmer Rouge. India wanted a comprehensive political settlement within Cambodia before the Vietnamese troops could be withdrawn. This settlement may have various political groups in a coalition except the Khmer Rouge. The final political settlement should also ensure a secure, neutral, independent, sovereign Cambodia (Kampuchea, the

[36] Atal Bihari Vajpayee, *Four Decades in Parliament, Vol. III* (Delhi: Shipra Publications, 1996), 381–384.

[37] Ibid., 384.

name changed under the Khmer Rouge regime), which involved some sort of international guarantees.

India was getting isolated on the Kampuchean issue, from ASEAN as well as the Western powers. ASEAN strongly reacted to India's position. While Thailand and Singapore took a very strong exception, Indonesia and Malaysia were somewhat resilient. Malaysia was also unhappy because India's recognition of the Heng Samrin regime kept India out of the ASEAN meeting for which Malaysia had lobbied hard. Indonesia had a balanced approach but could not ignore the other ASEAN members who were strategically sympathetic to the US and Chinese stakes in the issue and had their concerns regarding Vietnam's role in the region.[38] Despite the strains on its engagement with the ASEAN members, India could not change its Kampuchean policy. It could not let China dominate the Indo-China region. Vietnam being a powerful and independent factor in deterring China from doing so deserved India's unwavering support.

India pursued its Kampuchea policy through all possible international forums. In the Havana NAM Summit, Vietnam was spared of any criticism for intervening in Kampuchea. China escaped any attention as it had unilaterally withdrawn from Vietnam in March 1979. The Havana Conference also refused to recognize either the Pol Pot regime or the Vietnam-backed Heng Samrin regime as the legitimate Kampuchean representative, leaving the seat vacant until the resolution of the conflict. In July 1981, ASEAN and the USA called an International Conference on Kampuchea in New York which both India and Vietnam abstained. India continued to support its position in the UN and the NAM Summits. The New Delhi NAM Summit in 1983 adopted a resolution on Kampuchea that echoed the basic principles of India's Kampuchean stance. It said:

> The Heads of State or Government reaffirmed the right of the people of Kampuchea to determine their own destiny free from

[38] ASEAN reactions to India's support for Vietnam in Cambodia have been discussed in details in Sridharan, *The ASEAN Region in India's Foreign Policy*, 144–151; and also Ayoob, *India and Southeast Asia: Indian Perceptions and Policies* (Singapore: Routledge, 1990), 53–71.

> foreign interference, subversion and coercion and expressed the hope that through a process of negotiations and mutual understanding a climate conducive to the exercise of that right would be created. They also agreed that the humanitarian problems resulting from the conflicts in the region required urgent measures which called for the active cooperation of all the parties concerned. They urged all States in the region to undertake a dialogue which would lead to the resolution of differences among themselves and the establishment of durable peace and stability in the area, as well as the elimination of involvement and threats of intervention by outside powers.... (Para 113 of the Summit Declaration)[39]

Rajiv Gandhi actively pursued the Kampuchean issue. There was a realization in India that the best way to approach the issue was through those ASEAN countries which shared India's concern regarding the Chinese domination of the region. High-level political visits were exchanged for intensive discussion in this respect. On the basis of a broader political understanding thus evolved, Rajiv Gandhi appointed the then MOS for External Affairs K. Natwar Singh as a special envoy to work for the Kampuchean solution. Natwar Singh had this to say about his appointment:

> My sustained involvement with Cambodia began in January 1987 when I was on a visit to Hanoi. The accomplished and astute foreign minister Nguyen Co Thach took me aside. Hanoi had decided to pull out its troops from Cambodia by 1989. Could India convey this to the ASEAN countries? I naturally asked, 'why India'. His answer was gratifying. 'Because you have credibility'. For Vietnam this was a geopolitical question of the highest importance.
>
> I reported my conversation with Co Thach to Prime Minister Rajiv Gandhi, who at once saw the significance of this Vietnamese request. He asked me to visit all the ASEAN capitals. In Singapore, Kuala Lumpur, Manila and Bangkok I got a cold shoulder except in Phnom Penh, the capital of Cambodia. These countries did not

[39] United Nations, '7th Summit Conference of Heads of State or Government of the Non-Aligned Movement', 12 October 1983, http://repository.un.org/bitstream/handle/11176/65277/A_38_495%3BS_16035-EN.pdf?sequence=21&isAllowed=y, accessed 17 August 2018.

trust Vietnam, nor believed that its offer to withdraw troops from Cambodia was genuine.[40]

Through his extensive travels and intensive discussions with the ASEAN leaders during 1987–1988, and by playing an 'honest broker', Natwar Singh succeeded in breaking some ice. In January 1987, he secured assurances from Vietnam that it will withdraw its forces from Kampuchea by 1990 and was willing to accept any political coalition without Pol Pot. Vietnam was also willing to accept Prince Norodom Sihanouk as the principal Kampuchean negotiator and a possible partner in the post-Heng Samrin coalition government.[41] On the basis of these assurances, Natwar Singh managed to get a meeting arranged between Prince Sihanouk and Prime Minister Hun Sen from the Heng Samrin side. This meeting, called the Jakarta Informal Meeting, was to be held in Bogor, Indonesia, towards the end of July 1988. Before that, New Delhi hosted a meeting of NAM senior officials of Zimbabwe, Cuba, India, Indonesia and Vietnam on 15–16 July where the Kampuchean issue was also discussed. These discussions were followed in Harare from 15–17 August. The report submitted by the senior officials led to the setting up of the 14-member NAM Committee on Kampuchea by the NAM foreign ministers. NAM welcomed the Jakarta Informal Meeting of Kampuchean leaders held under Indonesian auspices.[42]

Efforts of India and other countries led to an International Conference on Cambodia, held in Paris in August 1989. It may be borne in mind that international context had become relaxed for this conference to be held. The process of normalization of relations between China and the Soviet Union had advanced. One of the conditions underwriting this process was the distancing of both China and the Soviet Union from the Kampuchean conflict. Relations between

[40] K. Natwar Singh, *Walking with Lions: Tales from a Diplomatic Past* (New Delhi: Harper Collins, 2013), 101–102.

[41] For details of Vietnam's assurances, see Ayoob, *India and Southeast Asia*; Singh, *Walking with Lions*, 60.

[42] For the complete text of India's engagement with the East in 1988–1089, see MEA's *Annual Report 1988–89*.

India and China were also looking up following Rajiv Gandhi's successful visit to China in December 1988. The MEA's version of this conference was: 'India co-Chaired the First Committee which dealt with the establishment of an International Control Mechanism. Although the Conference was unable to achieve a comprehensive settlement, important areas of agreement were identified, and India's contribution was appreciated'.[43] After this conference, Vietnam withdrew its troops from Cambodia in September 1989, which was witnessed by an official Indian delegation. India then started working with others on the UN role in resolving the Cambodian issue. As a result, another peace conference on Cambodia was held in Paris in October 1991 where the Cambodian Peace Accord was signed under the UN efforts.

India's role in resolving the Cambodian conflict was deeply engaged and intensive, though it may not be called decisive. The conflict had deep stakes of ASEAN, and was intricately trapped in great power rivalries between the USA, the Soviet Union and China. The Indian position was articulated on the basis of the ground reality of the presence of Vietnamese troops in Cambodia. It was also rationalized on the principles of human rights and the sovereign integrity of an Asian country. Above all, India was driven by its own security and strategic stakes in the region where it preferred domination of no major power, China, the USA or even Soviet Union. India's position was largely misunderstood by its ASEAN colleagues because of India's strategic proximity with the Soviet Union, highlighted through its treaty of peace and security signed with the Soviet Union in 1971. What the opponents of India's position in Cambodia failed to appreciate, despite best efforts on the part of the Indian leadership to explain, was that the treaty with the Soviet Union and its opposition to the USA and China was rooted in India's vital security interests within South Asia. They did not have much to do with Southeast Asia. In the larger

[43] For the complete text of India's engagement with the East in 1989–1990, see MEA's *Annual Report 1989–90*. For more details on the Paris Conference on Cambodia in August 1989, see Amitav Acharya, Pierre Lizee and Sorpong Peou, eds., *Cambodia—The 1989 Paris Peace Conference: Background Analysis and Documents* (Toronto: Centre for International and Strategic Studies, 1991), 592.

context, India, like many other ASEAN countries, did not want to facilitate China's domination in the Indo-Pacific region.[44] Looking at the developments from hindsight, there is no reason for India to be apologetic for what it did in relation to Cambodia.

Normalization of Relations with China

China constitutes the most critical aspects of India's eastward engagement. Since 1962, India's relations with China had remained in a frozen state. India could not afford to have two adversarial neighbours and, therefore, it was advisable to initiate a process of normalization of relations with China. The first step Mrs Gandhi took after coming to power was to de-freeze relations with China. In a statement in the Parliament on 22 December 1967, while blaming China for anti-India propaganda against the government and democratic institutions, she said: '[W]e do not harbor any evil intention towards the Chinese people, and we do hope that a day will come when they will realise that it is in the interest of all the countries of Southeast Asia that we should be friends…'.[45] Talking to the press on 1 January 1969, she was reported to have said that 'the Indian government would be prepared to try for ways of solving conflicts with China through talks which would not be based on preconditions'.[46] Answering a media question on China on 26 January 1970 she again said: '[W]e do not believe in permanent hostility towards any country'.[47] A positive signal to these statements came from China. In a diplomatic gathering, China's supreme leader Mao Zedong told India's Charge d' Affairs Brajesh Mishra on 1 May 1970: 'India is a great country and Indian people

[44] Details of India's approach to Cambodia have been discussed in Ayoob, *India and Southeast Asia*, 53–71. Also see Tridib Chakravarty, *India and Kampuchea: A Phase in their Relations, 1978–81* (Calcutta: Minerva Associates, 1985).

[45] Ministry of Information and Broadcasting, Government of India, *The Years of Challenge*, 401.

[46] As reported in Mohan Guruswamy and Zorawar Daulet Singh, *India China Relations: The Border Issue and Beyond* (New Delhi: Viva Books, 2009), 93.

[47] Ministry of Information and Broadcasting, Government of India, *The Years of Challenge*, 674.

are a great people. Chinese and Indian people ought to live as friends. They cannot always quarrel'.[48]

India announced its approach towards normalization of relations with China in November 1972. In a policy statement in the Parliament's Upper House (Rajya Sabha), the Minister of External Affairs said:

> India and China can and must normalize their relations on the basis of the Five principles of Peaceful Co-existence.... We hope and believe that in the larger interests of peace and stability in Asia, India and China would be able to take positive steps towards normalization of relations on the basis of mutual respect, equality and reciprocity.
>
> We can assure China that we have no desire or intention to interfere in her internal affairs. We regard Tibet as part of China, and any allegation that we are encouraging fissiparous tendencies in Tibet is totally unfounded and baseless. We hope that China will also respect our territorial integrity and sovereignty and not encourage any fissiparous elements in our country.[49]

This opened the way for functional and professional exchanges. Restoration of diplomatic representation took place in 1976, when K. R. Narayanan assumed the charge of India's Ambassador to Beijing. Encouraged by the leadership changes in China in 1978, when a liberal leader Deng Xiaoping took charge, the Janata Government's foreign minister, Atal Bihari Vajpayee, visited China in February 1979 to take the normalization forward. This was the first foreign-minister-level visit between the two countries in 19 years. The significance of this step was dented by the Chinese attack on Vietnam and Vajpayee's decision to cut short his visit in protest, as has already been mentioned. In Vajpayee's assessment, however, his China visit had brought in many positive results as it enabled him to raise critical issues of South Asian and Indo-China security as well as Tibet and Boundary dispute

[48] As quoted in Guruswamy and Singh, *India China Relations*, 93.

[49] For the complete text of India's engagement with the East in 1972–1973, see MEA's *Annual Report 1972–73*.

with the Chinese leaders.[50] The reciprocal Chinese visit to India took place when Chinese Foreign Minister Huang Hua visited Delhi in June 1981. Mrs Gandhi had a meeting with the Chinese premier in Cancun where both the leaders were attending the North–South Summit on International Development in October 1981.

As a result of these visits, official-level boundary talks were started between the two countries in May 1982, on annual basis. The ninth round of these talks was held in New Delhi in November 1987. While discussing sector-wise positions of the two countries, their differences in the eastern and western sectors of the boundary were brought to the table. The Chinese intrusion in the Samdorong Chu valley of the Tawang district of Arunachal Pradesh state of India in 1986 sharply focused on the seriousness of the differences in the Eastern sector. India strongly protested against these intrusions, but the series of talks was not disrupted.

The major landmark in the normalization process was Prime Minister Rajiv Gandhi's visit to China in December (19–23) 1988. An Indian prime minister was visiting China after a gap of 33 years. He had intensive discussion with the Chinese leaders including Deng Xiaoping on the issues of mutual interests. It was agreed that boundary question was complex and would take a long time to resolve. The mechanism of discussion on this issue was raised to a higher level by establishing a joint working group, which was also mandated to ensure peace and tranquillity on the border—the Line of Actual Control (LAC). While discussions on the boundary issue could continue to create a proper atmosphere for its resolution, India and China decided to expand their economic, cultural, and scientific and technical cooperation.[51]

India's urge for normalization of relations with China was an imperative of a number of evolving factors. To begin with, India was gradually gaining confidence after braving two wars of 1962 and

[50] For the detailed statement made by Vajpayee in Parliament on 21 February 1979, see Vajpayee, *Four Decades in Parliament*, 209–214.

[51] For the complete text of India's engagement with the East in 1988–1989, see MEA's *Annual Report 1988–89*.

1965. In April 1966, Mrs Gandhi told her audiences in New York that India was meeting the Chinese challenge not only ideologically and militarily in the bilateral context but also in the Afro-Asian world, for which there was 'little notice or thanks'. India's self-confidence got a boost with the most impressive outcome of the 1971 war with the birth of Bangladesh, 1974 peaceful nuclear explosion and 1975 integration of Sikkim. Rajiv Gandhi added to India's credibility of executing risk-prone strategic moves in Sri Lanka and Maldives and a bold, though unsuccessful, initiative for denuclearization of global arsenals during the latter half of the 1980s. India had realized that when great power equations were changing with the Soviet withdrawal from Afghanistan and rapprochement with China, China could not be ignored in shaping India's own relations in Asia and the world. China was also changing its strategic dimensions in Asia and emerging as an 'economic storehouse', and it was itself looking forward to making up with India in whatever limited way possible.

Expanding and Strengthening Bilateral Engagements

Even in the midst of diverse pressures generated by domestic demands, regional conflicts and great power turbulence, India tried to keep its bilateral engagements with the countries of the region. Referring to the Chinese support for subversion in the region and rise of nationalism in Southeast Asia, the MEA's *Annual Report 1969–70* observed that:

> This situation has created opportunities for India to improve the already good bilateral relations which exist with countries of the region and to give them deeper content particularly in the fields of economic, technological and cultural cooperation.[52]

Reiterating the same sentiment, the MEA report again underlined in its 1977–1978 edition:

[52] For the complete text of India's engagement with the East in 1969–1970, see MEA's *Annual Report 1969–70.*

> The sovereignty, independence and territorial integrity of the countries of the South-East Asia and stability in the region is of vital importance to India.... Having friendly relations both with the ASEAN countries and Indo-China States, India viewed with favour the progressive development of relations between them. So far as the development of the region was concerned, India expressed its willingness to share its resources, limited as they were, with the countries of South-East Asia to contribute towards their development.[53]

The sincerity of India's intent and the depth of its interests were reflected in the large number of visits exchanged between India and the Southeast Asian countries, especially at the high political levels. India organized several meetings of its envoys in the region to relate its interests with the ground reality and assigned specific diplomatic tasks to many special envoys that included secretary-level senior officials in the MEA as well as political heavyweights such as Dinesh Singh, Natwar Singh, Sardar Swaran Singh and P. N. Haksar.

India's deep involvement in the Indo-China conflicts, related to Vietnam and Cambodia, has been discussed earlier. India tried to help the Indo-China countries through economic assistance and support, possible within its capacity, and through training and agricultural support to Laos and Cambodia. The gift of buffaloes and introduction of water pumps massively enhanced the agricultural production in these countries, and both Laos and Vietnam gradually became rice-surplus countries. Under Indian Technical and Economic Cooperation (ITEC) programme, human resource development was enhanced in these countries. The Archaeological Survey of India also began to get involved in the restoration work of the Angkor Vat temples, which subsequently attracted the UN support. India's support for Vietnam, first in its war against the US intervention and then on the Kampuchean issue, consolidated strategic relations and expanded economic cooperation between the two countries. Towards the late 1980s, India was offered projects to explore and extract oil

[53] For the complete text of India's engagement with the East in 1977–1978, see MEA's *Annual Report 1977–78*.

in the Vietnamese maritime economic zone that China later claimed to be disputed.[54]

We have also noted earlier that a sudden change in Indonesia's approach towards India was witnessed with the change in regime in Indonesia in 1965 and the subsequent shift in Indonesia's policy of confrontation (*konfrontasi*) with Malaysia. Mrs Gandhi and Rajiv Gandhi expanded and strengthened relations with Indonesia. Indonesia was critical to India's engagement in the region for many reasons. It was the most powerful of the ASEAN members. It had a better understanding of India's own constraints and security interests—such as those related to India's close relations with the Soviet Union and Vietnam—and, therefore, was willing to coordinate its moves with India on the regional issues, like of Indo-China, despite differences in other areas. Indonesia was also an energy- and mineral-rich country and, being a member of the Organization of the Petroleum and Exporting Countries (OPEC), was a partner in the Indian moves to create a New International Economic Order during the early 1970s oil crisis. Mrs Gandhi sent Sardar Swaran Singh to plead with Indonesia for support in India's demand for dual oil pricing to compensate developing countries like India that had less per capita oil consumption.[55] Indonesia also stood with India on keeping the great powers' military presence out of the Indian Ocean. Within this framework of strategic synergy between the two countries, India's trade, investments and overall economic relations with Indonesia expanded fast.[56] India supported Indonesia on the question of East Timor in 1976.

India also built strong bilateral relationships with Singapore and Malaysia. As soon as these countries emerged as sovereign, independent entities, they sought India's help, including in defence

[54] For details of India's energy cooperation with Vietnam, see S. D. Muni and Girijesh Pant, *India's Energy Security: Prospects of Cooperation with Extended Neighbourhood* (New Delhi: Roopa & Co., 2005), 190–203.

[55] For the complete text of India's engagement with the East in 1980–1981, see MEA's *Annual Report 1980–81*.

[56] For details of trade and investments, see Navrekha Sharma and Baladas Ghoshal, *India's Relations with Indonesia* (Singapore: Market Books, 2014), 205–243.

and security matters. Singapore was keen to secure India's support in building its defence forces. India responded by offering training and other such facilities but could not rise up to their expectations. Neither did India have surplus capacities, particularly in view of its own requirements in the face of challenges from Pakistan and China, nor did it want to get into intra-regional rivalries and conflicts. This disappointed Singapore and Malaysia. Both these countries also took serious exception to India's support for Vietnam in the Kampuchean conflict of 1979. Gradually, however, India rebuilt its rapport with them, and they also realized that India was a key helpful player in the then unfolding regional strategic dynamics. Both India and Malaysia and also Singapore held economic promise for each other which was carefully harnessed, especially by Singapore.

Economies of the East including Japan, China and South Korea were turning into powerhouses of the global economic system. India too strived to catch up with these Eastern powerhouses as well as the ASEAN economies. Mrs Gandhi, in her second term, had asked the Planning Commission to explore the ways to liberalize the Indian economy,[57] and Rajiv Gandhi's promises for easing business procedures by introducing the concept of 'one window clearance' for business proposals may be recalled here. A former secretary in the MEA recalls:

> Economic liberalisation had begun in the early 1980s in a measured way. By the middle of the decade India's GDP growth rate had gone up to 7 percent. Even though India did not have any institutional contacts with ASEAN, bilateral relations with some ASEAN members like Indonesia, Singapore, Thailand were pursued through high level visits as well as traditional linkages of trade, culture, Indian diaspora, etc., with Japan and South Korea India's dialogue begun to develop.[58]

[57] Author's (S. D. Muni's) interview with former vice-chairman of the Planning Commission, Dr Abid Hussain.

[58] Sudhir T. Devare, 'India's Look East Policy: As Seen from a Vantage Point', in *Two Decades of India's Look East Policy Partnership for Peace, Progress and Prosperity*, ed. Amar Nath Ram (New Delhi: Institute for Southeast Asian Studies, 2012), 86.

Japan emerged as a strong supporter of India. It generously supported India to help meet its food and economic crisis.[59] By 1987, Japan became India's largest donor and also its third-largest trading partner. The volume of trade was not very significant though, accounting only for 7–8 per cent of the total trade turnover of India. Japan also facilitated India's entry into the Asian Development Bank as a founding member in December 1966. In December 1983, one of the most popular Maruti–Suzuki car manufacturing projects was launched in India. India's relations with Japan were institutionalized in several respects. An annual consultation mechanism at the level of foreign ministries was put in place from 1965 to 1966. In these consultations, besides bilateral issues, matters of mutual interest at regional and international levels were also thrashed out. The Indo-Japan Business Co-operation Committee was established at the non-governmental level and had had more than 20 rounds of meetings annually by the end of the 1980s. An Indo-Japan mixed commission was established to expand cultural and other areas of cooperation between the two countries. The Indo-Japan Science and Technology Committee had its first meeting in September 1986 in New Delhi. Japan's Prime Minister Yasuhiro Nakasone visited India in May 1984 after a gap of 23 years of prime ministerial visits, but he again came to India in less than a year later in October 1984 to attend Mrs Gandhi's state funeral.

Australia was another country which considerably helped India solve its food crisis during the late 1960s. Within the year 1966 itself, Australia made an emergency food gift to India worth A$17 million. More food aid followed from Australia in subsequent years. Australia and India also had close consultations on the Indian Ocean and the growing military presence of major powers in it. India also extended its outreach to the PIC. In Fiji, India was interested in the protection of legitimate rights of the PIOs since the beginning of Fiji's constitutional process in April 1970. Mrs Gandhi visited Fiji and Tonga islands as the first-ever Indian prime minister to do so. The May 1987 coup in Fiji that dislodged a democratically elected government dominated by the PIOs greatly upset India. India strongly criticized the move, raised

[59] The following information has been sourced from MEA's annual reports.

the issue internationally, imposed a trade ban on Fiji and called 'for the restoration of the democratically elected government, the revocation of Internal Security Decree and the return to racial harmony in Fiji'.[60] India also sought to mobilize support from Australia, but could not make much impact. India also developed relations with other Pacific island states like Nauru, Tonga and Vanuatu.

Having experienced conflicts with Pakistan and China on boundary-related issues, India decided to resolve all its border disputes. Driven by the self-confidence resulting from the emergence of Bangladesh in 1971, Mrs Gandhi moved to settle boundaries, including maritime, with all its neighbours, both immediate and Eastern. Negotiations on India–Indonesia maritime and continental shelf boundaries were completed in August 1974, and the agreement was ratified in December 1974. After resolving the continental shelf boundaries with Thailand, the agreements among all the three countries, since a tri-junction point was involved, were inked in New Delhi on 26 June 1978. India's then foreign minister, Atal Bihari Vajpayee, hosting a dinner for the foreign ministers of Indonesia and Thailand said:

> We feel privileged at the choice of New Delhi as the venue for the signing of the Indo-Thai Agreement on Seabed Boundary as well as the Agreement between Indonesia, Thailand and India on the Trijunction of the seabed boundaries in the Andaman Sea. This is an event of great significance and I am also glad to reaffirm the traditional friendship that my people have for the great peoples of Indonesia and Thailand.[61]

India's land boundary with Burma was settled in December 1967 and the maritime boundary agreement was concluded in December 1986. The maritime boundary issue was resolved with Sri Lanka and Maldives in June 1974 and December 1976 respectively.

[60] For the complete text of India's engagement with the East in 1988–1989, see MEA's *Annual Report 1988–89*.

[61] Vajpayee, *New Dimensions of India's Foreign Policy*, 211.

By the end of the 1960s, India's defence diplomacy in the region started showing signs of enhancement, going beyond providing training slots. The Indian Navy started paying goodwill visits to many countries in the region. In 1969, first the Indian naval ship called on the Fijian port. During 1969–1970, India's Naval Chief visited Thailand, Singapore, Australia and New Zealand. Subsequently, the Indian Navy and the Army started to have exercises with the countries of the Southeast Asian region. It may be interesting to note here that India's peaceful nuclear explosion of 1974 invoked only token disapproval. Maybe the smaller countries of the region wanted to have another Asian country besides China to have nuclear capabilities in the interest of the Asian balance. However, India's gradual naval expansion raised suspicions in the region, and India was accused of acquiring blue-water capabilities for offensive operations.[62] In 1987, India bought British navy's *Hermes* and inducted that in the Indian navy as INS *Viraat*. Next year, in 1988, India signed a three-year lease for INS *Chakra*—a Soviet nuclear-propelled submarine. In 1989, it secured a German license to produce conventional submarines. Some of the ASEAN countries which felt protected by the US naval presence and military alliances in the region found the rising Indian military capabilities uncomfortable. India's close ties with the Soviet Union and Vietnam had already become their sore point with India.[63] Alarmist reports by the American Department of Defense further heightened the suspicions. Countries of the region, particularly Indonesia and Australia, raised the alarm about India's intentions. India's peacekeeping operations in Sri Lanka were also used as an example of India's changing attitude towards the region. All this led to India being accused of militarizing the Indian Ocean and posing challenges before the long-term national security of these countries. India tried to explain that it neither had capacity to become a blue-water navy nor had any offensive intent in the region, as we shall see in the next chapter.

[62] For some details of India's acquisitions and naval expansion, see Ashley Tellis, 'Indian Naval Expansion: Reflections on History and Strategy', *Comparative Strategy* 6, no. 2 (1987): 185–219.

[63] Isabelle Saint-Mezard, *Eastward Bound—India's New Positioning in Asia* (New Delhi: Manohar Publishers, 2006), 283.

Appraisal

The foregoing discussion underlines that contrary to the perception of India neglecting its eastern neighbours, Nehru's successors had quite an intensive engagement with the East. There were, of course, phases where the intensity of the engagements was curtailed such as during 1980–1985, with the ASEAN region, following India's support for the Vietnamese-backed regime in Kampuchea. It was unrealistic to expect India to follow ideal norms of denouncing military intervention per say. India had to take a realistic position and see what were the issues involved. It could neither ignore its long-term strategic interests in the region nor overlook the genocidal character of the Khmer Rouge regime that was thrown out by the Vietnamese intervention. India was not guided by the ideological characteristics of the regime it was engaging with, as done by some in ASEAN.

But it would be unfair to blame India alone for such rough patches because the ASEAN and its member states had their own priorities and preferences and found that India did not fit well into them all the time. ASEAN and the USA had decided to ignore the question of human rights violations and the Chinese punitive aggression on Vietnam. On the question of India's proximity with Vietnam and the Soviet Union, many countries of the region refused to understand and appreciate India's vital security interests. However, as said earlier, in the long run, the ASEAN countries came round to India's position which proved to be credible and sustainable. It may be possible to argue that India did not measure up to the level of engagement expected by many countries in the region in the context of flux in the strategic dynamics of the region and political transformations within many of these countries. It may be relevant to keep in mind here that despite the scorn and embarrassment inflicted, India continued to seek association with the ASEAN.

India's engagement should also be seen in the comparative perspective. Besides its domestic concerns of security and economic/food difficulties faced initially, India had to confront considerable turmoil in its immediate neighbourhood. After the emergence of Bangladesh and the integration of Sikkim, the ethnic and political turbulence in

Sri Lanka and the Maldives kept India tied to South Asia. India also faced the serious energy crunch with the OPEC's decision to raise oil prices in the early 1970s. By the end of the 1970s came the Soviet intervention in Afghanistan which kept the whole Western front disturbed. The international resistance to the Soviet intervention not only left Afghanistan disturbed but also left Pakistan better armed and encouraged to confront India with cross-border terrorism.

After all the ups and downs, India was well placed vis-à-vis the whole of the Indo-Pacific region by the time the period of Nehru's successors came to an end. It had consolidated its relations with Indonesia, Singapore, Vietnam, Japan, South Korea and the countries of the Pacific Islands. It had normalized its relations with China where prospects of peace and economic cooperation started looking bright. India had started opening its economy for enhanced trade and investments so as to take advantage of the region's economic dynamism. And all this was done consistently, without being interrupted by the regime changes faced by New Delhi. India was now ready for greater integration with the whole region, both economically and strategically.

CHAPTER 5

Look East Policy (1992–2014)

Streamlining and Restructuring Engagement

Introduction

India's eastward engagement that had been unfolding as reactive, ad hoc and in a differentiated manner (based on country-wise approach), was renamed as the Look East Policy (LEP) by the beginning of the 1990s. This initiative is credited to former Indian Prime Minister P. V. Narasimha Rao. There are several opinions with regard to the genesis of naming the eastward engagement as the LEP. While some scholars consider that it began in 1994 with Rao's Singapore lecture, others, including former diplomats, have different takes on it. The then Secretary A. N. Ram, who was dealing with the MEA division devoted to Southeast Asia and others, is of the view that it was in 1992 when Look East found a place in the ministry's discourse. Former Foreign Secretary Salman Haidar, however, thinks that

> Initially, 'Look East' was a rather off-the-cuff slogan devised for Prime Minister Narasimha Rao's visit to the Republic of Korea in 1993. This was the first time an Indian Prime Minister was to go to Seoul and there was a need to give a distinctive focus to this pioneering journey, something to set it apart from the unending travels that constantly took the Prime Minister to all parts of the

> globe. So 'Look East' was invented, marking a deliberate inversion of the westward direction that had so long dominated Indian policy making.[1]

The name 'Look East' Policy was not used in any of the official documents initially. It did not figure even in Prime Minister Rao's Singapore Lecture delivered on 8 September 1994 that is marked as the comprehensive articulation of the policy. It appeared for the first time in the annual report of the MEA for 1995–1996, which by implication credits the policy officially to Rao's Singapore lecture.

Domestic and International Contexts

The policy was cast in the context of developments during the early 1990s that were full of uncertainties and anxieties, both internally and externally. At the international level, the collapse of the USSR and consequently the end of the Cold War and military-bloc politics, the onset of globalization, and the rise of the East Asian economies posed a whole new range of challenges for India. Externally, while the end of the Cold War opened up newer and greater opportunities for India in the absence of military alliances and blocs, there were also constraints inherent in coping with the post-Cold War 'unipolar world' dominated by the USA. The shrinking and weakening of Russia also left India with few friends. There was a need to redefine old adversarial strategic relationships and discover new friends and supporters.

A significant aspect of the new global and regional contexts for India was the resurgence of China, resulting from its sustained and high economic growth since the radical reforms introduced a decade earlier by Deng Xiaoping. There were two aspects of China's rise for India: one, to deal with it bilaterally, and another, to respond to it regionally. Bilaterally, India under Rajiv Gandhi's initiative had begun normalizing its relations with China, as seen in the previous chapter. China was also keen to normalize relations with India and start economic cooperation. This led the two giant Asian neighbours to build a mutual confidence and stabilize peace regarding the issues of mutual

[1] A. N. Ram, ed., *Two Decades of India's Look East Policy: Partnership for Peace, Progress and Prosperity* (New Delhi: Manohar Publications, 2012).

disputes and differences between them, such as the boundary question in the Himalayas. India was also concerned about the growing arms supplies from China to India's sensitive immediate neighbours such as Pakistan and Myanmar. India's concerns in such matters were communicated to China during the visit of Chinese Premier Li Peng to India in December 1991.[2] The countries in the Southeast Asian region had anxieties regarding the possibilities of a resurgent China asserting itself in the region. Their fears were that in a unipolar situation, the USA may reduce its presence and stakes in the region, and China may want to fill in the vacuum thus created. Such fears emanated from the USA's decision in 1992 to withdraw its naval base from the Philippines. The smaller Southeast Asian countries were seeking to augment their own military capabilities and draw other regional major players to participate in the dynamics of regional balance in the interest of stability and peace. India figured prominently in this respect, and some of the countries such as Malaysia, Singapore and Myanmar had started exploring India as a regional strategic option.

Besides the changing global and regional strategic contexts in the aftermath of the end of the Cold War, there were also many significant changes at the domestic level in India which had their impact on its foreign policy. First of all, the Congress came back to power after two interim minority governments of V. P. Singh (December 1989–November 1990) and Chandra Shekhar (November 1990–June 1991). Narasimha Rao was also only the second prime minister of a Congress-led government, after a long gap since Lal Bahadur Shastri (1964–1966), who did not come from the Nehru–Gandhi family. He led a minority government with just one ally, the All India Anna Dravida Munnetra Kazhagam (AIADMK) with 11 seats in the Lok Sabha (the Lower House of Indian Parliament). After being in power for nearly three years, in July 1993, the Rao government got support from some other smaller parties to survive a no-confidence motion. The Rao minority government was, therefore, generally free from coalition pressures on foreign policy except for the AIADMK's preference for the fishermen of Tamil Nadu in relation to Sri Lanka.

[2] For the complete text of India's engagement with the East in 1991–1992, see MEA's *Annual Report 1991–92*.

Rao's credibility and hold within the Congress party was not very strong either.

By the beginning of the 1990s, India was facing an acute economic crisis. It manifested itself first in the form of 'balance of payment' crisis. When Rao's government assumed office, India's foreign exchange reserves stood at a low of US$400 million and the Reserve Bank of India was struggling to ensure that India did not falter on loan repayments. The previous Chandra Shekhar government had borrowed from the International Monetary Fund (IMF), and there were conditions attached to the loan to be complied with, as the Rao government also wanted more IMF support. The thrust of deepening globalization was gradually weighing heavily on India's inward-looking mixed economy. In response to these pressures, Prime Minister Rao and his academic (economist) finance minister, Dr Manmohan Singh, expedited and widened the process of economic reforms and liberalization with the announcement of the New Economic Policy in 1991. This was done in the face of severe institutional resistance and internal political pressures from within the ruling party.[3] In pursuance of this policy, India launched a systematic campaign to mobilize investments and open India to the world in terms of trade, investments, technology and related areas of economic growth. Due to this economic drive, many analysts have seen the LEP as primarily an economic initiative. This may be a misunderstanding of the LEP. India's eastward engagement initiative has been driven by both economic and strategic factors, as we have seen in the previous chapter. The compulsion to articulate a comprehensive and systematic LEP was no exception to this.[4] It was a continuation of the previous approach, recast and redefined in response

[3] For an interesting detailed account of the making of Rao's economic policy, see Palakhumathu G. Mathai, 'The Untold Story–First 100 Days of the Rao Government', *The Telegraph*, 20 June 2013.

[4] See some of the studies on the subject: Frederic Grare and Amitabh Mattoo, eds., *The Politics of India's Look East Policy* (New Delhi: Manohar, 2001); Prakash Nanda, *Rediscovering Asia: Evolution of India's Look East Policy* (New Delhi: Lancer Publications, 2003); Sudhir Devare, *India and Southeast Asia: Towards Security Convergence* (Singapore: Institute of Southeast Asian Studies, 2006); and see Chak Mun, *India's Strategic Interest in Southeast Asia and Singapore* (New Delhi: Macmillan Publishers India, 2009).

to the new and emerging contexts. Rao had been Rajiv Gandhi's foreign minister and was associated with many of the initiatives in relation to the eastern neighbours. As will be seen in the following, he radically transformed them in order to carry them forward.

Articulation of the Look East Policy

While Rajiv Gandhi may be considered the pioneer in re-establishing India's eastward ties, it was Rao who set it on a firm footing and in a much more comprehensive manner. However, the biggest role was played, as mentioned earlier, by the fundamentally altered international situation, where the collapse of the Soviet Union, end of the Cold War politics and de-ideologization of foreign policies shaped the nature of the world politics. 'The role of Rajiv Gandhi in redefining relations with China, the US and Europe cannot be overstated and Rao endeavoured to build upon Rajiv Gandhi's legacy and essentially saw his role as continuing the well-established and tested parameters of foreign policy'.[5]

In that context, the role of Narasimha Rao in making structural changes in the foreign policymaking and syncing those with economic policy formulation deserves acknowledgement.

> It was Prime Minister Narasimha Rao, who gave concrete directions for the reorientation of India's policy towards its eastern neighbourhood. In order to grow economically by getting closer to Southeast Asia, India's strategy worked on two levels. It endeavoured to improve its relations both at the multilateral level, with ASEAN and, at the bilateral level, with each of the Association's member states. At Narasimha Rao's request, the Foreign Secretary J.N. Dixit, the primary official of the Ministry of External Affairs, took direct charge of Southeast Asian countries. The region formerly fell under a lower level official, the Secretary East, Mr. Dixit therefore found himself heading the Southern Division, as of the

[5] Amar Nath Ram, 'The First Decade of India's Look East Policy: An Insider's Account', in *Two Decades of India's Look East Policy: Partnership for Peace, Progress and Prosperity*, ed. A. N. Ram (New Delhi: Manohar Publications, 2012), 63.

second half of 1992, while at the same time, wielding direct control over the economic division.[6]

> If Rao was its chief architect and conceptualiser, Verma (Amar Nath Verma, Principal Secretary to the PM) and Dixit were its principal implementers. The roles of Ronen Sen at the prime minister's office, the then Finance Secretary, Montek Sing Ahluwalia and the Commerce Secretary Tajendra Khanna was also significant. Ahluwalia, specially, was very impressed with the ASEAN model of development and was instrumental in introducing far-reaching innovations in our economic policy, procedures and delivery systems, particularly at the cutting edge levels in the government.[7]

Prime Minister Rao was clearly aware of the fact that the for the new policy to succeed, it was necessary that 'bilateral relations with individual ASEAN countries improved and acquired mutually beneficial content, the LEP at the macro level would not amount to much'.[8]

It may also be noted here that much before Modi, it was Rao who conceptualized and implemented the idea of engaging the diaspora abroad. The hype and organization and the visibility of the diaspora at such a large scale as is evident now, however, was not there under Rao though. As A. N. Ram points out,

> Rao knew the importance of reaching out to the now influential and large Indian community and to the academics and intellectuals. His engagements in Bangkok and Chiang Mai included interactions with both these influential groups. He followed this practice during his other visits as well. The visit was a resounding success.[9]

Narasimha Rao's address at the Singapore Lecture Series in 1994 clearly explained the context as well as the main objectives of the

[6] Isabelle Saint-Mezard, *Eastward Bound: India's New Positioning in Asia* (New Delhi: Manohar, 2006), 41.

[7] Ram, 'The First Decade of India's Look East Policy: An Insider's Account', 66.

[8] Ibid., 67.

[9] Ibid., 69.

LEP.[10] The economic drive behind the policy was clear in his detailing of the reforms undertaken by India and emphasizing the need for investments. He told his audiences:

> I can assure this gathering that India not only welcomes but is worthy of your time and money. Investment in India is an investment in future—a future not only for the investor but for a population of one billion which will remain a force for stability in the world. In return, countries of Asia-Pacific will find India a reliable partner, a vast market, the process of whose development will simultaneously involve the renaissance of a great and noble civilization which we all share in some measure.[11]

He tried to set aside the doubts raised in the regional media, including in Singapore, regarding the slowing pace of economic reforms in India, saying:

> May I clarify that if we appear to have slowed down, it may only be because the pace of reforms over the past three years has been extremely rapid. Only last month my Government has further liberalised the currency regime to make the rupee convertible on current account. Meanwhile the Bombay Stock Exchange continues its bull run. Regarding our labour policy, one has to understand the Indian situation and spare a thought for the hundreds of millions of people who face the prospects of unemployment. A hire and fire policy in India would not only be inhuman, it would be economically unwise....[12]

He gave details of Indian economy's growing engagement with the world economy, especially the Asia-Pacific economies. In 1993 alone,

[10] This discussion is drawn on Rao's speech at Singapore. See P. V. Narasimha Rao, 'India and the Asia-Pacific—A New Relationship', *Selected Speeches, 1994–1995* (New Delhi: Publications Division, Ministry of Information and Broadcasting, Government of India, 1995), 390–405. The same speech was published with a slightly different title, 'India and the Asia-Pacific—Forging a New Relationship' (Singapore: Institute of Southeast Asian Studies, 1995).

[11] Ibid.

[12] Ibid.

20 per cent of the total foreign investments approved were from the Asia-Pacific Economic Cooperation (APEC) economies excluding the USA; 'Between January 1991 and June 1994, a total of 1904 foreign collaborations were approved with the APEC economies'. During this period, 'approximately 54 per cent' of the total foreign investments received by India were from the APEC region. Underlining the economic objective of his new approach, Rao said:

> Right now, the necessity of massive investment in infrastructure loom large.... I have come to extend my hand of partnership in this adventure.... My present endeavour is to draw, as much as possible investment and cooperation from the Asia-Pacific countries, in consonance with our common concept and solidarity and my faith in common destiny.[13]

The strategic underpinnings of the new policy were also clearly articulated by Rao. He welcomed the end of the Cold War but cautioned that the 'Cold War attitudes persist—not because there is anything permanently valid or inevitable about them, but because their removal takes time and even more than time, the genuine realisation that the change in human destiny needs a corresponding change in man's own mind set'. In his assessment, there was also a power shift in the world:

> While one cannot deny the overwhelming superiority of the United States, one cannot ignore the significant military developments of China, Japan, and Australia. The stakes in Asia-Pacific region are indeed high. They involve rights of passage through crucial waterways, security of navigation from piracy, claims over disputed lands, maritime zones and resources and hostilities through history that have been defused but not dispelled.[14]

Rao firmly asserted India's aspirations to play a larger strategic role in the changing world and the Asia-Pacific region. He strongly discounted the suspicions prevailing in the region about India's 'expansionist design, or its blue-water Navy'. Such suspicions had been

[13] Ibid.
[14] Ibid.

expressed earlier during and after Rajiv Gandhi period with which Rao was also associated. We have discussed them in the previous chapter. Rao found it necessary to remove these unfounded suspicions about India's expansionist plans in the Indian Ocean. He cited *The Australian Senate Report of 1991* in his support which said that 'India does not have the capability of sustained force projection far beyond its boundaries....' And yet, he said: '[W]hile India can be said to have been confined to its own strategic defence, this does not detract from its ability and willingness to exercise its role in global affairs'. This role would be based on India's principled non-alignment, which was not only relevant in the context of the military bloc politics but also reflected India's 'determination to decide our own destiny, independently according to our own lights and to ensure genuine international consensus on matters that concern the world community'.[15]

Economic and Strategic Imperatives

Rao's articulation of LEP in both its economic and strategic thrusts was based upon the Rao government's assessment of economic strengths and strategic imperatives of the region over a period of three years. In economic terms, the exchange of many high-level visits between India on the one hand and China, Japan and Korea on the other, before Prime Minister Rao's Singapore Lecture, were very important to convince India of the potential and possibilities in the Asia-Pacific region.

One may argue that contrary to popular belief, right from the beginning of the LEP in 1992, Prime Minister Narasimha Rao had his focus on both the Southeast Asian and the Northeast Asian countries. Many of his ideas articulated in the Singapore Lecture were shaped by his interaction with the countries of the Asia-Pacific region, particularly China, Japan, Korea and the ASEAN countries. Between 1991 and 1993, before going to Singapore, he had visited Japan in June 1992, and South Korea and China in September 1993. During these visits, Rao met major economic stakeholders and addressed business communities in these countries to project India's potential

[15] Ibid.

as a destination for investments and a market for trade. His visit to Korea was the first ever by an Indian prime minister. In Korea, he also addressed Indian heads of the missions in the north-eastern countries to explain to them India's new approach and efforts to enhance economic and strategic engagement. A number of ministerial and business delegations were welcomed in India, an important visit being by the then Chinese Prime Minister Li Peng in December 1991.[16] He had also sent his foreign and finance ministers to these countries and worked on the feedback brought by them.[17]

There was considerable emphasis during these visits to enhance trade with these countries and invite investments. The response from these countries was positive but cautious. India had just started liberalizing its economy then and everyone wanted to ensure that this trend will be sustained. Japan was the largest ODA (official development assistance) contributor to India, and by 1992–1993, it had emerged as the third-largest investor to India after the USA and Switzerland. A high-level economic delegation visited from Japan in January 1992 to assess the depth of the economic liberalization programme initiated by the Rao government and to explore the possibilities of investments and economic cooperation. India's trade with South Korea started showing promising prospects. Its EXIM Bank also extended credit to India exceeding US$500 million. China opened two sectors for border trade with India and finalized a trade protocol to enhance bilateral trade in 1992.[18] As Isabelle Saint-Mezard points out:

> There could be no better manifestation in organisational terms, of the economic rationale behind the diplomatic opening up to Southeast Asian countries.... The changes wrought in institutions handling bilateral cooperation also testifies to the new drive towards East Asia. A Joint Commission was set-up in 1990 with Thailand, in 1992 with Malaysia and in 1996 with South Korea as well as Indonesia.[19]

[16] For details on these visits, see MEA's annual reports for 1991–1992, 1992–1993 and 1993–1994.

[17] Ibid.

[18] Ibid.

[19] Saint-Mezard, *Eastward Bound*, 41.

Thus, a range of initiatives were taken to engage the countries of Southeast and East Asia through the LEP. Sheel Kant Sharma opines,

> India established resident diplomatic mission in Brunei Darussalam at the level of Ambassador. Prime Minister Narasimha Rao sent the ex-Maharaja of Jaipur to the court of the Sultan of Brunei as India's High Commissioner. The High Commissioner enjoyed close rapport with his hosts, both on and off the polo field and relations received a spurt as the Sultan paid a visit to India in 1992.[20]

Clearly, the rising Asian economic powerhouses and the Asian Tigers prompted India to forge closer ties with them as also benefit from their progress.

The strategic impetus to the Look East initiative came from three factors: the rising China, the turbulent Myanmar and the transforming ASEAN. There were two aspects of China's rise that was being gradually noticed in the region. The first was the shift in China's economic policies and regional approach since the beginning of Deng Xiaoping's leadership in the early 1980s and the second was an anxiety of whether a rising China would be more assertive in the region and seek to fill the vacuum created by reducing the US presence following the end of the Cold War. While the first aspect called for normalization of relations with China on India's part, the second one injected caution regarding the prospects of China's unfolding regional engagements. India's response to these two factors was marked by Rajiv Gandhi's visit to China, as mentioned in the previous chapter, that sought to normalize relations and build mutual confidence to avoid tensions on the unresolved border issue. The imperative of India's LEP was to sustain this approach and give momentum to it. Accordingly, Prime Minister Narasimha Rao visited China in September 1993, where he signed the Agreement on Maintenance of Peace and Tranquillity along the LAC in the India–China Border Area. Through this agreement, it was envisaged to put in place bilateral mechanisms to ensure peace on

[20] Sheel Kant Sharma, 'India's Look East Policy: Initial Years 1990–1994', in *Two Decades of India's Look East Policy: Partnership for Peace, Progress and Prosperity*, ed. A. N. Ram (New Delhi: Manohar Publications, 2012), 47.

the border, resolve differences in specific sectors and lead the process towards the final settlement of boundary.[21] In continuation of this, India and China concluded yet another confidence-building measure in the 'military field' along the LAC in November 1996 during the Chinese President Jiang Zemin's visit to India. Under this agreement, both India and China committed that:

> [N[either side shall use its military capabilities against the other side, and includes provisions for negotiating the reduction or limitation of forces from mutually agreed geographical zones along the Line of Actual Control, the prior notification of military exercises, the prevention of dangerous military exercises in border areas and service to service contacts.[22]

It was in continuation of this momentum of normalizing relations with China that in April 2005, during the Chinese Premier Wen Jiabao's visit to India, the two sides also signed the Agreement on the Political Parameters and Guiding Principles for resolving the boundary question. Though China's response to resolving the border issue slowed down after this agreement, India has continued its cautious approach towards sustaining its cooperative engagement with China. This is broadly summed up by then National Security Adviser Shivshankar Menon when he says:

> What India has successfully done with China since Rajiv Gandhi's 1988 visit and under successive governments of different political complexions has been to maintain the peace while strengthening itself, seeking partners in the extended neighbourhood and among major powers, and engaging China. Finding the balance between rivalry and incentives for good behaviour, between competition and cooperation, is among the hardest tasks in strategy.[23]

[21] For an excellent overview of China's territorial disputes, please see Sana Hashmi, *China's Territorial Disputes: Lessons and Prospects* (New Delhi: Knowledge World, 2016).

[22] For more details, see Ministry of Defence, *Annual Report 1996–97*.

[23] Shivshankar Menon, *Choices: Inside the Making of India's Foreign Policy* (New Delhi: Penguin Random House, 2016), 31.

While maintaining this strategic balance in its relations with China, India was cautious about China's growing cooperation with Pakistan and its expanding strategic presence in Myanmar and Bangladesh. The question of the Chinese nuclear support and supply of arms to Pakistan, and its supply of arms to Myanmar, was raised by India in meetings with the Chinese leaders. As this did not affect the Chinese much, India moved to shift its approach towards Myanmar.

There was considerable political turbulence in Myanmar with the rise of post–Ne Win military rule. The victory of Aung San Suu Kyi led democratic forces in 1989 aroused hopes for a new beginning, but these hopes were soon dashed with the junta's refusal to hand over power. On its part, India was isolated from *Tatmadaw*—the Myanmar's military regime—due to its traditional support for the democratic forces that continued until Rajiv Gandhi's period. The popular forces in Myanmar looked towards India for inspiration and encouragement in their struggle against the military order. China and Pakistan were supportive of Myanmar's new military leadership. On China's part, its support for the new junta in Yangon was also a reciprocal gesture for the Myanmar military leadership's endorsement of the Chinese government's position on the Tiananmen Square revolt of 1989. The political and strategic developments in Myanmar could not receive enough attention of the Indian policymakers in the beginning, which led to such a situation. India's ad hoc approach was reflected in New Delhi's inability to appoint an Ambassador to Myanmar for more than a year between July 1989 and August 1990. Preet Malik, who served as India's Ambassador to Myanmar during 1990–1992, explains:

> The fact that there had been no ambassador for a year was seen by some as a reaction of India's adversarial position on Myanmar. Little did they realise that it was not a position dictated by policy that had stood in the way of appointing an ambassador; it was merely that the Government of India (GOI) had not found itself able to select a person who would not wriggle out of a very uncomfortable position of ambassadorship that Indo-Myanmar relations represented. In fact, the then GOI, particularly the then Minister for External Affairs I. K. Gujral had come to the conclusion that

> they would have to look at the ranks of a politician (instead of a diplomat) to fill the post.[24]

At the critical moment when Myanmar was undergoing defining transitions, India could not act fast. Even on the political situation, New Delhi was unable to act swiftly. As Malik states,

> Discussions that I continued to have, at regular intervals at the policy level in Delhi, showed little clarity as to what we needed to do; by our refusal to do substantive business with the SLORC (State Law and Order Restoration Council—the name assumed by Myanmar's military rulers) leadership we were giving the Chinese an open field to further draw the Myanmar leadership deeper into the Chinese influence, much to the detriment of our strategic and security interests.[25]

Rising Chinese presence in South and Southeast Asia had become a major concern for India. This was particularly the case with countries such as Myanmar and Bangladesh.

> China's growing presence in Southeast Asia including the expanding economic relationship which was being encouraged by the adoption by ASEAN of the policy of 'constructive engagement' certainly made India take a good look at the policy that it needed to adopt to ensure that it was not ruled out as a player in this extremely important strategic region.[26]

Another major concern of India was the report that China had established listening posts in Myanmar's Indian Ocean islands to monitor developments in India's missile programme, which was just another manifestation of the rising China–Myanmar cooperation. India's security concerns related to the activities of the Northeast

[24] Preet Malik, *My Myanmar Years: A Diplomat's Account of India's Relations with the Region* (New Delhi: SAGE Publications, 2016), 6–7.

[25] Ibid., 71.

[26] Preet Malik, 'India's Look East Policy: Genesis', in *Two Decades of India's Look East Policy: Partnership for Peace, Progress and Prosperity*, ed. A. N. Ram (New Delhi: Manohar Publications, 2012), 33.

insurgent groups, growing flow of drugs and contraband along the India–Myanmar borders, and increasing Chinese strategic presence in Myanmar were raised by India with the U. Aye, a senior and influential officer of the Myanmar foreign office, during his visit to New Delhi in 1992. India's then foreign secretary, J. N. Dixit, during his visit to Myanmar in March 1993 also raised the question of growing Chinese presence with his hosts, expressing India's concerns at 'the possibility of Myanmar granting naval base facilities to China that would bring it into the Bay of Bengal and the Andaman Sea, pointing out that this would pose an unacceptable challenge to India's strategic and security interests'.[27] Pakistan, with the help and support of China, had started supplying military equipment to Myanmar's new military regime.[28] India shuddered at the prospect of Pakistan consolidating its position in Myanmar in view of strong Pakistani links with Bangladesh's security establishment and its propensity to support insurgencies in India's Northeast region.

> The fact that it was developing the infrastructure both within northern Myanmar and in Tibet that would have a direct impact on India's north-eastern states was not lost on the Indian establishment. It was also clear that attempts were being made to try and lock in both Myanmar and the north-eastern Indian states with the economies of relatively backward Chinese states of Szechwan and Yunnan. This expansion of Chinese interests was among the major reason why India had to evolve a definite strategic policy directed towards the countries not only in its immediate neighbourhood but also for the strategically important countries of Southeast Asia and the Far East particularly Japan and the Taiwanese and South Korean economies bringing them within its economic and strategic embrace.[29]

India could not afford to ignore Myanmar anymore in the face of these developments. The urgency for a basic shift in India's Myanmar policy

[27] Malik, *My Myanmar Years*, 93.

[28] S. D. Muni, 'China's Strategic Engagement with the New ASEAN', *IDSS Monograph No. 2* (Singapore: Institute for Defence and Strategic Studies, 2002).

[29] Malik, 'India's Look East Policy: Genesis', 35.

was injected by the deteriorating security situation in India's Northeast resulting from tribal insurgencies. Some of the insurgent groups, such as the Nagas, were seeking shelter in Myanmar by exploiting ethnic harmonies across the border. Myanmar's military regime could not care less in view of India's explicit support for their democratic adversaries. The policymakers in New Delhi saw the possibility of making up, at least partially, with Myanmar military junta as a way out of stabilizing the insurgency situation in its turbulent Northeast region. Underlining the importance of the Northeast in India's new Myanmar policy, an insider said that

> [There is an urgent] need to find lasting solutions that would ensure an end to the troubled northeast. This part of India had within it alienated groups that had in the past received material support from the PRC and continued to be supported by Pakistan which had established training centres within Bangladesh; retained from the days when that country was part of Pakistan. India's northeast insurgents continued to utilise the land routes of Myanmar for transit and tactical purposes.[30]

Thus, a cooperative and congenial relationship with Myanmar was also an imperative of India's internal (in the Northeast region) security concern.

While softening its approach towards the military rulers and exploring possibilities of cooperation with them, India also tried to keep engaged with the democratic forces, especially Aung San Suu Kyi, and tried to get her released. An obvious example of keeping the engagement was the conferring of Nehru Award for International Understanding for 1993 on her in recognition of her 'brave, non-violent and unyielding struggle for freedom, democracy and human dignity'.[31] Therefore, India's new Myanmar policy that was the harbinger of strategic shift towards the East was 'a two-track policy':

[30] Ibid.

[31] For the complete text of India's engagement with the East in 1995–1996, see MEA's *Annual Report 1995–96*. It is believed that then President K. R. Narayanan and a veteran journalist Nikhil Chakravarti has strongly lobbied for Nehru Award to Aung Sun Suu Kyi.

> [It] would continue to extend moral and political support to the democratic forces and leaders and it would also engage military government in order to improve and upgrade government to government relations. It was a calibrated and complex initiative to balance principles, values, interests and geo-political realities.[32]

Myanmar's joining of ASEAN in 1997 not only proved India's engagement right but also linked India with the Southeast through a possible land route.

India's security concerns regarding its North Eastern Region (NER) and the apprehensions of growing Chinese presence in the neighbourhood were also linked with Bangladesh. Serious initiative was taken to bring Bangladesh on board to accommodate India's sensitivities as Bangladesh moved from a military regime to a democratic order in 1991. India decided to meet Bangladesh's long-standing concerns in bilateral relations. The popularly elected Prime Minister of Bangladesh visited India in May 1992, where she appeared responsive to India's concerns and promised to extend cooperation in meeting these concerns. However, these promises could not be kept.[33]

While being driven by the strategic considerations in relation to China and Myanmar, India's LEP was also a response to the emerging changes in the ASEAN region. In order to cope with the consequences of the end of the Cold War, the prospects of a possible US withdrawal from the region and the rise of China, ASEAN was trying to internally consolidate the organization and reach out to other important regional players for ensuring a harmonious strategic balance. Internally, ASEAN not only gradually integrated its hitherto left out members,

[32] Rajiv Bhatia, *India-Myanmar Relations: Changing Contours* (New York, NY: Routledge, 2015), 101–102.

[33] For details, see Nancy Jetley, 'India and Bangladesh: Some Perspectives', in *Foreign Policy of Bangladesh*, ed. S. R. Chakravarty (New Delhi: Har Anand Publications, 1994). For a discussion on Indian thinking to cultivate Bangladesh, leading to Prime Minister Khaleda Zia's visit on 1992, see Krishnan Srinivasan, *The Jamdani Revolution: Politics, Personalities and Civil Society in Bangladesh, 1989–92* (New Delhi: Har Anand Publications, 2008). (Srinivasan was India's High Commissioner in Bangladesh and later Foreign Secretary. The book contains his diaries written during Dhaka posting.)

such as Vietnam, Laos, Myanmar and Cambodia, but also prepared itself strategically by establishing the ASEAN Regional Forum (ARF) as an important part of the ASEAN structure. India emerged as an important regional player to be brought into ASEAN. Many of the ASEAN members were reaching out to India for cooperation in the field of defence and security. Singapore, Malaysia, Vietnam and Laos took a lead in this respect.[34] India initiated the anti-submarine warfare exercises with Singapore in 1994.

> The upswing in defence ties is a result of a two-pronged strategy of economic and military cooperation—the Defence Cooperation Agreement in 2003 and the Comprehensive Economic Cooperation Agreement in 2005. In 2004, India granted the Singapore Army and Air Force training facilities on its soil—a significant departure from its traditional position of not allowing any foreign military presence.[35]

To be fair to the propounding father of the LEP, India did try to act on the defence aspect of its eastward engagement, but the trend could not continue for long thanks to the incapacities of India's defence sector. G. V. C. Naidu highlights that as early as in 1992,

> [D]uring the visit by the Malaysian Defence Minister, Najib Tun Abdul Razak, a wide range of defence ties was discussed. Prime Minister Mahathir Mohammad indicated in an interview that the level of cooperation between Malaysia and India would be upgraded with the Malaysian decision to buy the Russian MiG-29 fighter aircraft. He explained that India could extend service and training facilities and supply spare parts. India and Malaysia signed a Memorandum of Understanding on defence cooperation in February 1993, which, though primarily meant to train Malaysian

[34] The growing convergence between India and ASEAN in security matters has been discussed in Sudhir Devare, *India & Southeast Asia: Towards Security Convergence* (Singapore: Institute of Southeast Asian Studies, 2006), 45–87.

[35] For a detailed analysis of India Singapore defence ties, see Pankaj Jha and Rahul Mishra, 'Defence Cooperation: A Case Study of India and Singapore', *Air Power* 5, no. 2 (Summer, April–June 2010): 73–96.

> air force personnel, was fairly broad ranging to include joint development of certain defence systems of common interest...[36]
>
> India expanded facilities at the MiG-29 assembly factory to meet the Malaysian demand and at least 100 pilots and ground supporting staff were trained as part of this Memorandum of Understanding, although not much progress could take place with regard to joint development. Malaysia was keen to train its marine commando forces and service its naval boats in India, and have regular exchanges between the navies.[37]

Malaysia was also keen to acquire the Indian HAL (Hindustan Aeronautics Limited)-built Dornier 228 Maritime Patrol Craft and HAL-built *Chetak* helicopters for search and rescue, and the *Cheetah* light utility helicopters.[38] Likewise with Singapore and Vietnam, it is the agreement signed in the early 1990s that is driving the defence engagement even today.

India's relationship with Vietnam has been exceptionally good. The strategic dimensions of Indo-Vietnamese relations, which had begun during the 1980s, acquired a more structured and institutional shape during the 1990s. In September 1994, the two sides signed a Memorandum of Understanding on Defence Cooperation under which

> India not only offered training slots to Vietnamese defence personnel but also agreed to service their MIG-21 fighter aircrafts. The promise of the MoU however, did not take off in implementation. There were various factors behind this, including widening of Vietnam's economic and strategic relations with other powers, like the US, Japan and also China. During 1991–99, Vietnam was deeply engaged in resolving its boundary issue with China to ensure that in future China had no excuse of militarily intervening

[36] G. V. C. Naidu, 'Whither the Look East Policy: India and Southeast Asia', *Strategic Analysis* 28, no. 2 (April–June 2004): 331–346.

[37] Ibid.

[38] Ibid.

in Vietnam under the pretext of disputed boundary as was the case in 1979.[39]

The then Prime Minister of Singapore, Goh Chok Tong, even proposed in his National Day message in 1993 to cause a 'mild India fever' in Singapore. Later describing India as an essential part of the ASEAN economic growth, he said: 'I visualise ASEAN as a fuselage of jumbo plane with China as one wing and India, the other wing. If both wings take-off, ASEAN as a fuselage will also be lifted'.[40] Such thinking created a congenial atmosphere for India to look for greater engagement with the region and to explain its own position that it had no expansionist or aggressive designs towards the region.[41] The compulsions of the Cold War politics and the differing positions of India and ASEAN on the Cambodian issue had kept them away from each other, despite the two sides being fully aware of the mutual gains of a closer partnership. Rao was keen to correct this and to 'renew India's centuries-old civilizational bonds with Southeast Asia to our mutual advantage. He saw Southeast Asia as an essential added option and a foreign policy priority for India'.[42]

The LEP was, therefore, a response of felt need and perceived national interests on the part of both India and the countries of the East. It was a two-way approach. India's engagement with the East could not have been revived and expanded just because India wanted it so, unless there was an equal inclination to do so on the part of the ASEAN members and other countries in the region.

[39] For details, see S. D. Muni, 'The Turbulent South-China Sea Waters: India, Vietnam and China', *ISAS Insights,* no. 140, 11 October 2011, https://www.isas.nus.edu.sg/ISAS%20Reports/ISAS%20Insights%20140%20-%20Email%20-%20The%20Turbulent%20South-China%20Sea%20Waters-%20India%20Vietnam%20and%20China.pdf, accessed 16 August 2018.

[40] Goh Chok Tong's address at the ASEAN-India summit in 2002.

[41] Kripa Sridharan, *The ASEAN Region in India's Foreign Policy* (Singapore: Dartmouth, 1995), 176–179.

[42] Ram, 'The First Decade of India's Look East Policy: An Insider's Account', 65.

> Indeed, a large measure of the positive result of this approach can be attributed to the fact that India and the countries of the East have been able to correctly assess and judge the mutual need to start the dialogue and cooperation with each other at the same time.[43]

The Policy Unfolds Gradually

India's LEP is seen to have unfolded in various phases. The first phase can be described as being one of exploration and rehabilitation of India's interests and stakes in the region. As seen earlier, the policy prospects started getting explored since 1985, and the initiatives that are considered to have begun with the beginning of the 1990s took almost three to four years to be articulated in 1994 by Prime Minister Narasimha Rao in his Singapore Lecture. This articulation was not backed by a systematic policy campaign or projection as we see in the case of many other countries such as China, the USA and ASEAN members. Even by 1995, many senior officials in the Southeast Asian region had not even heard of the fact that India was consciously and systematically pursuing an LEP.[44] It remained confined to official engagements and events. Though the policy had a wider canvas and outreach, covering countries such as China and Japan, it was largely focused on the ASEAN region and its institutions. The apparent thrust of the policy was on economic issues of enhancing trade and mobilizing investments from the region, though its strategic underpinnings were not lost in the articulation and pursuance of the policy. This first phase of the LEP lasted almost for a decade.

[43] Sudhir T. Devare, 'India's Look East Policy: As Seen from a Vantage Point', in *Two Decades of India's Look East Policy: Partnership for Peace, Progress and Prosperity*, ed. A. N. Ram (New Delhi: Manohar Publications, 2012), 84.

[44] This is based on the impressions of one of the authors of this study (S. D. Muni) who interviewed many senior officials in Indonesia, Malaysia, Laos, Myanmar and Cambodia to find their reactions and responses to India's LEP. See S. D. Muni, 'ASEAN's Responses to India's "Look-East" Policy', A Draft Framework Report Submitted at the Institute of Southeast Asian Studies, Singapore, under Duncan Macneill's Visiting Fellowship Programme, July–September 1996 (Unpublished).

The announcement that the LEP had entered its second phase was made during the National Democratic Alliance (NDA) government led by the Bharatiya Janata Party (BJP) under Atal Bihari Vajpayee's leadership. Making this announcement, the then Foreign Minister Yashwant Sinha in his speech at Harvard University on 29 September 2003 said:

> The first phase of India's Look East policy was ASEAN centred and focussed primarily on trade and investment linkages. The new phase of this policy is characterised by an expanded definition of 'east' extending from Australia to East Asia, with ASEAN at its core. The new phase also marks a shift from trade to wider economic and security issues including joint efforts to protect the sea lanes and coordinate counter-terrorism activities.[45]

There were two important developments that might have prompted the characterization of the second phase. One was a new initiative taken by Australia to forge a regional grouping of the Indian Ocean Region. This offered a much wider theatre for Indian engagement, ranging from Australia to Africa. The Indian security establishments explored implications of such a wider grouping and found that India could not remain aloof from the new initiative but would have to ensure that it did not open prospects for bigger powers to dominate the Indian Ocean Region at the cost of its own vital stakes. A study officially commissioned in India to explore implications of the Australian initiative said:

> [T]he dominant naval presence of the US and Western Navies is a hard fact of Indian Ocean security situation. The advancement of IOR may reinforce this situation. There are both advantages and risks in India cooperating with this presence. Advantage lies in India coming out of its Cold War period isolation from the West's area of influence in the region and developing its

[45] The complete text of the speech is available via the MEA website, https://www.mea.gov.in/Speeches-Statements.htm?dtl/4744/Speech_by_External_Affairs_Minister_Shri_Yashwant_Sinha_at_Harvard_University, accessed 16 August 2018.

> professional knowledge and experience through bilateral exchanges and contacts. US is also a willing customer to utilise some of India's excellent naval facilities an infrastructure.... A prudent course for India would therefore be to build on selective areas of cooperation with the US in the region without compromising on its autonomy, resilience and long term interests.[46]

The second important development was the 9/11 attacks on the icons of the US economic, political and military power in Washington DC. This brought the issue of terrorism to the forefront of international politics and provided India an opportunity to dovetail its regional concerns of cross-border terrorism with the global counter-terrorism efforts. This also brought India and the USA strategically closer on the question of understanding the threat of terrorism. It may be recalled here that in 1998, India had declared its nuclear status, and while doing so, it had taken the USA into confidence because Chinese nuclear capabilities were identified as the major security concern of India. The USA was not impressed by this argument initially and claimed China to be a partner in ensuring security in South Asia.[47] Subsequently however, the US position was revised as it not only sought to improve its security relations with India but also accepted India's status as a nuclear weapon power. During the NDA regime, India's then Minister of Defence George Fernandes had publicly declared in May 1998 that 'China was India's potential threat no. 1'. He had also blamed China for supporting Pakistan's nuclear programme and supply of arms to Myanmar.[48] The NDA government had to soften this position to keep developing normal relations with China. The then Minister of Foreign

[46] The Joint Intelligence Committee of the Government of India commissioned a study in 1995–1996, on the security dimensions of the Australian Initiative for Indian Ocean Economic Community.

[47] This was underlined in a letter written by Prime Minister Atal Bihari Vajpayee to the US president, explaining the rationale of India's nuclear explosions and declaration of a nuclear power status. This letter was leaked by the US side and the USA not only imposed sanctions on India for its nuclear explosion but also called upon China to join in ensuring South Asian security.

[48] Manoj Joshi, 'China Is Potential Threat No. 1: Says George Fernandes', *India Today*, 18 May 1998, https://www.indiatoday.in/magazine/cover-story/story/19980518-china-is-the-potential-threat-no.-1-says-george-fernandes-826430-1998-05-18

Affairs Jaswant Singh was sent to China to undo the offensive thrust of Fernandes' statement. In 2003, Prime Minister Vajpayee visited China where he made a small and significant change by accepting 'Tibet as a part of Chinese territory' in the place of the traditional formulation of Tibet being 'an autonomous region of China'. In return, the Chinese had dropped their claims on Sikkim and accepted it as integral part of India.[49]

In view of these developments marked by India's growing capabilities, improving relations with the USA, firmed-up confidence-building measures with China and opening of new opportunities in the Indian Ocean Region, the deepening of strategic ties with the countries of the Southeast Asian region was a natural Indian response as underlined in Yashwant Sinha's statement. The second phase of the LEP was accordingly an acknowledgement of increasing naval exercises between India and the countries of the region as also growing economic as well as defence and security cooperation with them.

Looking at the phase II of the LEP, one feels that the real change that began was the slow but steady warming up of relations with the USA, which played a significant role in bringing the Southeast Asian countries closer to India. Such changes started taking shape by the time I. K. Gujral became the Prime Minister of India.

> Gujral wanted his extended neighbourhood policy to include all of the Asia-Pacific and accordingly, apart from ASEAN, he accorded priority to relations with China, Japan, South Korea, Australia, and the other Asia-Pacific countries. It is noteworthy that a number of technical and expert level visits and delegations were exchanged with Southeast Asia and the Asia-Pacific during his tenure first as foreign minister and subsequently as prime minister of India.[50]

For Gujral, Southeast and East Asian countries were part of his neighbourhood plan. As India's Minister of External Affairs, Gujral

[49] Amit Baruah, 'Taking a New Road', *Frontline* 20, no. 14, 5–18 July 2003, https://www.frontline.in/static/html/fl2014/stories/20030718006900400.htm, accessed 16 August 2018.

[50] Ram, 'The First Decade of India's Look East Policy: An Insider's Account', 72.

took keen interest in India's linkages with the countries of the East, which also helped him look at these countries in a larger and more comprehensive manner. As Malik points out:

> Another test for the emerging relationship was providing it with greater strategic depth, the factor of defence cooperation with Singapore and to an extent with Malaysia certainly opened doors in this direction. The fact that relations with the United States contained not only economic factors, albeit these were gradually drawing the Americans to look on India as a serious partner, that would be part of the security framework for the Indian Ocean was a factor that the countries east of India now took as a matter of significance and of strategic importance.[51]

There was no formal announcement of the third phase, but it was there on the minds of India's policymakers. With the US announcement of its 'rebalance strategy' in the Asia-Pacific region by 2011, the deepening of strategic proximity between India and the USA and the greater assertion of China in the region, including in South China Sea, the Indian Ocean and India's immediate neighbourhood, the consolidation and expansion of India in the Asia-Pacific region looked inevitable.[52]

There was also a greater emphasis on the role of India's Northeast in its LEP with the taking up of connectivity projects between India and the ASEAN region by 2010–2011.[53] It would not be far off the mark to consider the shift from 'Look-East' to 'AEP' under Prime Minister Modi as a concrete manifestation, with change in the nomenclature of the third phase. This will be discussed in the next chapter. It may, however, be useful to keep in mind that the different phases of the policy did not represent any radical shifts from the direction of the policy enunciated initially. There were differences only of the

[51] Malik, 'India's Look East Policy: Genesis', 36–37.

[52] Shivshankar Menon, then India's National Security Adviser, in an informal discussion with the author (S. D. Muni) in 2011 hinted that India's LEP was entering its third phase.

[53] S. Narayan and Laldinkima Sailo, eds., *Connecting India to ASEAN: Opportunities and Challenges in India's Northeast* (New Delhi: Manohar Publishing House, 2015).

nuances, pace, extent and outreach of the policy. The marking of the phases or attempts to rename them are often related to the identification of a given regime with the policy and to project it as its own unique contribution.

Gains of the Policy

One of the major gains for India of its LEP was that it managed to renew, reactivate and reinforce its relations with the countries of the region. Dr Manmohan Singh, who initiated and pursued the policy with Narasimha Rao as his finance minister, recorded the gains of the policy as Prime Minister of India in January 2007, saying that gains were:

> [A]mply demonstrated by the intensification of political dialogue and the steadily enlarging people-to-people contact encompassing all the countries of the region. Our bilateral relations with the countries of ASEAN has myriad facets and covers cooperation in diverse areas such as agriculture, fisheries, health, information technology, space technology, energy, defence, and combating international terrorism.[54]

Improving relations with the countries of the region was preconditioned on the shedding off of misgivings and suspicions about India's intentions in the region aroused during the Cold War years. India's closeness to the former Soviet Union was not strategically compatible with the ASEAN members and the other US allies in the region. India's support of Vietnam in the Kampuchean (Cambodian) conflict, therefore, was not acceptable to them. Added to this were the suspicions triggered by India's naval modernization programme during the late 1980s. India had acquired a second aircraft career in 1987 and 29 other warships. India also not only obtained a nuclear powered submarine on lease from the then Soviet Union in 1988 but also launched its indigenously built, with West German collaboration, submarine in

[54] The complete text of the speech is available via the Press Information Bureau website, http://www.pib.nic.in/newsite/erelcontent.aspx?relid=24032, accessed 16 August 2018.

October 1989.[55] The vision of building a blue-water navy by senior Indian naval officers had also raised eyebrows in Southeast Asia and Australia. The Prime Minister of Singapore had taken an exception to this by projecting that in any eventuality of the USA withdrawing its bases from Philippines and reducing its presence in the region, India and China would rush in to fill the vacuum.[56]

India's efforts to remove these misgivings had been initiated during Rajiv Gandhi's period, as discussed earlier. Narasimha Rao had also tried to explain India's non-expansionist intentions in his Singapore Lecture. These efforts along with India's sincerity in engaging with the region for cooperative development helped shed off these misgivings. This became evident when the countries of the region started showing interest in opening up the possibilities of security and defence cooperation. Singapore's Prime Minister Goh Chok Tong, who had publicly expressed misgivings about India during the late 1980s, said during his visit to India in January 1994 that 'while he was initially apprehensive about India's acquisition of a blue-water fleet, he acknowledged that India had a legitimate interest to have a good navy to defend its long coast line'.[57] This was backed by a serious rethinking at the policy level in Singapore as hinted by George Yeo, a minister in Goh's Cabinet when he said:

> As India integrates its economy into East Asia, India can also help to stabilise the region by counterbalancing the other heavyweights. Because the fear of China will grow with the growth of the Chinese economy, Japan and ASEAN will always value the strategic presence of India.[58]

The Singaporeans were perhaps concerned about China in view of Mao Zedong's earlier declaration in which he had said: 'We must

[55] Sridharan, *The ASEAN Region in India's Foreign Policy*, 175–177.

[56] Ibid., 176.

[57] See Chak Mun, 'Singapore-India Strategic Relations: Singapore Perspective', in *Merlion and the Ashoka: The Singapore-India Strategic Ties*, ed. Anit Mukerjee (Singapore: World Scientific Publishers, 2016), 55.

[58] As quoted in Sunanda K. Datta-Ray, *Looking East to Look West: Lee Kaun Yew's Mission India* (Singapore: ISEAS, 2009), 160.

have South-east Asia, including South Vietnam, Thailand, Burma, Malaysia and Singapore.... After we get the region, the wind from the East will prevail over the wind from the West.[59]

India's relations with the countries of the region unfolded gradually in a pattern which may be described as of differentiated engagement, depending on strategic and economic considerations as well as responses from the countries of the region, especially the ASEAN members. Hinting at the differentiated approach, India's then Minister of Foreign Affairs I. K. Gujral, underlined 'Southeast Asia, Indo-China and East Asia' separately.[60] Three or four of such categories could be identified in India's engagement with ASEAN. One was of the countries which were latecomers to ASEAN and belonged to the traditional Indo-Chinese region. These countries had not been originally included in ASEAN for their pronounced non-communist character under the US influence. In India's official policy lexicon, they came to be identified as CLMV (Cambodia, Laos, Myanmar and Vietnam) countries. A separate unit was set up in the Indian MEA to look after these countries. These countries are geographically closer and linked to India, through Myanmar, and they were not the part of the developed and Westernized Southeast Asia. They were later described by a Singapore leader as falling on the other side of the 'digital divide' in ASEAN. They had closer strategic relations with the former Soviet Union and China, and were economically underdeveloped. India had played an important role in the peace process in this region, earlier as a part of the UN Peace and Supervisory Commission established to overlook the implementation of Geneva Agreements of 1954 and later through its engagement with the resolution of the Cambodian conflict.[61]

[59] Ibid.

[60] I. K. Gujral, *A Foreign Policy for India* (New Delhi: External Publicity Division, Ministry of External Affairs, Government of India, 1998), 238.

[61] For a detailed analysis of India's economic relations and potential for expanding them with CLMV countries, see Ram Upendra Das, *India's Strategy for Economic Integration with CLMV* (New Delhi: Department of Commerce, Ministry of Commerce and Industry, Government of India, 2015).

Singapore could be put in another category for its special attention towards India. Singapore emerged as the most enthusiastic ASEAN member to get India integrated into the region. It developed unique and close defence cooperation arrangements with India where India allowed Singapore security forces to train in its territory. India's traditional engagement with Indonesia, Malaysia and Thailand could be seen as yet another category. Some of them were cautious, preferring a gradual approach for India's integration into the region. Comparatively, India had limited interaction with Brunei and the Philippines initially but developed them later. Finally, India's relations with China, Japan and Korea had their own pace and momentum. China is much more than an East Asian neighbour to India. It has a common, though unsettled, border and centuries-old cultural and civilizational contact with India. Economic relations with these dynamic economies gathered pace while strategic constraints and caveats continued to influence the overall thrust of engagement, especially in relation to China.

By the end of the 1990s, India and Japan started discovering the value of strategic cooperation between them. They joined hands in working for the UNSC reforms. In 2007, Japan also proposed a new definition of the Asia-Pacific region by calling it the Indo-Pacific region. Since then, India and Japan have been closely pursuing their cooperation to ensure peace and security in the Indo-Pacific region in cooperation with other major players. By July 2010, India and Japan established a 'Two Plus Two' dialogue process at the level of senior foreign and defence affairs officials to chart the course of bilateral cooperation in the region.[62] India's economic and strategic cooperation with Korea has also seen an impressive rise. Korea has also enhanced its economic cooperation with India—visible in the auto industry and consumer durable production—over the past decade and more. President Lee Myung Bak of South Korea was invited as the chief guest for India's 61st Republic Day celebrations in January 2010.

[62] For details of expanding relations between India and Japan, see Rajiv Sharma, 'India–Japan Ties Poised for Advance as Both Nations Eye China', *The Asia-Pacific Journal: Japan Focus* 8, no. 36 (September 2010), https://apjjf.org/-Rajeev-Sharma/3406/article.pdf

Institutional Integration: ASEAN

The other gain to India that resulted from improved bilateral relations with the Southeast Asian countries was its institutional integration in the region. The most important multilateral grouping in the region has been ASEAN. Narasimha Rao in his Singapore Lecture had said: 'Last year we commenced an economic dialogue with ASEAN. My visit to Singapore and earlier visits to other ASEAN countries have convinced me that the potential for India's partnership with this nucleus organization in the Asia-Pacific is immeasurable'.[63]

Institutionally, India was accepted as a sectoral dialogue partner by ASEAN in January 1992. The sectors identified for partnership were trade, investment, tourism and science and technology. By comparison, the areas of cooperation agreed to in May 1980, when India was first formally accepted to be part of the ASEAN process, were much broader than these, and it was not designated as 'sectoral partner', meaning that it was an unqualified status as a full dialogue partner. The status of sectoral dialogue partner was granted by ASEAN to both India and Pakistan at the same time. But soon the ASEAN countries realized that Pakistan had no inclination or potential to get economically engaged with the region. India on the other hand was very serious in pursuing its economic engagement with the regional grouping. As a result, India soon earned the status of a (full) dialogue partner by ASEAN at its fifth summit in December 1995.

The *Annual Report 1995–96* of India's MEA highlights the importance of ASEAN in India's LEP:

> As an integral part of India's 'Look East' policy in keeping with the rapid consolidation of ASEAN and the acceleration and expansion of the ASEAN Free Trade Area, India continued to engage the ASEAN in the four sectors of her Sectoral Dialogue Partnership with them. The second meeting of the

[63] Refer to Note 10 of this chapter.

> ASEAN–India Sectoral Dialogue Committee was held in February 1995, and ASEAN–India Round Table Conference involving policy makers and captains of industry on both sides was held in September 1995. Both these meetings gave an impetus to trade and investment between ASEAN and India whilst also establishing the necessary informational and institutional linkages.[64]

As mentioned in the *Annual Report 1995–96* of the MEA:

> This hope was realized when the Fifth ASEAN Summit in Bangkok on 14 and 15 December 1995 took the decision to upgrade India's Sectoral Dialogue Partnership to the status of full Dialogue Partnership. This is a major positive development for India having far-reaching implications.... Under this higher level of dialogue relationship, cooperation between ASEAN and India is bound to further intensify not only in the four select areas of trade, investment, science & technology, and tourism identified under the Sectoral Dialogue Partnership, but also in new areas expected to be mutually identified for bilateral cooperation. Moreover, the full Dialogue Partnership would enable comprehensive consultation and dialogue with ASEAN on all matters including political and security.[65]

The elevation from sectoral to full dialogue partnership was, however, not without political hurdles, notwithstanding a broad consensus on the economic aspects of India's engagement. Malaysia and Indonesia had strong reservations 'out of a sense of Islamic solidarity' as to why Pakistan was also not being elevated to the status of full dialogue partner, though there was no record to show that Pakistan was seriously interested in ASEAN, except to counter India.[66] The proposal for India's elevation was not accepted at the Senior Officers Meeting (SOM) at the Bangkok ASEAN summit.

[64] For the complete text of India's engagement with the East in 1995–1996, see MEA's *Annual Report 1995–96.*

[65] Ibid.

[66] Kishore Mahbubani and Jeffery Sng, *The ASEAN Miracle: A Catalyst for Peace* (Singapore: NUS Press, 2017), 121.

Kishore Mahbubani, who was then Singapore's permanent secretary at the foreign ministry says:

> In Bangkok, the ASEAN leaders retreated into a small room with no advisers present to deliberate a number of sensitive matters in private, including the question of India's admission. Before the meeting, Kishore warned Singapore Prime Minister Goh Chok Tong that Indonesia's President Suharto and Malaysia's PM Dr Mahathir were unlikely to agree to India's admission without Pakistan. PM Goh entered the room knowing that his chances of success were slim. When this meeting ended … PM Goh spotted Kishore in the crowd and gave him the thumps up, indicating that India had got it lone.[67]

China also did not seem to be in favour of India's elevation, because China itself took six months after India's elevation to get that status. India had been lobbying with the USA and was working in coordination with Singapore, which worked hard but quietly to help India's case. The US influence worked on the Philippines to tilt the last minute balance in India's favour at the Bangkok ASEAN Summit in December 1995. Dato Ajit Singh, a senior Malaysian official of Indian origin and a personal friend of Dr Manmohan Singh, being the Secretary General of ASEAN during the period of elevation, proved to be of immense help. To satisfy the opponents of India for elevation, ASEAN formally conveyed a strong message while elevating India. It said:

> [T]hough ASEAN countries were quite unhappy about India's past attitude and her policies towards South-east Asia, and disappointed at the tardy pace of substantive interaction and lack of focussed interest even after India was made a sectoral dialogue partner, ASEAN had nevertheless decided to upgrade India's status in the expectation that India would be more pro-active in the future.[68]

[67] Ibid.

[68] As quoted in Datta-Ray, *Looking East to Look West*, 288.

If at all ASEAN felt compelled to upgrade India's status, it could have been due to its concern for securing a balanced representation in the ARF that had been launched in 1993, but ARF's 'evolutionary procedures' for addressing conflicts in the region were finalized in 1995. Every full dialogue partner was a member of the ARF. India's membership of the ARF was considered desirable by the ASEAN.

Response to ASEAN's expressed caution about India's participation in ASEAN, was inherent in India's MEA report which took the ASEAN decision positively. This response was based on the then Minister of Foreign Affairs I. K. Gujral's statements made during his participation in the first Post-Ministerial Conference of ASEAN in Jakarta in July 1996 after India's elevation to the status of full dialogue partner. He conceded to his ASEAN colleagues that 'you may find political processes in India pluralistic and diffused. You may also occasionally get exasperated by the time taken by our democratic, legal, administrative as well as public opinion processes'. Then he assured them:

> [W]e will go beyond what we have achieved in every aspect of our relations thus far, because we believe that we have barely skimmed the surface of the intrinsic potential that exists. We will therefore, be forever scanning the ASEAN–India horizon to look at new areas of cooperation and innovative delivery mechanisms and methods that will invest the relationship with a special significance and priority down the line.[69]

In these statements, Gujral had detailed India's priorities and how it planned to proceed in strengthening its engagement with the ASEAN. While returning from Jakarta, he paid a visit to Singapore to express India's appreciation for Singapore's efforts in raising India's dialogue partner status.

The institutional engagement between India and ASEAN was further elevated with the convening of the ASEAN–India Summit in

[69] Gujral's three statements made during the participation in Jakarta meetings can be found in Gujral, *A Foreign Policy for India*, 219–242.

2002 in Phnom Penh, Cambodia.[70] Following China, India acceded to the TAC on 8 October 2003 during the Second ASEAN–India Summit in Bali, Indonesia. 'India's efforts and cooperation is also being sought by ASEAN on the entry of Laos, Cambodia and Vietnam into the WTO'.[71] India has been keen to get into all the ASEAN forums, particularly the Asia Europe Meeting (ASEM) and ASEAN+3 Summit between ASEAN and the three dynamic economies of the region: China, Japan and Korea. ASEAN's acceptance of India as a summit partner was in response to this Indian desire which made India an equal partner of ASEAN with others without disturbing the already established ASEAN structures. A watershed moment in India's ASEAN engagement was joining the EAS in 2005. In its commemorative meeting in 2012, India and ASEAN agreed to upgrade their relationship to that of a strategic partnership. The summit-level partnership made India integral to ASEAN processes and ensured its participation in all other ASEAN fora, like the ASEAN Defence Ministers Meeting + (ADMM +), which included all the 10 ASEAN members and China, Japan, Russia, New Zealand, Australia, India, South Korea and the USA. This forum was set up in 2010 to explore regional cooperation in areas such as maritime security, counter-terrorism, peacekeeping and humanitarian assistance.

S. Mahmud Ali opines:

> It is evident from this that the ASEAN members have found a congruence of shared interests with India, given its dramatic economic growth in recent years, its potential for further significant growth, its growing global economic and strategic footprint, and its implicit potential to balance—if not rival—China. India's sophisticated diplomacy and security approaches to the regional players juxtaposed with the growing regional insecurity vis-à-vis China and recent encouragement from the Obama administration

[70] For details, see the ASEAN website, http://www.aseansec.org/5738.htm, accessed 16 August 2018.

[71] Shankari Sundararaman, 'India and ASEAN', *The Hindu*, 19 November 2002, https://www.thehindu.com/2002/11/19/stories/2002111900771000.htm, accessed 16 August 2018.

(underscored in Obama's speech to a joint session of the Indian parliament during his visit to India in November 2010) for India not just to 'look East, but to engage East' suggest Delhi's strategic perspective on Southeast Asia is consonant with the US and ASEAN views of the regional security milieu. This has significantly boosted the efficacy of India's attraction as an emerging power among ASEAN states. The key to India's success has rested in its ability to persuade key ASEAN members of its non-threatening and supportive role. This voluntary acceptance of India's presence in their midst among most ASEAN member states underscores the achievement of Indian diplomacy in Southeast Asia. This delicate fruit will require sensitive and careful nurturing.[72]

Beyond ASEAN

India's LEP has taken its search for institutional integration in the region beyond ASEAN. This is evident in India's membership and participation in the Bay of Bengal Multi-Sectoral Initiative for Technical and Economic Cooperation (BIMSTEC), the Mekong–Ganga Cooperation (MGC) Initiative and the EAS. The first two groupings involve Southeast Asian countries and do not include China.

Initiative for the BIMSTEC came from Thailand as its 'Look West' policy to connect with South Asia for greater economic engagement. This initiative took the shape of the organization Bangladesh, India, Sri Lanka and Thailand–Economic Cooperation (BIST–EC) in June 1997. India had initial hesitation in Bangladesh joining the group, but this was given up on persuasion from Thailand. In December 1997, Myanmar joined, and the new name was BIMSTEC, taking the first alphabets of all the member countries' names. In 2004, Nepal and Bhutan joined the organization, renaming it as BIMSTEC. The organization has not been able to perform much due to various political and economic factors. In recent years, however, India is trying to energize and develop this as almost a parallel to SAARC (South

[72] Author's (Rahul Mishra) e-mail interview with Dr Mahmood Ali, Director of Research, Bangladesh Institute of Peace and Security Studies, 6 June 2011.

Asian Association for Regional Cooperation), as the latter has become dysfunctional on account of Pakistan's refusal to go along with the regional connectivity proposals and abandon the use of cross-border terrorism against other neighbours and SAARC members India, Afghanistan and Bangladesh.[73]

The MGC initiative fructified in November 2000 at the ministerial-level meeting of six countries at the Laos' capital Vientiane: India, Myanmar, Thailand, Laos, Cambodia and Vietnam. While India represented the river Ganges, the remaining five countries represented the Mekong basin. Both sides have had strong cultural and civilizational affinity and have forged a common platform not only to revive old bonds but also to harness their economic potential. The rest of the ASEAN members welcomed it as a move to facilitate the ASEAN integration process and help build a strong regional economic and strategic community. The sectors chosen for special emphasis in mutual cooperation, besides economic development, were tourism, culture, education, and transport and communication. By 2012, six ministerial meetings of MGC were held. The progress has been slow but the member countries are committed to carry forward their mutual agenda evolved under Hanoi Programme of Action in July 2001 and the Phnom Penh Road Map during June 2003 meetings.[74]

The EAS is a much bigger grouping. Its origin can be traced to the Malaysian Prime Minister Dr Mohammad Mahathir's call for establishing an East Asia Economic Group (EAEG) in response to the setting up of trade blocks by Western economies. He made this proposal in the presence of the then Chinese Prime Minister Li Peng in December 1990, with the idea of building an East Asia Economic Caucus (EAEC), EAEG was reformulated as EAEC in the face of Indonesian and US objections. Subsequently, after nearly

[73] For a detailed discussion of India's role in BIMSTEC, see Rahul Mishra and Sana Hashmi, 'Can India Take the Lead on BIMSTEC?', *East Asia Forum*, 23 September 2017, available at http://www.eastasiaforum.org/2017/09/23/can-india-take-the-lead-on-bimstec/, accessed 16 August 2018.

[74] For details, see the report 'Mekong–Ganga Cooperation: Breaking Barriers and Scaling New Heights', *Research and Information System and ASEAN–India Centre*, New Delhi, 2017.

two-decade-long efforts, the (EAS) was concretized in 2005 in the form of the Kuala Lumpur Declaration. There were initial objections to let countries such as Australia, New Zealand, India or the USA join this grouping, but due to the efforts of Japan and Singapore with the support of other ASEAN countries, such objections had to be withdrawn. The latter wanted to ensure that the grouping was not dominated by China in the long run. The first meeting of EAS took place in December 2005 where 16 countries participated: ASEAN 10 plus Australia, China, India, Japan, South Korea and New Zealand.[75] At the sixth EAS summit in 2011 in Jakarta, the USA and Russia also joined as its members. The EAS agenda has evolved to include economic, developmental, political and strategic/security issues to provide a broad platform for regional integration.

All these three groupings, BIMSTEC, MGC and EAS, have no conflict with ASEAN but are seen as a part of broader regional architecture. ASEAN is considered as the core of this architecture and the driving force of regional community. India's role in MGC and BIMSTEC is seen as conducive and helpful in the process of regional integration.

Trade, Investments and Development Cooperation

The most visible and tangible gain of the LEP has been in the economic sector covering trade, investments and development. Detailed figures of trade and investment between India and the Asia-Pacific region are appended in the annexures. After more than a decade of the initiative, India's Prime Minister Dr Manmohan Singh who was a part of the LEP initiative said while addressing the 5th India–ASEAN Summit in January 2007 (Cebu, Philippines):

> The results of India's 'Look east' policy are also amply demonstrated in our growing economic interaction with the region. India's trade with ASEAN has risen from US$2.4 billion in 1990,

[75] For a discussion on the formation of EAS and India's membership in it, see S. D. Muni, 'East Asia Summit and India', *ISAS Working Paper No. 13*, October 2006.

> to US$23 billion in 2005. Our trade with the countries of the East Asia Summit has similarly risen from the US$8 billion in 1990 to US$67.8 billion in 2005. This accounts for nearly 30 percent of our external trade.

India's trade with the region registered the fastest growth. According to Prabir De, India's merchandise trade with the world grew at the compound average growth rate of 18.3 per cent between 2000 and 2009, but during the same period, it showed an increase of 21.6 per cent between India and ASEAN.[76] For the past 20 years until the end of 2014, India registered a 20 times growth in its trade with ASEAN to reach over US$77 billion, making ASEAN its fourth-largest trading partner. China also emerged as the fastest growing trading partner of India, with Japan and the Republic of Korea registering impressive trade gains as well. On the whole, one-third of India's total global trade today is concentrated in its LEP policy region.

While growing trade ties with the East is a matter of celebration, there is no room for complacency as there is huge potential still to be harnessed. India's trade with the region is still far below that of other major players. As against India's nearly US$70 billion of trade, China accounted for US$350 billion, Japan for US$240 billion, the USA for US$206 billion and even Korea for US$135 billion. Except in 2012, targets set for trade by India and ASEAN have often fallen short in implementation. Enthused by a 30 per cent surge in trade soon after the launching of the LEP, then Minister of Foreign Affairs I. K. Gujral in 1996 hoped the trade target to be increased to US$180–200 billion by 2001, which still remains a far cry.[77] Following the conclusion of the free trade agreement (FTA) between India and ASEAN in 2009, the target for 2012, two decades after the LEP initiative, was set at US$70 billion, but it exceeded to US$74.9 billion, prompting a new target of US$100 billion for 2015 to be reset during the 10th

[76] Prabir De, 'ASEAN-India Connectivity: An Indian Perspective', in *ASEAN-India Connectivity: The Comprehensive Asia Development Plan, Phase II SRIA Research Project Report 2010, No. 7*, eds. Fukunari Kimura and So Umezaki (Jakarta: ERIA, 2011).

[77] Gujral, *A Foreign Policy for India*, 237.

India–ASEAN Summit. India is yet to achieve this target even in 2018, even after three years of renaming (Act East) and re-energizing the policy. India has been having a deficit trade with ASEAN, and this deficit has been growing over the years. It is hoped that as a result of the signing in 2014 of the ASEAN-India Trade in Services Agreement and ASEAN-India Investment Agreement, this deficit may be narrowed and the quantum of trade between India and ASEAN may increase. The levels of India's trade are also uneven with individual ASEAN countries, with Indonesia, Malaysia, Singapore, Thailand and Vietnam being India's bigger trading partners.

Among the factors that account for the shortfall in reaching the trade targets, two stand out for their negative impact: non-tariff barriers and connectivity. The problem of non-tariff barriers is more on India's side, and it concerns procedures and paperwork. Attention is being paid to improving connectivity in all the sectors of air, land and maritime. There are still huge problems of infrastructure within India, particularly in its Northeast region. Problems of infrastructure have started being addressed only for the past few years. Significant progress has been made in air connectivity, and India is now seriously pursuing its efforts to overcome the connectivity barrier in all the sectors.[78]

The trade story is also applicable to investment flows between India and the ASEAN countries. The LEP has helped investment flows to rise significantly between the two sides. Singapore has emerged as the largest ASEAN investor in India. There were more investments from India into ASEAN than from ASEAN into India. According to an assessment:

> In terms of FDI inflows, India–ASEAN region has significantly outpaced many other regions in the world. ASEAN drew more FDI than China for the second straight year in 2014....
>
> In the recent past investment flows have also expanded with US$25 billion FDI equity flowing into India from ASEAN countries and

[78] 'ASEAN-India Air Connectivity Report', *Research and Information System*, 2016, http://aic.ris.org.in/asean-india-air-connectivity-report-aic-ris-new-delhi-2016 accessed 16 August 2018.

> US$31 billion in outflows from India to ASEAN over the last seven years between the period of April 2007 to March 2014. It is expected that the increased economic relevance and dynamism of the ASEAN–India partnership will boost the bilateral FDI flows.[79]

But for this to happen, India will need to

> [E]nhance its business environment by reducing corruption and strengthening the rule of law, faster clearances for projects, develop infrastructure, boost manufacturing, simplify the taxation system, ease FDI regulations and increase awareness about its emerging cities, flexibility in Public–Private Partnership (PPP) contracts through negotiations, among others.[80]

Besides trade and investments, India's development cooperation with the countries of the Asia-Pacific region also covers a variety of other sectors. These include monetary and financial cooperation, energy, education, and science and technology. The scope of cooperation has, however, remained limited so far. In the field of energy, discussions have been focussed on renewable energy only. In the field of science and technology, India has provided considerable support in capacity building to the CLMV countries in the areas of information technology, agriculture and space. India has a great deal to offer to the ASEAN countries in the field of space technology, but procedural difficulties, competition from other providers and political considerations have not allowed matters to proceed.

Defence and Security

India's institutional integration with the region and its membership of some of the key ASEAN forums such as the ARF and ADMM+ provided impetus for India's greater cooperation with the countries of the region in defence and security matters. It has been noted earlier that the beginning of the LEP enabled India to get its eastern regional

[79] ASEAN-India Centre and Research and Information System, *ASEAN–India Development and Cooperation Report 2015* (New Delhi: Routledge, 2016), xxxiii.

[80] Ibid., xxvi.

neighbours shed off their ill-founded suspicions and anxieties about India's maritime ambitions. It may be recalled here that the countries of the Southeast Asian region made only token objections to India's nuclear explosion in May 1998, ignoring strong initial reactions of the USA, Japan, and Australia. The latter countries had also soon come to accept India as a de-facto nuclear weapon state. The first major concrete evidence of India's positive role in regional security came in April 2002 when India escorted US ships in the Malacca Strait to ward off threats from sea piracy. The USA was looking for protection to its important cargos in the aftermath of the 9/11 attacks, and no other country in the region was willing or equipped to come forward.[81] India's credibility as a security partner in the region was further enhanced in December 2004 with its collaboration with Japan, the USA and Australia and significant contribution in providing post-tsunami relief to the countries of the region, particularly Indonesia and Sri Lanka.

In 2002, LEP's second phase had been officially announced, as already noted, by then Minister of Foreign Affairs Yashwant Sinha. That reflected India's growing capabilities and self-confidence to extend its outreach in the region for cooperation in defence and security domains. Gradually that came to be known as India's role as a security provider in the region. Early indications were evident in India's officially declared maritime security doctrine, first announced in 2004, and revised and upgraded in 2007 and 2009 respectively.[82] In his foreword to the 2007 document, titled *Freedom to Use the Seas: India's Maritime Military Strategy*, the then Navy Chief Admiral Sureesh Mehta wrote:

> Our strategy recognises that the sea lines of communication passing through our region are critical for our economic growth and to the global community. Smaller nations in our neighbourhood

[81] Amit Baruah, 'Only "Escort Duties" in Malacca Strait', *The Hindu*, 23 April 2002.

[82] *Indian Maritime Doctrine*, Indian Navy, National Strategic Publication 1.1, www.indiannavy.nic.in/sites/default/files/India-Maritime-Doctrine-2009-Updated-12Feb16.pdf, accessed 18 August 2018.

> as well as nations depend(ent) on the waters of the Indian Ocean for their trade and energy supplies have come to expect that the Indian navy will ensure a measure of stability and tranquillity in the waters around our shores.[83]

Such resolve prompted other nations like the USA to look towards India as a new security provider in the Indian Ocean Region. In his address to the Shangri La Dialogue in Singapore on 30 May 2009, the then US Secretary of Defence, Robert Gates said: 'In coming years, we look to India to be a partner and net provider of security in the Indian Ocean and beyond'. India's former Minister of Defence A. K. Antony endorsed this expectation when on 12 October 2011, addressing Indian navy's top brass, he said that India would provide 'unstinted support for their security and economic prosperity to its maritime neighbours because Indian navy has been mandated to be a net security provider to island nations in the Indian Ocean Region'. Reiterating India's role as a 'security provider', the then Prime Minister Dr Manmohan Singh while laying down the foundation stone of Indian National Defence University on 23 May 2013 also said:

> India's security has never been stronger than it is today and our international relationships have never been more conducive to our national development efforts. Our engagement in our immediate neighbourhood has increased. We have deepened political, economic and strategic relations in the Asia-Pacific, Indian Ocean and West Asian regions. Our relations with all major powers have become stronger and more productive. We are also particularly participating in key global and regional forums ranging from Group of 20 to the East Asia Summit and the ASEAN groupings.
>
> … We have also sought to assume our responsibility for stability in the Indian Ocean Region. We are well positioned, therefore, to become a net provider of security in our immediate region and beyond.

India's role of providing security under the LEP focused on the areas of building capabilities, providing military support in terms of

[83] Ibid.

assistance and supply of equipment, and undertaking tasks through direct deployment for ensuring safety and security of the region, including the situations of disaster relief. Supply of weapons and military equipment has not come to India easily, partly because of its traditional principled stand to keep away from anything that leads to wars and conflicts, and partly due to limitations on India's defence production which hardly meets India's own requirements. Gradually, however, in response to the changing strategic context of the region and rising expectations from India, this has been changing. Over the years, India's defence cooperation has been strengthened, particularly with countries such as Vietnam, Singapore, Malaysia and Indonesia in ASEAN and with the USA, Japan, South Korea and Australia in the broader Asia-Pacific region.[84] A visible sign of India's growing cooperation in the defence and security affairs of the region has been in its fast upgrading participation in naval and military exercises with all these countries.[85] Some of these exercises have been listed as an annexure in this study.

In its defence and security cooperation under the LEP, India has been driven by two of its concerns for countering terrorism and keeping the region stable and free for navigation. There is a broad consensus between India and all the countries of the region that freedom of navigation in the Indo-Pacific region must be ensured at every cost. On specifics of terrorism, there may be differing perspectives and priorities between India and the countries of the region, but everyone agrees that radicalization and terrorist violence have to be fought resolutely. Towards its role in ensuring maritime security of the region, India has sought since 2001 to set up and strengthen a tri-service (army, navy and air force) command at the Andaman and

[84] For detailed analysis of India's role as a security provider and as a defence and security partner in the region, see S. D. Muni and Vivek Chadha, eds., *Asian Strategic Review 2015: India As A Security Provider* (New Delhi: Pentagon Press, New Delhi, 2015). Specially see the section on 'Indo-Pacific' in pages 145–286.

[85] Ibid., India's naval exercises with the ASEAN countries has been tabulated by Jagannath Panda in his chapter in East Asia on page 219. For a broader view of India's defence cooperation with various countries from 2002–2003 to 2013–2014, see Annexures from pages 359 to 392.

Nicobar Islands. Progress on this has been slow, but efforts are being pursued seriously.[86] Besides terrorism and maritime security, India has also taken keen interest in ASEAN's efforts at evolving a viable strategic architecture for the region. Without much regret for the absence of collective arrangements or institutions for security in Asia, India's then National Security Adviser Shivshankar Menon said at the Shangri La dialogue in Singapore on June 2010 that 'Asia is free to build the open, inclusive, plural, and flexible architecture required to deal with these new transnational dimensions of security … (where) ASEAN must remain the bedrock…'.

Summing Up

The foregoing discussion clearly underlines that the LEP succeeded in streamlining and restructuring India's engagement with its eastern extended neighbours that was hitherto done ad hoc. This policy had deep and strong roots and it unfolded gradually, moving from economic to strategic to people-to-people levels. From being a complete outcast in the strategic sense from the region, this policy rehabilitated India as a major player that had been predicted almost half a century ago by its first prime minister, Nehru. Both India and the region gained considerably as a result of this policy, although the policy failed to fulfil all its targets, and the full potential of their (India and the Indo-Pacific region) engagement remains to be harnessed.

[86] Anit Mukherjee, 'The Unsinkable Aircraft Career: The Andaman and Nicobar Command', in *India's Naval Strategy and Asian Security*, eds. Anit Mukherjee and C. Raja Mohan (New Delhi: Routledge, 2015). Also see Jeff M. Smith, 'Andaman and Nicobar Islands: India's Strategic Outpost', *The Diplomat*, 18 March 2014, https://the diplomat.com/2014/03/Andaman-and-nicobar-islands-indias-strategic-outpost/, accessed 16 August 2018.

CHAPTER 6

Act East Policy (2014–)

How Different, How Successful?

Introduction

The latest (seventh) wave of India's eastward engagement has been officially identified as the Act East Policy (AEP). The official renaming of the policy was done by Prime Minister of India Narendra Modi who assumed office in May 2014 after the BJP-led NDA coalition's convincing victory in the parliamentary elections. Since 2014, India's engagement with the countries of Southeast Asia, Northeast Asia, Mongolia, Australia, New Zealand, PIC, and regional and subregional organizations thereof have been included within the ambit of the AEP. Sometimes, deepening engagement with Bangladesh is also considered a part of this policy.[1] The emerging concept of Indo-Pacific has further widened the canvas of the AEP, with the USA and Japan actively supporting and encouraging India to play a larger and more active role as a powerful stakeholder in the region.

[1] 'Act East Policy Starts with Bangladesh: PM Modi', *Business Standard*, 19 December 2014, http://www.business-standard.com/article/news-ani/act-east-policy-starts-with-bangladesh-pm-modi-114121900599_1.html, accessed 16 August 2018.

Act East Policy

Prime Minister Modi made the formal announcement of the shift from the 'LEP' to 'AEP' on 12 November 2014 in his opening remarks at the India–ASEAN Summit in Myanmar's capital Nay Pyi Taw. He said: 'An era of economic development, industrialization and trade has begun in India. India's "Look East Policy" has become "Act East Policy"'. This was repeated the next day on 13 November, while addressing the EAS, when Modi said, 'Since entering office six months ago, my government has moved with a great sense of priority and speed to turn our "Look East Policy" into "Act East Policy". The EAS is an important pillar of this policy'.

The first official indication of the change in policy and its nomenclature came about three months before the prime minister's announcement. While addressing the Indian community in Hanoi (Vietnam), the Minister of External Affairs Mrs Sushma Swaraj said: 'Now it is time not just to look east but act. Under the (Narendra) Modi government, we will have an Act East Policy'.[2] Elaborating somewhat on Mrs Swaraj's idea of 'Act East', the official spokesman of the MEA, Syed Akbaruddin, said that Swaraj's visit to Vietnam was a part of 'Act East'. 'This Act East is in action. We began with focus on Neighbourhood and this has now moved on with focus on ASEAN.... Our Prime Minister is going to Japan. So, it further moves eastwards'.[3] Mrs Swaraj also had a brainstorming session with 15 of India's heads of diplomatic missions in the region where she asked them to be 'more dynamic and proactive' in strengthening ties with the East Asian countries. Soon after Mrs Swaraj's indication on the

[2] No authentic version of Mrs Swaraj's address to the Indian Community in Hanoi on 24 August 2014 is available from the MEA website. Reports of this meeting were available only in the newspapers. See, for instance, 'Time for Act East Policy and Not Just Look East: Swaraj', *Business Standard*, 24 August 2014, https://www.business-standard.com/article/pti-stories/time-for-act-east-policy-and-not-just-look-east-swaraj-114082400624_1.html, accessed 16 August 2018.

[3] 'Sushma Swaraj Tells Indian Envoys to Act East and Not Just Look East', *Economic Times*, 26 August 2014, economictimes.indiatimes.com/articleshow/40907671.cms?utm_source=contentofinterest&utm_medium=text&utm_campaign=cppst, accessed 16 August 2018.

Act East in Vietnam, the expression found a mention in the Indo-US joint statement issued on the occasion of Prime Minister Modi's visit to the USA. This was before Modi made a formal announcement of the name change from LEP to the AEP in Myanmar in November 2014. The US–India joint statement of 30 September 2014 said:

> Noting India's 'Act East' policy and the United States' rebalance to Asia, the leaders committed to work more closely with other Asia-Pacific countries through consultations, dialogues, and joint exercises. They underlined the importance of their trilateral dialogue with Japan and decided to explore holding this dialogue among their Foreign Ministers.[4]

Since 2014, the AEP has been projected as India's flagship policy to engage countries of the East, with a definite objective to move India's eastward engagement to the next level by making it wider, more multidimensional and action-oriented. Both the Prime Minister of India and his foreign minister have been emphasizing on widening the scope of India's eastward engagement by reaching out to all the countries of the region, beyond ASEAN, in their speeches on the AEP. The MEA, explaining the crux of this policy in its annual report for 2014–2015, noted:

> Our enhanced Look East Policy/Act East built upon what was enunciated in the early nineties as an economic initiative for Association of South East Asian Nations (ASEAN). It has acquired political, strategic and cultural dimensions and now extends beyond the ASEAN. It placed additional priority on security, connectivity and regional integration. India, as a major engine of growth in the regional and global economy, sought to leverage the opportunities for peace, prosperity and stability in the region. Our enhanced Look East Policy put a deep imprint in the region and beyond,

[4] The complete text of the US–India joint statement is available via the White House website, http://www.whitehouse.gov/the-press-office/2014/09/30/us-india-joint-statement, accessed 16 August 2018.

> complemented the regional approach of several partners and emerged as an integral component of our strategic agenda.[5]

Further elaborating on the basic features of the AEP, the MOS for External Affairs Gen. V. K. Singh, answering a parliamentary question on 23 December 2015, said:

> India's Act East Policy focuses on the extended neighbourhood in the Asia-Pacific region. The policy which was originally conceived as an economic initiative, has gained political, strategic and cultural dimensions including establishment of institutional mechanisms for dialogue and cooperation. India has upgraded its relations to strategic partnership with Indonesia, Vietnam, Malaysia, Japan, Republic of Korea (ROK), Australia, Singapore and Association of Southeast Asian Nations (ASEAN) and forged close ties with all countries in the Asia-Pacific region....
>
> The Objective of 'Act East Policy' is to promote economic cooperation, cultural ties and develop strategic relationship with the countries in the Asia-Pacific region through continuous engagement at bilateral and multilateral levels, thereby providing enhanced connectivity to the States of North Eastern Region, including Arunachal Pradesh, with other countries in our neighbourhood....
>
> The ASEAN–India Plan of Action for the period 2016–20 has been adopted in August 2015 which identifies concrete initiatives and areas of cooperation along three pillars of political-security, economic and socio-cultural. India continues with stepped up efforts to forge closer partnership with concerned regional and multilateral organisations such as ASEAN, ARF, EAS, BIMSTEC, ACD, MCG and IORA. On the civilisational front, Buddhist and Hindu links could be energised to develop new contacts and connectivity between people.[6]

[5] For the complete text of India's engagement with Southeast Asia in 2014–2015, see MEA's *Annual Report 2014–15*, page vi.

[6] 'Act East Policy', Press Information Bureau, Government of India, Ministry of External Affairs, 23 December 2015, http://pub.nic.in/newsite/PrintRelease.aspx?relid=133837, accessed 16 March 2018.

Thus, broadly, the AEP laid emphasis on four of its characteristic aspects:

1. Focused on integrating the NER with its neighbouring countries.
2. Go beyond ASEAN to reach out to other countries of the Indo-Pacific region, including through the regional and multilateral organizations.
3. Also, go beyond economic and commercial engagements to strengthen political and strategic/security cooperation.
4. Thrust on people-to-people connectivity, including through civilizational links.

A close, critical and comparative look at all these four aspects suggests that substantially there was not much new in the AEP from the LEP. There is more continuity than change, and the change is more on the quantitative side than qualitative one. Underlining the continuity from LEP to AEP, MOS for External Affairs Gen. V. K. Singh in another answer to the parliamentary question said: 'India's Look East Policy (LEP) has been a major pillar of our foreign policy since the early 1990s, in the second half of 2014, LEP was upgraded to Act East Policy (AEP)'.[7] As discussed in the previous chapter, the initial LEP move included Myanmar, where security of India's NER was a matter of primary concern. It is true that the development of the NER did not constitute the priority of the LEP initially, but gradually it made its place in the policy structure. It was as early as in October 1996 that the central government placed a special emphasis on the development of the NER. On the recommendation of the Planning Commission, a separate Department of the Development of the North East Region (DoNER) was created in 2001. This ministry was upgraded in 2004, and special funds were allocated to develop infrastructure of the region to link the region with its neighbouring countries, particularly Myanmar and Bangladesh. This brought the focus on the NER's connectivity with the ASEAN countries. The LEP from its early years had looked at the

[7] 'Lok Sabha, Unstarred Question No. 3121, Answered by Gen. V. K. Singh, the Minister of State in the Ministry of External Affairs on 16.03.2016', *Ministry of External Affairs*, 16 March 2016, http://mea.gov.in/lok-sabha.htm?dtl/26554/QUESTION_NO_3121_LOOK_EAST_AND_ACT_EAST_POLICY, accessed 16 August 2018.

region in its wider context while focusing on links with ASEAN. It has been noted in the previous chapter that India never closed its eyes on the countries of the region beyond ASEAN, especially China, Japan, South Korea and Australia. Even Fiji and the Pacific Islands were included in the canvass of India's engagements with the Indo-Pacific region. Nor were strategic and security issues ignored while emphasizing trade, investments and civilizational/cultural links. Narasimha Rao's Singapore Lecture in 1994 and the announcement of the 'second phase' of the LEP by the then Minister of External Affairs of India Yashwant Sinha in 2002 may be recalled here. This so-called second phase had widened the LEP to cover countries other than the ASEAN members in the region and issues other than economic to include security and strategic engagement, as discussed in the previous chapter.

The connectivity had also drawn attention to people-to-people relations, and economic dimensions of tourism were clearly highlighted under the LEP. No official statement on the LEP neglected the deep cultural and historical ties existing between India and its eastern extended neighbours. However, India was cautious in not highlighting the religious dimension. Under the AEP, the significance of Buddhist and Hindu linkages with the Asia-Pacific region is being highlighted, as also underlined in Gen. V. K. Singh's statement in Parliament given earlier. This raises some concern because of the omission of Islam that is an integral part of India's composite culture. It is true that unlike Hinduism and Buddhism, Islam did not originate from India. However, Islam got fully absorbed in India, and its character was enriched through the Islamic ideological schools of Deobandi and Berailvi, developed in undivided India to shape and explain the tenants of Islam. Indian contribution to soften Islam through the reinforcement of its Sufi traditions in India even today clearly distinguishes the Indo-Pacific Islam from the Wahabi-dominated Arabic Islam. The omission of Islam may in fact negatively affect India's engagement with the Islamic countries of the Indo-Pacific region such as Indonesia, Malaysia and Brunei. Muslim communities in the Philippines, Myanmar, Thailand and Singapore may also be marking out religious differentiation in India's approach. Modi's 2018 visits to the Istiqlal Mosque in Indonesia, Chulia Mosque (Singapore, 2018), Sheikh Zayed Mosque (Abu Dhabi) and Sultan Qaboos Mosque (Muscat) seem to be making an attempt to rectifying this flaw.

Renaming of the LEP

In view of the foregoing discussion of a comparison between AEP and LEP, it would be misleading to project or understand the AEP as a brand new policy. Since 2014, the government has been projecting AEP as a fine blend of India's diplomatic outreach, economic and trade partnerships, and strategic collaboration with the countries of Southeast Asia and the wider Indo-Pacific region. While at times, some in the government (primarily to cater to the domestic electoral politics) have claimed the AEP as a completely new initiative, the critics have labelled it as just a 'repackaged' form of the LEP which does not have much new to offer. It has also been argued that different phases of India's LEP and AEP are nothing but rebranding of India's engagement with Southeast Asia. While it is true that there have been elements of natural continuity in India's eastward engagement, it would be wrong to say that nothing fundamentally changed through the transition from Look East to Act East.

The question that arises here is that the direction and basic structure of the two policies being similar, what were the incentives or compulsions to change the name? Was it not possible to do under LEP what can be done under AEP? To begin with, there was international prodding to revisit the LEP for making it more active and effective. While the Modi government often claims to have initiated the AEP, interestingly, the first person to call upon India to 'Act East' rather than just 'Look East' was the then American President Barak Obama as has been noted in the first chapter. Recall his speech to the joint session of the Indian Parliament in November 2010, where he called upon India to not just 'Look East' but 'engage East'. President Obama said:

> India and the United States can partner in Asia. Today, the United States is once again playing a leadership role in Asia—strengthening old alliances; deepening relationships, as we are doing with China; and we're reengaging with regional organizations like ASEAN and joining the East Asia Summit—organizations in which India is also a partner. Like your neighbors in Southeast Asia, we want India not only to 'look East', we want India to 'engage East'—because it will increase the security and prosperity of all our nations.

Illustrating his desire by referring to the situation in Myanmar, Obama added:

> No one nation has a monopoly on wisdom, and no nation should ever try to impose its values on another. But when peaceful democratic movements are suppressed—as in Burma—then the democracies of the world cannot remain silent. For it is unacceptable to gun down peaceful protestors and incarcerate political prisoners decade after decade. It is unacceptable to hold the aspirations of an entire people hostage to the greed and paranoia of a bankrupt regime. It is unacceptable to steal an election, as the regime in Burma has done again for all the world to see....
>
> Faced with such gross violations of human rights, it is the responsibility of the international community—especially leaders like the United States and India—to condemn it. If I can be frank, in international fora, India has often avoided these issues. But speaking up for those who cannot do so for themselves is not interfering in the affairs of other countries. It's not violating the rights of sovereign nations. It's staying true to our democratic principles.[8]

Obama's desire for India to be more active in its LEP was reiterated subsequently by the then US Secretary of State Hillary Clinton. In her speech at the Anna Centenary Library in Chennai (India) in July 2011, Ms Clinton said:

> India's leadership will help to shape positively the future of the Asia Pacific. That's why the United States supports India's Look East policy, and we encourage India not just to look East, but to engage East and act East as well, because after all, India, like the United States, where we look to the Atlantic and to the Pacific, also looks both east and west. And its leadership in South and Central Asia is critically important.[9]

[8] The complete text of former United States President Barack Obama's Speech in the Indian Parliament on 8 November 2010 is available via the White House Website, https://obamawhitehouse.archives.gov/the-press-office/2010/11/08/remarks-president-joint-session-indian-parliament-new-delhi-india, accessed 16 August 2018.

[9] The complete text of former United States Secretary of State Hillary Rodham Clinton at Anna Centenary Library, Chennai, India, on 20 July 2011 is

Mrs Sushma Swaraj, then as the leader of BJP-led opposition in the Indian parliament claimed later that she had prompted Mrs Clinton on the 'Act East' aspect of LEP. That is why, perhaps, she was also the first in the Modi government to reiterate it. During a lecture at the Institute of South Asian Studies, Singapore, on 14 September 2011, she had said:

> I had the occasion to engage with US Secretary of State Mrs. Hillary Clinton during her visit to my country in June this year. During our extensive discussions at my residence, we talked about India's emerging role in the Asia and the focus naturally turned towards East and South East Asia. Emphasizing that it was the Bharatiya Janata Party that reshaped India's foreign policy priorities during its rule under the leadership of Shri Atal Bihari Vajpayee, I said the time had now come not only to 'Look East' but 'Act East'. It was most heartening to find the US Secretary of State incorporate many of the points we discussed in the course of her public lecture in Chennai a couple of days later. In fact, Mrs. Clinton articulated the issues so succinctly and powerfully that I believe it merits to be recalled in the context of today's lecture.[10]

It may be interesting to note that as suggested in the US–India Joint Statement of 30 September 2014, the USA had started perceiving the AEP as being dovetailed to its rebalance strategy in the Indo-Pacific region. Indian leaders have avoided making this linkage directly, though at one stage, in January 2015 addressing the India–US Business Summit, Modi said, 'when I look towards the East, I see the western shores of the United States'.[11] It may also be underlined here that the

---

available via the US Department of State website, https://2009–2017.state.gov/secretary/20092013clinton/rm/2011/07/168840.htm, accessed 16 August 2018.

[10] The complete text of then Leader of Opposition in Lok Sabha Sushma Swaraj's Speech at Institute of South Asian Studies, Singapore on 14 September 2011 is available via the BJP website, http://www.bjp.org/images/pdf/speech_14_2011_sushmaji.pdf, accessed 16 August 2018.

[11] The complete text of remarks by Indian Prime Minister Narendra Modi at the India–US Business Summit on 26 January 2015 is available via the Press Information Bureau website, http://pib.nic.in/newsite/PrintRelease.aspx?relid=114960, accessed 16 August 2018.

AEP has gained momentum with the growing strategic proximity between India and the USA under Modi's foreign policy.

The US impatience with the LEP was shared somewhat by other countries of the Indo-Pacific region. We have discussed in the previous chapter that the LEP did not meet its trade and investment targets. There was also serious delivery deficit on India's part, particularly on the connectivity projects. There was a general perception in the region that India was falling short on the expectations of the ASEAN and other regional countries regarding its role.[12] There was, therefore, a need to 'repackage' the LEP to reassure regional countries that India was serious and committed to playing a constructive and meaningful role. The AEP was a repackaging of the LEP in this respect, and a desirable one for that matter. Prime Minister Modi in his addresses to the India–ASEAN Summit as also the EAS summit on 12 and 13 November 2014, respectively tried to assure that he would seek to improve India's role and performance in the various areas of engagement. Through the AEP, the Government of India has 'expanded the scope and focus of Look East after sensing that Phase I and Phase II of the "Look East Policy" could not achieve their fullest potential, despite being success stories'.[13]

The last but not the least incentive for changing the name and 'repackaging' the LEP into the AEP came from the new government's strong desire to establish its ownership of the policy. It has been noted earlier that on assuming the office, Prime Minister Modi gave his new approach towards the immediate neighbours a new name, 'the neighbourhood first', and launched it with a great fanfare by inviting all the heads of the States/governments of the neighbouring countries to his swearing-in ceremony. It has been a constant refrain of the prime minister to distinguish his approach with that of his preceding

[12] Authors witnessed this in various meetings, conferences and seminars in the region from regional scholars and policymakers who wanted India to do more.

[13] Rahul Mishra, 'From Look East to Act East: Transitions in India's Eastward Engagement', *The ASAN Forum,* 1 December 2014, http://www.theasanforum.org/from-look-east-to-act-east-transitions-in-indias-eastward-engagement/, accessed 16 August 2018.

Congress/United Progressive Alliance (UPA) regimes. It has been argued by an analyst that

> [R]hetoric regarding the LEP is aspirational rather than a reflection of the reality of India's post-Cold War engagement with Southeast Asia. In this context, the launch of each phase often serves as a rebranding exercise as a new government seeks to differentiate its foreign policy approach from that of its predecessor.[14]

The marking of the second phase of the LEP during the earlier BJP-led government in 2002 may also be recalled here. Mrs Swaraj in her first statement in Vietnam in August 2014 almost blacked out the contribution made by the Narasimha Rao and succeeding governments in evolving and nursing the LEP.

The repackaging and rebranding of the LEP by the new government could also be justified on the basis of a radical transformation in the domestic as well as external geostrategic context in which the LEP was born during the early 1990s. Then, the Indian economy was in a crisis and the newly elected government was a minority government, not sure of its survival. Externally, it was surrounded by suspicion and alienation as the legacy of the Cold War period in the Indo-Pacific region and was groping for a new foreign policy framework on account of the collapse of the former Soviet Union. In contrast to this, India in 2014 was a reasonably strong economy with more than 6 per cent growth rate and around 1.5 per cent share in global trade, was already a signatory to more than a dozen multilateral FTAs and was actively negotiating one of the biggest mega trade blocks of Asia: the Regional Comprehensive Economic Partnership (RCEP). The domestic political situation of the country is stable with no apprehension of major internal upheavals unlike the troubled years of the early 1990s. On foreign policy domain, contrary to the desperation to reach out to new friends in view of loss of a superpower friend, this time around, the biggest power in the world—the USA itself—has been

[14] Chietigj Bajpaee, 'Dephasing India's Look East/Act East Policy', *Contemporary Southeast Asia* 39, no. 2 (August 2017): 348–372.

persuading India to *Act East.* For a country, which has religiously and rigorously maintained its independence and autonomy in foreign policymaking, it sounds odd that it is persuaded by another country to get more active. However, that coaxing is in India's own interests to widen and deepen relations with countries of the East, which are already very receptive of India. In case of the LEP, the first decade of the policy, until India signed the TAC and ASEAN–India Summit level dialogue started, was almost lost in socializing with ASEAN. This is no longer the case today.

Changing the name of a policy is not a major factor, but there is no evidence that a systematic discussion in India's policy portals had taken place in this regard. The implications of the name change in terms of planning and pursuing policy options were neither identified not assessed beforehand.[15] There was a general and a strong feeling in the new government that India will have to be more active and effective in the Indo-Pacific region following China's rise and assertion. But should it be done with a name change was neither felt compelling, nor made clear. That is why there was some confusion initially. It was seen as 'enhanced' LEP that was more 'proactive and pragmatic'. The annual report of the MEA for 2014–2015 says:

> The expansion and deepening of our engagement in our extended neighbourhood, particularly, after the new Government assumed office in 2014, led to the enhanced Look East Policy, acquiring a new dimension as 'Act East'. This new phase in our relations is characterized by a more pro-active and pragmatic approach to Foreign Policy with emphasis on concrete forms of cooperation in political, economic and cultural spheres and timelines for implementation.[16]

[15] Author's (S. D. Muni's) interviews with former senior officials of the MEA, Government of India. March 2018, in New Delhi and Bhubaneswar, India.

[16] For the complete text of India's engagement with Southeast Asia in 2014–2015, see MEA's *Annual Report 2014–15.*

Unfolding of the AEP

The AEP, being in its fourth year, is passing through its initial stages of evolution. Five of its policy directions that have emerged as its main thrust areas may be identified as follows:

1. Active and intensive political engagement with the region.
2. Integration of the policy with India's development and growth with focus on the integration of NER with its extended neighbourhood.
3. Sharp focus on security and defence cooperation.
4. Persistence of economic agenda.
5. Use of soft power.

Let us look at them in some detail.

Active and Intensive Political Engagement

There is wider recognition that the AEP is being pursued with considerable confidence and dynamism of the leadership. Prime Minister Modi's personal dynamism in this respect was backed by the absolute majority of his government in the parliament and by India's enhanced economic and strategic capabilities. The overall foreign policy framework has been redefined to reflect this confidence and dynamism. Soon after assuming office, Modi asked his senior diplomats to 'help India position itself in a leading role rather than just a balancing force'. Explaining this, former Foreign Secretary S. Jaishankar delivering Fullerton Lecture under the banner of the Singapore Chapter of IISS said on 20 July 2015: 'The transition in India is of great self-confidence. Its foreign policy dimension is to aspire to be a leading power, rather than just a balancing power. Consequently, there is also willingness to shoulder greater global responsibilities'.[17] The dynamism in India's foreign policy and diplomacy has also been taken

[17] The complete text of the IISS Fullerton Lecture by former Indian Foreign Secretary Dr S. Jaishankar in Singapore on 20 July 2015 available via the MEA's website, http://www.mea.gov.in/Speeches-Statements.htm?dtl/25493/iiss+fullerton+lecture+by+dr+s+jaishankar+foreign+secretary+in+singapore, accessed 16 August 2018.

note of by Chinese observers. The vice president of China's Institute of International Studies complimented India's diplomacy for being 'vibrant and assertive', and acknowledged that 'India's risk-taking ability has been on the rise under Modi'.[18]

One of the most convincing evidence of India's overall foreign policy activism, especially with regard to the Indo-Pacific region, has been the exchange of visits. Since his coming to power, Prime Minister Modi has travelled to 12 countries of the region, including eight of the ten ASEAN members, and the countries where he has not been able to go have been covered by the president, vice president and the external affairs minister. Modi himself has made nearly 25 visits to the region in a span of less than four years. Some of the countries such as the USA, China, Japan and Myanmar have been visited twice or more.[19] In some cases, Prime Minister Modi's visits broke the long absence of prime ministerial visit from India. For instance, his visit to Australia in November 2014 was after 22 years and to Fiji in May 2015 was after 33 years of the previous visit by an Indian prime minister to these countries. Some of these visits have been listed in Annexure A at the end of this study. Through these visits, Prime Minister Modi and other Indian leaders have been able to establish personal rapport with their respective regional counterparts. Commenting on some of Modi's visits, an Indian journalist wrote: 'Modi's visits to Japan, Australia and the US were filled with hype, humour and hyperactivity. The prime minister rarely missed a chance to emphasise his personal contacts with world leaders and his fierce ambitions to make India a global power'.[20]

[18] 'India's Risk-Taking Ability is on the Rise under Modi, Says China', *Economic Times*, 31 January 2018, available at https//economictimes.indiatimes.com/articleshow/62722930.cms?utm_source=contentofinterest&utm_medium=text&utm_campaign=cppst, accessed 16 August 2018.

[19] The USA is included here with the Asia-Pacific countries because of the USA's importance in India's engagement with this region. The affairs of this region have always formed a part of the core of discussions at the summit levels in contrast to other great extra-regional powers like Russia and the European countries.

[20] Subir Bhaumik, 'Narendra Modi's International Balancing Act', *Aljazeera*, 12 February 2015, available at https://www.aljazeera.com/indepth/features/2015/02/

The regional leaders have also reciprocated warmly and enthusiastically. Almost all the regional heads of the governments and/or States have visited India during the period of the AEP. All the ASEAN leaders were invited to India to be special guests on the Republic Day celebrations on 26 January 2018. This also became the occasion for a Commemorative India–ASEAN Summit to mark 25 years of the establishment of India's dialogue partnership with ASEAN. If we include the visits of the prime ministers, presidents, vice presidents and foreign ministers, the number of regional visits to India will come to nearly 50.

Besides high-level political visits, India has also tried to activate existing institutional mechanisms for regular discussions on issues of mutual interests and to also create new such mechanisms to keep the engagement active. The Indo-Cambodian (Kampuchea) Joint Commission that had not met for the past 10 years was revived through a meeting in New Delhi in July 2016. During the visit of New Zealand's Prime Minister John Key to India in 25–26 October 2016, it was agreed to set up an annual ministerial dialogue and also consultations on cyber security issues. An eminent persons group was set up to provide necessary momentum to bilateral relations. This group submitted its report in December 2016. An important development in this respect was the establishment of the Forum for India–Pacific Islands Cooperation (FIPIC) with the 14 Pacific Islands that form a Pacific community. Prime Minister Modi addressed the first meeting of this forum during his visit to Fiji in November 2014. The second meeting of this forum was held on 21 August 2015 in Jaipur. Indian foreign minister continued to participate in the think tanks networks between India and the Southeast Asian countries. A full-fledged diplomatic mission for ASEAN was set up in Jakarta in 2013 with a separate ambassador to coordinate activities. The first foreign-office-level consultation mechanism was established with Mongolia after the prime minister's visit. Task forces, mechanisms and institutional arrangements were also established between law

---

narendra-modi-international-balancing-act-150208044316333.html, accessed 16 August 2018.

enforcing agencies for legal and judicial cooperation, disaster relief institutions, etc., wherever required.[21]

Integration of the Act East Policy with India's Overall Development and the Northeast Region

India's foreign policy under Prime Minister Modi has mandated to link itself closely with India's national development, and the AEP is no exception to this. The annual report of the MEA for 2015–2016 clearly stated that

> Probably the most significant trend during the year was the increased emphasis placed by government in establishing close linkages between our foreign policy and our domestic developmental aspirations. Over the past 12 months, our international outreach has been carefully tailored and directed to create the most propitious climate for domestic growth, including by working towards a regional security environment that allows us to focus on our economic goals.[22]

The development of the NER and its connectivity with the Indo-Pacific region has acquired a special place in the AEP in this respect. In the General Budget of 2015–2016, the Union Finance Minister Arun Jaitley announced that

> [India would set up] manufacturing hubs in CMLV countries, namely, Cambodia, Myanmar, Laos and Vietnam. Presenting the General Budget 2015–16 in the Lok Sabha, the Finance Minister stated that the 'Act East' policy of the Government endeavours to cultivate extensive economic and strategic relations in South-East Asia. In order to catalyse investments from the Indian private sector in this region, a project development company will set-up the

[21] For the complete text of India's engagement with Southeast Asia in 2014–2015, 2015–2016 and 2016–2017, see MEA's annual reports.

[22] For the complete text of India's engagement with Southeast Asia in 2015–2016, see MEA's *Annual Report 2015–16*.

manufacturing hubs in CMLV countries through separate Special Purpose Vehicles (SPVs).[23]

Moreover, India is now inviting countries such as Japan and Singapore to invest in India's Northeastern states. Even in terms of engaging the CLMV countries, India has been doing quite a lot of work to link them with India's Northeast. 'Government of India has approved constituting a Special Purpose Vehicle as a project development fund to help and facilitate investment by Indian business houses/groups in CLMV countries, as part of initiative on the Act East Policy'.[24]

When the LEP was started in 1992, one of the reasons pertaining to the Northeastern states of India was that India was in dire need of curbing insurgency in the region. The support of Myanmar was of key importance at that point. With the beginning of the phase II of LEP, the situation in India's Northeastern states had improved. Initiatives such as Kaladan Multimodal project and the India–Myanmar–Thailand Trilateral Highway were conceptualized and launched at that time. However, the region, which was marred by decades of insurgency, acute neglect and rampant corruption, could not get back on track in such a short time. It would be an exaggeration to state that the level of physical, digital and economic connectivity in the Northeastern states of India is the same as in mainland India. Over the past 25 years, however, the situation has improved, just as the rest of India and the level of economic growth and development of other states have also improved since 1991.

Nevertheless, a lot needed to be done to bring the Northeastern states of India to the level where they could even attempt to link with countries of the ASEAN region.[25] Here, an element of logical fallacy

[23] 'Act East Policy of the Government', *Press Information Bureau, Government of India, Ministry of Finance*, 28 February 2016, available at http://pib.nic.in/newsite/PrintRelease.aspx?relid=116168, accessed 16 August 2018.

[24] For the complete text of India's engagement with Southeast Asia in 2015–2016, see MEA's *Annual Report 2015–16.*

[25] For studies on Look East and NER, see ISAS (Institute of South Asian Studies) reports published over the years.

catches the analysts who wish to compare the LEP with the AEP. The fundamental difference on this count is that Look East is assessed for what it delivered in 25 years, within its limited role in shaping the domestic agenda in the age of coalition governments, whereas Act East is projected on the basis of the promise it makes to develop and integrate the NER.

The thrust in the AEP on the NER has been clear and serious from the very beginning. The pursuance of the AEP so far clearly underlines that the NER is attracting more attention of Delhi than ever before. The ruling party seems to have firmly decided to open the NER both for its development as well as political outreach and consolidation. This has been seen in the overall perspective of India's development, and its linkages with the neighbouring region encompassed by the Indian Ocean. AEP has been a part of this broader perspective, like the concept of SAGAR (Security and Growth for All in the Region),[26] enunciated by Prime Minister Modi in Mauritius on 12 March 2015 and the project of 'Sagarmala' aimed at developing ports along India's western and eastern seaboards to improve connectivity and trade with its eastern and western Indian Ocean neighbours.

The policy debate on linking the NER with the AEP was started when the then President Pranab Mukherjee, while addressing the 47th Conference of Governors, said on 10 February 2015 that 'connectivity of the Northeastern States must be improved by strengthening road and rail network. There is need for progressive policy for industrial investment and promotion in the hilly mountainous States'. It was interesting to note that this statement came from him because in his earlier avatars as India's defence minister, he was not comfortable with the idea of opening up the NER on account of security considerations. At this meeting, the governors of NER asked for a briefing on the AEP which was organized in October 2015. Addressing these governors on 6 October 2015, Minister of External Affairs Mrs Swaraj described the NER as a 'natural partner in India's Act East Policy' and also a 'land bridge to ASEAN', with AEP as 'a means to strengthen the stability, economy and prospects of our Northeast region'. Various

[26] *The Hindu*, 'Mr. Modi's Ocean View', 17 March 2015.

proposals related to border trade, connectivity, people-to-people contacts, cultural exchanges and enhancing capabilities of the NER were discussed at this meeting. This enabled the MOS in the MEA, Gen. V. K. Singh, to say in answer to a parliamentary question:

> The North East of India has been a priority in our Act East Policy (AEP). AEP provides an interface between North East India including the state of Arunachal Pradesh, and the ASEAN region. Various plans at bilateral and regional levels include steady efforts to develop and strengthen connectivity of Northeast with the ASEAN region through trade, culture, people-to-people contacts and physical infrastructure (road, airport, telecommunication, power), etc.[27]

Mrs Swaraj again had an interactive session with the Governors of NER on the eve of the India–ASEAN Commemorative Summit of January 2018 to prepare India's position on this issue. There was no specific mention of NER linkage with ASEAN in the summit's *Delhi Declaration* issued in Delhi on 25 January 2018, but India's commitment to expedite the work to complete the Trilateral (India–Myanmar–Thailand) Highway and extend it to Lao PDR (People's Democratic Republic), Cambodia and Vietnam was reiterated (para 35). The NER has, however, been actively aspiring for connectivity to the neighbouring countries as a precondition to its development. Following on the interactive session with the foreign minister, Mrs Swaraj, the Governor of Assam, Jagdish Mukhi, disclosed that the central government had big plans to make Guwahati, the largest city of Assam, a trading hub for ASEAN and connect it to all the eastern countries by air. He also disclosed that India would soon encourage neighbouring countries to open consulates in Guwahati.[28] The Assam government has also taken a lead in creating a separate ministry of 'Act

[27] 'Act East Policy', Press Information Bureau, Government of India, Ministry of External Affairs, 23 December 2015, available at http://pib.nic.in/newsite/PrintRelease.aspx?relid=133837, accessed 16 August 2018.

[28] 'Act East: Centre Plans to Link North East India to South East Asia, says Assam Governor Jagdish Mukhi', *The Indian Express*, 26 November 2017, available at https://indianexpress.com/article/india/act-east-centre-plans-to-link-north-east-india-to-south-east-asia-says-assam-governor-jagdish-mukhi-4955476/, accessed 16 August 2018.

East' at the state level to pursue the broader objective of 'connectivity, commerce and culture' in relation to the eastern extended neighbours. The Assam state government has also established a new Centre of Southeast Asian Studies to create academic and intellectual back up for this purpose. The support for Assamese initiatives and aspirations has come from Prime Minister Modi, who, after the India–ASEAN Commemorative Summit, addressing a business conclave in Assam, said 'we created Act East Policy and the Northeast is at the heart of it' and declared that the central government had allocated ₹13 billion for the National Bamboo Mission which will greatly help the Northeast farmers.[29] India has also extended a credit line of US$1 billion for facilitating physical and digital infrastructure connectivity between India and ASEAN, with a focus on the NER.[30]

Progress is being made gradually to build NER's connectivity with rest of India and its neighbours. A definite development that has happened under the Act East is the linking of the Northeastern states with Southeast Asian capitals through direct flights. In the context of railway connectivity, in January 2018, the MOS for Railways Rajen Gohain remarked,

> The capitals of Agartala, Arunachal Pradesh and Assam are already connected by broad gauge railway lines and works for extension of railway lines in Mizoram, Manipur and Nagaland are going on with top priority basis, while in Sikkim and Meghalaya, some land related problems have become a hurdle.[31]

[29] 'Northeast Is at Heart of Act East Policy: PM Modi', *ANI News*, 3 February 2018, available at https://www.aninews.in/news/national/general-news/northeast-is-at-heart-of-act-east-policy-pm-modi201802031447410002/, accessed 16 August 2018.

[30] The complete text of Delhi Declaration is available via the ASEAN website, available at http://asean.org/storage/2018/01/Delhi-Declaration_Adopted-25-Jan-2018.pdf, accessed 16 August 2018.

[31] 'Modi's "Act East" Policy Boosted Infrastructure in Northeast: Union Minister', *Business Standard*, 5 January 2018, available at https://www.business-standard.com/article/news-ians/modi-s-act-east-policy-boosted-infrastructure-in-northeast-union-minister-118010501072_1.html, accessed 16 August 2018.

He further announced that 'by 2020 all the remaining state capitals would be linked by broad gauge railway line'. On 5 January 2018, Tripura's capital 'was linked with Bengaluru by Humsafar Express, becoming the second city in the northeast to get a newly introduced train, equipped with modern facilities'.[32] In terms of boosting connectivity within the Northeastern states of India, in May 2017, the prime minister inaugurated the Bhupen Hazarika Setu which ensures connectivity between upper Assam and eastern part of Arunachal Pradesh.[33] In response to a parliamentary question asked in the Rajya Sabha, MOS in MEA, M. J. Akbar stated:

> A Line of Credit of US $1 billion has been offered by our Prime Minister at the ASEAN–India Summit for enhancing physical and digital connectivity between India and ASEAN. A flagship ASEAN–India project is the establishment of a Tracking, Telemetry and Data Reception Centre and Data Processing Facility near Ho Chi Minh City in Vietnam. ISRO has already initiated the project.[34]

During the 14th ASEAN–India Summit and the 11th EAS held in Laotian capital Vientiane on 7–8 September 2016, Modi announced the augmentation of the ASEAN–India innovation platform to facilitate commercialization of low-cost technologies, and cooperation in capacity building in solar energy. He also offered the facilities of India's indigenously developed GPS-aided GEO Augmented Navigation (GAGAN) to the ASEAN member states.

[32] Ibid.

[33] 'Lok Sabha Unstarred Question No. 1743 Answered by Gen. V. K. Singh, the Minister of State in the Ministry of External Affairs on 26.07.2017', *Ministry of External Affairs*, 26 July 2017, available at http://www.mea.gov.in/lok-sabha.htm?dtl/28721/QUESTION_NO1743_ACT_EAST_POLICY, accessed 16 August 2018.

[34] 'Rajya Sabha Unstarred Question No. 26 Answered by M. J. Akbar, the Minister of State in the Ministry of External Affairs on 02.02.2017', *Ministry of External Affairs*, 2 February 2017, available at http://www.mea.gov.in/rajya-sabha.htm?dtl/27982/QUESTION+NO26+ACT+EAST+POLICY, accessed 16 August 2018.

Further, within the NER, building up on agenda of establishing land custom stations and border *haats* (markets) along India–Myanmar border, the government has been working on opening up the Moreh Integrated Check Post (ICP) which was conceptualized a decade ago. Among the eight Northeastern states, Manipur has traditionally been considered India's domestic gateway to Southeast Asia (externally, Myanmar has been looked as India's linking bridge to Southeast Asia). Though Arunachal Pradesh (Nampong aka Pangsau pass) and Nagaland (Avangkhu) also offer possibilities for land custom stations, both have not taken off yet. Keeping that in view, both the central government and Manipur's state government have been trying to make the Moreh Land Custom Station a hub of trade between India and Myanmar for several years now. Attempts have also been made to upgrade the Moreh Land Custom Station to an ICP. The Modi government has also been actively supporting the idea and has actively worked on the same. However, the change that has been brought about is that in addition to Moreh, the Modi government opened the Zokhawthar Land Custom Station in Champhai district of Mizoram in March 2015 with the objective to open new vistas of bilateral border trade between India and Myanmar. Churachandpur district in Manipur is also likely to get a land custom station along the Indo-Myanmar border soon.

Opening Mizoram to external trade is definitely an addition made by the Modi government in terms of linking India with Southeast Asia in general and Myanmar in particular. While inaugurating the 60 MW Tuirial hydroelectric power project in December 2017, Modi stated that India will actively work towards developing the Rih-Tiddim road as also to establish several rural haats along the Mizoram–Myanmar border. During his address at the function, Modi stated that 'his government would soon make Mizoram the gateway to Southeast Asian countries'. This is an important development in terms of linking the Northeastern region with the AEP. Having common boundaries with both Myanmar and Bangladesh, a high literacy rate and an English speaking population, Mizoram indeed serves as an anchor to make Act East a success in the Northeastern region.

The challenge of linking the NER with its neighbouring countries, however, is not easy to meet. There are security issues and serious gaps in the intra-NER connectivity. A great deal of work remains to be done on the ground to prepare the NER for being an integral part of AEP.[35] To energize the Northeastern states on AEP, Minister of External Affairs Swaraj also invited a meeting of the chief ministers of the Northeast in May 2018. The focus of discussion was development of infrastructure and facilitating the flow of goods and people across the state boundaries as also between the Northeast states and their eastern neighbours across international border. The chief ministers asked the central government to help their states develop road, rail, air and water ways for such connectivity. They also drew attention towards changing and improving the customs facilities and rules for promoting trade across the borders.[36]

Security and Defence Cooperation

The emphasis on the NER in the AEP was the result of focus on connectivity. Another area of focus in the AEP was on defence and security. The MEA *Annual Report 2014–15* had clearly underlined the priorities in AEP as on 'connectivity, security and regional integration'. It would be stretching the point a bit too far, as is often done rhetorically, that security cooperation with the region started with the launching of the AEP. We have noted in the previous chapter that cooperation in the field of defence and security with its extended eastern neighbours was very much a part of the LEP and even before the LEP was initiated. What the AEP has aimed at is continuing with this cooperation, and deepening and expanding it wherever possible and desirable.

[35] Radhabinod Koijam, 'Act Northeast before Act East', *The Hindu*, 6 July 2016.

[36] For details, see Jayanth Jacob and Kumar Uttam, 'Act East Policy Talks: Sushma Swaraj Calls Meeting of all Northeast CMs', *The Hindustan Times*, 30 April 2018; Prabin Kalita, 'Sushma Swaraj Looks East, Meet CMs of Northeast', *The Times of India*, 5 May 2018; Kangkan Acharyya, 'Sushma Swaraj Meets North East Chief Ministers to Propel Act East Policy Towards Action-oriented Results', *Firstpost*, 4 May 2018; and 'Sushma Swaraj Chairs Meet with Northeast CMs', *The Asian Age*, 5 May 2018.

This has been pursued in various ways. To begin with, India's strategic partnerships have been reinforced and upgraded with the countries of the region. It would be futile to define the parameters or the precise nature of the concept of 'strategic partnership' which is used these days in a wide and varied manner. Generally used in corporate terminology and European discourse, it has come to acquire increasing salience in international relations and it covers economic, political, defence and security, technology and people-to-people partnerships.[37] These partnerships, in content, differ from country to country and depend upon the nature of political and strategic understanding between the two or more given partners at any point of time as there is no legal binding. Strategic partnership is not an alliance.

Under the AEP, strategic partnerships have been reinforced with a number of countries, especially Australia, Japan, Vietnam, Indonesia and Singapore. India's strategic partnership with Australia established in 2009 has been upgraded into a Framework for Security Cooperation in 2014. While hosting the Australian Prime Minister Tony Abbot in Delhi in 5 September 2014, Modi said that the two countries have decided to 'increase security and defence cooperation'. During this visit, Australia also agreed to have civil-nuclear cooperation with India, an issue that was under discussion for a long time. This led to the first ever bilateral week-long naval exercise between the two countries in the Bay of Bengal on 11–17 September 2015.

During Prime Minister Modi's visit to Japan on 1 September 2014, the Strategic and Global Partnership between the two countries was elevated to a Special Strategic and Global Partnership. At the joint press briefing with his host Prime Minister Shinzo Abe, Modi explained the elevation by saying:

[37] For some discussion of the concept and its usage, see Razvan-Alexandru Gentimir, 'A Theoretical Approach on the Strategic Partnership between European Union and the Russian Federation', *CES Working Papers* VII, no. 2 (2015): 299–295, available at http://www.ceswp.uaic.ro/articles/CESWP2015_VII2_GEN.pdf, accessed 16 August 2018; 'Strategic Partnership. Really?', *The Hindu*, 13 January 2017; and Arvind Gupta, 'Evaluating India's Strategic Partnerships Using Analytic Hierarchy Process', *IDSA Comment*, 17 September 2011.

It is a strategic partnership because Japan will play an increasingly important role in India's economic transformation and development. Today, Prime Minister Abe has pledged a qualitatively new level of Japanese support and partnership for India's inclusive development, including transformation of India's manufacturing and infrastructure sectors. Today, he has announced his intention to realise 3.5 trillion Yens, or USD 35 billion, or ₹2,10,000 crores, of public and private investment and financing to India over the next five years. I am deeply grateful to him and the people of Japan....

Second, our relations are not confined to economic cooperation, but it is comprehensive and broad-based. We have agreed today to intensify our political dialogue and cooperation. We intend to give a new thrust and direction to our defence cooperation, including collaboration in defence technology and equipment, given our shared interest in peace and stability and maritime security. We have also decided to expand our cooperation in advanced technology, science and technology, people-to-people exchanges, educational exchanges, etc....

It is global because,

We are the two oldest democracies in Asia and among its three biggest economies. Our relationship is not only regional in its framework, but will have a global impact. This is because if the 21st century is an Asian century, then Asia's future direction will shape the destiny of the world.

India and Japan will work for a peaceful and prosperous world drawing upon the message of Lord Buddha and in partnership with all countries of this region and beyond.

We are also intensifying cooperation on non-proliferation, UN reforms, space security, cyber security and in regional forums of this region, such as East Asia Summit.

Equally important, we will forge a partnership for development in other regions and interested countries across the world. The relationship is special because:

> The importance and priority that we will both give this relationship will see a qualitative increase.[38]

It may be useful to keep in mind that India's early initiative during the LEP to build economic and strategic relations with Japan received only a guarded response. The relationship, however, picked up momentum with the warming up of Indo-US relations and the growing assertion of China in the region. Under the AEP, Japan started occupying a lot of attention of Indian policymakers. While it is true that India's LEP actually began with Japan, and it was Japan which played a crucial role in helping India when it was on the brink of economic collapse in the early 1990s, this time the focus was on moving beyond the framework of a donor–recipient relationship and work towards building a multi-dimensional Indo-Japan partnership. The role of the leaders, namely, Shinzo Abe, Dr Manmohan Singh and Narendra Modi, cannot be overlooked in that context. The warmth in the Modi–Abe relationship has definitely benefited the India–Japan partnership. The ministries, media and common people, all look towards each other with greater hope now than in the past. It is with the efforts of Modi and Abe that Japan has finally agreed to supply nuclear technology to India. Japan is also mulling over the possibility of providing India with the amphibious U2 aircrafts. Japan has become the first country to finally launch a bullet train in India (between Ahmedabad and Mumbai), the work on which was inaugurated on 14 September 2017 by Shinzo Abe and Modi during the former's visit to India. Unlike the Look East phase, now Japan is investing in India's infrastructure sector on a massive scale and is willing to be a proactive partner in India's capacity-building efforts, which may be considered an achievement of the AEP. According to the 2015 India–Japan joint statement:

> Japan and India are committed to leverage the synergy between India's 'Act East' policy and Japan's 'Partnership for Quality

[38] The complete text of the remarks by Prime Minister Narendra Modi at the joint press briefing with Prime Minister Shinzo Abe of Japan on 1 September 2014 is available via the Public Information Bureau website, at http://www.pib.nic.in/newsite/erelcontent.aspx?relid=109222, accessed 16 August 2018.

> Infrastructure' to develop and strengthen reliable, sustainable and resilient infrastructures that augment connectivity within India and between India and other countries in the region. Japanese ODA's contribution to the building of social and physical infrastructure in India was acknowledged. The total commitment of Japanese ODA yen loan to India in FY 2015 reached around 400 billion yen, the highest ever provided to India.[39]

India and Japan have also agreed to make efforts to invest in India's Northeastern states. Few years back, this was unimaginable considering the troubled Second World War history involving Japan and the Northeastern states.

Another important partnership for India is with Vietnam. Both sides established a strategic partnership in 2007, which was upgraded to a comprehensive strategic partnership in September 2016 during the visit of Prime Minister Modi to Vietnam. The two countries had also adopted a Joint Vision Statement on Defence Cooperation on 26 May 2015, during the visit of Vietnamese Minister of National Security Phung Quang Thanh. Under this vision statement, India committed itself to help in Vietnam's defence modernization and capacity-building. The Vietnamese President Tran Dai Quang, during his visit to India in March 2018, appreciated the role of AEP and the contribution of the upgraded strategic partnership under which '[p]olitical, defence, and security cooperation has all been expanded and become strategic pillars in our bilateral relations'.[40] The strategic partnership agreement with Singapore was signed in November 2015.

[39] The complete text of the 2015 Joint Statement between India and Japan is available via the MEA's website, http://www.mea.gov.in/bilateral-documents.htm?dtl/26176/Joint_Statement_on_India_and_Japan_Vision_2025_Special_Strategic_and_Global_Partnership_Working_Together_for_Peace_and_Prosperity_of_the_IndoPacific_R, accessed 16 August 2018.

[40] The text of the speech distributed at the end of his address at the Nehru Memorial Museum and Library, New Delhi on 4 March 2018. Also see his interview, Dipanjan Roy Chaudhury, 'Welcome India's Efforts in Act East Policy: Tran Dai Quang, Vietnamese President', *The Economic Times*, 1 March 2018, available at https//economictimes.indiatimes.com/articleshow/63119555.cms?utm_source=contentofinterest&utm_medium=text&utm_campaign=cppst, accessed 16 August 2018.

An enhanced defence cooperation agreement was also signed along with that to upgrade the initial defence cooperation agreement signed in 2003 which had established a unique security partnership between the two countries as discussed in the previous chapter. Under the November 2015 agreement, an annual defence ministers' dialogue was also established between the two countries, the second round of which was held in New Delhi in November 2017. India has also enhanced its strategic partnership with Malaysia. Defence and security cooperation between India and Indonesia has 'witnessed a qualitative and quantitative enhancement' under the AEP according to MEA's annual report (2014–15, p. ix).

An important aspect of enhanced security and defence cooperation with the Indo-Pacific countries has given a spurt to India's military diplomacy in the region. Important aspects of this have been India's help in training and capability enhancement, military exercises and ship visits, increasing participation from the region in India's Milan naval exercises and the annual Indian Ocean Naval Symposium organized by the Indian Navy. The Annexure at the end of the study gives an idea of India's military and naval exercises with its Indo-Pacific neighbours. A new and significant development in India's military diplomacy under the AEP is the willingness to sell weapons to the countries in the region. For this purpose, for the first time in September 2016, during Modi's visit to Vietnam, India even extended a line of credit of US$500 million to Vietnam to buy weapons, 'for deepening defence relationship'. This is reflective of the shift in India's arms sales policy. However, in terms of joint productions and exporting defence equipment, India has so far fallen short in meeting demands and expectations of the countries such as Vietnam, Indonesia and Malaysia. According to Kishan S. Rana, under the AEP:

> India is looking at significantly increasing defence cooperation with neighbouring countries, not just in South Asia but also in Southeast Asia. A vital aspect in this is the expansion of the 'Make in India' concept to the defence sector. India is looking at making more defence and security assets and exporting them. A key focus that is important to both India and its prospective partners in Southeast Asia is the maritime sector. Such developments will not only be

> to the interest of India but also Southeast Asia. Indeed, the region needs more options and avenues for cooperation.[41]

In April 2018, Minister of Defence Nirmala Sitharaman called all of India's defence Attachés posted in Indian embassies and missions abroad for a meeting on promoting India's military exports. It was disclosed that India was seriously considering the export of Brahmos and Akash missile systems. She told the defence Attachés: 'India is one of the top importers in defence. The time has come to change that as we are silently but steadily growing our manufacturing'.[42] The Indo-Pacific region would be an important market for India in this respect.

India's concerns in the domain of security have continued, as under the LEP, to be focused on peace and stability, counter-terrorism, maritime security and building a strategic architecture for the region. On evolution of strategic architecture, India continues to emphasize 'inclusive, open, balanced and equitable' regional architecture, as was the case under LEP. The AEP has laid greater emphasis on counter-terrorism and maritime security. Despite basic differences in the nature of terrorism confronted by the Indo-Pacific region as a whole and by India, two important aspects of counter-terrorism may be noticed in the AEP: mobilization of support from the region on India-specific terrorist challenge, especially cross-border terrorism from Pakistan, and building mutual understanding and cooperation on countering and containing Jihadi threats posed to India and to the region as a whole. A flavour of this two-way approach on terrorism could be discerned during the commemorative summit between India and ASEAN in January 2018. The Summit Declaration said:

> 9. Deepen cooperation in combating terrorism in all its forms and manifestations, violent extremism and radicalization through

[41] Kishan S. Rana, 'Modi Acts East: The Emerging Contours of India's Foreign Policy', *Institute of Strategic and International Studies (ISIS),* 13 March 2015, available at http://www.isis.org.my/files/IF_2015/IF4/ISIS_Focus_4_-_2015_1.pdf accessed 16 August 2018.

[42] Rajat Pandit, 'India in Talks with Friendly Nations for Sale of Missiles', *The Times of India*, 10 April 2018.

> information sharing, law enforcement cooperation and capacity building under the existing ASEAN-led mechanisms…
>
> 11. Reiterate commitment and promote comprehensive approach to combat terrorism through close cooperation by disrupting and countering terrorists, terrorist groups and networks, including by countering cross border movement of terrorists and foreign terrorist fighters and misuse of Internet including social media by terror entities; strengthen cooperation to stop terrorism financing efforts, and prevent recruitment of members of terrorist groups; support efforts in targeting terrorist groups and sanctuaries; and take further urgent measures to counter and prevent the spread of terrorism, while stressing that there can be no justification for acts of terror on any grounds whatsoever.
>
> 12. Work together with the international community to ensure compliance with the relevant United Nations Security Council resolutions regarding counter-terrorism, and to note efforts on the negotiations of the Comprehensive Convention on International Terrorism (CCIT) at the United Nations.[43]

While Para 9 underlined cooperative approach to fighting Jihadi terrorism, Paras 11 and 12 addressed India-specific concerns hinting at Pakistan-sponsored terrorism and China's resistance to naming Pakistan-based terrorists at the UN.

Concerning maritime security, thrust was on freedom of navigation in general but with a specific focus on the South China Sea where China had adopted an assertive posture and been encroaching on the territorial waters and claims of its Southeast Asian neighbours. The Commemorative India–ASEAN Summit of January 2018 said in this respect:

> 6. Reaffirm the importance of maintaining and promoting peace, stability, maritime safety and security, freedom of navigation and overflight in the region, and other lawful uses of the seas and

[43] The complete text of Delhi Declaration is available via the ASEAN website, available at http://asean.org/storage/2018/01/Delhi-Declaration_Adopted-25-Jan-2018.pdf, accessed 16 August 2018.

> unimpeded lawful maritime commerce and to promote peaceful resolutions of disputes, in accordance with universally recognised principles of international law, including the 1982 United Nations Convention on the Law of the Sea (UNCLOS), and the relevant standards and recommended practices by the International Civil Aviation Organization (ICAO) and the International Maritime Organization (IMO). In this regard, we support the full and effective implementation of the Declaration on the Conduct of the Parties in the South China Sea (DOC) and look forward to an early conclusion of the Code of Conduct in the South China Sea (COC).[44]

In both bilateral and multilateral forums, India has become more vocal in expressing its strategic interests, concerns and long-term goals—something which used to be expressed earlier with a little hesitation. For years, India was extremely cautious in expressing its views on the South China Sea dispute. Concerns expressed on the South China Sea with regard to Chinese aggressive posture were very measured. Recall an incident in December 2012 when the then Navy Chief of India, D. K. Joshi, reacting to the Chinese objections on the Oil and Natural Gas Commission's (ONGC) joint exploration of oil with Vietnam in the latter's economic zone in South China Sea, said that if and when required in India's national interests, 'we are prepared' to go there. The then National Security Adviser Shivshankar Menon, who was on a visit to China at that time, sought to underplay this statement by saying that media had 'manufactured' the story.[45] Some of the former Indian Navy Chiefs like Admiral Arun Prakash (chief during 2004–2006) also tried to underline that India neither had capabilities nor will to project power in the South China Sea. In the context of a similar issue of India's reaction to Chinese objections on oil exploration in Vietnamese waters, he wrote in 2011, 'At this juncture it would be imprudent sustaining a naval presence some 2500 nautical miles from home to bolster ONGC Videsh Ltd's stakes in South China

[44] Ibid.

[45] For details, see Zachary Keck, 'India's South China Sea Gambit', *The Diplomat*, 5 December 2012; Ananth Krishnan, 'China Opposes Unilateral Energy Exploration in South China Sea', *The Hindu*, 5 December 2012.

Sea hydrocarbons'.[46] The present Navy Chief Sunil Lanba, however, has been questioning Chinese tendency to 'conveniently ignore' territorial sovereignty of the island states. He has been preparing the Indian Navy to ensure 'free and secure Oceans for legitimate use by all countries', decrying 'narrow and over-nationalistic attitude', and asking for 'Integrated Ocean Government for facing the forthcoming challenges in the Indian Ocean'.[47]

As noted earlier, with the AEP, India has shown signs of getting more vocal in registering its concerns on the issue of Chinese assertions in the South China Sea. According to Carl Thayer, under the Modi government, India–Vietnam cooperation has increased. Highlighting that India has gone bolder on the issues of South China Sea with the AEP, David Scott argues,

> Significant development under the Modi administration is how the South China Sea has featured in their Joint Statements drawn up in President Mukherjee's trip to Vietnam in September 2014 and the visit by Vietnam's Prime Minister to India in October 2014. These Joint Statements' formulaic reiteration of freedom of navigation in the South China Sea, and adherence to international law, are an implicit criticism of China. The October 2014 visit also saw a slew of increased military assistance programmes by India to the Vietnamese navy.[48]

Since 2015, especially after India resolved its boundary dispute with Bangladesh through international arbitration, the situation has changed in a decisive fashion as India has been projecting its approach towards maritime dispute resolution as a model against China's

[46] Arun Prakash, 'India Must Pause Before Venturing into Choppy Waters', *Rediff*, 26 September 2011, available at http://www.rediff.com/news/column/column-india-must-pause-before-venturing-into-choppy-waters/20110926.htm, accessed 16 August 2018.

[47] 'South China Sea Situation is Cause of Concern: Navy Chief'. *The Times of India*, 15 October 2017.

[48] David Scott, 'India's Incremental Balancing in the South China Sea', *E-International Relations*, 26 July 2015, available at http://www.e-ir.info/2015/07/26/indias-incremental-balancing-in-the-south-china-sea/, accessed 16 August 2018.

intrusive behaviour in the South China Sea as also regarding other territorial disputes. In 2014, Modi said:

> For peace and stability in South China Sea, everyone should follow international norms and law. This includes the 1982 United Nations Convention on the Law of the Sea. We also hope that you will be able to successfully implement the Guidelines to the 2002 Declaration on Conduct and that the Code of Conduct on South China Sea can be concluded soon on the basis of consensus.[49]

In 2015, at the EAS, Modi clearly highlighted the diplomatic achievement of India in not only resolving the dispute peacefully but also acting benign by happily accepting the international arbitration results that went in favour of a close and smaller neighbour like Bangladesh. Modi stated:

> India and Bangladesh recently settled their maritime boundary using the mechanism of UNCLOS. India hopes that all parties to the disputes in the South China Sea will abide by the Declaration on the Conduct on South China Sea and the guidelines on the implementation. Parties must also redouble efforts for early adoption of a Code of Conduct on the basis of consensus.[50]

Speaking at the 14th ASEAN–India Summit in Vientiane, Lao PDR, on 8 September 2016, Modi reiterated:

> The sea-lanes of communications passing through this region are life lines of global trade. As such, they are directly linked to regional

[49] The complete text of the remarks by the Indian Prime Minister Narendra Modi at 12th India–ASEAN Summit, Nay Pyi Taw, Myanmar on 12 November 2014 is available via the MEA's website, http://www.mea.gov.in/Speeches--Statements.htm?dtl/24236/Remarks_by_the_Prime_Minister_at_12th_IndiaASEAN_Summit_Nay_Pyi_Taw_Myanmar, accessed 16 August 2018.

[50] The complete text of the remarks by the Indian Prime Minister Narendra Modi at the 10th EAS in Kuala Lumpur on 22 November 2015 is available via the MEA's website, http://www.mea.gov.in/Speeches--Statements.htm?dtl/26053/Remarks_by_Prime_Minister_at_the_10th_East_Asia_Summit_in_Kuala_Lumpur_November_22_2015, accessed 16 August 2018.

> peace, prosperity and stability. Securing the seas is, therefore, a shared responsibility. On our part, India supports freedom of navigation, over-flight and unimpeded commerce, based on the principles of international law, as reflected in the United Nations Convention on the Law of the Sea. And, we are ready to play our part in partnership with ASEAN.[51]

In her remarks during the Fifth EAS Foreign Ministers' Meeting in Kuala Lumpur in 2015, Mrs Swaraj, the Minister for External Affairs, not only made the Indian standpoint clear but also suggested that the South China Sea disputants (read China) should follow the Indian approach, which undoubtedly was an unprecedented stand keeping in view India's traditional approach on the matter. She stated:

> India supports freedom of navigation in international waters, including the South China Sea, the rights of passage and overflight, unimpeded commerce and access to resources in accordance with principles of international law, including the 1982 UN Convention on the Law of the Sea. Territorial disputes must be settled through peaceful means, as was done by India and Bangladesh recently using the mechanisms provided under UNCLOS. India hopes that all parties to the disputes in the South China Sea will abide by the guidelines on the implementation of the Declaration on the Conduct of Parties in the South China Sea. We further support efforts for the early adoption of a Code of Conduct on the South China Sea on the basis of consensus.[52]

[51] The complete text of the remarks by the Indian Prime Minister Narendra Modi at the 14th ASEAN–India Summit in Vientiane, Lao PDR on 8 September 2016 is available via the MEA's website, http://www.mea.gov.in/Speeches--Statements.htm?dtl/27551/Remarks_by_Prime_Minister_at_the_14th_ASEANIndia_Summit_in_Vientiane_Lao_PDR_September_08_2016, accessed 16 August 2018.

[52] The complete text of the remarks by MOS for External Affairs at the 5th East Asia Summit Foreign Ministers' Meeting, Kuala Lumpur on 6 August 2015 is available via the MEA's website, http://www.mea.gov.in/Speeches--Statements.htm?dtl/25654/Remarks_by_Minister_of_State_for_External_Affairs_at_the_5th_East_Asia_Summit_Foreign_Ministers_Meeting_Kuala_Lumpur_August_06_2015.

The initiative for India to play a larger role in the South China Sea was originally triggered by the perceptions that the USA was unwilling to put in its best for the security of the Indo-Pacific region in the face of increasing Chinese assertion. This brought India and Japan closer since 2006, mostly at the Japanese initiative. In a book published in 2007, Japan's Prime Minister Shinzo Abe wrote that he would not be surprised if 'in another decade, Japan–India relations overtook Japan–US and Japan–China ties'.[53] This has not exactly happened, but India–Japan strategic relations have definitely become much closer than what they were five years earlier. The decisive phase in India's approach towards the South China Sea dispute seems to have come about with the USA also pushing India for a greater role in the region, particularly since the launching of former President Obama's Asian 'pivot' strategy. It has been noted earlier that Obama was the first to publicly ask India to 'Act East'. The South China Sea dispute[54] was mentioned for the first time in a joint statement released by India and the USA in 2014.[55]

There is no doubt that the USA's growing strategic proximity in the Indo-Pacific region and its support has been an important factor in India's increased strategic role in the region. The USA's encouragement to play a larger role in the Indo-Pacific region has not only enhanced India's self-confidence to do so but also encouraged other major players in the region to seek greater strategic cooperation and understanding in regional affairs with India, both bilaterally and multilaterally. The triangular strategic axis between India, Japan, and the USA that began in 2011 can be seen as a concrete manifestation of this. This relationship has been further strengthened with Japan joining the India–US Malabar exercise in 2017, for which India invited

[53] Brahma Chellaney, 'Asia's Emerging Democratic Axis', *The Japan Times*, 31 January 2014.

[54] The complete text of the 2014 U.S.-India Joint Statement is available via the White House website, at https://obamawhitehouse.archives.gov/the-press-office/2014/09/30/us-india-joint-statement, accessed 16 August 2018.

[55] 'In a First, India-US Joint Statement Mentions South China Sea', *The Times of India*, 2 October 2014, available at https://timesofindia.indiatimes.com/india/In-a-first-India-US-joint-statement-mentions-South-China-Sea/articleshow/44028687.cms, accessed 16 August 2018.

Japan in January 2014 when Abe was India's Special Guest for the Republic Day celebrations. These three countries have also set up the Trilateral Infrastructure Working Group which met in Washington in February 2018 and decided to collaborate in facilitating connectivity in the Indo-Pacific region to counter the impact of Chinese Belt and Road Initiative (BRI) and Maritime Silk Route projects. In the ninth trilateral meeting of this group at the senior officials' level, it was decided to expand other players in the region to strengthen the 'Indo-Pacific construct'. The meeting also discussed the 'freedom of navigation' issue in the light of the suspension of a Spanish project of offshore oil exploration in the South China Sea under the Chinese pressure.[56]

India entered into another similar tie with Japan and Australia in 2015. In November 2017, the quadrilateral (Quad) strategic tie-up between India, Japan, the USA and Australia has been revived. An earlier exercise for such a grouping had been attempted during 2007–2008, but did not sustain, as Australia was hesitant to do anything that could displease China.[57] India has joined the present initiative but is expected to move cautiously. After the first meeting of the officials of the Quad countries in Manila on the sidelines of the EAS and ASEAN summits (12–14 November 2018), India's then Foreign Secretary S. Jaishankar called it a meeting of the 'middle level officials', to discuss Indo-Pacific affairs.[58] All the four countries issued separate statements after the meeting emphasizing the need for 'rules-based order in the Indo-Pacific region'. Countries issued separate statements of their respective positions on this meeting suggesting that much groundwork for building Quad as a viable grouping was still to be done.[59] The AEP, when situated in the wider canvass of

[56] Dipanjan Roy Chaudhury, 'India–US–Japan Discuss South China Sea Tensions; Indo-Pacific Region', *The Economic Times*, 4 April 2018.

[57] Tanvi Madan, 'Rise, Fall and Rebirth of the Quad', *War on the Rock*, 16 November 2017 available at https://warontherocks.com/2017/11/rise-fall-rebirth-quad/, accessed 16 August 2018.

[58] Dhruva Jaishankar, 'India's Strategic Dilemma: Here Is What Makes the Quad Both Valuable and Necessary', *Deccan Herald*, 5 February 2018.

[59] These were brief statements. Their texts can be accessed from the respective websites of foreign offices of the participating countries on 12 November 2017.

policy initiatives taken by other major stakeholders gains more salience. Japan's Democratic Security Diamond and Partnership for Quality Infrastructure (PQI), China's Twenty-first Century Maritime Silk Road, which is a component of the One Belt, One Road (OBOR) or the BRI, the four-nation Quad discussion involving the USA, Japan, India and Australia, and the three mini-laterals involving India, Japan and the USA; India, Japan and Australia; and Japan, the USA, and Australia, make India's AEP more important. Today, the catalytic external determinants are more powerful in influencing and shaping India's eastward engagement than in the past. The difference between the past and now is that, in the past, even when India took the positive initiatives, such initiatives were a result of New Delhi's own calculations; others, particularly major powers, either had no stand on India's position or were against it. That has changed in India's favour now. For instance, the Trump administration of the USA in its policy document entitled *National Security Strategy of the United States of America* has made its intentions and plans clear with regard to India. As per the US NSS paper:

> We welcome India's emergence as a leading global power and stronger strategic and defense partner. We will seek to increase quadrilateral cooperation with Japan, Australia, and India.... We will deepen our strategic partnership with India and support its leadership role in Indian Ocean security and throughout the broader region.[60]

Clearly, today, the USA considers India a major partner with the potential to form the bulwark in shaping the global international order. The other major stakeholders of the Indo-Pacific and Southeast Asian region look towards India with the expectation that it will positively and decisively contribute to shaping the tectonic shifts in Indo-Pacific politics in the favour of greater stability and for the good of other 'democratic countries'.

[60] The complete text of the NSS of the USA released in December 2017 is available via the White House website, at https://www.whitehouse.gov/wp-content/uploads/2017/12/NSS-Final-12-18-2017-0905.pdf, accessed 16 August 2018.

It remains to be seen as to how India's role in these groupings will unfold in pursuance of its interests. There are a host of factors that will influence and shape this role, most important being the Chinese behaviour in the region and the USA–China rivalry therein. India will also be governed by the considerations of balancing its strategic autonomy in relation to the growing strategic proximity with the USA.

Persistence of Economic Agenda and Development Cooperation

Under the AEP, one of the core objectives of the LEP, of deeper economic integration with the region through trade and investment, has also been pursued vigorously. At the beginning of the AEP, the possibilities of expanding trade and mobilizing investments looked promising. However, India's trade with the region has not grown on expected lines. The value of trade that stood at nearly US$75 billion during 2013–2014 has come to less than US$70 billion during 2017–2018, and the inflow of investments, except from Japan and Singapore, also does not look very good. It was hoped that the entry into force of the ASEAN–India Agreement on Trade in Services and Investments on 1 July 2015, after almost a decade-long effort, would help boost trade, but that has not happened. The FTA in services is definitely a step forward on promoting trade and economic cooperation through better linking of economies of the ASEAN with India. The FTA in services aptly complements the ASEAN–India Free Trade Agreement in Goods and Services, which has been in operation since 1 January 2010. It is hoped that completion of connectivity projects and better linking of India with the ASEAN region physically will help trade to grow and facilitate economic integration between the two.

In order to move forward in terms of integrating with other Asian economies, India decided to join the Regional Comprehensive Economic Partnership (RCEP) conceptualized in 2011. So far as the evolution of RCEP is concerned, in November 2011, the ASEAN Framework for RCEP was adopted during the 19th ASEAN Summit in Bali, Indonesia. In April 2012, during the 20th ASEAN summit in Phnom Penh, Cambodia, the members reiterated the ASEAN

Framework for RCEP. In the same year, in August 2012, during the first ASEAN economic ministers (AEM) plus FTA partners' consultations held in Siem Reap, Cambodia, the members adopted the Guiding Principles and Objectives for Negotiating the RCEP, and later, in November 2012, during the 20th ASEAN Summit, the *Joint Declaration of Ministers for the launch of RCEP negotiations* was adopted in Phnom Penh, Cambodia. The guiding principles and objectives of RCEP are devising a modern, comprehensive, high quality and mutually beneficial economic partnership agreement. It has been agreed that negotiations on trade in goods, trade in services, investment and other areas will be conducted in parallel to ensure a comprehensive and balanced outcome. The member countries have also decided to take into consideration different levels of development of the participating countries.

Later, in 2013, it was decided by the member states to set up the RCEP Trade Negotiations Committee as the apex negotiating body for RCEP.

> The RCEP is an ambitious project which for the first time intends to bring in Asia's three biggest economies: China, India and Japan, into a regional trading arrangement. Concomitantly, the proposed trade area will be the largest in terms of population, with a combined GDP of around US$19 trillion. When fully established, it will become the largest trade bloc in the world.[61]

RCEP is a vital component of the ASEAN vision of realizing the ASEAN economic community. The significance of the RCEP in regional economic relations has been enhanced following the US withdrawal from the Trans-Pacific Partnership (TPP) under the Trump administration. The RCEP is a prime multilateral and regional tool for India to engage with the Asia-Pacific economies on issues of trade, commerce and investments. Led by the ASEAN, the RCEP

[61] Rahul Mishra, 'RCEP: Challenges and Opportunities for India', *RSIS Commentaries,* 25 July 2013, available at https://www.rsis.edu.sg/rsis-publication/rsis/2028-rcep-challenges-and-opportuni/#.Wlt6ikuLlok, accessed 16 August 2018.

negotiations aim at building a region-wide free trade area encompassing the 10 ASEAN member countries and their six dialogue partners—China, Japan, South Korea, India, Australia and New Zealand. These countries are also the six FTA partners of ASEAN. Geographical contiguity and diverse market sizes make RCEP attractive for all potential members. Keeping that in view, the RCEP members have agreed to include appropriate forms of flexibility including provision for special and differential treatment. Another point of agreement is that RCEP members will have broader and deeper engagement with significant improvements over the existing ASEAN + 1 FTAs while recognizing the individual and diverse circumstances of the participating countries.

So far as the challenges before RCEP are concerned, one of the most prominent ones is that it intends to build a structured regional institution to cover a vast and diversified region, with economies at different levels and power being asymmetrical between the larger and the smaller countries. This is not easy for economic as well as political reasons.[62] Then many of the major countries still do not have free trade agreements between them. These countries are Australia–India, China–India, China–Japan; India–New Zealand, Japan–Korea and Japan–New Zealand. China may be actively supporting the RCEP in the hope that it may lead the grouping and use it as an instrument of building and legitimizing its regional identity, and hopefully its dominance.[63] With regard to the RCEP rationale for India, it will lead to diversification and expansion of India's export markets. The RCEP would provide access to raw materials, intermediate products and capital goods for value-added manufacturing. It would help in attracting foreign investment to stimulate manufacturing, generate employment and improve competitiveness. The politico-diplomatic initiative of 'Act East' resulting in FTAs with the ASEAN, Japan

[62] Suisheng Zhao, 'From Soft to Structured Regionalism: Building Regional Institutions in the Asia-Pacific', *Journal of Global Policy and Governance* 2, no. 2 (November 2013): 145–166.

[63] Rafel Leal-Arcas, 'China and the Regional Comprehensive Economic Partnership', *Journal of Global Policy and Governance* 2, no. 2 (November 2013): 287–304.

and South Korea will most likely further integrate India with the economies of the region.

In view of this, it is clear that joining RCEP fits in well with the AEP. Moreover, India, being such a large economy, cannot afford to be out of a mega trade block whose participants cover more than one-fourth of global trade and GDP. If looked at purely from trade point of view, it is also clear that competitors to the Indian economy in different sectors would gain preferential market access to the markets of India's export interest, if India fails to join the RCEP. The RCEP also provides India the opportunity to leverage regional value chains under RCEP, where the investment flows would be dictated by the reduction of trade and investment barriers. However, along with opportunities, RCEP has also thrown open a range of challenges for the Indian economy and its bidding industries. This has led to domestic resistance, apprehensions and concerns. Highlighting India's concerns on RCEP, Modi stated in 2014:

> It (RCEP) can be a springboard for economic integration and prosperity in the region. However, we should aim for a balanced Agreement, which is beneficial to all; and, is truly comprehensive in nature, by equally ambitious agenda with similar timelines for goods and services.[64]

While some of India's concerns and apprehensions about RCEP are genuine, others are simply a manifestation of the protectionist nature of the industry sectors and their desire to keep dominating sectors without offering the best services and prices to the consumer. This has been the case with India's iron and steel industries, cement industries and several other subsectors of heavy industries in India.

[64] The complete text of the remarks by the Indian Prime Minister Narendra Modi at the 14th ASEAN–India Summit in Vientiane, Lao PDR on 8 September 2016 is available via the MEA's website, http://www.mea.gov.in/Speeches--Statements.htm?dtl/27551/Remarks_by_Prime_Minister_at_the_14th_ASEANIndia_Summit_in_Vientiane_Lao_PDR_September_08_2016, accessed 16 August 2018.

Unfortunately, India is still outside the other major multilateral trade pacts of the region, which indicates that India is yet to overcome several hurdles before it becomes an active part of regional supply chain mechanism. India's candidature for the APEC membership, for which it had first applied for in 1997, is still unattended. APEC is a multilateral forum that has countries of Asia and the Pacific on board, ranging from Australia to Canada, and from Russia to the USA and Vietnam. APEC is based on the model of open regionalism and thus enshrines the idea that common agenda, rather than geographic proximity and contiguity, should guide an organization. Over the years, the APEC has served as a platform for interactions among the economies of East and Southeast Asia with Oceania, North America, Eurasia and Latin America.

Even in the China-led Free Trade Area for Asia Pacific (FTAAP), possibilities of India becoming a part are almost bleak, leave alone the TPP, which claims to be the 'twenty-first century free-trade pact of gold standards'. This means that in TPP, the phytosanitary and labour norms will be of very high standards. Meeting such standards would naturally be a difficult task for most of the developing economies, especially those which depend on subsistence agriculture and cheap labour sources—sometimes child labour also—like India. Thus, on the multilateral trade front, the AEP faces difficulties.

Nonetheless, if India manages to meet the expectations of other potential RCEP members and finally lowers down the tariff rates, it will be able to join RCEP, which will be a boon for the Indian economy and a success for the multilateral trade dimension of the AEP. Arguably, India's RCEP membership might also open new doors for India to join APEC, a dream which has remained unfulfilled since the heydays of the LEP.

Another mega initiative, of which India is a prominent member, is the Asian Infrastructure Investment Bank (AIIB). China, India and Russia are the three largest shareholders, taking a 30.34 per cent, 8.52 per cent, 6.66 per cent stake, respectively. Accordingly, their voting shares are calculated at 26.06 per cent, 7.5 per cent and

5.92 per cent, respectively. China with the largest voting rights in the AIIB and it may virtually have a veto power on some key decisions despite its assurance that it is not keen to possess such powers.[65]

Besides the mega regional groupings, India's AEP has also worked to give momentum to other subregional groupings. The Modi government has tried to bring in some energy to the BIMSTEC, which has the unique distinction of working as a bridge between South and Southeast Asia. The countries of both South Asia as well as Southeast Asia (Thailand and Myanmar) are members of BIMSTEC. With the inclusion of two landlocked states—Bhutan and Nepal—the BIMSTEC has not remained confined to the Bay of Bengal subregion only. That BIMSTEC may get more attention than it has got in the past, and it might work as an important subregional tool, was amply signalled when during the BRICS (Brazil, Russia, India, China and South Africa) Summit in Goa in October 2016, India invited the BIMSTEC leaders to join the BRICS outreach summit. Clearly, a stalled SAARC, on account of Pakistan's persisting problems with its neighbours such as India, Afghanistan and Bangladesh, has created a larger space for the BIMSTEC. Diplomatic deadlock with Pakistan at the SAARC has been a major propelling factor in persuading the Indian policymakers to look for a multilateral regional/subregional unit that is devoid of Pakistan. And there, the BIMSTEC becomes critically important. Already the BIMSTEC Secretariat has been set up in Dhaka, and India has also provided some corpus money to the secretariat for its smooth functioning. It has also been decided to regularly host the summit meetings so that it is ensured that the BIMSTEC keeps moving forward. The Modi government's focus on the BIMSTEC might lead to some constructive results, though much remains dependent on how things move on the ground.

Soft Power: Religion, Yoga and Diaspora

India's AEP has carried forward the trilogy of 'commerce, connectivity and culture' vigorously. The infusion of culture in the conduct of

[65] For more details, see Rahul Mishra, 'Asian Infrastructure Investment Bank: An Assessment', *India Quarterly* 72, no. 2 (May 2016): 163–176.

India's foreign policy may not be new under Prime Minister Modi, but it has become multidimensional, robust and a far more clearly visible aspect. It began with the recognition of Yoga as the 'holistic approach to health and wellbeing' by the UN on 11 December 2014. 21 June was designated as the International Yoga Day, and since 2015 is celebrated all over the world every year.

India has centuries-old religious ties with the Indo-Pacific region, especially based on Hinduism and Buddhism. The AEP has been used in activating and expanding these ties through the holding of international conferences, improving of facilities at the places of pilgrims and developing them as tourist hubs for pilgrimage travels. One gets a feeling that Islam has not been adequately integrated into this approach, perhaps because Islam, unlike Hinduism and Buddhism, was not born in India. However, as noted earlier, Islam has been enriched in India and given specific characteristics that are moderate and softer in comparison to the Wahhabi thrust. Islam as prevalent in India and the Southeast Asian countries, displays a strong Sufi trend that can counter the forces of radicalization and violence dominating political Islam in the world today. This was strongly argued by Prime Minister Modi in his address to the World Islamic Sufi Conference held in New Delhi on 17 March 2016.[66] India would do well to own Islam and make it a part of composite cultural package for projection at the global level, especially in the Indo-Pacific region. It will also get India diplomatic and strategic mileage in Islamic countries of the region.

Engagement with diaspora has emerged as a major component of India's soft power projection under the AEP. Contrary to popular perception, it was P. V. Narasimha Rao who had for the first time in the past 25 years, addressed the Indian diaspora during his visits abroad. Former Prime Ministers I. K. Gujral and Atal Bihari Vajpayee also repeated that, albeit less frequently. Indeed, it is Prime Minister Narendra Modi who has made interaction and engagement with the Indian diaspora a part of his foreign visits. However, the sole purpose

[66] The complete text of Indian prime minister's speech at the World Islamic Sufi Conference in New Delhi is available via the website of Press Information Bureau, Government of India, Prime Minister's Office, at http://pib.nic.in/newsite/PrintRelease.aspx?relid=138124.

of engaging the diaspora is not only for India's stronger relations with the East. The objectives are not confined to gains in foreign policy, but clearly transcend beyond that and into the domestic politics of India. This is evident from the fact that the BJP, the ruling party which also leads the NDA coalition, keeps engagement with diaspora as an important component. The 2014 election manifesto of the BJP stated: 'The NRIs, PIOs and professionals settled abroad are a vast reservoir to articulate the national interests and affairs globally. This resource will be harnessed for strengthening Brand India'.[67]

Though Modi has been criticized for raking domestic issues with the diaspora community, he has been lauded for bringing diaspora's attention to India. In countries such as Malaysia, he took a politically bold step to talk with them, which is a clear departure from his predecessor Dr Manmohan Singh who had even refused to speak to the Indo-Malay community and listen to their grievances. Modi inaugurated 'Little India' in Malaysia, which was difficult to imagine during the UPA government.

India's diaspora engagements have been institutionalized under 'Pravasi Bhartiya Divas' (PBD or Day for the PIOs) for biennial meetings. Now annual regional PBD has been institutionalized for closer engagement. The issues raised regarding the problems and expectations of the Indian diaspora are addressed and the diaspora's strength is harnessed for India's outreach, development and specific policy issues. A special regional PBD was organized in Singapore in January 2018 to commemorate the 25th anniversary of the India–ASEAN relations. The first conference of the PIO parliamentarians was also held in New Delhi on 9 January 2018.

Appraisal

The AEP is only about four years old. It may not be fair to expect the policy to meet all its goals within such a short time. It may, therefore,

[67] The complete text of the 2014 election manifesto of the BJP is available at https://www.bjp.org/images/pdf_2014/full_manifesto_english_07.04.2014.pdf, accessed 16 August 2018.

not be proper to attempt an objective and balanced assessment of the policy. Yet some of its major trends may be identified.

There is no doubt that the policy has injected considerable energy and activism in India's eastward engagement. Under the AEP, many of the gaps in terms of visits, upgrading of bilateral relations, and integrating with regional and multilateral organizations have been advanced. There exist much better personal relationships and rapport at the levels of top leadership between India and the Indo-Pacific region. The visibility of India's engagement with this region has also been enhanced, both internally within the country and externally in the region. The visit of the 10 ASEAN leaders at India's Republic Day celebrations in January 2018 stands out as a unique and concrete example in this respect.

India's relationship with the region regarding defence and security has also been enhanced substantially. Strategic partnerships have been made concrete and substantial. India is now more active in its military diplomacy and has strengthened its role as a security provider by coming forward in supplying weapon systems and technologies. It has also become a favoured recipient of sophisticated weapons and technologies from those who are better off than India in these areas. The emergence and strengthening of multilateral partnerships like the India–US and Japan grouping, and the Quad formed by the USA, India, Japan and Australia, has opened new opportunities for India to take advantage of in building its capabilities and meeting its potential challenges. Some of these institutions are still evolving, and one can hope that they would help maintain strategic balance in the region and preserve its peace and stability.

The AEP's principal objective was to improve upon the performance of the LEP, particularly in the three areas of commerce, connectivity and culture. There is general acceptance of the fact that India's cultural engagement with the Indo-Pacific region has been deepened and expanded. The same, however, does not seem to be the case with the other two areas of commerce and connectivity. India's overall trade with the region has declined during the AEP years so far. It was hoped that the operationalization of the services and investment

FTA between India and the ASEAN would help boost the bilateral trade, but such hope stands belied so far. Trade flows have also confronted problems from non-tariff barriers and poor connectivity. The question of non-tariff barriers is trapped in the procedural and institutional efficiencies or the lack of them, which remains to be addressed seriously.

India has taken steps to perform better on connectivity, but the results are still slow to come. Take for instance the question of utilizing the US$1 billion facility created by India to boost connectivity projects. Since the facility has been extended through the Axim Bank, the bank procedures and conditionality have blunted the incentives offered. The countries of the region are also deterred by the conditionality that 85 per cent of the goods and services related to such projects must be obtained from India.[68] Such problems are rooted into the faulty structure of India's line of credit (LoC) approach. Announcements of the LoC are often made at the political level even without making firm budgetary allocations. The terms and conditions offered are not always competitive and attractive. Serious problems of coordination exist between the Ministry of Finance and the MEA in funding and supervising the projects that cause delays. The Indian missions in the countries where the LoC projects are carried out lack technical competence and manpower to monitor the execution of such projects. Then there are only a small number of preferred companies that manage to corner most of the projects, and sometimes they deliver products that lack adequate quality and precision. A Development Partnership Administration (DPA) was constituted between the MEA and the Ministry of Finance, but due to lack of coordination and operational synergy between the two ministries, it has remained weak and ineffective. Unless the whole question of the LoC policy is revised and streamlined, India's delivery deficit in development cooperation will not be improved.[69]

[68] Sushant Singh, 'Three Years, No Takers for India's $1-billion Credit Line for ASEAN Digital Links', *The Indian Express*, 4 April 2018.

[69] Anil Trigunayat, 'India's Lines of Credit Dilemma', *Vivekananda International Foundation*, 16 May 2018.

India has made serious moves towards completing its obligations on projects like the trilateral highway (India–Myanmar–Thailand). The work was awarded to the National Highway Authority of India at the end of 2017, and it is hoped that construction would now move faster.[70] With regard to performance on such projects, there are serious bottlenecks in coordination between the MEA and the Ministry of Finance. Even interventions by the Prime Minister's Office have not been able to resolve such bottlenecks.[71]

In view of these difficulties, some scepticism on the performance of India's AEP persists in the region.

[70] Sunny Verma, 'South-East Asia Link: India, Thailand Hope to Overcome Challenges for Early Completion', *The Indian Express*, 30 March 2017.

[71] Author's (S. D. Muni's) interviews with two of India's former foreign secretaries who do not wish to be identified.

CHAPTER 7

Prospects

Challenges of Deeper and Wider Engagement

India's eastward engagement has been driven by its civilizational and cultural inheritance, economic aspirations and strategic requirements. It will, therefore, deepen and widen in the years to come. The latest evidence of this may be seen in Prime Minister Narendra Modi's address to the Shangri La Dialogue held in Singapore on 1 June 2018.[1] The Shangri La Dialogue has been organized in Singapore by the IISS, London, since 2002, as a regional platform for security discourse. India has been participating in it mostly at the level of defence ministers and national security advisers. In 2017, India had no official-level participation. However, in 2018, for the first time, Prime Minister Modi decided to raise the level of India's participation and articulate India's interests and stakes in contributing to peace and prosperity in the Indo-Pacific region.

Modi's outlining of India's role in the Indo-Pacific had strong elements of continuity and consistency, cutting across bipartisan political lines, that could be seen in the statements made at this forum earlier

[1] The complete text of the speech is available via the MEA's website, https://www.mea.gov.in/Speeches-Statements.htm?dtl/29943/Prime+Ministers+Keynote+Address+at+Shangri+La+Dialogue+June+01+2018, accessed 16 August 2018.

by former Minister of Defence Pranab Mukherjee in 2006, former National Security Adviser Shivshankar Menon in 2010, former Minister of Defence A. K. Antony in 2012, and former Minister of Defence Manohar Parrikar in 2016. Therefore, what Modi said at Shangri La should be seen in a wider context as articulation of India's policy towards the region, and not simply as that of the Modi government's. Modi underlined both the factors that propel India's engagement with the region as also the core concerns and the directions that India's role will follow in pursuance of its interests. The factors that have driven India's eastward engagement and will continue to do so, as highlighted by Modi, fall mainly into three categories: civilizational links, economic growth of India and of the Indo-Pacific region as a whole, and critical security challenges arising out of uncertainty in the region. As far as India's approach in the region is concerned, Modi listed six basic elements:

> 1. Stand for open and inclusive Indo-Pacific region. 2. Southeast Asia remains at the centre of the Indo-Pacific region. 3. The necessity to evolve through dialogue, a common rule-based order. 4. All nations should have equal access as a right under international law to use common places on the sea and in the air. 5. Solutions cannot be found within walls of protectionism but in embracing change. 6. If connectivity initiatives have to be successful, they must be built on bridges of trust highlighting need to respect the sovereignty and territorial integrity.[2]

Accordingly, he defined India's commitment to the region as:

> We will promote democratic and rule based international order, in which all nations, small and large, thrive as equal and sovereign. We will work with others to keep our seas, space and airways free and open; our nations secure from terrorism; and our cyber spaces free from disruption and conflict. We will keep our economy open and our engagement transparent. We will share our resources, markets and prosperity with our friends and partners. We will seek

[2] Ibid.

> a sustainable future for our planet, as through the new International Solar Alliance together with France and other partners.[3]

Let us look at prospects of these drivers and directions of India's eastward engagement and the related aspects in some detail.

Drivers of Engagement

Modi referred to the civilizational links between India and the Indo-Pacific region since the pre-Vedic age and prior to the Indus Valley Civilization. He also referred to Buddha's teachings as a bond between India and the Indo-Pacific region. It has been noted in the previous chapters that Indian leaders, from Nehru down to those in the period of LEP, have been acutely conscious of India's cultural and civilizational links with the countries of the region. Dr Manmohan Singh, addressing the plenary session of India–ASEAN Commemorative Summit in New Delhi on 20 December 2012, said:

> People, ideas, trade, art and religions have long criss-crossed this region. A timeless thread of civilisation runs through all our countries. While each one of us has a unique and rich heritage, there are abiding linkages of culture and custom, of art and religion and of civilisation, all of which create a sense of unity in the diversity and pluralism in our region.[4]

His foreign secretary, speaking at the 10th Meeting of Bangladesh, China, India and Myanmar (BCIM) grouping on connectivity, said on 18 February 2012:

> India has long standing civilizational bonds with countries in East and South East Asia. In spiritual and cultural values, by name and

[3] Ibid.

[4] The complete text of the speech is available via the MEA's website, http://mea.gov.in/Speeches-Statements.htm?dtl/20981/Opening+Statement+by+Prime+Minister+at+Plenary+Session+of+IndiaASEAN+Commemorative+Summit/, accessed 16 August 2018.

> language, through dance and art, there is a historical tradition of contact between India and the East. It is against this larger backdrop that we have located our Look East Policy or LEP.[5]

However, the civilizational and cultural dimension had not been front-loaded in the LEP as it has been done under the AEP. The earlier hesitation of using religion for foreign policy purposes has been completely shed off. There also seems to be an attempt to widen the cultural thrust in the AEP as evident in Prime Minister Modi's visits to prominent mosques in Indonesia and Singapore. In the Shangri La address, he hailed Singapore's experience of 'embrace diversity at home … (to) seek an inclusive world outside'. On earlier occasions of visit to this region and elsewhere, Modi's ceremonial visits had been limited to Hindu and Buddhist temples. This is a clear shift in favour of India's broader composite culture being used as a part of its soft power projection. In his Shangri La address, he also highlighted 'foundations of our civilizational ethos—of pluralism, coexistence, openness and dialogue', to be practiced both internally and externally. This civilizational dimension may gain strength in India's foreign policy in general and its approach towards the Indo-Pacific region in particular, irrespective of who is in power in India. The opposition in India led by the Congress Party is also identifying itself with Hinduism, while opposing its political use by the BJP through 'Hindutva', as could be seen during the Karnataka assembly elections held in May 2018.[6] Cultural drivers of the AEP are, therefore, expected to be consolidated and reinforced. Even in a situation of regime change in India, the importance of cultural drivers is not likely to be diminished in India's eastward engagement.

[5] The complete text of the speech is available via the MEA's website, http://www.mea.gov.in/Speeches-Statements.htm?dtl/18855/Speech+by+Foreign+secretary+on+Indias+Look+East+Policy+at+the+10th+Meeting+of+the+BCIM+Bangladesh+China+India+Myanmar+Cooperation+Forum, accessed 16 August 2018.

[6] A strong argument of difference between Hinduism and Hindutva has been made by Dr Shashi Tharoor, a prominent Congress leader in his latest book. See Shashi Tharoor, *Why I Am Hindu* (New Delhi: Aleph Book Company, 2018).

With regard to the economic driver, India is confident of its sustained growth and its linkage with the Indo-Pacific region in the long run. Modi clarified this linkage at the Shangri La Dialogue saying:

> We will sustain growth of 7.5 to 8 percent per year. As our economy grows, our global and regional integration will increase. A nation of over 800 million youth knows that their future will be secured not just by the scale of India's economy, but also by the depth of global engagement. More than anywhere else, our ties will deepen and out presence will grow in the region.[7]

This is supported by independent analyses and projections. The Center for International Development at the Harvard Kennedy School came with estimates in June 2017 that the 'pole of global growth has moved over the past few years from China to neighbouring India where it is likely to stay over the coming decade'. According to these projections, India tops the list of fastest-growing economies in the world and in Asia. This is because 'India has made inroads in diversifying its export base to include more complex sectors, such as chemicals, vehicles and certain electronics'.[8] These projections also underlined that Southeast Asian countries such as the Philippines, Vietnam, Indonesia and Thailand will dominate the global and Asian growth story.

India's growth projections have also been endorsed by the World Bank and the IMF. There are suggestions from the IMF for India to introduce reforms by removing 'trade and non-trade barriers'. India's statutory tariffs are pegged on at 15 per cent, which is much higher than that of any other country in the region. These tariffs can be brought down.[9] Trade issues are also being intensely debated between

[7] The complete text of the speech is available via the MEA's website, at https://www.mea.gov.in/Speeches-Statements.htm?dtl/29943/Prime+Ministers+Keynote+Address+at+Shangri+La+Dialogue+June+01+2018, accessed 16 August 2018.

[8] 'New 2025 Growth Projections Predict China's Further Slowdown', *Harvard Kennedy School*, 28 June 2017, https://www.hks.harvard.edu/announcements/new-2025-global-growth-projections-predict-chinas-further-slowdown, accessed 16 August 2018.

[9] 'India's Role in Development of Indo-Pacific Region to Expand: Says IMF', *Livemint*, New Delhi, 21 April 2018, http://epaper.livemint.com/epaper/viewer.aspx, accessed 16 August 2018.

India and other countries in RCEP and in other forums. In this debate, India's position has been to have balance in trade, investments and services, which has been stated by India earlier and was also reiterated by Modi in his Shangri La address, where he also clearly asserted India's opposition to protectionism.

As highlighted in the previous chapters, India has always seen its growth and prosperity linked with the economic dynamism of the East including the Indian Ocean.[10] The experience of India's LEP and the AEP has reinforced these linkages. India would, therefore, continue to look towards the Indo-Pacific region for export markets and investment sources. With planned expansion of India's growth story by expediting the development of India's Northeast states and undertaking projects like the Sagarmala, where India's port facilities will be expanded on the eastern front, greater integration and developmental linkages with the Indo-Pacific are inevitable. For preparing the Northeast to have greater engagement with its ASEAN neighbours, Minister of External Affairs Sushma Swaraj called a meeting of the Northeast chief ministers to brief them on the AEP and the relations with BIMSTEC. Major connectivity projects such as the Kaladan Multimodel transport hub and the Trilateral Highway (India–Myanmar–Thailand) were discussed to highlight their importance. Various other aspects of connectivity, including waterways, and communication linkages with the neighbouring ASEAN countries were also explored. It was agreed that expeditious completion of these projects will boost the meagre 1 per cent trade between India and the ASEAN that presently passes through the Northeast region out of a total of nearly US$70 billion. The other infrastructure projects that are work-in-progress in India like the 'Sagarmala', when completed, will also boost economic and strategic engagement with the Indo-Pacific region. It is estimated that by 2030, the Indo-Pacific region may have 21 of the top 25 global sea and air trade routes, carrying around two-thirds of global energy trade and '1/3rd of world's bulk cargo

[10] Sanjay Baru, 'India and the Indian Ocean Region: The New Geo-economics', *India Foundation*, https://www.indiafoundation.in/india-and-the-indian-ocean-region-the-new-geo-economics-by-sanjaya-baru/, accessed 16 August 2018.

movement' which in turn will enhance India's economic prospects and opportunities in the region.[11]

The most important precondition for protecting and promoting India's cultural and economic stakes in the region is peace and stability. The challenge to regional peace and stability in the Indo-Pacific emanates from uncertainty. Modi's comments in this respect in his Shangri La address may be recalled where he said:

> The Foundations of the global order appear shaken. And the future looks less certain. For all our progress, we live on the edge of uncertainty, of unsettled questions and unresolved disputes; contests and claims; and clashing visions and competing models....
>
> We see growing mutual insecurity and rising military expenditure; internal dislocations turning into external tensions; and new fault lines in trade and competition in global commons. Above all we see assertion of power and recourse to international norms. In the midst of all this, there are challenges that touch us all, including the unending threats of terrorism and extremism.

There is a consistency in India's position in this respect as all Indian participants in the Shangri La and other relevant international forums have been emphasizing the insecurity emerging out of uncertainty.

The power shift to Asia and the rise of an assertive China are seen as the root causes of this uncertainty because the prevailing power hierarchy and international norms have been put under stress by this power shift. While India rejoices the rise of Asia including China, the matter of concern for India is the Chinese assertion and intent to change the prevailing rules of engagement in the region. China has developed Anti-access and Area Denial (A2AD) capabilities by deploying multiple missile launchers on its Hainan Island in the South China Sea to deter any US intervention. It is fast expanding the Peoples' Liberation Army Navy (PLAN) to mark its presence in the wider Indian Ocean. China's push, particularly in South Asia and

[11] Kevin Andrews, 'India Is a Key Partner in Indo-Pacific Region', *The Hindu*, 1 September 2015.

the Indian Ocean, is squeezing India's long cherished strategic space and its territorial claims backed by rapid militarization of territorial waters in the South China Sea and the East Asia Sea have sparked of numerous disputes and counterclaims that can disturb the peace and stability in the region any time, notwithstanding a general assessment that neither China nor any of its neighbours want or can afford.

Uncertainty in the Indo-Pacific region has been fuelled further by the indications and perceptions that the USA is reducing its commitment to the stability and peace in the region. To discount them, the USA launched its rebalancing strategy for the region and has been asserting that it will not allow China or any other country to disturb the existing order in the region and violate international norms regarding the freedom of navigation in sea and the air. Almost everyone else supports these freedoms and the respect for existing international norms. Asia and the Indo-Pacific region seem to be getting polarized around the US–China rivalry, that goes beyond the questions of regional order in the Indo-Pacific and cover even the bilateral US–China issues of trade and human rights. The USA sees challenge to its interests in the Indo-Pacific region emanating from the 'revisionist powers of China and Russia'. In its NSS document adopted in December 2017, the sharpening of fault lines with China is clearly identified:

> Every year competitors such as China steal US intellectual property valued at hundreds of billions of dollars (p. 21).... China seeks to displace the United States in the Indo-Pacific region, expand the reaches of its state driven economy model, and reorder the region in its favour (p. 25).[12]

The NSS has laid down a road map to show how the USA would not let this happen.[13]

One of the biggest sources of anxiety and uncertainty in the region is the question as to how the US–China competition and rivalry will

[12] 'The National Security Strategy of the United States of America December 2017', *White House*, December 2017, https://www.whitehouse.gov/wp-content/uploads/2017/12/NSS-Final-12-18-2017-0905.pdf, accessed 16 August 2018.

[13] Ibid.

unfold. There are three possible scenarios in answers to this question. China is asking for a 'new framework of great power relations', which if accepted by the USA would mean the USA accepting Chinese dominance in the region or at best sharing influence in the region with China—*a la* G-2 or the Group of Two, dominating the region. Analysts generally believe that this may not happen since the USA has heavy and deep stakes and is still economically and militarily hugely powerful to let these stakes be compromised. The second possibility is that a simmering rivalry and competition sharpens between them, leading to 'escalating strategic conflict and potentially even a full blown Cold War'. Under this scenario, both of them 'would almost certainly engage in an arms race that fuels overall global risk, while extending their strategic conflict to the world's most unstable areas, potentially through proxy wars'.[14] Since neither of them can afford to get 'enmeshed in such a conflict', the third more likely possibility is a 'managed strategic conflict' between them where their mutual 'economic disengagement' takes place 'gradually and not completely'. Also while asserting their respective military capabilities, they do not engage in proxy wars by providing military support to 'forces engaged in military conflict with the other party'.[15] The management of a deepening strategic conflict would depend upon several factors such as the leadership, regional political and strategic dynamics involving other players and accidental triggers of a wider conflict. The uncertainty arising out of this situation is leading almost every country in the region to pile up weapons, build up their capabilities and deterrence, and craft complex strategic equations amongst themselves, including with the two principal competitors, the USA and China. India cannot be an exception in this respect.

India's position in the competition and rivalry between the USA and China has been and is most likely to remain that of a balancing player. The Indo-US strategic partnership has considerably improved since the beginning of this century, and the USA is projecting India as 'the linchpin', in its rebalancing strategy and a major strategic

[14] Minxin Pei, 'Asia Will Pay a High Price for a US-China Conflict', *Hindustan Times*, 10 June 2018.

[15] Ibid.

partner for the region. The former US Secretary of State Rex Tillerson declared that the USA was having a 'planned partnership for entire 21st century' with India. During the past four years of the Modi regime, strategic proximity between India and the USA has been considerably enhanced, creating an impression that India was heavily tilting towards the USA not only in search of technological capabilities but also to restraint China in its assertion and hegemonic aspirations in the region.

> Uncertainties and apprehensions regarding China's approach towards India are two of the fundamental driving forces for India looking for closer defense and strategic partnerships with the United States and Japan. The more unpredictable and assertive Beijing is with Delhi, the more salience Washington and Tokyo acquire in Delhi's politico-military calculus, thus enmeshing multi-nodal dynamics in India-China relations.[16]

Modi's informal summit with the Chinese President Xi Jinping in Wuhan on 27–28 April 2018, held in the aftermath of the more than 70 days' standoff between the two Asian giants in the Himalayas (Dokalam at the tri-junction of India, China and Bhutan), has widely been seen as an attempt by India to reset its relations with China. In his address at the Shangri La Dialogue in Singapore on 1 June 2018, Modi disclosed that '[n]o other relationship of India has as many layers as our relations with China'. India has been underplaying its participation in 'Quad', the four power grouping of the USA, Japan, Australia and India. It was not even mentioned by Modi at the Shangri La Dialogue, and the Chinese appreciated Modi's Shangri La address despite a wield criticism of China on so many issues. A balanced approach towards US–China relationships underlines India's 'strategic autonomy' which has characterized India's foreign policy since its Independence.

[16] For a detailed analysis of challenges of hedging and balancing ties between China and the USA, see Rahul Mishra, 'Challenges of Hedging Under Trump and Xi: An Indian Perspective', *National Commentaries, The ASAN Forum*, July–August 2018, http://www.theasanforum.org/an-indian-perspective/, accessed 16 August 2018.

India's Approach

India has its Nehru moment in the Indo-Pacific region. Recall Nehru's projection, underlined in the first chapter, that Atlantic domination will decline and the Indo-Pacific would emerge as the most dynamic region of the world where India will play a significant role in contributing to its stability and prosperity. We have also seen in Chapter 3 that Nehru contested the great power dominance in the region and worked for mobilizing Asian solidarity. Nehru's framework for a strategic order in the region was clearly laid down in his Asian relations and Afro-Asian conferences as also in his commitments to the freedom and stability of the countries of the region like Indonesia and Myanmar; and peace and stability in Korea and Indo-China. Echoes of this Nehruvian perspective could be easily discerned in Prime Minister Modi's maritime security vision with Indonesia and Singapore and in his Shangri La Dialogue's call to resist the 'return to the age of great power rivalries', and ensure that 'contests must not turn into conflicts'.[17]

The prevailing atmosphere of anxiety and uncertainty in the Indo-Pacific region will go away only under a stable and peaceful strategic order. India has repeatedly argued its vision of the regional strategic order which should be 'free, open, equal, inclusive, multipolar and transparent'. It cannot be a 'club of limited members', nor 'a grouping that seeks to dominate'. This order must be 'democratic and rule based'. Crafting such an order and sustaining it may be easier said than done, as underlined by India's former National Security Adviser Shivshankar Menon. Such an order cannot also be a coherent integrated structure. It would most likely be a network of multiple institutions and organizations. There are ASEAN and its related institutions. Then there are EAS, the AIIB and the Indian Ocean Rim Association, surrounded by various regional groupings such as BIMSTEC, MGC Initiative, APEC, RCEP and the like. An integrated perspective of all these differentiated institutions and groupings create the framework of a regional order that should be bound by internationally accepted

[17] Pratap Bhanu Mehta, 'The Shangri-La Moment', *The Indian Express*, 6 June 2018.

norms and consensual terms of engagement that are free from unilateral assertions and from use of force and violence.

India sees the centrality of ASEAN in evolving and sustaining such an order, and for good reasons. ASEAN is spread out in most of the region from the Bay of Bengal to the South China and East Asian seas. ASEAN has also evolved a unique style of operation, the 'ASEAN way', which is based on 'consensus, consultations and cooperation'. The centrality of ASEAN is also essential to prevent any strategic vacuum that may be filled in by hegemonic and assertive forces. The possibility of the ASEAN centrality becoming somewhat problematic cannot be ruled out as situations are developing to put ASEAN under pressure both internally and externally. ASEAN foreign ministers failed for the first time in July 2012 in issuing a joint statement in want of a consensus on the South China Sea dispute in the Scarborough Shoal area between the Philippines and China. Cambodia as a host of this meeting, and under the Chinese influence, refused to bring this issue in the joint statement, which was not acceptable to other members—Philippines and Vietnam. Analysts have blamed China for breaking ASEAN's internal cohesion through coercion and economic inducement. China had also taken exception in 2017 to a more than 40-year-old practice of military exercises between Singapore and Taiwan. There are also issues related to the nature and pace of building and consolidating the ASEAN community, economically, strategically and socioculturally as the member countries are diverse.

Any weakening of internal cohesion in the grouping will cost ASEAN heavily in terms of its centrality in Indo-Pacific regional architecture, where the South China Sea disputes have emerged as a major and sensitive hot spot. Underlining this, Singapore Prime Minister Lee Hsien Loong in a lecture delivered on 13 March 2018 said:

> One area where ASEAN countries do not have a unified stance and for fundamental reasons, is our strategic outlook. A clear instance of the impact of this, and how ASEAN members can find common ground despite our differences is South China Sea dispute, or issue. Not all ASEAN members are claimant states. Even among the four

> claimant states—Vietnam, Malaysia, Brunei, Philippines—there are different concerns and attitudes and nuances. ASEAN has to recognise this diversity.[18]

Conscious of the challenges ahead, in his capacity as the Prime Minister of ASEAN coordinating country, Lee added:

> Looking ahead, ASEAN must continue working hard to remain an effective and central player in the region. The 21st century is a different world.... Southeast Asia today is largely peaceful and stable but there will always be hotspots and difficult issues to deal with from time to time. We also have to adjust to a strategic balance which is shifting both globally and in the region. New powers are growing in strength and influence, especially China and India. Individual ASEAN countries must adapt to the new and changing strategic landscape. Countries have to take into account the policies and interests of new powers, while maintaining their traditional political and economic ties...
>
> ...At the same time, the ASEAN grouping has to get used to new internal dynamics, as each member feels the influence of the different powers to different degrees. We must accept the reality of these tidal pulls without allowing them to lead to fault lines forming within the ASEAN group.[19]

A realistic and sobering assessment indeed. Therefore, if India has to ensure the centrality of ASEAN in the regional strategic order, it will have to not only vigorously compete for strategic space in ASEAN but also contribute creatively in helping ASEAN preserve its internal cohesion and solidarity.

The concept of Asian Century was inherent in Nehru's endeavours for Asian resurgence and solidarity, but regional and international developments were then not propitious to realize his vision. The rise of the Indo-Pacific appears to be far more compatible and conducive

[18] Complete text of the speech is available via the Ministry of Foreign Affairs of Republic of Singapore, https://www1.mfa.gov.sg/Newsroom/Press-Statements-Transcripts-and-Photos/2018/03/press20180314, accessed 16 August 2018.

[19] Ibid.

in this respect. Asian Century has assumed a central place in the regional and international discourse related to Asia's rise and search for a strategic order in this region. Periodically there are claims and counterclaims of the Asian Century being led by India or by China. The Chinese leaders have left no doubt in anyone's mind that they would redefine the rules and terms of engagement in the Indo-Pacific region, and in the wider global context. The Indian leaders have also periodically indulged in exaggerated aspirational rhetoric assuming India's leadership of the Asian Century project. Participating in the ASEAN summit in Manila in November 2017, Prime Minister Modi commented: 'If 21st century is considered to be Asian Century, then it becomes our duty to make it India's century, and I say, it is possible'. At more serious moments, however, India has entertained no doubt that building of the Asian Century has to be a collaborative effort on the part of both India and China. India's Minister of External Affairs Sushma Swaraj presented at the Second India–China Media Forum on 1 February 2015 a six-point proposal for India and China to jointly realize the dream of the Asian Century. Prime Minister Narendra Modi reiterated in his Shangri La Dialogue in Singapore that 'Asia of rivalry will hold us all back. Asia of cooperation will shape this century'. This is shared by the Chinese leadership as well. Recall Deng Xiaoping's saying that 'Only when India and China had developed, a real century of Asia will emerge'. Echoing this, President Xi Jinping on the occasion of his visit to India in September 2014 wrote in an article: 'I am confident that as long as China and India work together, the Asian Century of prosperity and renewal will surely arrive at an early date'.[20]

These hopes and promises at the leadership levels are, however, mostly promises and popular sentiments. In concrete terms, India and China working together for Asian Century means working for their respective developments and working jointly with each other both economically and strategically. Economically, both India and China are growing at their own respective paces that are impressive. They are carrying out structural reforms and addressing domestic challenges

[20] Xi Jinping, 'Towards and Asian Century of Prosperity', *The Hindu*, 17 November 2014.

of equity, unemployment and delivery of services. China's growth rate has slowed down but it is still impressive and promises to make China the world's largest economy. India has started growing faster but may not be able to match China in the overall weight of economy until at least 2050. Despite their repeated assurances to each other, China and India are not opening enough to each other for trade, investments and services. There are issues of heavy trade imbalance in China's favour and its unfair trade practices, as also security concerns on India's part that keep China cooperating with each other only at the suboptimal level bilaterally.

The real challenge of the two together creating Asian Century is in the strategic context and there they are faced with serious bilateral as well as regional issues. China's spreading out economically in the region through its mega projects such as the BRI and Maritime Silk Road, and its acquisition of formidable military capabilities have created a widespread impression that China is driving for a unipolar Asia and a China-dominated Asian Century. This will be resisted by India and all other countries in the Indo-Pacific region. China has to ask itself that why has it created bilateral and multilateral conflicts with its Asian neighbours such as India, Japan and those in the South China Sea and why is it not resolving these conflicts through peaceful negotiations.

India has been seeking peaceful coexistence with China since the early 1950s. Even after 1962, it was India that took initiatives to normalize relations with China and to seek a common ground in regional and bilateral engagements. The Wuhan Summit and the institutionalization of 'informal summit' to have regular strategic communication have been the latest examples of such Indian initiatives. India has also been cautious in blindly participating in the moves like the India–US–Japan–Australia Quad grouping with military overtones, as already noted. China has been taking note of such Indian caution and is appreciating them. But China still seems reluctant to move on the issues of bilateral contention like the border dispute and propping up of Pakistan. China has assertively frontloaded the sovereignty question in its engagement with its neighbours but is indifferent to India's protestations regarding the violation of India's sovereignty in

Pakistan-occupied Kashmir under its BRI projects. China needs to understand that lack of creative response from its side to India's primary security concerns and the continued indifference and assertion will only push India closer to those forces that China considers inimical to its interests. It must be recalled that in the aftermath of the 1962 offensive, India was forced to seek military support from the USA and the UK that had hitherto been stoutly avoided.

It has been argued elsewhere that there are clearly two mutually competing narratives of India–China relations. The first one is based on peaceful coexistence, rooted back in the period of the first to the seventeenth and eighteenth centuries. Then, India and China together accounted for more than 50 per cent of the world's wealth without any mutual conflict. This narrative had also characterized their engagement during the first decade of their resurgence in the late 1940s. The second narrative is that of rivalry and conflict that is landmarked by China's unexpected war imposed on India in 1962 and that keeps manifesting in China's nuclear and military propping up of Pakistan and Dokalam-like standoffs. The contention that Asian Century cannot be built by following the second narrative cannot be disputed.[21]

To escape the unexpected fallout of the global and regional uncertainty as well as to guard against China's unpredictability and hegemonic aspirations, India has been building its own capabilities and has been widening and deepening its strategic engagements in the region. Some of the key directions of this approach are discernible. India is building close bilateral and trilateral strategic partnerships with the key regional stakeholders like the USA and Japan. Emphasis in these partnerships is to acquire technologies and expand markets for trade and investments. India is systematically collaborating with Japan and the USA even in carrying out infrastructural projects in the Indo-Pacific region to present alternatives to the Chinese BRI projects. Gradually upgrading military, especially naval, exercises are also preparing these partners for joint action in the region, as and when the situation

[21] For a detailed argument on these lines, see S. D. Muni, 'India, China and the Asian Century', *Diplomatist*, March 2015, https://www.diplomatist.com/dipo201503/article009.html, accessed 16 August 2018.

demands, including in the area of disaster relief, humanitarian operations and anti-piracy actions. While doing so, India is also mindful of maintaining its strategic resilience towards China as indicated in steps like the Wuhan Informal Summit and through the forums like the India–Russia–China trilateral equations and active participation in the Shanghai Cooperation Organisation. India then is integrating itself fully with the regional institutions and multilateral groupings in the region, as already mentioned. Through its active participation in these institutions and grouping, attempts are made to strengthen international norms and commitment to regional commons such as freedom of sea-lane navigation and airways, avoidance of force in mutual engagement and negotiated resolution of disputes.

India is also keen to fortify its position in the Indo-Pacific waterways—the Bay of Bengal, Malacca Strait and South China Sea—keeping in view China's fast expanding, assertive and sizable economic and strategic presence. India is activating and strengthening the BIMSTEC to consolidate its presence in South Asia and the Bay of Bengal area. This process may not be easy and smooth in view of the diversity of strategic perspectives of the BIMSTEC members but India looks determined to carry its approach forward.

In the strategically vital Malacca Strait, India's approach is concentrated at two levels. First, to strengthen Andaman and Nicobar as the tri-service base for its formidable geostrategic location in the Strait, and second, by cultivating littoral states of the Malacca Strait, in particular Singapore and Indonesia. India's naval access to Sabang port in Sumatra and the signing of a Joint Maritime Vision Statement with Indonesia in May 2018, as already discussed, marks a major move forward in this direction. India has left no one in doubt that it is a major stakeholder in the peace, stability and freedom of navigation in South China Sea, in view of its growing trade passing through this region. There is no doubt that mutual interests will bring India and Vietnam much closer economically and strategically and that India will also be able to widen its cooperative interaction with the Philippines. Beyond South China Sea, India's initiative to form a forum of Pacific Island Nations will also gather momentum gradually. India's attempts to bridge its areas of trust deficit with Russia are expected to energize its South China Sea stakes in view of increasing flow of oil to India from Russia's Sakhalin reserves.

Looking Ahead

India today is better placed to realize Nehru's dream of Asian resurgence and solidarity in the Indo-Pacific region. There has been significant accretion to India's economic and military capabilities, and the countries in the region are far more receptive to India's initiatives and enhanced presence. The dynamics of power relations and strategic moves of the bigger players in the region are different from what they were during the 1950s and the 1960s, but the spirit of Asian consensus to keep the hegemonic powers away and have a multipolar, free and independent Asia is as strong as ever. In its approach to this region, the Indian leadership, however, has to learn from and internalize the reasons of Nehru's failure. To begin with, there is no room for arrogance and complacence in India's approach, howsoever benign it could be. The region has witnessed a huge surge in nationalism and identity, and no country—small, weak or poor—can be taken for granted. India needs to be sensitive and accommodative to the aspirations of all its neighbours in the Indo-Pacific region. India also needs to be careful in avoiding any indication that it is working to assume leadership of the region. In a multi-polar Asia, there are many leaders and more may be emerging. The third lesson from Nehru's experience is that in India's approach, personally amicable relations at the leadership levels are welcome but they cannot be a substitute for hard-core national interests. It may also be underlined in this respect that 'mutual trust' is a two-way street. Every country has to closely monitor the movements on this street to ensure that it is not taken by a surprise at any stage as India had experienced in the past. Nation states perceive and respond to the regional and international systems to meet domestic needs and aspirations. While the countries in the Indo-Pacific region are economically active and dynamic, they are also undergoing significant domestic political turbulence. Their regional policies are shaped by this turbulence, and India's approach towards them must be sensitive and accommodative towards the implications of their respective internal turbulences. An example to learn lessons in this respect is the changing responses of Western Indian Ocean island country of Seychelles for granting development projects and naval access to India on its military base on Assumption Island.[22]

The best of the lessons drawn from the Nehru era is that for visions and aspirations to be realized fully, they need to be backed by capabilities and resources. India is growing fast and it has the potential to grow faster. It has to strengthen its manufacturing sector and seek possibilities of getting integrated with the global and regional value chains. Singapore's Minister of Foreign Affairs Dr Vivian Balakrishnan, speaking at Singapore Symposium in New Delhi, offered help to 'forge closer links between India and Southeast Asia through transforming global value chains and enhancing maritime, aviation and digital connectivity'. He also advised India to liberalize its aviation sector which can have a spin-off effect in generating employment and facilitating businesses.[23] India is also being pressured to liberalize its trade. Elements of stagnation in India's trade with the region, as already discussed in the previous chapters, are a matter of concern. Similarly, India's defence production has to gain momentum to make its military diplomacy in the region effective.

In the previous chapters, India's delivery deficit—delays and failures in delivering on promises—has been underlined as a serious weakness in India's eastward engagement. Problems of coordinating projects and providing adequate financial support have created serious bottlenecks in this respect, besides bureaucratic procedures. It has been noted that between the finance and the foreign ministries, the DPA has been constituted and reconstituted, but without satisfactory results as yet. Similarly, we have drawn attention to India's lines of credit policy, which is so unrealistic that the friendly countries find it

[22] *The Indian Express* (New Delhi), 17 June 2017 (front page), http://epaper.indianexpress.com/1247973/Indian-Express/June-17,-2017#page/1/1, accessed 16 August 2018.

[23] The complete text of the speech is available via the Ministry of Foreign Affairs, Singapore, https://www.mfa.gov.sg/content/mfa/overseasmission/new_delhi/press_statements_speeches/2017/Nov/visit-by-minister-for-foreign-affairs-dr-vivian-balakrishnan-to-.html, accessed 16 August 2018. (S. D. Muni was present at the Singapore Symposium.)

extremely difficult to take advantage of the offers made by India. It is hoped that as India's AEP moves forward, these problems would be attended with seriousness. India's private sector is a significant partner in India's engagement with the Indo-Pacific region. While the private sector is expected to be driven by its business interests and profit motives, it must also get sensitized to India's long-term strategic stakes in the region to strike a balance between the corporate interests and the national interests. The Indian government may make institutional arrangements in collaboration with various business and industrial chambers to update companies and entrepreneurs on the changing strategic scene in the region and India's stakes in these changes.

The broader policy-level challenge for India in the Indo-Pacific region is to cope with the uncertainty precipitated by the Sino-US rivalry, which is gradually also preparing the ground for trade wars between them. China is not giving any indication of letting up in its assertive stance in the region. It will be unlikely to see any softening in China's approach towards India in the region. On the question of NSG (Nuclear Suppliers Group) membership, India's application remains stalled largely due to China's obstruction. Maldives also continues to flout all democratic norms and practices of its own constitution, largely on the basis of China's support for the ruling regime. India can only continue with its present two-way policy to plead cooperation and coexistence with China on the one hand while availing of all possible options and opportunities to prepare itself for any untoward and unexpected development.

ANNEXURE A

Exchange of Visits

Table A.1 *A Narendra Modi's Visit to the Indo-Pacific Region*

S. No.	*Date*	*Who Visited*	*Countries Visited*	*Outcome*
1	31 May–2 June 2018	Narendra Modi	Singapore	The following MoUs were signed: (a) mutual recognition agreement on nursing; (b) logistics and services support for naval ships, submarines and naval aircraft visits; (c) cyber security; (d) combat illicit trafficking in narcotic drugs, psychotropic substances and their precursors; (e) cooperation in the field of personnel management and public administration; (f) constitution of a joint working group (JWG) on Fintech between India and Singapore; and (g) cooperation in the field of planning between NITI Aayog and Singapore Cooperation Enterprise (SCE).
2	31 May 2018	Narendra Modi	Malaysia	PM Narendra Modi made a brief stopover in Kuala Lumpur, Malaysia, on 31 May 2018 to meet the newly elected Prime Minister of Malaysia, H. E. Dr Mahathir Mohammad.
3	29–31 May 2018	Narendra Modi	Indonesia	Agreements were signed for (a) cooperation in the field of defence, including exchange of strategic information, military education, training and exercise, and cooperation among the armed forces and (b) cooperation in the exploration and uses of outer space for peaceful purposes. MoUs were signed on: (a) scientific and technological cooperation in the field of information and communication technology, marine science and technology, energy research, disaster management, geospatial information, applied chemistry, etc.; (b) technical cooperation in the railways sector; (c) health cooperation; (d) pharmaceutical, biological and cosmetics regulatory functions;

(continued)

Table A.1 *(Continued)*

S. No.	*Date*	*Who Visited*	*Countries Visited*	*Outcome*
				(e) policy dialogue between governments and interactions between think tanks; (f) Lal Bahadur Shastri National Academy of Administration of India and National Institute of Public Administration of Indonesia (NIPA); and (g) plan of activities to celebrate 70 years of diplomatic relations.
4	12–14 November 2017	Narendra Modi	Philippines This is the first prime ministerial visit from India to the Philippines in 36 years.	The following agreements were signed: (a) defence cooperation and logistics; (b) agriculture, including International Rice Research Institute opening its South Asian branch in Varanasi; (c) micro, small and medium enterprises; (d) cooperation between the Indian Council for World Affairs (ICWA) and Philippines Foreign Services Institute; (e) establishment of Indian cultural relations chair at Philippines University.
5	14 November 2017	Narendra Modi	Philippines 15th ASEAN–India Summit and the 12th East Asia Summit	The prime minister invited all ASEAN countries for the India–ASEAN Connectivity Summit in December and then for business summit from 22 to 24 January in Delhi.
6	5–7 September 2017	Narendra Modi	Myanmar	The following MoUs were signed: (a) on maritime security cooperation; (b) women's police training centre at Yamethin, Myanmar; (c) cultural exchange programme from 2017 to 2020; (d) sharing white shipping information between navies; (e) technical agreement for a coastal surveillance system; (f) MoU on regulation of medical products; (g) cooperation in the field of health and medicine; (h) extension of MoU on the establishment of MIIT: (i) extension of MoU on the establishment of the India–Myanmar Center for Enhancement of IT-Skill;

				(j) cooperation between the Myanmar Press Council and the Press Council of India; and (k) MoU in the field of elections.
7	25–26 June 2017	Narendra Modi	USA 70 years of diplomatic relations	Trump reaffirmed the support of the USA for India's permanent membership on a reformed UN Security Council, membership in the Nuclear Suppliers Group, the Wassenaar Arrangement and the Australia Group and for a UN Comprehensive Convention on International Terrorism. The USA has offered for India's consideration the sale of Sea Guardian unmanned aerial systems. Leaders announced their intention to build on the implementation of their 'white shipping' data-sharing arrangement, which enhances collaboration on maritime domain awareness.
8	10–12 November 2016	Narendra Modi	Japan	Agreement on Cooperation in the Peaceful Uses of Nuclear Energy Following MoUs were signed: (a) between ISRO and JAXA concerning cooperation in the field of outer space; (b) mutual collaboration in marine and earth science and technology; (c) agriculture and food-related industry that includes food value chain networking and protecting the geographical indication (GI) of agriculture products; (d) transport and urban development; (e) capacity-building measures for the Textiles Committee and aligning the Indian quality control measures in line with Japanese market and technical standards; and (f) MoU between the state government of Gujarat and Hyogo Prefectural Government, Japan. The MoU seeks to promote mutual cooperation between Gujarat and Hyogo in the fields of academics, business, cultural cooperation, disaster management and environmental protection. Memorandum of Cooperation (MoC) on (a) manufacturing skill transfer promotion programme; (b) cultural exchange; (c) cooperation in sports. Under this MOC, the two sides would seek to promote the training of athletes, training of coaches, programmes for sports science and anti-doping, etc.

(continued)

Table A.1 *(Continued)*

S. No.	*Date*	*Who Visited*	*Countries Visited*	*Outcome*
9	7–8 September 2016	Narendra Modi	Lao PDR To attend the 14th ASEAN–India Summit and the 11th East Asia Summit	Three declarations were discussed in EAS: Vientiane Declaration on Promoting Infrastructure Development Cooperation in East Asia; an EAS Declaration on Strengthening Responses to Migrants in Crisis and Trafficking in Persons; and an EAS Statement on Non-Proliferation. A Joint Statement on the Regional Comprehensive Economic Partnership (RCEP) Negotiations adopted at a separate ceremony after the EAS.
10	2–3 September 2016	Narendra Modi	Vietnam First bilateral visit at the prime ministerial level to Vietnam in the last 15 years. The last such bilateral visit took place when the then Prime Minister Atal Bihari Vajpayee went in 2001.	Talk with Prime Minister of Vietnam Nguyen Xuan Phucapart.
11	6–8 June 2016	Narendra Modi	USA Theme: The United States and India: Enduring Global Partners in the 21st Century	Following agreements were signed: (a) technical arrangement between the Indian Navy and the United States Navy concerning unclassified maritime information sharing; (b) exchange of terrorist screening information; and (c) information exchange agreement concerning aircraft carrier technologies and HA-DR (humanitarian assistance and disaster relief).

				Following MoUs were signed: (a) enhance cooperation on energy security, clean energy and climate change; (b) enhance co-operation on wildlife conservation and combating wildlife trafficking; (c) development of an international expedited traveller initiative (the Global Entry Programme); and (d) increase the understanding of the geologic occurrence, distribution and production of natural gas hydrates along the continental margin of India and in the USA.
12	31 March–1 April 2016	Narendra Modi	USA Nuclear Security Summit (31 March–1 April 2016)	To discuss measures required to prevent terrorists and other non-state actors from gaining access to sensitive nuclear materials and technologies. The Prime Minister of India also met the Prime Minister of New Zealand. They discussed the issues of dairy technology, tourism, free trade areas and direct flight between both countries, etc.
13	23–24 November 2015	Narendra Modi	Singapore	Cooperation in the field of defence, science, trade, finance transport, maritime, smart city and skill development. Promotion of culture and education.
14	21–23 November 2015	Narendra Modi	Malaysia To attend the 13th ASEAN–India Summit, the 10th East Asia Summit as well as participate in a bilateral visit to Malaysia	The foreign ministers of our countries have adopted an ASEAN–India plan of action for the period 2016–2020 which is called the Partnership for Peace, Progress and Shared Prosperity. India will enhance the ASEAN–India Science and Technology Development Fund from the current US$1 million to US$5 million. Decided to cooperate in the field of space, solar and wind energy, science, etc. Electronic visa facility to all 10 ASEAN countries.

(continued)

Table A.1 *(Continued)*

S. No.	*Date*	*Who Visited*	*Countries Visited*	*Outcome*
				India has announced at this meeting a US$1 billion line of credit to facilitate connectivity projects under the ASEAN–India Strategic Partnership. ASEAN-Study Centre at the North-Eastern Hill University in Shillong. Settlement of disputes on South China Sea according to the principles of international law including the 1982 UN Convention on the Law of the Sea. India wants all parties to the disputes in the South China Sea to abide by the 2002 declaration on the conduct of parties. With Malaysia, India signed MoUs on (a) cyber security; (b) culture exchange programme; and (c) PEMANDU, to develop cooperation in the areas of performance management, project delivery and monitoring related to government programmes.
15	23–24 September 2015	Narendra Modi	USA	Issues discussed with President of the USA include comprehensive convention on suppression of terrorism and cooperation in the field of cyber security, space, climate change, solar energy, technology, etc. No joint statement was signed.
16	18–19 May 2015	Narendra Modi	Republic of Korea	Agreements were signed on (a) avoidance of double taxation and the prevention of fiscal evasion with respect to taxes on income and (b) cooperation in audio-visual co-production. MoUs were signed for (a) cooperation between the National Security Council Secretariat of the Republic of India and the Office of National Security of the

Republic of Korea and (b) cooperation in the field of electric power development and new energy industries.

MoUs were signed for (a) cooperation in youth matters through participation in events and activities; (b) framework of cooperation in the field of road transport and highways; and (c) cooperation in the fields of maritime transport and logistics.

To substantiate the special strategic partnership, the two sides agreed to the following: (a) establish annual summit meetings, in either country, or on the margins of plurilateral events; (b) hold joint commissions led by the two foreign ministers annually; (c) facilitate greater parliamentary exchanges to strengthen democratic institutions in their respective regions; (d) strengthen the partnerships between Indian and Korean institutions of defence education, including the National Defence College of India and the National Defense University of Korea, by activating the dispatch of military officers for education; (e) further strengthen regular consultations between the National Security Council structures of the two countries on security, defence and cyber-related issues; (f) establish a joint vice-ministerial-level defence and foreign affairs dialogue in the '2+2' format; (g) encourage greater cooperation between their shipyards for defence needs; (h) pursue further deepening of defence cooperation through commencement of staff level talks between the two navies and regular exchanges of visits between the two armed forces; (i) seek the means of the cyber security cooperation to prepare against transnational cyber threats; (j) cooperate appropriately in the area of UN peacekeeping; and (k) hold a track 1.5 dialogue annually between the Institute of Foreign Affairs and National Security of ROK (IFANS) and ICWA.

(continued)

Table A.1 *(Continued)*

S. No.	*Date*	*Who Visited*	*Countries Visited*	*Outcome*
17	14–18 November 2014	Narendra Modi	Australia	Agreements were signed on (a) social security—it will provide for social security and superannuation benefits for those who have been residents of the other country on the basis of equality of benefit, export of benefits and avoidance of double coverage—and (b) agreement concerning transfer of sentenced persons. MOUs were signed on (a) combating narcotics trafficking and developing police cooperation; (b) cooperation in the field of arts and culture; and (c) field of tourism. Framework for security cooperation between India and Australia: (a) annual summit and foreign policy exchanges and coordination; (b) defence policy planning and coordination; (c) counter-terrorism and other transnational crimes; (d) border protection, coast guard and customs; (e) disarmament, non-proliferation, civil nuclear energy and maritime security; (f) disaster management and peacekeeping; and (g) cooperation in regional and multilateral fora.
18	11–13 November 2014	Narendra Modi	Myanmar To participate in the Ninth East Asia Summit and the 12th India–ASEAN Summit Six bilateral meetings	All of these meetings were his first meetings. In essence, they were meetings where the prime minister was able to explain his views on how he sees India progressing and seek the cooperation of various countries and their leadership in the India story. Discussion with ASEAN was focused on RCEP (Regional Comprehensive Economic Partnership), FTA, solar energy, etc. For FTA, Modi urged the Philippines, which is the last country to sign on this, to complete the process so that this can be implemented at the earliest.

				India discussed housing and infrastructure development with Malaysia, and tri-lateral highway and skill development with Myanmar.
19	26–30 September 2014	Narendra Modi	USA	USA agreed to help India in smart city and other infrastructure development. To enhance 'Make in India' USA also decided to help in manufacturing. Both countries agreed to work together on counter terrorism, space, defence, security, MTCR, NSG, against counterfeit currency and cybercrime, clean energy and technology development.
20	30 August–3 September 2014	Narendra Modi	Japan	Agreement on a commercial contract for manufacturing and supply of rare earth chlorides from India to Japan. Japan pledges 50 billion yen loan for the Guwahati Sewerage Project in Assam. Establishment of a group for setting up of a 10 MW canal-top grid connected solar photovoltaic (PV) power plant in Gujarat as a model for next-generation infrastructure. Signing of the loan agreement for the super-critical coal-fired power project in Meja in Uttar Pradesh. Signing of two memoranda between the Japan Society for the Promotion of Science (JSPS) and the Indian Council of Historical Research (ICHR), and between the JSPS and the Indian Council of Social Science Research (ICSSR).

Source: http://www.mea.gov.in/prime-minister-visits.htm

Table A.2 *Indo-Pacific Visit from India: Presidents and Vice-Presidents*

		Presidents		
S. No.	*Date*	*Who Visited*	*Countries Visited*	*Any Outcome*
1	30 April–2 May 2016	Pranab Mukherjee	New Zealand	Air services agreement
2	14–17 September 2014	Pranab Mukherjee	Vietnam	Agreement on cooperation and mutual assistance in customs matters MoUs on (a) US$100 million line of credit for defence procurement; (b) animal health; (c) setting up of Pangasius breeding and farming in India; (d) cooperation in youth affairs and skill development; (e) letter of intent between ONGC Videsh Limited, India, and Vietnam Oil and Gas Group (PetroVietnam); and (f) MoU between Jet Airways (India) and Vietnam Airlines Company Limited.
3	24–30 July 2011	Pratibha Patil	Republic of Korea	Agreement in the peaceful uses of nuclear energy. Administrative arrangements for social security agreement. MoU on media exchanges.
4	31 January–9 February 2006	A. P. J. Abdul Kalam	Interaction with Academician and Students, Speech in National Assembly	No agreement was signed.

Vice Presidents				
S. No.	*Date*	*Who Visited*	*Countries Visited*	*Any Outcome*
1	6–7 March 2017	Hamid Ansari	Indonesia IORA (Indian Ocean Rim Association) Leader's Summit	The vice-president announced India's willingness to set up an IORA Centre of Excellence for strengthening maritime domain awareness in one of the coastal cities of India. In order to rekindle the cultural linkages that existed between countries adjoining the Indian Ocean, India has launched initiatives like Project Mausam. India is committed to working with other member states of IORA to realize the region's untapped potential and to ensure that the Indian Ocean becomes a zone of prosperity and harmony.
2	3–5 February 2016	Hamid Ansari	Thailand	Address by vice-president at Chulalongkorn University, Bangkok: 'India, Thailand and ASEAN: Contours of a Rejuvenated Relationship'.
3	1–3 February 2016	Hamid Ansari	Brunei	MoUs were signed on (a) health cooperation—exchange of doctors, information, etc.; (b) defence cooperation—training of military officers, joint exercise, etc.; and (c) cooperation in youth and sports affairs.
4	1–4 November 2015	Hamid Ansari	Indonesia	MoUs were signed on (a) cooperation in new and renewable energy sector and (b) cooperation in the cultural field. Aim to enhance trade, technological and space cooperation.

(Continued)

Table A.2 *(Continued)*

		Vice Presidents		
S. No.	*Date*	*Who Visited*	*Countries Visited*	*Any Outcome*
5	15–17 September 2015	Hamid Ansari	Lao PDR	Air services agreement between India and Lao PDR. Agreement on quick impact projects related to agriculture sector. For this, Lao proposed three projects. The first one is the establishment of a National Biofertiliser Production Centre. The second is the promotion of Indian goats and sheep in Lao PDR. The third is an integrated spices and grapes cultivation project Discussion started on new MoU on agriculture, defence, double tax avoidance, etc.
6	15–17 September 2015	Hamid Ansari	Cambodia	Two MoUs were signed: (a) quick impact projects signed under Mekong–Ganga Cooperation. Quick impact projects are related to health, agriculture and women empowerment. (b) tourism: Assistance in conservation of culture and heritage such as Angkor Wat and Ta Prohm temple, etc. Grant of US$50,000 for the already existing Entrepreneurship Development Centre, which has already been functioning with Indian assistance since 2004. Increasing vocational and English training centres.
7	14–17 January 2013	Hamid Ansari	Vietnam	Speech of Shri M. Hamid Ansari, Hon'ble Vice-President of India at the closing ceremony of the India–Vietnam Friendship Year in Hanoi.

Sources: http://www.mea.gov.in/president-visits.htm; http://www.mea.gov.in/vice-president-visits.htm.

Table A.3 *Manmohan Singh's Visit to the Indo-Pacific*

S. No.	*Date*	*Who Visited*	*Countries Visited*	*Any Outcome*
1	3–4 March 2014	Manmohan Singh	Myanmar BIMSTEC Summit	Memorandum of Association on the Establishment of the BIMSTEC Permanent Secretariat. Memorandum of Association Among BIMSTEC Member Countries Concerning Establishment of a BIMSTEC Centre for Weather and Climate. Memorandum of Understanding (MoU) on the Establishment of the BIMSTEC Cultural Industries Commission (BCIC) and BIMSTEC Cultural Industries Observatory (BCIO) in Bhutan. Agree to implement the BIMSTEC Poverty Plan of Action adopted at the Second BIMSTEC Ministerial Meeting on Poverty Alleviation held in January 2012 in Nepal. Also decided to enhance cooperation in the field of energy, physical connectivity in BIMSTEC region, tourism cooperation, fisheries, health sector, including on traditional medicine, environmental protection and sustainable development and to promote capacity building in the area of disaster management.
2	10–12 October 2013	Manmohan Singh	Indonesia	MoUs were signed on the following: (a) health, in the field of child and maternal health, traditional medicine and research, etc.; (b) cooperation in combating corruption; (c) combating illicit trafficking in narcotics, drugs, psychotropic substances and their precursors; (d) cooperation in the field of disaster management; (e) encourage and promote cooperation in the area of training of public officials and capacity building; and (f) promote friendly, cooperative and

(Continued)

Table A.3 *(Continued)*

S. No.	*Date*	*Who Visited*	*Countries Visited*	*Any Outcome*
				collaborative institutional relations through facilitation of dialogue involving eminent persons from the fields of diplomacy, culture, economy, trade, education, international relations, sciences, social sciences, communications and the media.
3	9–10 October 2013	Manmohan Singh	Brunei 11th India–ASEAN Summit and Eighth EAST Asian Summit	India ratified the Third Protocol of the Treaty of Amity and Cooperation in Southeast Asia (TAC) on 28 March 2012. To mark the 20th Anniversary of ASEAN–India Dialogue Relations and the 10 years of summit-level partnership, India successfully hosted the ASEAN–India Commemorative Summit in New Delhi on 20–21 December 2012, under the theme 'ASEAN-India Partnership for Peace and Shared Prosperity', where the leaders declared the ASEAN–India partnership to be elevated to a strategic partnership and adopted the ASEAN–India Vision Statement. The ASEAN–India Eminent Persons Group (AIEPG), Delhi dialogue, ASEAN-India Network of Think Tanks (AINTT) has evolved for the discussion on strategic political and economic issues facing the region. SOMTC (Senior Officials on Transnational Crime)+India decided to work together on combating transnational crime, drug trafficking, trade, IT, education, training, agriculture, climate change, renewable energy and natural disaster.
4	30–31 May 2013	Manmohan Singh	Thailand	Treaties on (a) extradition and (b) transfer of sentenced persons—signed on 25 January 2012 have been ratified by both sides. MoUs were signed on the following: (a) establishment of the India–Thailand

				Exchange Programme; (b) cooperation in the field of mapping and geospatial technology applications; (c) cooperation in the exchange of intelligence related to money laundering and financing terrorism; and (d) establishment of the ICCR Hindi Chair of Indian Studies (Hindi Language).
5	27–29 May 2013	Manmohan Singh	Japan	India and Japan have agreed to institutionalize bilateral naval exercises, to conduct them regularly and with increased frequency. The Japanese government has offered to sell the US-2 amphibious aircraft to India. After DMIC, Japan will also support the Chennai–Bengaluru Industrial Corridor. Joint feasibility study on the possible introduction of high-speed railways or Shinkansen on the Mumbai–Ahmedabad route in India. In the joint statement there is agreement to work together for India's full membership in all the four export control regimes.
6	19 November 2012	Manmohan Singh	Cambodia 10th ASEAN–India Summit	Manmohan Singh emphasized that improved connectivity between India and ASEAN will be vital for deepening economic integration as well as strategic partnership. India and ASEAN have a shared interest in maritime security, counter-terrorism, anti-piracy and disaster management. India's large markets and rapid growth offer enormous opportunities for investments. Conclusion of the Agreement on Trade in Services and Investments, together with our existing Agreement on Trade in Goods, will be a springboard for rapid expansion in our economic relations.
7	27–29 May 2012	Manmohan Singh	Myanmar	Agreements signed on the following: (a) cooperation between Institute of Defence Studies and Analysis (IDSA) and Myanmar Institute of Strategic and International Studies (MISIS), and (b) Air Services Agreement between India and Myanmar.

(Continued)

Table A.3 *(Continued)*

S. No.	*Date*	*Who Visited*	*Countries Visited*	*Any Outcome*
				MoUs were signed on the following: (a) India–Myanmar Border Area Development; (b) setting up of Myanmar Institute of Information Technology; (c) establishment of the Advanced Centre for Agriculture Research and Education (ACARE), Yezin Agriculture University and Nay Pyi Taw, Myanmar; (d) establishment of a Rice Bio Park (Paddy and Rural Prosperity) at the Department of Agriculture Research, Nay Pyi Taw, Myanmar; (e) establishment of border haats across the border between India and Myanmar; (f) establishment of the Joint Trade and Investment Forum; (g) Cultural Exchange Programme 2012–2015; (h) US$500 million credit line between Export-Import Bank of India and Myanmar Foreign Trade Bank.; (i) MoU between Calcutta University, Kolkata, and Dagon University, Yangon; and (j) cooperation between the Indian Council of World Affairs (ICWA) and MISIS.
8	24–26 March 2012	South Korea	Manmohan Singh	Agreement on visa simplification was signed.
			Nuclear Security Summit	MoUs were signed on the following: (a) cooperation between the Indian Space Research Organization (ISRO) and the Korea Aerospace Research Institute (KARI); (b) cooperation between the Foreign Service Institute and Korean National Diplomatic Academy.
				Upgrading of the Joint Committee on Science and Technology to the ministerial level as a foundation for common growth.
				India and South Korea have Comprehensive Economic Partnership Agreement (CEPA) since January 2010.

9	17–20 November 2011	Manmohan Singh	Indonesia Ninth India–ASEAN Summit and Sixth East Asia Summit	India–ASEAN Free Trade Agreement for Trade in Goods has come into effect in all ASEAN member states and India following its ratification by Cambodia on 1 August 2011. The ministers have agreed to a structured, private sector engagement in the five areas of pharmaceuticals, innovation and skills training, information technology, manufacturing and infrastructure. The Indian prime minister (PM) seeks support for early conclusion of a commercially meaningful services and investment agreement. This would create a positive atmosphere for the implementation of the India–ASEAN Comprehensive Economic Cooperation Agreement as envisaged in our Framework Agreement of 2003. The first ASEAN–India Meeting on Agriculture was held in October 2011, and the first meeting of the India–ASEAN Green Fund was held in Cambodia in October 2011. Greater physical connectivity between India and ASEAN remains our strategic objective. There are several proposals under consideration with regard to land and sea connectivity. These include the India–Myanmar–Thailand Highway, its extension to Laos and Cambodia and the development of a new highway also linking Vietnam. Both countries also have a study on a Mekong–India Economic Corridor conducted by the Economic Research Institute for ASEAN and East Asia which proposes the linking of corridors in the peninsular, and possibly the northeast regions of India with the East Asian region.

(Continued)

Table A.3 *(Continued)*

S. No.	*Date*	*Who Visited*	*Countries Visited*	*Any Outcome*
10	30 October 2010	Manmohan Singh	Vietnam Eighth India–ASEAN Summit and Fifth East Asia Summit The theme of the summit: From vision to action	Discussion on implementing the India–ASEAN Trade in Goods Agreement by all ASEAN States. The conclusion of a services and investment agreement would be an important step in achieving goal of comprehensive economic cooperation. India decided to extend visa on arrival facility to nationals of Cambodia, Vietnam, Philippines and Laos with effect from 1 January 2011. Upgrade the level of youth exchanges as well as establish vocational training centres in ASEAN countries. Cooperation in space and security.
11	24–26 October 2010	Manmohan Singh	Japan Annual Summit	The two PMs directed their relevant authorities to work towards early entry into a CEPA and its smooth implementation. The two PMs decided to steadily expand security and defence cooperation between India and Japan. In this context, they welcomed the launch of India–Japan Shipping Policy Forum and mutual exchange of schedules of escort operations by the Indian Navy and Japan Self-Defense Forces in the Gulf of Aden. They instructed relevant authorities to realize the full potential of the Action Plan to Advance Security Cooperation signed in 2009, based on the Joint Declaration on Security Cooperation between India and Japan. The two PMs welcomed the establishment and the holding of the Committee on India-Japan ICT (Information and Communication Technology) strategy for economic growth and India–Japan ICT regulatory policy talk. Both also decided to cooperate in the field of climate change, counterterrorism, nuclear non-proliferation, etc.

12	27 October 2010	Manmohan Singh	Malaysia	The agreement on CECA which specified timelines, both for the signing by 31 January and for the implementation by 1 July, was indeed hailed as a corner-stone of these talks and of the visit. Malaysia expressed full support for counterterrorism cooperation with India including the setting up of a joint working group. Malaysia had opened visa facilitation centres which would help particularly for issue of business visas in Hyderabad and Mumbai. Decided to set up the Joint Talent Development Consultative Committee (JICTDC). Setting up of a joint working group on new and renewable energy.
13	22–26 November 2009	Manmohan Singh	USA 'India and the United States: Partnership for a Better World'	Agreement to jointly develop technology to improve weather forecasting, in particular, monsoon prediction. Agreed on MoUs for the following: (a) collaboration on R&D in solar and wind energy and (b) agreed on a new MoU on counterterrorism cooperation. Agreed to launch the US–India Financial and Economic Partnership to strengthen engagement on economic-, financial- and investment-related issues. Launched a new Obama–Singh 21st Century Knowledge Initiative to increase university linkages. Agreed to establish a Regional Global Disease Detection Center in India and to build a partnership with the US Centres for Disease Control and Prevention. An important outcome was establishing a green partnership which would address inter-related challenges of energy security, climate change and food security.

(Continued)

Table A.3 *(Continued)*

S. No.	*Date*	*Who Visited*	*Countries Visited*	*Any Outcome*
				India and the United States reiterated their intention to realize the full potential of the Agreement on Civil Nuclear Co-operation signed on 10 October 2008 through the speedy implementation of its provisions. On Copenhagen process, the two leaders reaffirmed their commitment to the UNFCCC and the Bali Action Plan as basis for deliberations at Copenhagen.
14	22–25 October 2009	Manmohan Singh	Thailand Seventh India–ASEAN Summit and Fourth East Asia Summit	India signed with ASEAN a Partnership Programme for Peace, Progress and Shared Prosperity in 2004 at the time of the Vientiane Summit which was held in Laos. That programme has more or less come to end in 2009, and a new programme is on the anvil for the period 2009 to 2015. Keeping that in mind, the Indian PM announced a series of initiatives, which was widely welcomed by all the leaders. The first was the establishment of an India–ASEAN Round Table comprising think tanks, policymakers, scholars, and media and business representatives to bridge the knowledge gap. Another was the intensification of negotiations on an open skies policy between India and ASEAN so that people-to-people exchanges took place at all levels. Cooperation in the application of space technologies such as sharing of satellite data for management of natural disasters, launching of small satellites, scientific payloads for experiments in remote sensing and communication for space agencies, and most importantly space technology for academic institutions in ASEAN countries. This was a major point in the PM's initiatives. India also offered help in establishing IT and English centres.

				Vietnam signed the India–ASEAN trade in goods agreement as the last signatory during this meeting, so that all 10 members of ASEAN are now on board on the Trade in Goods Agreement, and so that its implementation can begin as agreed from 1 January 2010. Indian PM also met PMs of Japan, Thailand and Cambodia and China in this meeting.
15	23–27 September 2008	Manmohan Singh	United States of America	India emphasized on civil-nuclear cooperation deal. Agreed to open two additional consulates in the USA at Seattle and Atlanta. The USA has opened its consulate in Hyderabad. On WTO, PM emphasized that India was interested in a rule-based trading system and that the most important part of our approach was our concern for our subsistence farmers, and President Bush expressed understanding for this from the fact that he supported the need to accommodate this.
16	13–15 January 2007	Manmohan Singh	Philippines Fifth India–ASEAN Summit and Second East Asia Summit	CEBU declaration on East Asian Energy Security on 15 January 2007. It emphasized on cleaner and lower emission technologies, and increased capacity and reduced costs of renewable and alternate energy sources. The Indian PM emphasized on early conclusion and implementation of India–ASEAN FTAs. India offered to host 10 students from each of the 10 member countries of ASEAN on a trip of the sights and sounds of modern and ancient India.

(Continued)

Table A.3 *(Continued)*

S. No.	*Date*	*Who Visited*	*Countries Visited*	*Any Outcome*
17	20–22 November 2007	Manmohan Singh	Singapore Sixth ASEAN–India Summit and Third East Asia Summit	Adopted the Singapore Declaration on Climate Change, Energy and the Environment on 21 November 2007. Discussion on India–ASEAN Free Trade Agreement, physical connectivity, collaborative R&D and technology development. Concluded Memorandums of Understanding for the establishment of Centres for English Language Training in Cambodia, Lao PDR and Vietnam. Indian PM proposed to set up an India-ASEAN Green Fund. He also proposed India-ASEAN Health Care Initiative providing basic drugs at low cost to our public health systems through steps such as joint production of medical formulations. A second focus could be to develop a framework for cooperation in traditional medicine systems, which are popular in these countries.
18	14–16 December 2006	Manmohan Singh	Japan	Discussed the implementation of the Joint Statement on the India-Japan Partnership in a New Asian Era: Strategic Orientation of the India-Japan Global Partnership and the Eight-fold Initiative for Strengthening India-Japan Global Partnership, signed between the PMs of the two countries on 29 April 2005 in New Delhi. The Indian side welcomed the Japanese plan to establish a consular post in Bangalore. They welcomed the coming into force of the Regional Cooperation Agreement on Combating Piracy and Armed Robbery against Ships in Asia (ReCAAP) and signing of Memorandum on Cooperation between the Coast Guards.

Constituting a joint task force to undertake the inter-governmental negotiations on the Bilateral Economic Partnership Agreement/Comprehensive Economic Partnership Agreement (EPA/CEPA) was agreed during the visit.

The two leaders announced an India-Japan Special Economic Partnership Initiative (SEPI).

MOUs were signed on the following: (a) Delhi–Mumbai Industrial Corridor. (b) cooperation in science and technology between (i) Department of Science & Technology (DST) of India and RIKEN, and (ii) scientific cooperation programme between DST and Japan Science and Technology Agency or JST (in addition to the existing MOU between DST and Japan Society for the Promotion of Science or JSPS on the Core University Program). The two leaders also welcome the collaboration between the National Institute of Advanced Industrial Science and Technology (AIST) of Japan and Indian research institutions, particularly the Council of Scientific and Industrial Research, DST, Department of Biotechnology and Jawaharlal Nehru Centre for Advanced Scientific Research, in advanced industrial science and technology fields including nano-technology and materials, energy and environment (clean coal and biomass resources), life sciences and information and communication technology. (c) Cooperation between the Indian Council for Cultural Relations and the Japan Foundation.

Source: http://www.mea.gov.in/prime-minister-visits.htm

Table A.4 *Incoming Visits from Indo-Pacific*

S. No.	*Date*	*Who Visited*	*Outcome*
1	8–11 July 2018	Mr Moon Jae-in	Memorandums of Understanding (MoUs) were signed on the following: (a) trade remedies; (b) future strategy group thrust areas including the Internet of Things (IOT), artificial intelligence (AI), 'big data', 'smart factory', 3D printing, electric vehicles, advance materials and affordable healthcare for the elderly and disabled; (c) cultural exchange programme for the period 2018–2022; (d) cooperation in the field of scientific and technological research; (e) cooperation between Research Design and Standards Organization (RDSO) and Korea Railroad Research Institute (KRRI); (f) cooperation in the field of biotechnology and bio-economics; (g) cooperation in the field of ICT and telecommunications; (h) cooperation in the field of micro, small and medium enterprises; (i) Government of Gujarat and Korea Trade Promotion Agency (KOTRA) to enhance industrial and investment relations; and (j) Queen Suriratna Memorial Project to facilitate upgradation and expansion of the existing monument commemorating Princess Suriratna.
2	2–4 March 2018	President of Vietnam Tran Dai Quang	The following MoUs/work plans were signed: (a) MoU on economic and trade cooperation; (b) work plan for the years 2018–2022 to promote cooperation in transfer of technology and exchange of visits of technical experts in the fields of agriculture and allied; and (c) MoU to strengthen the technical cooperation in the field of atomic energy for peaceful purposes.
3	24–27 January 2018	Prime Minister of Cambodia Hun Sen	(a) MoU for cultural exchange programme with Cambodia for the years 2018–2022; (b) Agreement Credit Line Agreement between the EXIM Banks for a line of credit to finance the Stung Sva Hab Water Resource Development Projects; (c) MoU for mutual legal assistance in criminal matters; and (d) MoU on Cooperation for Prevention of Human Trafficking.

4	30 March–4 April 2017	Prime Minister of Malaysia Mohd Najib Tun Abdul Razak	The following agreements and MoUs were signed: (a) Air Services Agreement; (b) MoU for cooperation in the proposed development of a urea and ammonia manufacturing plant in Malaysia and offtake of the existing surplus urea from Malaysia to India; (c) MoU on cooperation in the field of sports; (d) MoU between the Malaysian Human Resource Fund (HRDF)/Pembangunan Sumber Manusia Berhad (PSMB) and EDII, Ahmedabad, for cooperation in training, etc.; (e) MoU between the Association of Indian Universities (AIU), India, and Malaysian Qualifications Agency (MQA), Malaysia, on mutual recognition of the educational qualifications; (f) MoU between Malaysian Palm Oil Board (MPOB) and Institute of Chemical Technology (ICT) India; (g) MoU between MIGHT Technology Malaysia and AP Economic Development Board on implementation of Fourth-Generation Technology Park in AP.
5	12–13 December 2016	President of Indonesia Joko Widodo	Agreed to cooperate to ensure the safety and security of the sea lanes, in disaster response and environmental protection. The joint statement on maritime cooperation outlines the agenda of both countries engagement in this field. The partnership will also extend to combating terrorism, organized crime, drugs and human trafficking. Both countries agreed that early implementation of the India–ASEAN Free Trade Agreement (FTA) in Services & Investment, and finalization of the Regional Comprehensive Economic Partnership. Both countries agreed to speed up establishment of Chairs of Indian and Indonesian Studies in each other's universities. They also agreed to expand our scholarship and training programmes. For direct connectivity between both countries Garuda Indonesia's decided to commence direct flights to Mumbai.

(Continued)

Table A.4 *(Continued)*

S. No.	*Date*	*Who Visited*	*Outcome*
6	17–18 October 2016	State Counsellor Aung San Suu Kyi	(a) MoU for designing an academic and professional building programme for insurance industry of Myanmar; (b) MoU on Cooperation in the field of Power Sector; (c) MoU on banking supervision between RBI and Central Bank of Myanmar.
7	3–7 October 2016	Prime Minister of Singapore Lee Hsien Loong	The following bilateral documents were signed during the visit: 1. MoU in the field of Industrial Property Cooperation between Department of Industrial Policy and Promotion (DIPP) and Intellectual Property Office of Singapore. 2. MoU on Collaboration in the Field of Technical and Vocational Education and Training between the National Skill Development Corporation and ITE Education Services, Singapore. 3. MoU on Collaboration in the Field of Technical and Vocational Education and Training between the Government of Assam and ITE Education Services, Singapore.
8	27–30 August 2016	President of Myanmar U Htin Kyaw	(a) MoU on cooperation in the construction of 69 Bridges including AP Approach Roads in the Tamu-Kyigone-Kalewa Road Section of the Trilateral Highway in Myanmar; (b) MoU on Cooperation in the Construction/Upgradation of the Kalewa–Yagyi Road Section; (c) MoU on Cooperation in the Field of Renewable Energy; and (d) MoU on Cooperation in the field of Traditional Systems of Medicine.
9	16–18 June 2016	Prime Minister of Thailand General Prayut Chan-o-cha	The following agreements were signed during the visit: 1. Executive Programme of Cultural Exchange (Extension of CEP) for 2016–2019. 2. MoU between Nagaland University, India and Chiang Mai University,

			Thailand. Both sides also agreed to pursue negotiations on combating human trafficking, revision of air services agreement, FTA, bilateral investment treaty and for controlling narcotic drugs.
10	8–11 February 2015	President of Singapore Dr Tony Tan Keng Yam	Issues discussed were the following: Specific initiatives to develop smart cities and urban rejuvenation; promote skill development; measures to speed up connectivity and coastal and port development; strengthening linkages with the Northeast states of India; projects to scale-up investments in the new development initiatives launched in India; and enhancing exchanges with the State of India. They agreed on sharing of experiences in science and technology, space and other areas to enhance productivity and efficiency as well as broaden cooperation in fighting terrorism.
11	27–28 October 2014	Prime Minister of Vietnam Nguyen Tan Dung	MoUs were signed on the following : (a) establishment of Nalanda University; (b) conservation and restoration of the world heritage site of My Son, Quang Nam Province, Vietnam; (c) Establishing the Centre for English Language and Information Technology (IT) training at the Telecommunications University, Ministry of Defense, Vietnam; (d) Cultural Exchange Programme for 2015–17; (e) Exchange of audio-visual programmes between Prasar Bharti and the Voice of Vietnam; (f) Heads of agreement between ONGC Videsh Limited and PetroVietnam for hydrocarbon; and (g) MoU between ONGC and PetroVietnam.
12	10–12 July 2012	Prime Minister of Singapore Lee Hsien Loong	MoUs were signed during this visit for the following: (a) cooperation in the field of vocational education and skills development; (b) conduct of joint military training and exercises in India; and (c) setting-up of a the Greenfield World Class Skills Development Centre in Delhi to provide state of the art facility for skills development.

(Continued)

Table A.4 *(Continued)*

S. No.	*Date*	*Who Visited*	*Outcome*
13	24–26 January 2012	Prime Minister of Thailand Ms Yingluck Shinawatra	The following MoUs were signed: (a) MoU on defence cooperation between India and Thailand; (b) treaty for transfer of sentenced prisoners; (c) second protocol to amend the framework agreement between India and Thailand; (d) MoU for cooperation in the fields of science technology for the years 2012–2014; (e) MoU for a cultural exchange programme between India and Thailand for the years 2012–2014; and (f) MoU between ICCR and Chulalongkorn University for setting up a Chair at the India Studies Centre.
14	12–15 October 2011	President of Myanmar U Thein Sein	During the visit, the following documents were signed: (a) MoU for the Upgradation of the Yangon Children's Hospital and Sittwe General Hospital and (b) Programme of Cooperation in Science & Technology for the period of 2012–2015. The Prime Minister of India announced that India would extend technical and financial support for following new projects: (a) setting up an Advanced Centre for Agricultural Research and Education (ACARE) in Yezin; and (b) setting up a Rice Bio Park demonstrating the various techniques in rice biomass utilisation in the Integrated Demonstration Farm at Nay Pyi Taw. Both sides decided to cooperate in the implementation of the Tamanthi and Shwezaye projects on the Chindwin River Basin in Myanmar.
15	11–12 October 2011	President of Vietnam Truong Tan Sang	The following MoUs were signed: (a) extradition treaty between Republic of India and the Socialist Republic of Vietnam; (b) MoU **on the 'Vietnam-India Friendship Year 2012'; (c) MoU on cooperation between PetroVietnam and ONGC Videsh**

			Limited in oil and gas sector; (d) work plan for the years 2011-2013 in the field of agricultural and fishery research and education; and (e) cultural exchange programme for the years 2011-2014.
16	4–5 April 2011	Prime Minister of Thailand Abhisit Vejjajiva	The two sides discussed enhancing connectivity, to cooperate in natural disaster, FTA, cooperation in combating terrorism. They agreed to establish a regular high-level dialogue on defence cooperation and that the extradition treaty, the Mutual Legal Assistance Treaty in Civil and Commercial Matters and the agreement on transfer of sentenced persons will be concluded at the earliest. India announced support to the India Studies Centre set up at the Thammasat University in Thailand.
17	24–26 January 2011	President of Indonesia Dr Susilo Bambang Yudhoyono	MoUs were signed on the following: (a) development of an industrial complex based on heavy minerals resource utilization; (b) railway line for transporting coal, and a coal terminal from Tanjung Enim to Tanjung Api-api; (c) infrastructure (railway and seaport); (d) aluminium smelter; (e) setting up an operationalized gas-based power plant with a capacity of 2x1100 MW or 3X660 MW; (f) training and internships for civil servants and the National Electric Company; (g) mining, and construction of a steel plant and its infrastructure; (h) setting up of an airport at Kulon Progo, Yogyakarta; (i) Off-take fertilizer; (j) IT; (k) financing of a coal-based power plant; (l) setting up of an airport at Buleleng, Bali; (m) building cargo ships, and an oil and gas terminal; (n) road infrastructure for mine and port; (o) IT security transfer of technology; (p) dredging of Batanghari River and construction of a coal terminal in Jambi; (q) establishment and management of an innovation institute; and (r) free trade zone cooperation.

(Continued)

Table A.4 *(Continued)*

S. No.	*Date*	*Who Visited*	*Outcome*
18	19–23 January 2010	Prime Minister of Malaysia Mohd Najib Tun Abdul Razak	First Prime Ministerial visit from Malaysia in six years (last one was in December 2004 by Abdullah Badawi).
19	20–23 May 2008	Sultan Haji Hassanal Bolkiah of Brunei	During the visit, the following MoUs/Agreements were signed: (a) agreement on reciprocal promotion and protection of investments; (b) MoU of cooperation in information and communication technology; (c) MoU on cooperation in the fields of culture, arts and sports; (d) MoU on the establishment of a joint trade committee; and (e) MoU on cooperation in the operation of the telemetry tracking and telecommand station for satellite and launch vehicles and for cooperation in the field of space research science and applications.
20	26–30 August 2008	President of Laos Choummaly Sayasone	The following MoUs/agreements were signed during the visit: agreement on line of credit of US$33 million for (a) Paksong S/S–Jiangxay 115 KV, double circuit transmission line project; (b) Nam Song 7.5 MW hydropower project; and (c) Equipment for rural electrification Phase-2 project. India decided to establish an Air Force Academy in Laos. India also gifted 50 parachutes to Lao Defence Forces on its 60th anniversary in 2009.
21	7–10 December 2007	Prime Minister of Cambodia Hun Sen	The following agreements and MoUs were signed: (a) agreement on transfer of sentenced persons; (b) MoU on cooperation in the field of water resources management; (c) MoU on foreign office consultations; (d) work plan under MoU on agricultural cooperation for 2007 and 2008; (e) credit line agreement between the Government of Cambodia and the EXIM bank; (f) MoU on cooperation and

			technical assistance between the ONGC Videsh Limited and the Cambodian National Petroleum Authority; and (g) agreement on defence cooperation.
22	4–6 October 2007	President of the Philippines H. E. Gloria Macapagal Arroyo	After the conclusion of the bilateral talks, the following declarations/agreement/MoUs were signed: • Declaration on a Framework of Bilateral Cooperation • Agreement on the Establishment of a Joint Commission on Bilateral Cooperation • Joint Declaration for Cooperation to Combat International Terrorism • Memorandum of Agreement on Exemption of Visa Requirements for Diplomatic Passport holders • Memorandum of Agreement on Enhanced Cooperation in the Field of Renewable Energy • MoU on Cooperation between the Foreign Service Institutes of India and the Philippines • MoU between the Exim Bank of India and the Government of Philippines on the extension of a US$15 million LoC to the Philippines
23	4–6 July 2007	Prime Minister of Vietnam Mr Nguyen Tan Dung	MoUs were signed on cooperation in the field of fisheries and aquaculture and on the cultural exchange programme between India and Vietnam for the period 2007–2009, and a work plan in the field of agriculture for the period 2007–2009.
24	25–27 June 2007	Prime Minister of Thailand General Surayad Chulanont	Two important agreements were signed—MoUs on enhanced cooperation in the field of renewable energy and on the cultural programme. The visit of the Prime Minister of Thailand took place in the 60th anniversary year of the establishment of diplomatic relations between the two countries.

Source: http://www.mea.gov.in/incoming-visits.htm?1/incoming_visits

ANNEXURE B

India's Trade with ASEAN and Its Dialogue Partners

Table B.1 *India's Total Trade with ASEAN and Its Dialogue Partners (1980–1991)**

Country	Partner	1980	1981	1982	1983	1984	1985	1986	1987	1988	1989	1990	1991
		US$ Million											
India	Brunei	0.02	0.10	0.03	0.07	0.67	0.33	0.05	0.00	1.88	0.00	0.29	0.68
India	Cambodia	0.79	3.18	0.14	0.02	0.00	0.12	0.16	0.11	0.12	0.00	1.31	0.02
India	Indonesia	74.95	96.59	112.07	44.04	80.69	48.60	93.78	71.89	81.68	103.01	265.19	212.35
India	Lao PDR	0.19	0.02	0.00	0.00	0.00	0.00	0.00	0.00	0.00	0.00	0.44	0.04
India	Malaysia	409.41	288.12	311.67	329.42	509.26	463.00	459.14	644.40	705.25	498.86	671.12	593.84
India	Myanmar	12.39	7.65	24.29	25.30	62.92	27.49	29.63	32.08	45.28	174.55	91.57	55.06
India	Philippines	20.24	17.44	25.93	13.33	15.52	12.84	10.09	17.13	23.26	53.80	25.53	95.84
India	Singapore	602.01	557.97	564.30	477.84	569.99	424.43	425.54	498.18	583.65	862.39	997.36	697.61
India	Thailand	70.86	99.18	51.24	113.09	116.88	89.05	95.17	97.69	167.39	208.36	263.31	247.69
India	Vietnam	76.73	14.55	17.63	12.08	10.88	18.53	17.77	16.75	26.71	126.42	67.74	51.39
India	**ASEAN**	1,267.59	1,084.80	1,107.30	1,015.19	1,366.81	1,084.39	1,131.33	1,378.23	1,635.22	2,027.39	2,383.86	1,954.52
India	China	111.98	129.29	146.92	79.21	76.54	125.38	150.65	118.08	145.91	182.04	48.75	69.24
India	Japan	1,590.90	1,437.47	2,089.03	2,099.35	1,911.75	2,284.17	2,948.48	2,940.23	3,295.07	3,630.38	3,456.83	3,018.26
India	Korea	236.74	213.48	328.11	245.18	197.88	278.89	334.24	373.88	428.03	566.59	489.06	554.97
India	**ASEAN+3**	3,207.21	2,865.04	3,671.36	3,438.93	3,552.98	3,772.83	4,564.70	4,810.42	5,504.23	6,406.40	6,378.50	5,596.99
India	Australia	334.43	270.17	516.44	273.07	176.49	514.43	442.78	473.10	584.83	625.97	940.09	763.74
India	New Zealand	35.90	54.30	46.98	36.66	44.82	41.38	53.87	61.87	64.86	73.59	81.55	92.56
India	**ASEAN+5**	3,577.54	3,189.51	4,234.78	3,748.66	3,774.29	4,328.64	5,061.35	5,345.39	6,153.92	7,105.96	7,400.14	6,453.29
India	World	23,262.36	21,376.25	23,906.16	21,750.12	23,345.55	24,594.22	24,186.54	27,635.30	32,226.70	35,135.00	41,802.90	37,380.90

*All the tables in Annexures B to D are from the Data Base of India-ASEAN Centre, Research and Information System for Developing Countries (RIS), India Habitat Centre, New Delhi.

Table B.2 *India's Total Trade with ASEAN and Its Dialogue Partners (1992–2002)*

						US$ Million						
Country	*Partner*	*1992*	*1993*	*1994*	*1995*	*1996*	*1997*	*1998*	*1999*	*2000*	*2001*	*2002*
India	Brunei	0.85	0.23	1.41	4.99	6.50	3.23	3.05	1.88	2.98	2.51	4.38
India	Cambodia	2.81	2.34	1.65	30.72	1.66	3.78	7.21	8.10	8.93	11.58	18.44
India	Indonesia	216.95	287.99	535.82	884.36	1,147.39	1,174.31	1,053.18	1,217.11	1,308.15	1,421.38	2,048.66
India	Lao PDR	0.05	0.11	0.04	0.33	0.43	0.33	0.98	1.35	5.00	4.05	2.09
India	Malaysia	756.15	459.54	682.11	1,125.11	1,391.15	1,661.25	1,864.78	2,335.85	1,956.53	1,905.18	2,137.90
India	Myanmar	108.27	131.63	144.39	181.70	194.26	260.58	221.25	205.25	227.23	401.00	417.17
India	Philippines	90.17	55.03	105.38	137.08	194.49	249.81	183.60	188.78	249.13	305.55	532.49
India	Singapore	1,203.64	1,320.55	1,457.97	1,772.40	1,916.88	1,993.40	1,920.68	2,130.75	2,307.53	2,243.41	2,711.39
India	Thailand	308.67	371.43	520.24	607.43	609.96	594.06	589.90	731.58	845.36	999.48	1,081.70
India	Vietnam	77.17	66.15	93.15	112.66	128.32	131.43	134.70	158.05	220.21	234.01	334.20
India	**ASEAN**	2,764.73	2,695.00	3,542.16	4,856.78	5,591.04	6,072.18	5,979.33	6,978.70	7,131.05	7,528.15	9,288.42
India	China	187.94	544.74	836.91	1,094.39	1,244.56	1,720.90	1,602.25	1,751.07	2,206.83	2,724.72	4,322.73
India	Japan	3,027.03	3,033.01	3,763.41	4,364.73	4,211.49	4,080.87	4,099.13	4,195.33	3,782.83	3,288.30	3,689.49
India	Korea	606.02	595.79	972.65	1,111.19	1,339.86	1,452.58	1,644.08	1,738.00	1,445.93	1,584.14	2,028.33
India	**ASEAN+3**	6,585.72	6,868.54	9,115.13	11,427.09	12,386.95	13,326.53	13,324.79	14,663.10	14,566.64	15,125.31	19,328.97
India	Australia	1,058.48	931.41	1,154.39	1,295.74	1,470.41	1,868.58	1,855.28	1,571.93	1,472.80	1,608.72	1,811.76
India	New Zealand	97.42	100.70	119.15	119.95	135.68	153.16	147.78	156.88	147.15	136.52	144.17
India	**ASEAN+5**	7,741.62	7,900.65	10,388.67	12,842.78	13,993.04	15,348.27	15,327.85	16,391.91	16,186.59	16,870.55	21,284.90
India	World	42,426.70	42,257.30	49,679.20	65,022.90	68,378.40	75,518.50	75,827.30	83,822.10	92,961.90	93,457.00	109,408.70

Table B.3 *India's Total Trade with ASEAN and Its Dialogue Partners* (2003–2016)

(US$ Million)

Country	*Partner*	*2003*	*2004*	*2005*	*2006*	*2007*	*2008*	*2009*	*2010*	*2011*	*2012*	*2013*	*2014*	*2015*	*2016*
India	Brunei	4.89	5.29	34.26	231.12	250.50	378.96	510.58	228.69	1,615.15	791.07	900.11	1,013.29	615.37	530.32
India	Cambodia	19.27	17.60	23.32	46.55	55.66	51.10	45.11	68.75	96.60	120.92	100.68	157.41	123.90	111.85
India	Indonesia	2,989.88	3,663.28	4,278.82	5,744.94	6,786.40	8,639.43	10,736.44	14,291.00	20,855.80	20,346.37	16,995.28	16,201.04	14,454.44	12,976.66
India	Lao PDR	0.85	2.14	4.86	3.45	3.65	8.59	20.85	28.27	81.68	168.21	153.66	123.56	189.63	187.62
India	Malaysia	2,758.18	3,147.87	3,528.87	5,843.71	8,079.15	9,981.87	8,386.81	9,549.03	13,039.13	13,945.97	13,387.46	13,843.02	12,029.25	11,725.92
India	Myanmar	476.77	504.76	607.27	851.12	976.81	1,106.15	1,405.04	1,394.26	1,724.16	1,883.26	1,236.42	1,495.39	1,488.03	2,132.82
India	Philippines	481.67	542.72	697.53	744.98	804.94	945.77	1,016.72	1,200.85	1,455.00	1,609.07	1,070.50	1,350.12	1,706.62	1,838.36
India	Singapore	3,871.75	5,835.81	8,247.30	10,863.63	14,503.51	15,600.13	12,768.96	16,363.63	24,377.34	22,295.75	20,388.75	19,399.84	16,485.51	15,635.12
India	Thailand	1,353.10	1,627.35	2,156.99	2,964.19	3,879.18	4,502.87	4,276.24	6,093.66	8,291.96	8,919.11	8,599.83	8,597.33	7,830.29	7,708.20
India	Vietnam	428.13	567.80	777.16	1,068.20	1,619.38	2,043.20	2,149.44	3,481.74	4,942.10	5,665.47	5,236.64	5,593.24	5,124.88	5,826.54
India	**ASEAN**	12,384.49	15,914.62	20,356.38	28,361.89	36,959.18	43,258.07	41,316.19	52,699.88	76,478.92	75,745.20	68,069.34	67,774.25	60,047.93	58,673.40
India	China	6,448.10	10,251.77	16,398.83	23,722.75	34,887.10	39,939.86	38,994.60	58,851.60	74,412.40	67,311.20	65,491.65	70,649.81	71,654.08	71,194.78
India	Japan	4,207.81	4,831.91	6,247.53	7,229.32	9,497.34	10,499.81	9,571.94	13,094.86	16,859.85	19,099.93	15,692.45	15,095.71	12,971.40	12,860.20
India	Korea	3,237.24	4,016.15	5,930.91	7,088.33	8,497.25	11,658.73	11,588.50	13,578.75	17,261.33	17,632.02	17,555.96	18,057.16	16,270.15	15,616.08
India	**ASEAN+3**	26,277.64	35,014.45	48,933.65	66,402.29	89,840.87	105,356.47	101,471.23	138,225.09	185,012.50	179,788.35	166,809.40	171,576.93	160,943.56	158,344.46
India	Australia	2,885.37	3,994.48	5,463.10	7,391.98	8,723.48	9,633.67	12,059.12	13,726.54	15,512.06	16,285.28	11,686.19	10,937.36	11,750.21	10,140.54
India	New Zealand	159.68	188.02	324.19	666.50	563.23	580.94	671.40	840.83	953.90	1,076.58	902.10	956.66	859.82	854.51
India	**ASEAN+5**	29,322.69	39,196.95	54,720.94	74,460.77	99,127.58	115,571.08	114,201.75	152,792.46	201,478.46	197,150.21	179,397.69	183,470.95	173,553.59	169,339.51
India	World	135,188.50	175,220.50	237,955.60	297,133.00	388,784.00	459,164.00	422,842.00	573,705.00	772,147.00	787,674.00	739,960.62	739,857.70	633,356.96	596,538.94

Note: Columns showing the figures for financial years 2014, 2015 and 2016 are highlighted to show the developments since the launch of the Act East Policy.

ANNEXURE C

India's Exports to ASEAN

Table C.1 *India's Export to ASEAN and Its Dialogue Partners* (1980–1991)

		US$ Million											
Country	*Partner*	*1980*	*1981*	*1982*	*1983*	*1984*	*1985*	*1986*	*1987*	*1988*	*1989*	*1990*	*1991*
India	Brunei	0.02	0.08	0.03	0.05	0.37	0.09	0.04	0.00	1.88	0.00	0.27	0.57
India	Cambodia	0.79	3.18	0.14	0.02	0.00	0.12	0.16	0.10	0.11	0.00	1.31	0.02
India	Indonesia	50.36	74.51	96.17	26.99	38.54	10.72	16.53	20.22	25.43	49.81	92.25	145.09
India	Lao PDR	0.19	0.02	0.00	0.00	0.00	0.00	0.00	0.00	0.00	0.00	0.07	0.04
India	Malaysia	67.71	48.02	52.78	57.32	66.59	59.71	64.39	69.90	84.49	138.89	125.58	202.75
India	Myanmar	4.77	1.95	7.23	2.53	1.44	1.73	1.04	0.86	1.31	0.00	1.43	3.84
India	Philippines	8.70	4.51	9.56	7.56	6.05	4.23	5.04	11.40	18.50	40.53	21.32	64.37
India	Singapore	126.84	94.83	125.96	129.18	124.68	103.03	172.89	188.27	218.00	370.81	308.30	386.47
India	Thailand	46.63	41.26	29.75	45.37	27.12	21.52	38.46	59.42	84.70	131.86	201.07	198.94
India	Vietnam	74.43	12.11	17.63	11.63	10.48	12.99	13.08	8.79	16.98	0.00	8.26	12.93
India	**ASEAN**	**380.44**	**280.47**	**339.25**	**280.65**	**275.27**	**214.14**	**311.63**	**358.96**	**451.40**	**731.90**	**759.86**	**1,015.02**
India	China	28.55	50.08	27.01	9.11	10.85	21.45	8.13	8.29	23.13	143.11	18.02	48.27
India	Japan	775.83	557.07	909.60	834.23	826.65	920.61	1,017.31	1,198.49	1,420.58	2,136.67	1,656.00	1,653.96
India	Korea	64.20	42.27	61.61	83.36	74.09	73.44	83.29	106.73	123.30	282.39	163.60	241.29
India	**ASEAN+3**	**1,249.02**	**929.89**	**1,337.47**	**1,207.35**	**1,186.86**	**1,229.64**	**1,420.36**	**1,672.47**	**2,018.41**	**3,294.07**	**2,597.48**	**2,958.54**
India	Australia	124.23	95.71	110.54	89.63	118.22	102.59	110.68	130.27	159.83	193.31	183.32	202.90
India	New Zealand	24.95	19.50	21.51	15.61	18.82	14.06	15.00	20.17	23.19	41.35	21.10	24.21
India	**ASEAN+5**	**1,398.20**	**1,045.10**	**1,469.52**	**1,312.59**	**1,323.90**	**1,346.29**	**1,546.04**	**1,822.91**	**2,201.43**	**3,528.73**	**2,801.90**	**3,185.65**
India	World	8,440.16	6,826.45	8,271.36	7,857.42	8,230.25	8,265.22	9,135.14	10,797.30	13,192.00	15,837.50	17,811.50	17,871.50

Table C.2 *India's Export to ASEAN and Its Dialogue Partners (1992–2002)*

		US$ Million										
Country	*Partner*	*1992*	*1993*	*1994*	*1995*	*1996*	*1997*	*1998*	*1999*	*2000*	*2001*	*2002*
India	Brunei	0.74	0.23	1.30	4.96	6.49	3.23	3.05	1.80	2.80	2.21	4.05
India	Cambodia	0.18	0.31	1.45	1.84	1.30	2.65	5.03	7.35	7.90	10.51	17.70
India	Indonesia	143.50	200.27	252.62	500.69	569.04	475.93	248.45	290.73	385.80	470.77	753.80
India	Lao PDR	0.05	0.11	0.04	0.33	0.43	0.33	0.98	1.35	5.00	4.05	1.97
India	Malaysia	221.76	232.17	250.17	355.40	457.25	500.20	363.75	415.75	567.93	778.17	755.45
India	Myanmar	4.20	14.49	23.96	21.24	45.89	48.28	34.90	33.10	48.05	55.57	71.53
India	Philippines	76.90	48.12	95.37	122.33	173.93	224.93	148.70	137.30	187.83	230.33	415.95
India	Singapore	515.06	727.40	737.97	806.63	942.63	829.15	583.05	633.90	826.00	909.51	1,309.26
India	Thailand	242.04	317.92	374.39	461.19	434.10	369.78	326.75	417.45	509.98	595.10	691.68
India	Vietnam	18.53	22.11	42.94	97.31	127.28	124.48	125.70	147.15	208.03	216.76	307.59
India	**ASEAN**	**1,222.96**	**1,563.13**	**1,780.21**	**2,371.92**	**2,758.34**	**2,578.96**	**1,840.36**	**2,085.88**	**2,749.32**	**3,272.98**	**4,328.98**
India	China	94.13	286.13	214.55	282.92	542.48	692.20	499.90	511.05	758.23	915.57	1,719.60
India	Japan	1,522.83	1,656.54	1,923.53	2,130.40	2,077.97	1,925.35	1,713.63	1,677.05	1,767.23	1,532.13	1,775.63
India	Korea	196.38	230.44	278.62	394.29	503.83	480.33	347.83	434.43	457.25	452.31	601.48
India	**ASEAN+3**	**3,036.30**	**3,736.24**	**4,196.91**	**5,179.53**	**5,882.62**	**5,676.84**	**4,401.72**	**4,708.41**	**5,732.03**	**6,172.99**	**8,425.69**
India	Australia	232.16	245.59	313.40	351.09	381.26	425.08	400.13	399.33	405.25	391.05	482.64
India	New Zealand	33.30	30.34	48.87	57.59	62.78	70.43	60.60	62.43	63.55	60.82	66.33
India	**ASEAN+5**	**3,301.76**	**4,012.17**	**4,559.18**	**5,588.21**	**6,326.66**	**6,172.35**	**4,862.45**	**5,170.17**	**6,200.83**	**6,624.86**	**8,974.66**
India	World	19,230.10	20,988.50	24,193.40	30,536.40	32,323.60	34,622.10	33,665.20	35,921.60	42,625.80	43,313.60	50,496.30

Table C.3 India's Export to ASEAN and Its Dialogue Partners (2003–2016)

US$ Million

Country	*Partner*	*2003*	*2004*	*2005*	*2006*	*2007*	*2008*	*2009*	*2010*	*2011*	*2012*	*2013*	*2014*	*2015*	*2016*
India	Brunei	4.56	4.80	33.47	16.97	9.91	15.65	24.42	21.26	895.62	33.12	35.19	46.74	37.47	39.64
India	Cambodia	18.91	17.35	22.68	45.17	53.11	48.43	41.39	61.07	88.15	110.54	93.29	149.44	114.07	89.28
India	Indonesia	1,053.10	1,251.22	1,368.30	1,866.11	2,126.36	2,427.75	2,872.53	4,572.19	6,860.40	6,070.57	3,963.98	3,952.08	2,741.42	2,872.74
India	Lao PDR	0.72	2.07	4.77	3.15	3.47	8.21	20.65	8.23	14.63	27.46	48.26	67.28	54.66	25.44
India	Malaysia	856.91	970.46	1,142.41	1,268.70	2,251.77	3,215.02	3,463.78	3,551.32	3,917.17	3,788.17	5,212.49	4,074.93	3,901.28	4,012.35
India	Myanmar	86.00	104.71	111.32	132.72	174.02	212.23	209.78	273.26	466.46	533.37	351.50	659.80	474.04	1,094.70
India	Philippines	359.15	375.79	474.06	560.57	609.62	704.95	699.84	804.09	1,008.14	1,116.61	782.27	1,051.02	1,333.73	1,523.24
India	Singapore	1,949.02	3,377.84	5,069.12	5,908.02	7,042.89	7,997.11	6,721.49	9,093.86	16,147.30	14,692.50	9,117.68	8,270.21	5,794.29	5,874.46
India	Thailand	801.56	849.97	1,031.83	1,352.09	1,717.02	1,935.63	1,592.29	2,144.92	3,224.45	3,455.33	3,498.63	3,045.26	2,618.19	2,587.18
India	Vietnam	392.17	497.44	657.00	909.62	1,447.43	1,697.21	1,722.47	2,485.12	3,403.00	3,671.46	2,882.70	3,132.33	2,655.16	3,013.83
India	**ASEAN**	**5,522.10**	**74,51.65**	**9,914.96**	**12,063.12**	**15,435.60**	**18,262.19**	**17,368.64**	**23,015.32**	**36,025.32**	**33,499.13**	**25,985.99**	**24,449.09**	**19,724.31**	**21,132.87**
India	China	2,710.18	4,178.48	6,473.30	7,910.25	10,195.10	9,663.86	10,155.00	17,519.00	19,113.10	14,904.00	17,046.05	16,412.57	13,394.90	11,759.57
India	Japan	1,747.97	1,910.52	2,392.92	2,767.34	3,606.01	3,214.07	3,186.04	4,812.81	5,663.55	6,697.23	**7,079.04**	**6,981.90**	**4,867.38**	**4,669.73**
India	Korea	734.86	913.29	1,630.83	2,342.85	2,767.53	3,705.82	3,732.14	3,641.06	4,824.63	4,142.32	6,180.17	5,274.67	4,240.57	4,242.25
India	**ASEAN+3**	**10,715.11**	**14,453.94**	**20,412.01**	**25,083.56**	**32,004.24**	**34,845.94**	**34,441.82**	**48,988.19**	**65,626.60**	**59,242.68**	**56,291.25**	**53,118.23**	**42,227.16**	**41,804.43**
India	Australia	564.26	661.35	796.03	898.91	1,093.74	1,357.05	1,315.32	1,652.84	2,087.96	2,665.38	2,450.30	2,954.38	3,796.09	3,466.76
India	New Zealand	81.41	87.95	129.73	413.00	244.73	179.02	243.96	189.04	240.74	303.52	348.20	421.67	417.44	408.84
India	**ASEAN+5**	**11,360.78**	**15,203.24**	**21,337.77**	**26,395.47**	**33,342.71**	**36,382.01**	**36,001.10**	**50,830.07**	**679,55.30**	**62,211.58**	**59,089.75**	**56,494.28**	**46,440.69**	**45,680.03**
India	World	61,118.50	75,385.20	98,201.60	120,532.00	153,768.00	177,698.00	165,184.00	222,922.00	307,071.00	297,261.00	284,347.77	288,416.02	254,396.39	249,736.85

Note: Columns showing the figures for financial years 2014, 2015 and 2016 are highlighted to show the developments since the launch of the Act East Policy.

ANNEXURE D

India's Imports from ASEAN

Table D.1 *India's Imports from ASEAN and Its Dialogue Partners (1980–1991)*

		US$ Million											
Country	*Partner*	*1980*	*1981*	*1982*	*1983*	*1984*	*1985*	*1986*	*1987*	*1988*	*1989*	*1990*	*1991*
India	Brunei	0.00	0.02	0.00	0.02	0.30	0.24	0.01	0.00	0.00	0.00	0.02	0.11
India	Cambodia	0.00	0.00	0.00	0.00	0.00	0.00	0.00	0.01	0.01	0.00	0.00	0.00
India	Indonesia	24.59	22.08	15.90	17.05	42.15	37.88	77.25	51.67	56.25	53.20	172.94	67.26
India	Lao PDR	–	–	0.00	0.00	0.00	0.00	0.00	0.00	0.00	0.00	0.37	0.00
India	Malaysia	341.70	240.10	258.89	272.10	442.67	403.29	394.75	574.50	620.76	359.97	545.54	391.09
India	Myanmar	7.62	5.70	17.06	22.77	61.48	25.76	28.59	31.22	43.97	174.55	90.14	51.22
India	Philippines	11.54	12.93	16.37	5.77	9.47	8.61	5.05	5.73	4.76	13.27	4.21	31.47
India	Singapore	475.17	463.14	438.34	348.66	445.31	321.40	252.65	309.91	365.65	491.58	689.06	311.14
India	Thailand	24.23	57.92	21.49	67.72	89.76	67.53	56.71	38.27	82.69	76.50	62.24	48.75
India	Vietnam	2.30	2.44	0.00	0.45	0.40	5.54	4.69	7.96	9.73	126.42	59.48	38.46
India	**ASEAN**	887.15	804.33	768.05	734.54	1,091.54	870.25	819.70	1,019.27	1,183.82	1,295.49	1,624.00	939.50
India	China	83.43	79.21	119.91	70.10	65.69	103.93	142.52	109.79	122.78	38.93	30.73	20.97
India	Japan	815.07	880.40	1,179.43	1,265.12	1,085.10	1,363.56	1,931.17	1,741.74	1,874.49	1,493.71	1,800.83	1,364.30
India	Korea	172.54	171.21	266.50	161.82	123.79	205.45	250.95	267.15	304.73	284.20	325.46	313.68
India	**ASEAN+3**	**1,958.19**	**1,935.15**	**2,333.89**	**2,231.58**	**2,366.12**	**2,543.19**	**3,144.34**	**3,137.95**	**3,485.82**	**3,112.33**	**3,781.02**	**2,638.45**
India	Australia	210.20	174.46	405.90	183.44	58.27	411.84	332.10	342.83	425.00	432.66	756.77	560.84
India	New Zealand	10.95	34.80	25.47	21.05	26.00	27.32	38.87	41.70	41.67	32.24	60.45	68.35
India	**ASEAN+5**	**2,179.34**	**2,144.41**	**2,765.26**	**2,436.07**	**2,450.39**	**2,982.35**	**3,515.31**	**3,522.48**	**3,952.49**	**3,577.23**	**4,598.24**	**3,267.64**
India	World	14,822.20	14,549.80	15,634.80	13,892.70	15,115.30	16,329.00	15,051.40	16,838.00	19,034.70	19,297.50	23,991.40	19,509.40

Table D.2 *India's Imports from ASEAN and Its Dialogue Partners (1992–2002)*

		US$ Million										
Country	*Partner*	*1992*	*1993*	*1994*	*1995*	*1996*	*1997*	*1998*	*1999*	*2000*	*2001*	*2002*
India	Brunei	0.11	0.00	0.11	0.03	0.01	0.00	0.00	0.08	0.18	0.30	0.33
India	Cambodia	2.63	2.03	0.20	28.88	0.36	1.13	2.18	0.75	1.03	1.07	0.74
India	Indonesia	73.45	87.72	283.20	383.67	578.35	698.38	804.73	926.38	922.35	950.61	1,294.86
India	Lao PDR	0.00	0.00	0.00	0.00	0.00	0.00	0.00	0.00	0.00	0.00	0.12
India	Malaysia	534.39	227.37	431.94	769.71	933.90	1,161.05	1,501.03	1,920.10	1,388.60	1,127.01	1,382.45
India	Myanmar	104.07	117.14	120.43	160.46	148.37	212.30	186.35	172.15	179.18	345.43	345.64
India	Philippines	13.27	6.91	10.01	14.75	20.56	24.88	34.90	51.48	61.30	75.22	116.54
India	Singapore	688.58	593.15	720.00	965.77	974.25	1,164.25	1,337.63	1,496.85	1,481.53	1,333.90	1,402.13
India	Thailand	66.63	53.51	145.85	146.24	175.86	224.28	263.15	314.13	335.38	404.38	390.02
India	Vietnam	58.64	44.04	50.21	15.35	1.04	6.95	9.00	10.90	12.18	17.25	26.61
India	**ASEAN**	1,541.77	1,131.87	1,761.95	2,484.86	2,832.70	3,493.22	4,138.97	4,892.82	4,381.73	4,255.17	4,959.44
India	China	93.81	258.61	622.36	811.47	702.08	1,028.70	1,102.35	1,240.02	1,448.60	1,809.15	2,603.13
India	Japan	1,504.20	1,376.47	1,839.88	2,234.33	2,133.52	2,155.52	2,385.50	2,518.28	2,015.60	1,756.17	1,913.86
India	Korea	409.64	365.35	694.03	716.90	836.03	972.25	1,296.25	1,303.57	988.68	1,131.83	1,426.85
India	**ASEAN+3**	**3,549.42**	**3,132.30**	**4,918.22**	**6,247.56**	**6,504.33**	**7,649.69**	**8,923.07**	**9,954.69**	**8,834.61**	**8,952.32**	**10,903.28**
India	Australia	826.32	685.82	840.99	944.65	1,089.15	1,443.50	1,455.15	1,172.60	1,067.55	1,217.67	1,329.12
India	New Zealand	64.12	70.36	70.28	62.36	72.90	82.73	87.18	94.45	83.60	75.70	77.84
India	**ASEAN+5**	**4,439.86**	**3,888.48**	**5,829.49**	**7,254.57**	**7,666.38**	**9,175.92**	**10,465.40**	**11,221.74**	**9,985.76**	**10,245.69**	**12,310.24**
India	World	23,196.60	21,268.80	25,485.80	34,486.50	36,054.80	40,896.40	42,162.10	47,900.50	50,336.10	50,143.40	58,912.40

Table D.3 *India's Imports from ASEAN and Its Dialogue Partners (2003–2016)*

US$ Million

Country	*Partner*	*2003*	*2004*	*2005*	*2006*	*2007*	*2008*	*2009*	*2010*	*2011*	*2012*	*2013*	*2014*	*2015*	*2016*
India	Brunei	0.33	0.49	0.79	214.15	240.59	363.31	486.16	207.43	719.53	757.95	864.92	966.55	577.91	490.68
India	Cambodia	0.36	0.25	0.64	1.38	2.55	2.67	3.72	7.68	8.45	10.38	7.38	7.97	9.83	22.57
India	Indonesia	1,936.78	2,412.06	2,910.52	3,878.83	4,660.04	6,211.68	7,863.91	9,718.81	13,995.40	14,275.80	13,031.30	12,248.96	11,713.02	10,103.92
India	Lao PDR	0.13	0.07	0.09	0.30	0.18	0.38	0.20	20.04	67.05	140.75	105.41	56.29	134.97	162.18
India	Malaysia	1,901.27	2,177.41	2,386.46	4,575.01	5,827.38	6,766.85	4,923.03	5,997.71	9,121.96	10,157.80	8,174.97	9,768.09	8,127.97	7,713.56
India	Myanmar	390.77	400.05	495.95	718.40	802.79	893.92	1,195.26	1,121.00	1,257.70	1,349.89	884.92	835.58	1,013.99	1,038.11
India	Philippines	122.52	166.93	223.47	184.41	195.32	240.82	316.88	396.76	446.86	492.46	288.22	299.10	372.89	315.13
India	Singapore	1,922.73	2,457.97	3,178.18	4,955.61	7,460.62	7,603.02	6,047.47	7,269.77	8,230.04	7,603.25	11,271.07	11,129.64	10,691.21	9,760.66
India	Thailand	551.54	777.38	1,125.16	1,612.10	2,162.16	2,567.24	2,683.95	3,948.74	5,067.51	5,463.78	5,101.21	5,552.07	5,212.11	5,121.01
India	Vietnam	35.96	70.36	120.16	158.58	171.95	345.99	426.97	996.62	1,539.10	1,994.01	2,353.94	2,460.91	2,469.72	2,812.70
India	**ASEAN**	6,862.39	8,462.97	10,441.42	16,298.77	21,523.58	24,995.88	23,947.55	29,684.56	40,453.60	42,246.07	42,083.35	43,325.17	40,323.61	37,540.53
India	China	3,737.92	6,073.29	9,925.53	15,812.50	24,692.00	30,276.00	28,839.60	41,332.60	55,299.30	52,407.20	48,445.60	54,237.23	58,259.17	59,435.21
India	Japan	2,459.84	2,921.39	3,854.61	4,461.98	5,891.33	7,285.74	6,385.90	8,282.05	11,196.30	12,402.70	8,613.41	8,113.81	8,104.03	8,190.47
India	Korea	2,502.38	3,102.86	4,300.08	4,745.48	5,729.72	7,952.91	7,856.36	9,937.69	12,436.70	13,489.70	**11,375.79**	**12,782.49**	**12,029.59**	**11,373.82**
India	**ASEAN+3**	**15,562.53**	**20,560.51**	**28,521.64**	**41,318.73**	**57,836.63**	**70,510.53**	**67,029.41**	**89,236.90**	**119,385.90**	**120,545.67**	**110,518.15**	**118,458.70**	**118,716.40**	**116,540.03**
India	Australia	2,321.11	3,333.13	4,667.07	6,493.07	7,629.74	8,276.62	10,743.80	12,073.70	13,424.10	13,619.90	9,235.88	7,982.97	7,954.12	6,673.78
India	New Zealand	78.27	100.07	194.46	253.50	318.50	401.92	427.44	651.79	713.16	773.06	553.90	534.99	442.38	445.66
India	**ASEAN+5**	**17,961.91**	**23,993.71**	**33,383.17**	**48,065.30**	**65,784.87**	**79,189.07**	**78,200.65**	**101,962.39**	**133,523.16**	**134,938.63**	**120,307.94**	**126,976.66**	**127,112.90**	**123,659.48**
India	World	74,070.00	99,835.30	139,754.00	176,601.00	235,016.00	281,466.00	257,658.00	350,783.00	465,076.00	490,413.00	455,612.85	451,441.68	378,960.56	346,802.09

Note: Columns showing the figures for financial years 2014, 2015 and 2016 are highlighted to show the developments since the launch of the Act East Policy.

ANNEXURE E

FDI Inflows and Outflows between ASEAN and India

Table E.1 *India's FDI Outflow to ASEAN Countries*

	Brunei	*Cambodia*	*Indonesia*	*Laos*	*Malaysia*	*Myanmar*	*Philippines*	*Singapore*	*Thailand*	*Vietnam*	*India's Total FDI Outflow to ASEAN Countries (US$ Million)*
2008	–	–	40.31	4.03	117.04	42.21	11.98	4,547.60	126.29	45.97	4,935.43
2009	–	–	55.03	2	9.01	20.24	18.78	4,680.30	61.92	6.68	4,853.96
2010	–	–	257.80	2	75.63	45.25	42.44	12,071.87	6.53	19.88	12,521.40
2011	–	0.02	104.16	2.06	393.54	9.72	35.81	7,185.36	35.29	59.52	7,825.48
2012	2.25	10.03	96.23	0.2	124.39	1.76	45.60	4,184.39	22.42	1.64	4,488.91
2013	–	0.85	47.88	1.03	7.20	16.09	9.25	4,672.76	55.72	11.62	4,822.40
2014	–	0.01	164.30	1.09	61.77	4.44	27.07	6,410.88	73.59	15.72	6,758.87
2015	–	0.52	101.9	0.8	452.94	1.55	25.39	5,277.31	21.24	22.24	5,903.89
2016	–	1.45	43.99	0.9	113.19	0.44	5.33	4,842.44	8.74	17.49	5,033.97
Total	2.25	12.88	911.60	14.11	1,354.71	141.70	221.65	53,872.91	411.74	200.76	57,144.31

Source: ASEAN-India Centre (AIC) based on RBI.

Table E.2 *India's FDI Inflow from ASEAN Countries*

	Malaysia	*Myanmar*	*Philippines*	*Singapore*	*Thailand*	*Vietnam*	*Indonesia*	*India's Total FDI Inflow from ASEAN Countries (US$ Millions)*	*India's Total FDI Inflow from World (US$ Millions)*	*Share of Total FDI Inflow from ASEAN Countries to World (%)*
2010	8.6	–	–	1,076.9	12.8	–	432.6	1,530.8	7,179.1	21.32
2011	6.7	–	0.3	1,609.6	4.6	–	0.0	1,621.2	11,172.0	14.51
2012	2.9	–	2.7	1,489.7	8.4	–	0.1	1,503.7	9,020.6	16.67
2013	34.4	–	3.3	2,129.0	10.4	0.1	0.0	2,177.2	9,240.5	23.56
2014	87.5	–	0.0	3,751.7	9.0	0.0	9.9	3,858.1	13,047.7	29.57
2015	16.5	0.0	0.8	6,301.8	20.7	0.1	1.1	6,341.0	20,427.7	31.04
2016	21.6	0.0	95.0	5,623.7	42.2	0.1	1.6	5,784.0	37,671.4	15.35
Total	178.1	0.0	102.0	21,982.3	108.1	0.3	445.4	22,816.0	107,759.1	21.17

Source: ASEAN-India Centre (AIC) based on RBI.

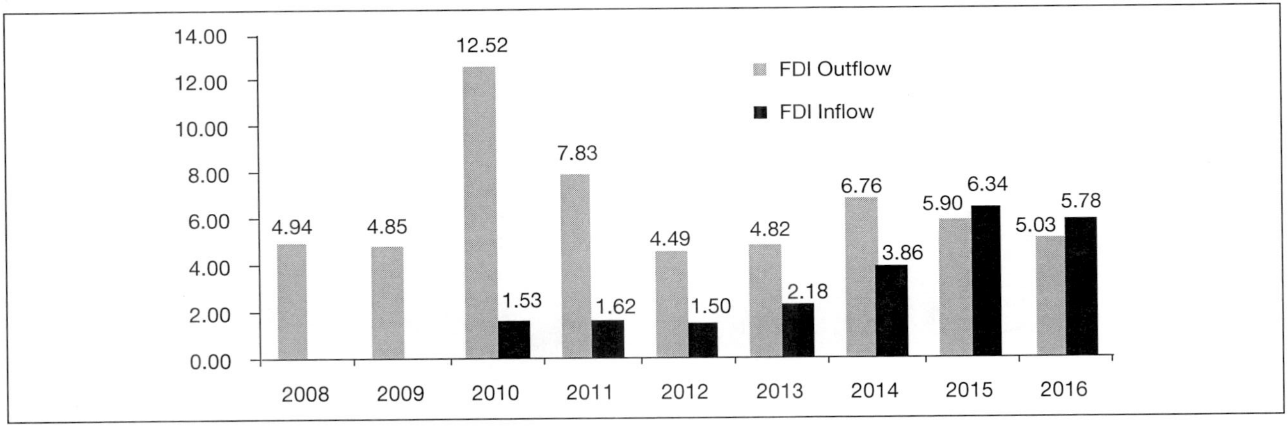

Figure E.1 *FDI Inflow and Outflow between India and ASEAN (US$ Billions)*

Source: RBI.

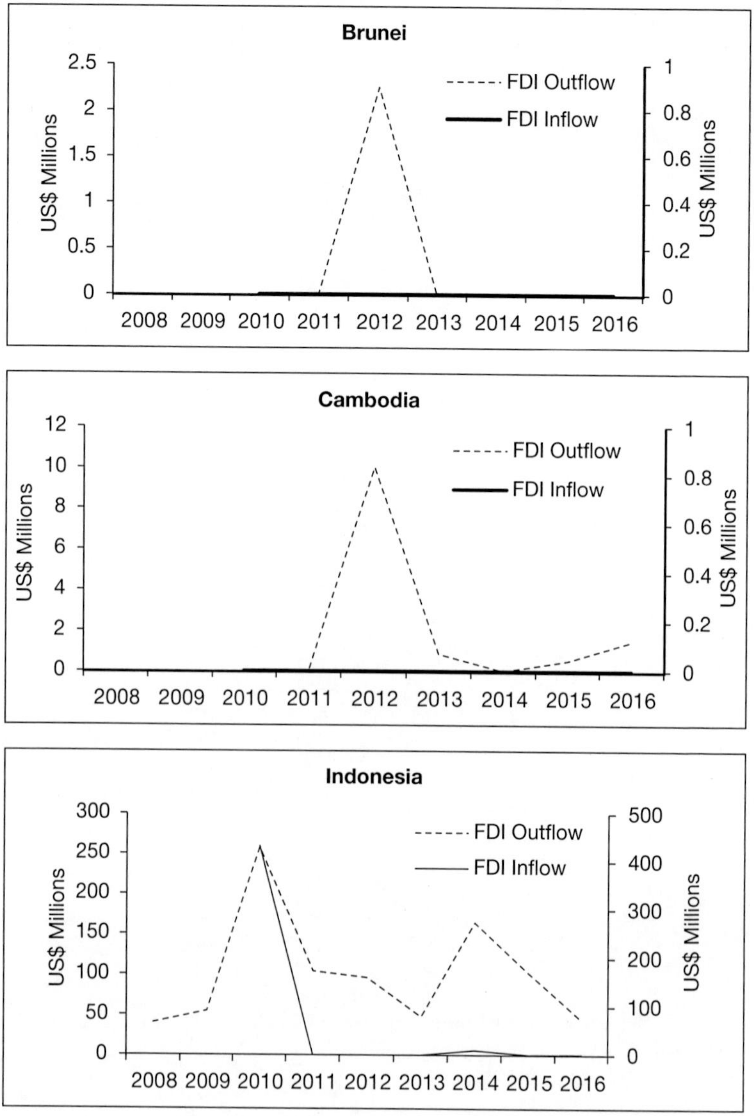

Figure E.2 *Trends in FDI Inflow and Outflow of ASEAN Countries*

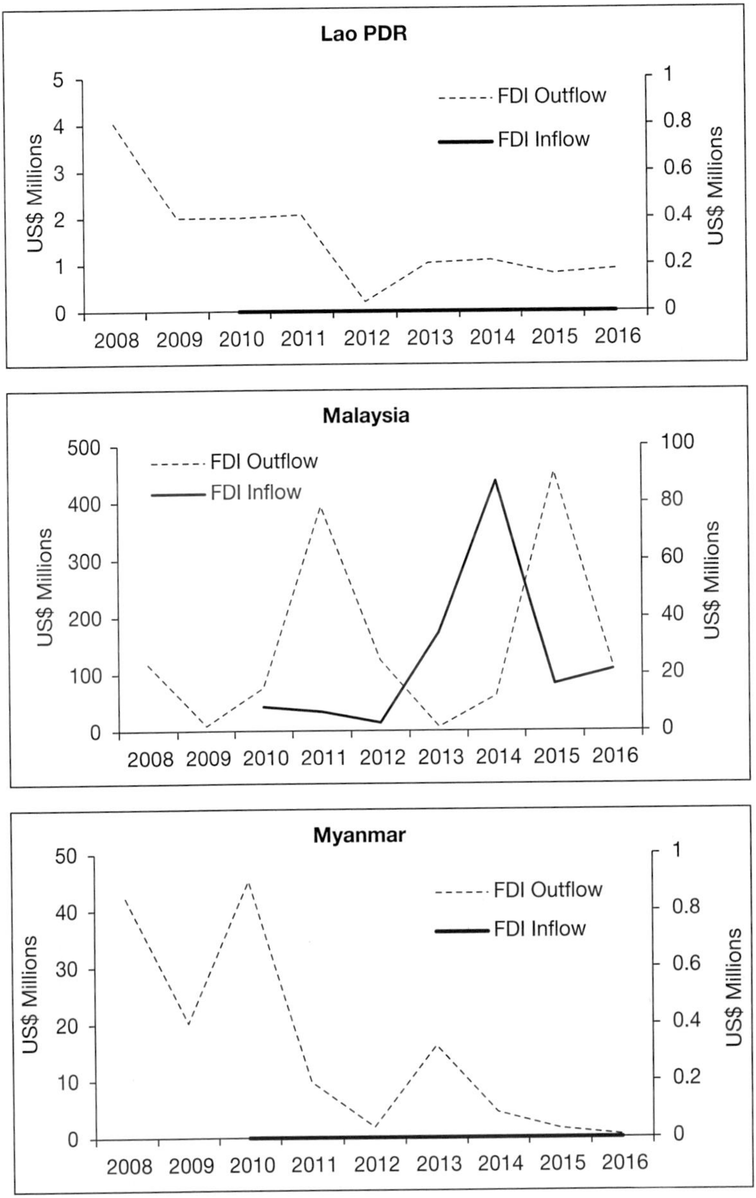

Figure E.2 *(Continued)*

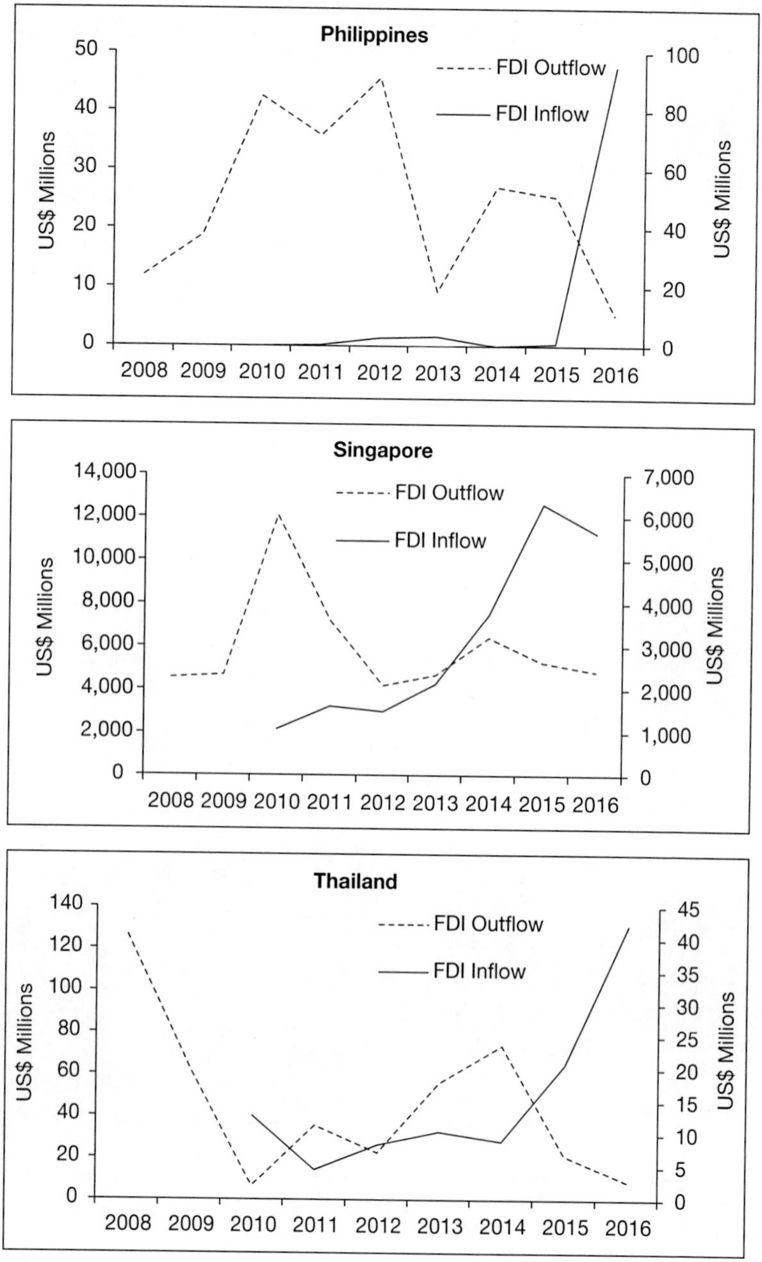

Figure E.2 *(Continued)*

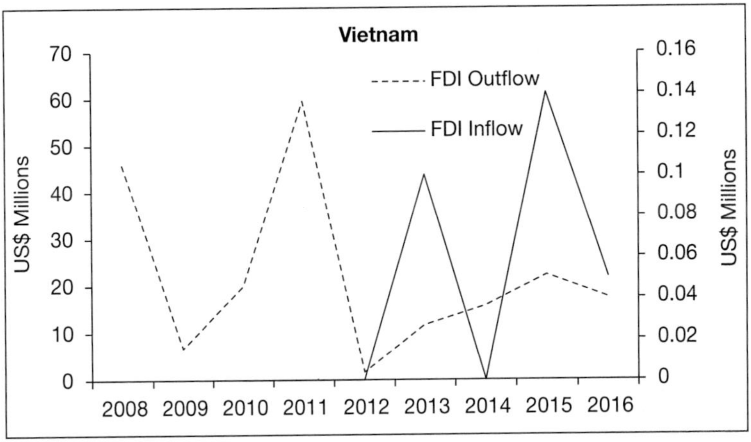

Figure E.2 *(Continued)*

ANNEXURE F

Military Exercises

Table F.1 *India and Indo-Pacific Army Exercise*

S. No.	*Country*	*Exercise Name*
1	USA	Yudh Abhyas (started in 2004)[a] and Vajra Prahar (started in 2010)[b]
2	Japan	–
3	Australia	AUSTRA HIND[c]
4	New Zealand	–
5	Indonesia	Garuda Shakti (started in 2012)[d]
6	Malaysia	Harimau Shakti (started in 2018)[e]
7	Vietnam	VINBAX (started in 2018)[f]
8	Singapore	Bold Kurukshetra[g] and Agni Warrior[h]
9	Thailand	Maitree[i] and Cobra Gold[j]
10	Cambodia	–
11	Myanmar	IMBAX (started in 2017)[k]
12	Philippines	The Philippines-India Joint Defence Cooperation Committee has been set up[l]
13	Brunei	MoU signed for joint military exercise in 2016[m]
14	Laos	–
15	ASEAN +	Force 18[n]

Sources: [a] http://zeenews.india.com/india/india-and-us-to-conduct-joint-military-exercise-yudh-abhyas-2017-in-september-2040360.html, accessed 22 August 2018.
[b] http://indianexpress.com/article/india/indo-us-joint-military-exercise-vajra-prahar-to-be-held-in-seattle-5026208/, accessed 22 August 2018.
[c] http://www.pibregional.nic.in/PressReleseDetail.aspx?PRID=1484819, accessed 22 August 2018.
[d] http://pib.nic.in/newsite/PrintRelease.aspx?relid=137499, accessed 22 August 2018.
[e] https://www.financialexpress.com/defence/harimau-shakti-2018-whats-special-about-india-and-malaysias-joint-counter-guerrilla-operations/1158278/, accessed 22 August 2018.
[f] https://economictimes.indiatimes.com/news/defence/indian-vietnamese-armies-hold-first-military-exercise/articleshow/62699234.cms, accessed 22 August 2018.
[g] http://www.pibregional.nic.in/PressReleseDetail.aspx?PRID=1484819, accessed 22 August 2018.
[h] Ibid
[i] Ibid.
[j] Ibid.
[k] https://www.hindustantimes.com/india-news/first-indo-myanmar-joint-military-exercise-begins-in-meghalaya/story-uU6qctYcF5hbTa6UiOliDP.html, accessed 22 August 2018.
[l] http://newdelhipe.dfa.gov.ph/index.php/newsroom/embassy-news/305-2nd-philippines-india-joint-defense-cooperation-committee-jdcc-meeting-new-delhi-24-march-2017, accessed 22 August 2018.
[m] https://thewire.in/diplomacy/india-brunei-to-conduct-joint-military-exercises-explore-joint-production, accessed 22 August 2018.
[n] http://www.rediff.com/news/column/exercise-force-18-takes-indias-act-east-policy-to-the-next-level/20160308.htm, accessed 22 August 2018.

Table F.2 *India and Indo-Pacific Naval Exercise*

S. No.	*Country*	*Exercise Name*
1	USA	Salvex (started in 2005),[a] Malabar (started in 1992)[b] and RIMPAC-Multilateral (started in 1971)[c]
2	Japan	Sahyog-Kaijin (started in 2000)[d] and JIMEX (started in 2013)[e]
3	Australia	Ausindex (started in 2017)[f]
4	New Zealand	–

(Continued)

Table F.2 *(Continued)*

S. No.	*Country*	*Exercise Name*
5	Indonesia	CORPAT (started in 2002),[g] IND-INDO BILAT (started in 2015)[h] and KOMODO (HADR) multilateral exercise (started in 2014)[i]
6	Malaysia	ARFDIR Ex (started in 2008)[j]
7	Vietnam	Started first naval exercise in May 2018[k]
8	Singapore	SIMBEX (started in 1993)[l]
9	Thailand	CORPAT (started in 2006)[m]
10	Cambodia	Goodwill visit since 2003. Joint training exercise started in 2015[n]
11	Myanmar	IMCOR[o]
12	Philippines	Regular port visits[p]
13	Brunei	–
14	Laos	–
15	Australia, Bangladesh, Indonesia, India, Malaysia, Myanmar, Singapore, Sri Lanka and Thailand	Milan exercise was participated by 20 ships from nine countries.[q]

Sources: [a] https://www.naval-technology.com/news/news106338-html/, accessed 22 August 2018.

[b] https://timesofindia.indiatimes.com/india/malabar-naval-exercise-all-you-need-to-know-in-10-points/articleshow/59522548.cms, accessed 22 August 2018.

[c] https://www.moneycontrol.com/news/india/rimpac-from-june-27-india-among-26-participant-countries-2579397.html, accessed 22 August 2018.

[d] Anit Mukherjee and C. Raja Mohan, *India's Naval Strategy and Asian Security* (New York, NY: Routledge Publication, 2016), https://books.google.co.in/books?id=mQQBCwAAQBAJ&pg=PA164&lpg=PA164&dq=when+sahyog+kaijin+exercise+started&source=bl&ots=CQgq6h-9wn&sig=gKaDDlmZrATbpvnFbcNtQwMdDaE&hl=en&sa=X&ved=0ahUKEwjggrfTwbXbAhUTb30KHbGXAe84FBDoAQg7MAQ#v=onepage&q=when%20sahyog%20kaijin%20exercise%20started&f=false & http://pib.nic.in/newsite/PrintRelease.aspx?relid=101825, accessed 2 June 2018.

[e] Ibid

[f] https://thediplomat.com/2017/06/indian-warships-arrive-in-australia-for-military-exercise/, accessed 22 August 2018.

[g] http://pib.nic.in/newsite/PrintRelease.aspx?relid=151567, accessed 22 August 2018.

[h] Ibid.

[i] https://www.indiannavy.nic.in/content/exercise-komodo, accessed 22 August 2018.

[j] http://www.thehindu.com/todays-paper/tp-international/India-Malaysia-hold-naval-exercise/article15215678.ece, accessed 22 August 2018.

[k] https://timesofindia.indiatimes.com/india/with-an-eye-on-china-india-to-hold-naval-exercise-with-vietnam/articleshow/64241913.cms, accessed 22 August 2018.
[l] https://www.indiannavy.nic.in/content/simbex-14, accessed 22 August 2018.
[m] https://www.indiannavy.nic.in/sites/default/files/press_release_document/PRel_120424_Indo-US-Ex-14thCORPAT-completed.pdf?download=1, accessed 22 August 2018.
[n] http://www.indembassyphnompenh.org/gallery.php?album=90, accessed 22 August 2018.
[o] http://pib.nic.in/newsite/PrintRelease.aspx?relid=136531, accessed 22 August 2018.
[p] https://www.indiannavy.nic.in/content/visit-indian-warships-subic-bay-philippines, accessed 22 August 2018.
[q] https://milan18.org/history.php, accessed 22 August 2018.

Table F.3 *India and Indo-Pacific Air Force Exercise*

S. No.	*Country*	*Exercise Name*
1	USA	Red Flag-Multilateral (India started participating in 2008)[a]
2	Japan	–
3	Australia	–
4	New Zealand	–
5	Indonesia	–
6	Malaysia	–
7	Vietnam	–
8	Thailand	SIAM BHARAT (started in 2017)[b]
9	Singapore	Joint military training[c]
10	Cambodia	–
11	Myanmar	–
12	Philippines	–
13	Brunei	–
14	Laos	–

Sources: [a] https://timesofindia.indiatimes.com/india/IAF-may-take-part-in-combat-exercise-in-US/articleshow/47335354.cms, accessed 22 August 2018.
[b] http://www.pibregional.nic.in/PressReleseDetail.aspx?PRID=1484819 accessed 22 August 2018.
[c] https://idsa.in/system/files/jds/jds_11_3_2017_international-military-exercises.pdf accessed 22 August 2018.

Index

Abbot, Tony, 219
Abe, Shinzo, 219, 221, 230
Acharya, Amitav, 8, 67, 90
Act East Policy (AEP), 12, 28, 196, 249
  active and intensive political engagement, 208–211
  features of, 200
  integration with India and north eastern region (NER), 211–218
  Narendra Modi formal announcement of shift from Look East, 197–202
  objective of, 199, 241–243
  persistence of economic agenda and development cooperation, 233–238
  renaming of LEP, 202–207
  security and defence cooperation, 218–233
  soft power, use of, 238–240
Afro-Asian Conference (1955), 78
Ajanta caves, 29
Akbar, M. J., 216
Akbaruddin, Syed, 197
All India Anna DMK (AIADMK), 154
Amravati, 33, 46
Andrews, C. F., 67
Angkor Wat, Cambodia, 2, 37
Anti-Access and Area Denial (A2AD), 250
Antony, A. K., 25
Apartheid, 91
Arabic Islam, 5
Arabs, 4
Archaeological Survey of India, 144
Arthashastra (Kautilya), 33, 40
ASEAN +3 Summit, 185
ASEAN 10 plus, 188
ASEAN Commemorative Summit (2012), New Delhi, 215, 246
ASEAN Defence Ministers Meeting + (ADMM+), 185
ASEAN Europe Meeting (ASEM), 185
ASEAN Regional Forum (ARF), 169, 184
ASEAN–India innovation Platform, 216
ASEAN–India Summit (2002), Cambodia, 185
ASEAN–India Plan of Action for the period 2016–2020, 199
Ashoka, 39
Asia Pacific Economic Cooperation (APEC), 159, 237, 254
Asian Century, concept of, 256, 257
Asian Council, 128
Asian decolonization, 105
Asian Development Bank, 147
Asian federation, 60
Asian Infrastructure Investment Bank (AIIB), 237
Asian Relations Conference (1947), 16, 66, 69, 79–80
Asian Relations Organisation (ARO), 80
Association of South East Asian Nations (ASEAN), 23, 89, 95, 112, 122, 126–133, 150, 198, 199

centrality of operations, 255
future challenges, 256
Australia, 13, 22, 82, 123, 134, 148, 149, 159, 173, 178, 185, 188, 196, 199, 201, 209, 219, 231, 232
Aye, U., 166
Azad Hind Fauj or Indian National Army (INA), 62–63, 75, 76

Bak, Lee Myung, 180
Balakrishnan, Vivian, 262
balance of payment crisis, 155
Bali Jatra, 18
Bali temples, 2
Bandung Conference (1955), 66, 69, 85–87
post-Bandung setback for India, 87–94
Bangladesh, 148, 168
Bangladesh, India, Sri Lanka, and Thailand–Economic Cooperation (BIST-EC), 186
Bangladesh
liberation war (December 1971), 26
Barakatallah, 59, 62
Bay of Bengal, 260
Bay of Bengal Multi-Sectoral Initiative for Technical and Economic Cooperation (BIMSTEC), 186, 188, 199, 238, 249, 254, 260
Bayon, 37
Belgrade conference, 92
Belt and Road Initiative (BRI), 232, 258
Bhagat, Bali Ram, 128
Bharatiya Janata Party (BJP), 173, 196, 204, 240, 247
Bhaskara Ravi Varman plate, 38
Bhupen Hazarika Setu, 216
Bodh Gaya, 46
Borobudur temple, 2, 37
Bose, Nandalal, 56
Bose, Rash Behari, 45, 58, 62
Bose, Subhas Chandra, 13, 45, 50, 55, 62–63, 68, 75
Brazil, Russia, India, China, South Africa (BRICS) Summit (2016), Goa, 238
Broader Asia, 19
Buchan, Alastair, 123
Buddhism, 3, 12
emergence of world class centres of learning, 43–44
in East and Southeast Asia, 39–43
Bumiputra, 46
Burma (Myanmar), 96–100

Cambodge, 33
Cambodia (Kamboja), 8
Cambodia, Laos, Myanmar and Vietnam (CLMV), 179
Campbell, Kurt, 21
Center for International Development, 248
CENTO, 89
Chagla, M. C., 128
Champa civilization, Vietnam, 3, 33
Chauhan, Y. B., 130
Chetak helicopters, 170
Chhath Pooja, 2
China, 1, 3, 14, 40, 55, 82, 86, 89, 124, 207
aspects of rise, 153
Rajiv Gandhi role in redefining relations with, 156
resistance in naming Pakistan based terrorists at UN, 225
support for Pakistan nuclear programme, 174
China Day, 63
Chola Kingdom, 37
Christian era, 6, 7
civilizational exchanges, 2–5
Clinton, Hillary, 203

Code of Conduct in the South China Sea (COC), 226
Coedes, George, 12, 14, 31, 32
Cold War, 10, 159
colonial rule, 50
colonialism, 66
Commemorative India–ASEAN Summit (2018), 225
Commonwealth Conference, 106
Communist Party of Burma, 96
Comprehensive Convention on International Terrorism (CCIT), 225
Comprehensive Economic Cooperation Agreement (2005), 169
Conference on Indonesia (1949), 78
Council of a Consular Commission, 81
Council of Asia, 128
cultural diffusion, 2–5, 9
Cunningham, Maura, 18

Declaration on the Conduct of the Parties in the South China Sea (DOC), 226
Defence Cooperation Agreement (2003), 169
Democratic Security Diamond, Japan, 232
Desai, Morarji, 116, 131
  critical view of China's role in Southeast Asia, 124
Development Partnership Administration (DPA), 262
diaspora, Indian, 50–52
Dixit, J. N., 166

East
  Buddhism in, 39–43
  Hindus engagement with, 32–39
  phases of India's engagement with, 30
  strategic dimensions of India's engagement with, 52–55
East Asia Economic Group (EAEG), 187
East Asia Summit (EAS), 187, 188, 197
eastward engagement, transition in India's, 14–19
economic dimensions between India and East, 10–14
economic liberalization, 146
Ellora caves, 29
EXIM Bank, 161

farthest India, 14
Fatimids, in Egypt, 5
Fernandes, George, 174
Forum for India–Pacific Islands Cooperation (FIPIC), 210
Framework for Security Cooperation (2014), 219
Free Trade Area for Asia Pacific (FTAAP), 237
freedom struggle
  in Asia, 55–56, 59–62
  in India, 58–59

Gandhi, Indira, 115
  assassination in 1985, 121
  resistance to great power interventions and military groupings, 122–124
Gandhi, Rajiv, 116, 122, 132, 142, 143, 160
Gandhi, Sanjay, 132
Geneva Agreements of 1954, 179
Geneva Conference, 108
Ghoshal, U. N., 5
Gohain, Rajen, 215
Gonsalves, Eric, 131
GPS Aided Geo-Augmented Navigation (GAGAN), 216
greater India, 14
Greater India Society, 6, 9
Group of Two (G-2), 252

Gujral, I. K., 164, 175, 184, 189, 239

Haidar, Salman, 152
Haksar, P. N., 144
Harsono, Ganis, 120
Harvard Kennedy School, 248
Hatta, Mohd., 55
Hindu colonization, 8
Hinduism, 3, 12, 32
Hinduization, 31
Hindutva, 247
Hsien, Fa, 41
Hurgronje, Snouck, 48

imperialism, 66, 111
India–Japan Joint Statement (2015), 221
India–Pakistan conflict of 1965, 13
India–U.S. Business Summit, 204
India–US Malabar exercise (2017), 230
Indian Maritime Doctrine, 24
Indian National Congress, 50, 59–62, 66–68, 71, 72, 75
Indianization, 14, 30, 32, 35
India–ASEAN Summit (2012), New Delhi, 25
Indo–China relations
  efforts to build peace and stability in, 133–140
  expansion and strengthening of bilateral engagement, 143–150
  normalization of, 140–143
Indo–China war of 1962, 66, 94–96
Indo–Japan Mixed Commission, 147
Indo-Pacific Friendship and Cooperation treaty, 23
Indo-Pacific relations, 19–28
Indo–Pak War of 1965, 118
Indonesia, 34, 78, 248
Indonesia Day, 61
Indonesia
  India's role in independence of, 80–85
  Islam in, 5
  Shailendra dynasty of, 43
  supporter of concept of Indo-Pacific, 22
  threatened to blockade Andaman Nicobar Islands, 13
Indonesian Herald, 119
Indus Valley civilization, 246
Industrial Revolution, 18
INS Chakra, 149
INS Viraat, 149
International Civil Aviation Organization (ICAO), 226
International Institute of Strategic Studies (IISS), London, 123, 208, 244
International Maritime Organization (IMO), 226
International Monetary Fund (IMF), 248
International Solar Alliance, 246
International Technical and Economic Cooperation (ITEC) programme, 144
Islam, 3
Islam in Southeast Asia, emergence of, 44–50
Islamising courts of Southeast Asia, 48

Jaishankar, S., 208, 231
Jaitley, Arun, 211
Janata Party, 116
Janatha Vimukti Peramuna, 116
Japan, 1, 6, 13, 14, 19, 41, 42, 134, 161, 201, 220
  aggression in East and Southeast Asia, 63
  annexation of Korea in 1910–1911, 57
  relations with India, 109
  supporter for India in food and economic crisis, 147
  victory over Russia, 62

Jatakas, 33
Jiabao, Wen, 163
Jinping, Xi, 257
Joint Session of the Indian Parliament (November 2010), 202
Joshi, D. K., 226

Kanishka, 39
Karmarkar, D. P., 117
Karna, 2
Kaul, T. N., 128
Kauthara, 33
Kaveri delta, 46
Key, John, 210
Khilji, Muhammad bin Bakhtiyar, 43
King Dharmapala, 43
Kripalani, Acharya J. B., 61
Kuala Lumpur Declaration, 188
Kunti, 2

Laffan, Michael, 48
Lanba, Sunil, 227
Levi, Sylvain, 5
Line of Actual Control (LAC), 142, 163
Lines of Credit policy, 262
Linga Parvat (Mountain with a Shiv Linga), 38
linkage birth, between India and East leaders, 55–56
Lippmann, Walter, 78
little India, 14
Lohiya, Ram Manohar, 61
Look East Policy (LEP), 12, 28, 132, 247
  articulation of, 156–160
  beyond ASEAN, 186–188
  cooperation in defence and security sector, 191–195
  domestic and international context, 153–156
  economic and strategic imperatives, 160–172
  gain in economic sector, 188–191
  gains for India, 177–181
  institutional integration of ASEAN, 181–186
  origin of, 152–153
  phases of, 172–177
  renaming of, 202–207
  shift towards Act East Policy, 197–202
Luang Prabang, Laos, 2

Madurai, 46
Mahabharata, 2, 29
Mahathir, Mohammad, 187
Mahatma Gandhi, 45, 55, 57, 58, 60, 65, 67
Mahayana Buddhism, 32, 39, 40
Majumdar, R. C., 6, 9, 32, 34
Make in India concept, 223
Malabar, 4
Malacca Strait, 260
Malcolm, Howard, 16
Maldives, 143, 148, 151
Malik, Adam, 130
Manigramam Chetties, 37
map (modern) of India, 15
Maritime Silk Road, 258
Matanga, Kashyapa, 41
Mathai, Ranjan, 25
Mattis, John, 22
Mauryan, 50
Mehta, Sureesh, 192
Mekong-Ganga Cooperation (MGC), 186–188, 254
Menon, Krishna, 98
Menon, Shivshankar, 163, 195, 226, 245, 254
Middle East, 28
Minh, Ho Chi, 104, 108
Ministry for the Development of the North East Region (DoNER), 200
Modi, Narendra, 28, 217, 221, 239
  drivers of engagement between India-Pacific relations, 246–253

maritime security vision, 254
new approach towards neighbours, 206
role in Indo-Pacific relations, 244–246
Shangri La Dialogue on 2018, 244
Moreh Integrated Check Post (ICP), 217
Morgulov, Igor, 23
Mughal Empire, 4
Mukherjee, Pranab, 213, 245
Mukhi, Jagdish, 214

Nag, Kalidas, 6, 26, 27, 33, 36, 56
Naga insurgency, 101
Nahdlatul Ulama (Islamic Party of Indonesia), 118
Nalanda University, 43
Nanadesis, 37
Narayanan, K. R., 141
Narikeladvipa, Kathadvipa (Kedah, Malaysia), 29
National Bamboo Mission, 215
National Democratic Alliance (NDA) government, 173, 196
National Security Strategy (NSS), 251
Nationalist Revolution in China (1911), 58
Nehru, Jawaharlal, 7, 16, 45, 50, 55, 59–62, 261–262
and beginning of eastward engagement, 65–68
and Korean crisis, 102–104
and relations with Thailand, 109–110
evolution of eastward engagement under, 68–79
inaugural speech in Indonesia international conference in 1949, 81–82
peace making efforts between India and China, 104–109
period and contribution towards eastward engagement, 110–113
relations with Japan, 109
role in Indian politics, 66
support to Burma (Myanmar), 96–100
thoughts on foreign policy, 67
turbulent transition after, 115–117
New World Order, 81
New York Times, 88
Non-cooperation movement, 58
Nu, U., 97, 100
Nuclear Suppliers Group (NSG), 263

Obama, Barack, 202, 230
Oil Producing and Exporting Countries (OPEC), 145
One Belt, One Road (OBOR), 232
oriental civilizations, 69

Pakistan Occupied Kashmir, 259
Pali language, 43
Pali Nidesa, 29
Pallava, 33
Pandavas, 2
Pande, G. C., 9
Pandit, Vijaya Lakshmi, 91
Panduranga, 33
Panetta, Leon E., 21
Panikkar, K. M., 37
Partnership for Quality Investment (PQI), Japan, 232
Pataliputra (Patna), 46
Patel, Sardar, 67
Peng, Li, 154, 161
Peoples' Liberation Army-Navy (PLA-N), 250
Persons of Indian Origin (PIO), 240
Philippines, 248
Phizo, Angami Zapu, 101
Pingle, Vishnu Ganesh, 59
post-Mauryan, 50
Prakash, Arun, 25, 226
Prakrit language, 43

Prambanan, 37
Prasad, Rajendra, 63, 96
Pravasi Bhartiya Divas (PBD—Day for the Persons of Indian Origin), 240
Prayag (Allahabad), 46
pre-Mauryan, 50
Proto-Australoids (or the Pre-Dravidians), 36
Public–Private Partnership (PPP), 191

Rai, Lala Lajpat, 62
Rajagopalachari, C., 67
Ram, A. N., 152
Ramayana, 2, 3, 10, 29
Rana, Kishan S., 223
Rao, Nirupama, 24
Rao, P. V. Narasimha, 132, 152, 172, 177, 206
Rau, B. N., 96
Regional Comprehensive Economic Partnership (RCEP), 206, 233, 235, 236
regional cooperation, 128
Renaissance, 18
Rennell, James, 15
Ricci, Ronit, 4
Roy, M. N., 62

Sagarmala project, 249
Samsin, Heng, 132
Samudragupta, 17
San, Aung, 55
Sanchi, 46
Sanskritization, 32
Saran, Shyam, 25
Sardesai, D. R., 106, 111
Sarnath, 46
schools of thought, 5–10
Security and Growth for all in the Region (SAGAR), 213
Sen, Kshitimohan, 56
Sen, Satyendra Nath, 59
Shanghai Cooperation Organisation, 260
Shastri, K. A. Nilakanta, 6
Shastri, Lal Bahadur, 13, 115, 117–121, 154
Shek, Chiang Kai, 55
Shekhar, Chandra, 154, 155
Shrenis (trade guilds), 50
Singh, Charan, 116
Singh, Dato Ajit, 183
Singh, Dinesh, 144
Singh, Jaswant, 174
Singh, Manmohan, 155, 177, 183, 188, 193, 221
Singh, Natwar, 144
Singh, Sardar Swaran, 144
Singh, V. K., 199, 201, 214
Singh, V. P., 154
Sinha, Yashwant, 173, 175, 192, 201
Sitharaman, Nirmala, 224
Soekarno, 55
South China Sea, 226, 260
Southeast Asia Day, 61
Southeast Asian Treaty Organisation (SEATO), 89, 112
Sri Lanka, 116, 128, 143, 148, 149, 151, 154
Sri Vijaya Empire, 38
Sribijiyalakshmi, 7
State Law and Order Restoration Council (SLORC), 165
Subramaniam, C., 120
Sun Temple, Odisha, 2
sun worshippers, 1–2
Sung dynasty, 5
Surya Namaskar, 2
Suu Kyi, Aung San, 164, 167
Suvarnabhumi (Myanmar), 29, 33
Suvarndvipa, 29
Swami Vivekananda, 62
Swaraj, Sushma, 197, 204, 213, 214, 229, 257
Swarnbhumi (Land of Gold), 11
Swarndeep (Golden Island), 11

Tagore, Rabindranath, 6, 56–58, 62, 67
Tamralipti, 46
Tang dynasty, 41
Taw, Nay Pyi, 197
Thailand, 248
The Australian Senate Report of 1991, 160
Tibet, 141
Tilak, Bal Gangadhar, 67
Time Magazine, 88
Tipu Sultan, 12
Tong, Goh Chok, 178
Trans Pacific Partnership (TPP), 237
Treaty of Amity and Cooperation (TAC) 2003, 185
Treaty of Peace and Friendship, 98
Tsang, Huan, 41

Ujjain, 46
UN International Control Commission, 108
UN Peace and Supervisory Commission, 179
Union of Soviet Socialist Republics (USSR), 153
United Nations Convention on the Law of the Sea (UNCLOS), 226, 228, 229
United Nations Security Council, 81, 83
United Progressive Alliance (UPA) government, 240
upper India, 14

Vajpayee, Atal Bihari, 129, 130, 141, 148, 173, 204, 239
Van Leur, J. C., 8, 32
vedic civilization, 2
Vidisha, 46
Vietnam, 3, 26, 99, 104, 105, 107, 211, 219, 223, 227, 248, 256
Vijaya, 33
Vikramshila University, 43
Vishwa Bharti delegation, 56

Washington Post, 88
Western colonialism, 111
Widodo, Joko, 23, 28
Win, Ne, 121
World Bank, 248
World Islamic Sufi Conference (201), New Delhi, 239
Wuhan Informal Summit, 260

Xiaoping, Deng, 153, 257

Yat-Sen, Sun, 55, 58–59
Yavodvipa, 29
Yew, Lee Kuan, 13, 117
Yi-Tsing, 41
Yoga, 2

Zamin, Jiang, 163
Zedong, Mao, 140, 178
Zone of Peace, Freedom and Neutrality (ZOPFAN), 129

About the Authors

S. D. Muni is Professor Emeritus at the School of International Studies, Jawaharlal Nehru University (JNU), New Delhi. He is also a member of the Executive Council of the Institute for Defence and Strategic Analyses, New Delhi. He taught and conducted/guided research at JNU, New Delhi; National University of Singapore, Singapore; Banaras Hindu University, Varanasi; and Rajasthan University, Jaipur. He was India's Special Envoy for Southeast Asian Countries for the UN Security Council Reforms (2005–2006) and also served as India's Ambassador (1997–1999) to Lao People's Democratic Republic. He was nominated to the first-ever constituted National Security Advisory Board of India in 1990–1991. Professor Muni also addressed the UN Special Committee on Indian Ocean in Socci (former Soviet Union). In 2005, the Sri Lankan president bestowed him with the 'Sri Lanka Ratna', the country's highest national award for a foreigner. Sri Venkateswara University, Tirupati (Andhra Pradesh), honoured him in 2014 with the 'Life Time Achievement Award' in South and Southeast Asian Studies.

Author and editor of about 30 books and monographs, Professor Muni has published nearly 250 articles and research papers in Indian and international journals. He has extensively travelled on academic assignments and has had associations with several international think tanks and research centres in Europe, the Americas and Asia.

Rahul Mishra is Associate Professor, Centre for Indo-Pacific Studies, Jawaharlal Nehru University, and Senior Research Fellow, German-Southeast Asian Center of Excellence for Public Policy and Good Governance, Thammasat University, Thailand. He was a visiting research fellow at S. Rajaratnam School of International Studies, Nanyang Technological University, Singapore. Prior to that, he was affiliated with the National University of Singapore. Dr Mishra is a recipient of Department of Foreign Affairs and Trade, Government of Australia fellowship (2007–2008), and Government of Korea fellowship (2016).

He has published widely, and he regularly contributes articles in leading journals, magazines and newspapers. He has been interviewed by the BBC, Channel NewsAsia, Phoenix TV, DD News, LS TV, RS TV, CCTV, Deutsche Welle and ABC Radio on Indo-Pacific affairs. He has co-edited *BCIM Economic Corridor: The Road Ahead* (2015), *The Peacock and the Garuda: An Overview of India–Indonesia Relations* (2015) and *Integrating North East in India's Act East Policy* (2017). He is the author of *One Belt, One Road: Mapping China's Strategy for Shaping the International Order* (2019).